THE AGE OF
ACRIMONY

The Virgin Vote: How Young Americans Made Democracy Social, Politics Personal, and Voting Popular in the Nineteenth Century

THE AGE OF
ACRIMONY

HOW AMERICANS FOUGHT

TO FIX THEIR DEMOCRACY,

1865–1915

JON GRINSPAN

BLOOMSBURY PUBLISHING

NEW YORK · LONDON · OXFORD · NEW DELHI · SYDNEY

BLOOMSBURY PUBLISHING
Bloomsbury Publishing Inc.
1385 Broadway, New York, NY 10018, USA

BLOOMSBURY, BLOOMSBURY PUBLISHING, and the Diana logo are trademarks
of Bloomsbury Publishing Plc

First published in the United States 2021

Bloomsbury Publishing Plc does not have any control over, or responsibility for,
any third-party websites referred to or in this book. All internet addresses given in
this book were correct at the time of going to press. The author and publisher regret
any inconvenience caused if addresses have changed or sites have ceased to exist,
but can accept no responsibility for any such changes.

ISBN: HB: 978-1-63557-462-3; EBOOK: 978-1-63557-463-0

LIBRARY OF CONGRESS CATALOGING-IN-PUBLICATION
Names: Grinspan, Jon, author.
Title: The age of acrimony: how Americans fought to fix their democracy, 1865–1915 /
Jon Grinspan.
Other titles: How Americans fought to fix their democracy, 1865–1915
Description: New York: Bloomsbury Publishing, 2021. | Includes bibliographical
references and index.
Identifiers: LCCN 2020053954 (print) | LCCN 2020053955 (ebook) |
ISBN 9781635574623 (hardcover) | ISBN 9781635574630 (ebook)
Subjects: LCSH: United States—Politics and government—1865–1933. |
Kelley, William D. (William Darrah), 1814–890. | Kelley, Florence, 1859–1932. |
Social problems—United States—History—19th century. | Women social reformers—
United States—Biography. | United States. Congress. House—Biography. |
Legislators—United States—Biography. | Philadelphia (Pa.)—Biography. |
Classification: LCC E661 .G756 2021 (print) | LCC E661 (ebook) |
DDC 303.48/40922 [B]—dc23
LC record available at https://lccn.loc.gov/2020053954
LC ebook record available at https://lccn.loc.gov/2020053955

2 4 6 8 10 9 7 5 3 1

Typeset by Westchester Publishing Services
Printed and bound in the U.S.A. by Berryville Graphics Inc., Berryville, Virginia

To find out more about our authors and books visit www.bloomsbury.com and
sign up for our newsletters.

Bloomsbury books may be purchased for business or promotional use. For information on
bulk purchases please contact Macmillan Corporate and Premium Sales Department at
specialmarkets@macmillan.com.

For Solomon

CONTENTS

PREFACE

Nearly every day while writing this book, I would walk across the National Mall. I'd pass tourists wearing MAKE AMERICA GREAT AGAIN caps and protesters waving THIS IS NOT NORMAL signs, and head into the secure vaults of the Smithsonian's National Museum of American History. Beyond the recently collected riot shields and tiki torches, I would settle into the cool, quiet aisles that preserve the deep history of our democracy.

There, century-old objects told a forgotten drama, more heated than anything we've seen. Torches from midnight rallies. Uniforms from partisan street gangs. Ballots from stolen elections. Shifting between the fractious twenty-first century and those furious nineteenth-century objects started to feel like digging at opposite ends of the same tunnel, struggling to connect in the dark. In between lay the norms of political behavior that most of us grew up with, or imagine, from America's more stable twentieth century. But the objects on the other end of that tunnel seemed to cry out: "Your normal was abnormal."

In our arguments over democracy, we have missed out on the most vital, most urgent, most relevant period of American history. Twentieth-century America's expectations of restrained public politics were a historical outlier. That civility was an invention, the end result of a brutal fight over the nature of democracy that raged across American life in the late 1800s. The objects in the Smithsonian are wreckage from that conflict; the diaries and letters stored elsewhere are battlefield reports.

We barely remember it, but this was the origin story of normal politics, the dirty tale of how democracy got clean.

Americans claim that we are more divided than we have been since the Civil War, but forget that the lifetime *after* the Civil War saw the loudest, roughest political campaigns in our history. From the 1860s through the early 1900s, presidential elections drew the highest turnouts ever reached, were decided by the closest margins, and witnessed the most political violence. Racist terrorism during Reconstruction, political machines that often operated as organized crime syndicates, and the brutal suppression of labor movements made this the deadliest era in American political history. The nation experienced one impeachment, two presidential elections "won" by the loser of the popular vote, and *three presidential assassinations*. Control of Congress rocketed back and forth, but neither party seemed capable of tackling the systemic issues disrupting Americans' lives. Driving it all, a tribal partisanship captivated the public, folding racial, ethnic, and religious identities into two warring hosts.[1]

Critics came to consider this era democracy's "forty years in the wilderness," when America's politics threatened America's promise.[2]

But these were not just a cartoonish "bad old days." Those eligible to vote did so as never before—averaging 77 percent turnout in presidential elections—and those denied that right fought to join in.[3] These were the years when nationwide voting rights for African Americans and women went from utopian dreams to achievable realities. Wild rallies, bustling saloons, street-corner debates, a sarcastic press, and a love of costumes, fireworks, barbecue, and lager beer all helped heat campaigns into vibrant spectacles. The public grew used to seeing ten thousand Democrats throw their top hats in the air all at once, or watching phalanxes of Republican women dressed as goddesses float down Main Street, or eavesdropping on young girls arguing politics on streetcars. Participation was highest among the working class and poorer citizens, and often incorporated recent immigrants, young voters, and newly enfranchised African Americans.[4] For all of the era's political ugliness, Americans chose to participate in their government as few people in world history ever had.

In an age of disruption and isolation, many found identity, friendship, and meaning in that participation. The same competitive zeal that shouted down independent thought, or sparked atrocious violence, also made politics gripping, joyful, fun. Living through a partisan American election, one critic wrote in 1894, was like watching two speeding locomotives race across an open plain. Each bystander felt irresistibly compelled to cheer for one train, to be "jubilant when it forges ahead, or mortified if it falls behind. It becomes for the time being *his* train, *his* locomotive, *his* railroad." Complain as they might about politics, Americans couldn't look away.[5]

This is the fundamental paradox of their era—and perhaps of our own. Americans bemoaned the failure of their democracy, but also joined in its worst habits with a zealous fixation. An already overworked citizenry devoted incredible amounts of unpaid labor to politics. Why bother? Why turn out? In particular, why participate in a government that so many agreed was broken, rigged, and rotten?

How could a system be so popular and so unpopular at the same time?

This paradox has not been resolved, partly because we tend to associate this period with the politics of conspiracy. At the time, bigots blamed the nation's problems on Reconstruction's African American politicians, or Irish Catholic machines, or German anarchists, or Jewish socialists. Since the Progressive Era, many have focused on the (far more real) guilt of tycoons and lobbyists, in an age of yawning income inequality.

But this focus on conspiracy misses how fundamental America's political problems were. There were, to be sure, a fantastic number of scams and schemes in this era, but they were outweighed by the votes and passions of tens of millions of partisan citizens who had a greater cumulative impact. The system evolved to convince citizens to care about their government, they did, and the results were maddening. Massive public participation made it harder, not easier, to tackle the inequities of their era. It was an engaged majority, not scheming minorities, that made politics so fascinating and so frustrating.

The underlying issue of so many midnight rallies, barroom debates, drawing room lectures, and bedroom spats was the question of whether this democracy could be reformed. And then it was. While the partisan divisions of the mid-1800s ended in an atrocious civil war, Americans managed to peacefully calm the heated politics of the late nineteenth century. An incredible transformation of American politics took place around 1900, reconfiguring a public, partisan, passionate system into a more private, independent, restrained one.

It was the boldest change in political behavior since the writing of the Constitution, reprioritizing Americans' relationship with their government, with each other, and with themselves. How it happened is one of the greatest mysteries in our history.[6]

It took a terrible bargain. The well-to-do victors of the Gilded Age's class wars chose to trade participation for civility. They restrained the old system, decreasing violence and partisanship, but diminishing public engagement along with it. Turnout crashed, falling by nearly one-third in the early twentieth century, especially among the working class, immigrants, young people, and African Americans.[7] Our engagement has yet to recover. In the twentieth century, much of the dynamism of American public life lived outside "capital P" electoral Politics.[8]

Instead of fixing their system, reformers broke it in a different way, one that we got used to. Much of what Americans value about their democracy was not passed down by the Founders but invented by restrainers a century later: our views on voting rights, public service, corruption, independent journalism, partisan outrage, and political violence. Few twenty-first-century Americans would want to participate in elections as they looked in 1868 or 1884. Indeed, most simply could not. And the social reforms of the Progressive Era—the child labor laws and pure food acts and vaccination campaigns that made modern life livable—were only possible because a generation first quieted their politics. But much of what is wrong with our politics is of this same vintage—our inferior turnout rates, our class- and race-based divisions, our systemic discouragements for participation.

No era better highlights the nuanced trade-offs at the core of the study of history, yet, perhaps because of this, it has mostly been forgotten. So the return of angry partisanship and obsessive campaignism in the twenty-first century seems "unprecedented." It's not that our problems are the same as those of the late nineteenth century—often they are strikingly different—but that the era in between was so unusual. As the restraints of the 1900s erode, we are seeing old tendencies peek through. To understand what seems to be going wrong with our politics today, we have to ask how we got that "normal" twentieth-century democracy to begin with.

～

FOR ALL THE acrimony of its politics, the late nineteenth century was not a dismal era. The sun still shone in the Gilded Age. This same period gave American culture brilliant gifts: the cocktail and the bicycle, the hot dog and pop music, participatory democracy inching toward the premise of one person, one vote.[9]

Among this era's most brilliant gifts was a forgotten father-daughter dynasty. As I rifled through the Smithsonian's collections, hints of this family's incredible story kept showing themselves. Cartoons mocking the radical father. Pamphlets from the daughter's public crusades. Again and again, the charming, frustrating, fantastically ubiquitous Kelley family kept popping up, their rich but stormy relationship tracing the arc of American democracy from 1865 to 1915.

The lives of William Kelley and his daughter Florence Kelley seem to reach everywhere and connect to everyone, taking them from Philadelphia slums to Washington ballrooms to Swiss socialist meetings. He was a congressman; she was a labor activist. His enemies called him "Pig Iron Kelley," hers called her "that fire-eater in the black dress." Over two lifetimes they fought a sustained crusade for the rights of working people, playing key roles in the rise of popular democracy, abolition, voting rights for African Americans, women's suffrage, an expanded money supply, the tariff, the battle against child labor, the settlement movement, and the rise of social security. They even contributed to the official designation of the tomato as a vegetable. Leafing through their letters, I stumbled across notes they received from Frederick Douglass and Friedrich Engels, Abraham Lincoln and Lincoln Steffens, Susan B. Anthony and W. E. B. Du Bois. In between the big names, Will and Florie corresponded with voters and factory laborers, reform activists and party thugs, athletes and professors and gunmen and church ladies.[10]

And through all the elections and protests, assassination attempts and ugly divorces, Will and Florie learned from each other, mixing the personal and the political in a bond that tested the limits of family and democracy.

William Kelley's body was a textbook of his era. Long and lean, he bore a scar on his eye from a childhood of hard labor, another on his arm from a fellow congressman's knife, and cancer building in his throat from a lifetime in smoke-filled rooms. His victories were those his era would allow; his defeats marked the limits of his age. From the 1830s to the 1890s, Will Kelley campaigned and legislated and fought, starting movements and jumping parties, struggling to maintain his independence amid the two political machines that ruled American life. He was widely considered an Honest Man, but his life shows how little an Honest Man could do against the irresistible momentum of that mass political system, that locomotive hurtling nowhere.

Florence "inherited her father's ability," then spent a lifetime making it her own. She lived a life of persistence, triumphing over epidemic disease, Victorian sexism, industrial tycoons, and the political system that dragged her father down. She was funnier than her father, harsher too, an "explosive, hot-tempered, determined" woman who charted a path out of the political world she grew to disdain. Florence Kelley built a life of public influence along the lines of the twentieth century's emerging political model. Doing so required a terrible rupture with her family, even as she worked to remain true to the intellectual and political apprenticeship she received from her father, learning the family business.[11]

William and Florence Kelley tell the story of their democracy as it went through a painful re-formation. Because they pursued consistent ends—of protecting working people—but had to work through the evolving means of their successive generations, they highlight how dramatically American politics changed. Their dinner table talks and fierce letters offer a study of a phase change in democracy, the same points argued by those objects in the Smithsonian. It is a story and a study that we might benefit from today, to understand that reform is possible, and to appreciate what it cost to cool our democracy.

PART ONE

PURE DEMOCRACY, 1865–1877

CHAPTER ONE

"The One Question of the Age Is *Settled*"

F lorie's Papa had sent a letter. It came from Washington like all the others, pages covered with black or purple ink, each word leaning into the next. Just how her Papa talked, a flood of thoughts and jokes bubbling out. There had been a lot of letters lately, and usually Florie's Mamma gathered the children to read them aloud, telling all about Papa's important work and faraway adventures. About The War. But sometimes she kept them to herself, looking worried, disappearing into her chambers upstairs.[1]

Their big house, with so many rooms and hallways, with dark walnut paneling perfect for a little girl to trace with her fingers, was quiet when Papa was away. Called the Elms, their mansion stood shielded by towering trees, its shutters thrown open to a cheerful Pennsylvania lane. But inside, the house felt still without Papa. His library was dim, and Florie would count the days until he would come home and bathe all those gorgeous books in warm light and nonstop talk.[2]

Florie could not go to Washington, D.C., to see her Papa. Mamma said that it was a noisy, dusty city with no little girls at all. Five-year-olds did not belong there. It sounded fascinating though, with a great deal of business for her Papa to do in a big building on a hill.[3]

She worried about her Papa. He never stopped moving, never stopped talking. As soon as she could write, she had her Mamma send her letters down to Washington, scratching out messages like "DEAR PAPA I HOPE YOU ARE W-ELL. I HOPE YOUR COUG-H HAZ LEFT YOU." She stared at each word, a serious little girl, sallow and sickly, with a weak chin but deep-diving brown eyes. The same eyes in each photo, all through her life. Demanding eyes that would one day win her a reputation for fierceness, what she later called a habit of "persistent asking." It was all there in her five-year-old face.[4]

Florie Kelley wanted to know what was in those letters from her Papa. What was he doing, and why were things so busy down in dusty Washington?

SLAVERY WAS DYING in that big building on the hill. All around Will Kelley, the House of Representatives buzzed and croaked, packed with gossipers and speechifiers fighting out a constitutional amendment. Though Congressman William Darrah Kelley had defined his career fighting slavery, he had another priority on January 31, 1865. He had to tell his family. His abolitionist wife, Carrie, would want to know. So would Florie, with her endless questions. But the bandage wrapped round his left hand, and the aching knife wound within it, made writing difficult.[5]

Kelley scrawled nonetheless. It was typical of the ranty, loving congressman that he chose this moment to write to "Dear Carrie" and the kids. As a politician, as a husband, as a father, Will Kelley was always passionate, and always operating on his own timeline. In Congress, he would often stretch out his impossibly long frame—skinny legs propped on green-felt writing desk, floppy hair falling over his low brow—and absent-mindedly pare an apple while some representative droned. Then he would spring up with surprising grace, intoning "Mr. Speak-*arr*—Mr. Speak-*arr*" when he felt moved to disagree. As a judge in Philadelphia in the 1850s, he would grow distracted and lovesick during legal proceedings and jot letters to Carrie, his dark-haired, blue-eyed bride.[6]

And so Kelley hunched his long frame over his desk, pinned some pages down with his bandaged left hand, and scribbled with his right, trying to capture the momentous scene.

Around him Congress pulled to and fro, fighting over "the most important question submitted to the House in more than half a century."[7] Not far to the south the Civil War raged, and throughout the nation many were still enslaved. Lincoln's bold Emancipation Proclamation had freed millions, theoretically, but only applied to those men and women living in rebel territory. The many still within the Union, in nonseceded states like Maryland or Kentucky, were left enslaved, as were those in some regions held by the Union Army. And Lincoln's Emancipation was achieved only through the vague war powers of the president. A democratically elected Congress would have to make Emancipation federal law for slavery to truly die. So Will Kelley and his allies pushed for an amendment, a final federal death blow, a test of what popular democracy could achieve.

It had been an unforgivingly cold January, but the massive structure on the hill warmed with the heat of so many agitated bodies. Their voices echoed and banked across the coffered ceiling. The elevated galleries, Will wrote to Carrie, "swarm with people," uniformed Black soldiers, female lobbyists, and shabby reporters, all breathing the same "miserable air." The flickering gaslights stank, and half the speeches were inaudible, but a kind of mass expectation intoxicated everyone present. "How I regret that you are not in the diplomatic gallery," Will told Carrie.[8]

On the packed floor, small clutches of congressmen gathered and fractured, navigating around writing desks and overfull spittoons. Supreme Court justices and most of President Lincoln's cabinet circulated, chatting amiably about how to swing a few key votes. Kelley broke away from his letter writing to learn the newest count or watch some stiff-necked Democrat defend slavery. One Kentucky politician began "croaking forth in much scriptural language a last plea for the dying institution," Kelley smirked to his wife. "Poor fellow, he honestly believes that he is defending the Constitution."[9]

Kelley was free to write his wife because no one in Congress thought that they might change his vote. Kelley placed himself on the radical fringe of the Radical Republicans of 1865, a rare supporter of abolition, women's rights, workers' rights, and many other unusual, crankish causes. He had spent the past few years sharing stages with his friend Frederick Douglass and mentoring Anna Dickinson, an electrifying twenty-year-old "girl orator." Few White men in America would have done the same; Kelley was totally out of the mainstream. At a time when slavery still remained in limbo, when most White Americans were publicly and unabashedly racist, Kelley attacked the "hypocritical lip-service" with which Americans talked about the notion of equality.[10]

His timing may have appeared radical, but Will's sense of the possible was astute. Somehow, across one of the longest careers in American politics, he consistently managed to be noisily on the vanguard, attracting piles of adoring, bemused, or hateful commentary. People just loved to write about the guy. The elite, effete Philadelphia diarist Sidney George Fisher may have captured him best, when he wrote with disdain that Congressman Kelley "is an abolitionist. He was formerly a democrat. He is a man of obscure birth and vulgar manners, but has ability, is a fluent speaker not without a coarse popular eloquence, and, tho a good deal of a demagogue, is, I believe, generally considered an honest man."[11]

Kelley's appearance won even more attention. Journalists and memoirists often commented on his unusual physique—"long, lean, lean and cadaverous Pig-Iron Kelley, towered aloft six feet nine inches, more or less." In reality he stood six foot three, but his slimness and unexpected "lightness of step" made him seem taller. Kelley's handsome, simian face, with full beard, protruding ears, sharp blue eyes, and tousled hair hanging low over his forehead, made him a perfect victim for cartoonists. Few mocked his right eye, however, which bore a nasty scar from a childhood of hard labor.[12]

Nearly everyone mentioned his uncanny voice, a classically trained rumble, a voice, wrote the *Chicago Tribune*, "like an eloquent graveyard."[13]

Lately, that deep voice had been calling for radical change, and that lanky body had been bearing the consequences. Two weeks before the vote on the Thirteenth Amendment, Will introduced a bill to guarantee voting rights for many African Americans.[14] He had argued that a government that "deprived thousands of men of the right of suffrage" had "invested them with the acknowledged right to rebel against a tyrant who will not listen to their voice." Give people rights, or they would be justified in taking them. The republic only makes itself "safer when she binds all her children to her by protecting the rights of all." Kelley's view of democracy—the bigger the better, the louder the safer—captured the populist tone of nineteenth-century politics.[15]

Supporters printed half a million copies of his speech, and an African American admirer wrote to Kelley, promising that "if the present does assault you," he should nonetheless be proud of standing up for "the great principles of the age."[16]

The predicted assault came a few days later. Will had joined some ladies and gentlemen for a late supper at Washington's ornate Willard Hotel. There, while the party dined, a burly older man with a Kentucky drawl and a gap-toothed smile forced his way into their circle. The would-be congressman Alexander Pope Field began to heckle "Judge Kelley." Will responded; the two pushed back and forth. When Kelley dismissed Field as a man "who behaves in the presence of ladies as you are now doing," Field snapped. Hollering "God damn you, you must give me satisfaction," he drew a blade and sliced at Will again and again, catching his outstretched left hand, slashing down to the bone. Will caught Field by the lapels, bloodying his white collar while the pair wrestled. Bystanders intervened, dragging them apart. Field shouted at Kelley that he would "shoot him before I go to bed."[17]

Newspapers reported that Congressman Kelley was bleeding to death, but he survived. Bandaged, dosed with sedatives, Will wrote to Carrie from his F Street boardinghouse, his penmanship faint but reassuring. It would not be the last letter Will sent to Carrie begging her to disregard some awful news in the papers about him.[18]

He would go on to make grander speeches and anger stronger enemies. Over his many years in Congress, Will Kelley became beloved, hated, "almost better known throughout the world than any other man in American public life." Somehow, this single individual shook Andrew Jackson's hand in 1833, informed Abraham Lincoln that he had won the Republican nomination in 1860, helped the transcontinental railroad link America in 1869, wrote the bill guaranteeing voting rights for men of all races in 1870, proposed the creation of Yellowstone as America's first national park in 1871, organized America's centennial celebration in 1876, reshaped America's industrial economy in the 1880s, and helped dedicate the Statue of Liberty in 1886.[19]

And on January 31, 1865, Will Kelley sat in Congress with a bandaged left hand, preparing to end the 246-year-old travesty of American slavery.

The counting began. That massive hall, never fuller, held its breath as men representing so many corners and constituents intoned their "Aye" or "Nay." Every swing Democrat's "Aye" won cheers from the galleries. Ex-slaves who had seen battle in a blue uniform, old women who begged church members to sign their emancipation petitions, leaned out over the boxes to hear. Kelley quickly summed up his letter with "love and Kisses to the children and you / I am as ever your Will," so he could vote to kill slavery.[20]

The final tally was 119 for, 56 against, 8 absent. Just two more votes than the two-thirds needed to pass. There was a long, quiet moment, a "disbelieving hollow silence." How could a room that full feel that still? Then it shattered, hundreds of men and women on their feet, hollering and whistling, throwing their hats, climbing on the desks. The galleries fluttered with ladies waving handkerchiefs. Democrats turned away as Republicans hugged and shook hands. African American spectators in the galleries struggled to comprehend how dramatically their reality had just changed. One dignified Black spectator, reluctant to show his joy in that mixed crowd, quietly excused himself, stepped quickly to an empty anteroom across the hall, and exploded in a full-body shimmy, silently dancing with jubilation.[21]

Kelley broke away from his backslapping friends, finding his desk among the throng. He leaned his long frame over this letter to Carrie and the kids, dipped his pen in fresh ink, and added an almost glowing postscript:

"The bill is carried."[22]

THE NEXT DAY, jubilant crowds gathered before the White House. They cheered the passage of the Thirteenth Amendment and serenaded President Lincoln. In extemporaneous remarks before that jostling crowd, Lincoln called the amendment "a King's Cure for all the evils," referring to a common medicinal tonic, used to treat everything from bunions to cholera. His words hinted at a sweeping, end-of-history view of the moment, unusual for a man so careful with language, and with slavery. Many celebrants agreed. One thrilled Californian wrote home to his wife that with the passage of the Thirteenth Amendment, "the one question of the age is *settled.*"[23]

Words like *cure* and *settled* capture the anticipation of many in the victorious North in 1865, convinced that their nation stood on the threshold of a new era. The war was not yet over, and no one knew how to reconstruct the nation, but it was clear that American democracy was about to change. It was time, Will Kelley told an African American social club in Philadelphia, to "perpetuate a pure democracy, with powers subject only to the revision of the people."[24]

What Kelley called "pure democracy," the belligerent New York congressman Roscoe Conkling called a "moral earthquake." Things were about to get a lot less "settled." It was time to shake loose the old bonds that had restrained politics for far too long, to ensure that "the will of the majority must be the only king; the ballot-box must be the only throne." Three elements converged around 1865 to give that ballot box new and unprecedented power: the end of slavery, the widening of political participation by the laboring classes, and the economic disruptions that began with the war and only increased after. Together they would remake American politics. No one could define "pure democracy," but millions felt invested in some kind of stripping away of the old limitations that had held back the will of the majority.[25]

It was easy for northern Republicans to boast about majorities in 1865. They had the numbers. In the defeated Confederacy, many grumbled that they would never vote again, and in the North conservative Democrats accused the Republican Party of conspiring to "carry out its spite / to elevate the black man and trample on the white." But the Republican Party held unprecedented sway, controlling over 70 percent of the seats in Congress in 1865, soon to rise to 80 percent. The next census would find that three-quarters of Americans lived outside the former Confederacy, with more people in New York, Pennsylvania, and Ohio than in all the formerly seceded states combined. If the four million newly freed African Americans were able to win political rights, they would further strengthen this ruling alliance.[26]

Looking back on this moment, Americans have so focused on the myths of the Lost South that they have ignored the ascendant North. Never in American history, except possibly for the Virginians of the founding generation, was one bloc of Americans so dominant as the postwar northern Republicans.

By killing slavery, this majority unsettled a careful balance that had long shaped American politics. For decades, before it caused civil war, slavery had often restrained American political behavior. Terrified of disunion, careful politicians—"Great Compromisers" like Henry Clay or "doughface" appeasers like James Buchanan—worked to avoid conflict over the issue, engineering artful compromises, preserving the Union at the expense, over and over again, of the enslaved. Every deal postponed a reckoning. Congress suppressed discussion of the issue with "gag rules," states disenfranchised Black voters, and angry mobs targeted abolitionists. The Democratic Party itself was created, in the 1820s, as an "antidote for sectional prejudices."[27]

But a lively, popular democracy could not keep quiet about slavery forever. In the 1850s, the matter took center stage. Soon parties splintered, crowds gathered, idealists and hotheads pushed the sides farther from each other. Southern Democrats made impossible demands on their northern allies. The first entirely sectional party emerged with the rise of the northern Republicans. It is no accident that secession followed the highest turnout election in U.S. history to that point, with 81.2 percent of eligible voters weighing in on the booming 1860 campaign.[28] Public outrage was replacing restrained compromise on the eve of the Civil War.

To most in the Union, the time had come to confront slavery. Even those Whites who had no interest in liberating African Americans were willing to take up arms to defend their nation's political system. Many came to believe that a cabal of southern aristocrats, called the Slave Power, was strangling democracy, for free White men as well as the enslaved. They pointed to the unhealthy status of politics in the Deep South, where some states still denied voting rights to men without property, where voter turnout was often abysmally low, where public dissent was squashed, where the Democrats often ran uncontested, and where Confederates were willing to leave the Union because they lost an election.[29]

Democracy was under threat, and the whole world was watching. The *New York Times* pointed out that, on the eve of war, conservatives in Europe were hollering "We told you so" across the Atlantic at America's naive faith in popular self-government. The *Times* titled its article "IS DEMOCRACY A FAILURE?"[30]

Four years later, the death of the slaveholders' republic looked like a new birth for democracy. By killing "the Slave Power," the cobbler-turned-populist-politician Henry Wilson argued, "the business of self-government is now in the hands of the people" for the first time in history. A New Hampshire preacher went further, claiming that the defeat of the southern aristocracy meant "the last class government in the United States had been swept away." Instead, Americans "found themselves face to face with a pure democracy from one end of the country to the other."[31]

The unleashing of voters, and soldiers, against the Slave Power over-lapped with another trend revolutionizing mid-nineteenth-century America. Faith in popular self-government was reaching an unprecedented peak. The Republic was not created as a democracy (the word does not even appear in the Constitution), but for several decades Americans had been unwrapping the bonds that kept most people out of most governments for most of history.

Today, we can see the many ways that the politics of the 1800s were bigoted and exclusionary, but at the time, they looked revelatory. A series of quiet revolutions had distributed power to ordinary citizens: offering suffrage to White men who did not own property, electing common-born men like Andrew Jackson or Abraham Lincoln to high office, organizing wild political campaigns that engaged thousands, and drawing the highest voter turnouts in American history. It is hard to overstate how revolutionary these steps were at the time; even these limited rights cannot be taken for granted as inevitable. In some states foreign citizens could vote, in others Black men participated, and a few seriously debated women's suffrage. Activists like Frederick Douglass, Susan B. Anthony, and Will Kelley began to talk about "impartial suffrage"—voting rights regardless of identity. Though far from twenty-first-century expectations of inclusivity, and never following a steady line of progress, America was just about the most democratic place on earth by the standards of world history up to the nineteenth century.

To the inheritors of this political revolution, pure democracy meant killing the Slave Power, but also sweeping away "class government." Even those who fiercely opposed racial inclusion, like the bigoted vice president Andrew Johnson, hoped to "go on elevating our people, perfecting our institutions," until the whole world could see that in America, "the voice of the people is the voice of god."[32]

The fight against slavery, and the widening of popular politics, had taken decades, but everything seemed to accelerate with the war. The conflict exaggerated economic and social trends already showing themselves across the striving nineteenth century. "All previous tendencies," wrote one journalist, "intensified into a whirl."[33] During the war three million men saw combat, but more than thirty million citizens took on new roles—wives running businesses, inventors debuting designs, laborers increasing output. The growing nation was six times more populous than in 1800, continuously pushing west, devouring a continent. Industry drove forward, laying more miles of railroad track than Britain, Germany, and France combined. Government spent twenty-one times more in 1865 than it had a decade before. And American culture outpaced itself, boasting more breweries, better eating houses, bolder comedians, bigger brothels. Americans could choose from over four thousand newspapers nationwide, up from seven hundred a generation before.[34]

That growth set a nation loose. Millions migrated to this booming republic, millions more relocated within it, freed from conformity but also cut off from community. As the economy and the war shook ambitious men and women loose, and the widening of democracy and the end of slavery severed past restraints, old aristocrats had to cede their dominance. The snide but observant Henry Adams—himself descended from two presidents and as close to nobility as America got—suggested that a newly mobilized generation had empowered strivers and bounders who had little interest in the old rules of behavior, men and women who "naturally and intensely disliked to be told what to do."[35]

It seemed like nothing could hold this victorious majority back. A great unsettling had crushed slavery, broadened politics, and accelerated change. With so many obstacles pushed away, what else could American democracy achieve?

Success pushed idealists to reimagine politics in ways that had long seemed impossible. Emancipation heated their expectations. Before the war, only a tiny minority supported abolition, but once it succeeded, millions "fell into line," claiming that "we are all Abolitionists since the emancipation of the slaves." The generation who watched Emancipation take place at a formative moment in their upbringing would spend the rest of the nineteenth century looking for an issue—women's rights, class revolution, social Darwinism—"as meaningful as abolition."[36]

Others began to fantasize about destroying partisanship. The nation seemed to be moving in that direction: the tectonic stress of the past decade had crumbled the old parties, killing the Whigs, giving rise to the Know-Nothings and the Republican Party, and splitting the old Democratic Party over and over. Millions actually had switched parties. In an era of political fluidity, when nothing seemed permanent, President Lincoln went so far as to temporarily replace the Republican Party with the so-called Union Party, a vehicle that made room for moderate Democrats as well as Republicans.[37]

Will Kelley hoped to be done with partisanship. He had left the Democrats over slavery and now imagined a future where, to express their views, Americans would dig deeper than simply "naming a party." Political machines had empowered leaders whose views were as fleeting "as pepper is hot in the mouth," whose "intellectual vision is from the back of their heads." It was time to reimagine politics entirely, Kelley told Congress in his speech calling for Black voting rights. "Ours is a new age. We are unfolding a new page in national life."[38]

America's unleashed democracy was as rich with disruptive possibility, Kelley thundered, as the invention of the steam engine or the printing press. No need to cling to old parties or identities. "The past is gone forever," he told Congress. "There is no abiding present: it flies while we name it. It is our duty to provide for the thick-coming future."[39]

Of course, "pure democracy" was a joke, a fantasy of exuberant radicals. But so were hopes that the nation might just return to the old way of doing things, "the Constitution as it was" that conservative Democrats kept hollering for. A moderate majority would have to settle somewhere in between. But change was coming, that was certain. "The Civil War had made a new system in fact," Henry Adams observed. "The country would have to reorganize the machinery in practice and theory . . . All that had gone before was useless." A political system that had spent decades reined in by gag rules and compromises was breaking free.[40]

The Civil War obliterated many of the checks on the power of the ballot box. It was impossible to see, in 1865, that this stripped-down, sped-up vision of democratic progress brought with it a new, in some ways more fundamental, challenge: How to cope with popular government once you had it? How to navigate the big, loud, populist political system with dangerously high expectations for what it could achieve?

One thing is certain: neither the death of slavery nor the grinding down of the war would "settle" American democracy. Over the next generation, Americans would face a long crisis of popular government, self-inflicted and eventually self-cured. A political disruption that ricocheted from optimism through rage to disillusionment to boredom before reform was possible. And it was spelled out, vote-for-vote and fight-for-fight, in the letters and talks of the idealistic Will Kelley and his persistent daughter Florie.

The cautious, the conservative, they had better hang on, Florie's Papa had thundered in that hill-top Capitol: "These are terrible times for timid people."[41]

CHAPTER TWO

"The Great American Game"

"Made a very good speech—spoke for two hours. Mem.: an empty stomach & two good cups of black tea greatly provocative of eloquence."

"Speaking for two hours on an empty stomach gives one an appetite . . . Celebration of Ale & Oysters after."

"Supper without meat—I nearly starved . . . One of the miseries of country canvassing."[1]

Ignatius Donnelly campaigned on his stomach. From one muddy midwestern settlement to the next, raw Atlantic oysters powered one of the nation's wildest political orators. When he had eaten right, Donnelly could ignite a Minnesota town hall. Sometimes the village was seedy, the men rat-faced, the crowd "Drunken Norwegians," the audience "very stupid & myself more so." But more often, everything clicked. "What a joy it is to find such a hall and such an audience," Donnelly enthused after one Republican event, "where one's words fall like showers of electric sparks, kindling a blaze wherever they touch!"[2]

Donnelly's words lit blazes up and down the Midwest in the mid-1860s, as he canvassed for himself and other Republicans in race after race.

Broad-faced and pudgy, the thirtysomething Donnelly stood out for his speaking skills and his nonstop campaigning. Though born near Will in Philadelphia, the Irish American Donnelly left behind the "Philie" machine and settled in Minnesota, putting his gab to use among the taciturn locals. During the Civil War years, he won office as a young congressman serving alongside Kelley. He became a national icon and a go-to stumper for Republicans in need of an eloquent boost. Donnelly would claim to have traveled 5,326 miles in the 1868 presidential race alone, slurping oysters and savaging Democrats.[3]

Donnelly's strength was also his weakness, and spoke to a political system driven by such charismatic campaigners. Once he got talking, he just could not stop himself. He did not have a particularly resonant voice, or a consistent message, but he built up a kind of rhetorical momentum that won debates and stunned crowds. He would veer from party politics to barnyard humor to pseudoscientific predictions, taking a break from attacking the president to wonder whether "dragons of fairy lore represent the now extinct pterodactyl."[4]

The result was that, though a fiery political entertainer, Donnelly developed a reputation for taking things too far. Politicians complained that he talked until he ruined his best ideas. One newspaper declared that he "sickened the legislature with his verbosity." William Allen White, the Kansan journalist, looking back on Donnelly decades later, wondered whether his "burning eloquence" was matched by something like insanity, a "soft place in his brain." Donnelly worried about what he called the "softening of the brain" as well, and the rest of his career would bear out concerns for his mental health.[5]

But in the second half of the 1860s, Donnelly looked like the tribune of a dawning democratic age, a mouthy Irishman come west to spread the good news. He was like a funhouse mirror image of Will Kelley—fat to Kelley's thin, emotion to Kelley's empiricism, wild to Kelley's warmth. But they both agreed that the end of the war meant a new wave of democratic progress, with "no return to this forward moving flood." Donnelly put his faith in mass politics even more strongly than Kelley had in his Black suffrage speech. "I am not one of those," Donnelly declared, "who believe that politics is a mere base struggle for place and plunder—where the profoundest rascality and the deepest purse always win the game." Instead, capturing all the optimism of northern Republicans in the postwar moment, Donnelly declared that to participate in politics meant "to make some one better for your having lived. This lifts us above the worms & vermin and makes up part of the great enginery of God."[6]

And God needed Republicans to work that enginery, to build a great machine. The party that emerged from the Civil War was, to Donnelly, "the friend of the poor, the oppressed, the down trodden—the lifter up of the slave & the friend of our national life." Like Kelley, Donnelly expressed a bold, populist faith in American politics: a combination of the old Jacksonian belief that the majority must be right, with a post-Emancipation confidence that an active government could be a force for good. Throughout history, Donnelly believed, immoral laws "sooner or later result in wars"— echoing Kelley's claim that expanding democracy made the state safer.[7]

And, more prophetically, the oyster-slurping, stump-speaking Donnelly voiced the premise driving the next phase of American political life. It was always the case, Donnelly shouted during one of his rolling speeches, "that the representative men of a community"—the politicians—"will never attain a higher moral standard than their constituency." The voting public would have to determine the direction of that "forward moving flood."[8]

In the middle to late 1860s, it was clear how those constituents could express their moral standards. They could leave their houses and their shops and join in the vast, stomping political campaigns that dominated popular culture. They could light stinking oil torches, don shimmering uniforms, burn effigies, roll floats, push coffins (with the names of rival politicians scribbled on their sides), sing serenades, build bonfires, light fireworks. They could argue all night in saloons, or shout down strangers on railcars, or help load the celebratory cannons. They could illuminate their homes with hundreds of candles, or shoot their revolvers in the air, or barbecue hogs for celebrations, or heave brickbats from their roofs into teeming rallies of the other party. They could stand for hours, held rapt by fiery speeches, or post broadsides on walls with a sticky paste, or pour out campaign whiskey for thirsty marchers. They could smell, taste, and feel democracy pulsating all around them. Newly emboldened African Americans could participate in the kind of campaign wildness they had observed, from the sidelines, for years. Those campaigns were, sniped the urbane *Atlantic Monthly*, "the theatre, the opera, the base-ball game, the intellectual gymnasium, almost the church, of the people."[9]

One veteran politician, explaining campaign tricks to a newcomer, reminded him: "Never allow yourself to lose sight of the fact that politics, and not poker, is our great American game."[10] And "nobody ever dreams of organizing a reform movement in poker."[11]

Visitors agreed. European publications struggled to explain the democratic carnival that preceded American elections, an event "oddly unlike anything with which we are familiar." One stunned correspondent for the *London Daily News* tried to take his readers through the scenes, as "people living as far asunder as the population of Paris is from that of St. Petersburg" simultaneously broke "out into flags, placards, portraits and symbols." Nearly "every leading street of every city will have huge transparencies of the rival candidates suspended high in air . . . The rival effigies will blister in the sun of Broadway, New York . . . will span the narrow, formal and busy Chestnut Street, Philadelphia, and adorn the broad, crude, unfinished spaces of Pennsylvania avenue, Washington . . . The motley crowd—American, Irish, Mexican, and Chinese—that stream every day along Montgomery street, San Francisco" would march under party banners.[12]

As if they had "sprung suddenly out of the earth," huge parades of thousands of Republicans or Democrats would come marching through the nighttime, blinding stunned English newspapermen with the "ruddy glow of a vast parade of torchbearers." Among the marchers, "startling oddities will break out"—clubs and companies wearing military uniforms, capes, helmets of medieval knights, or caps with blazing torches fixed to the top. Down America's main streets would pour men "in scarves and chimney-pot hats, the German Turnverein, the Fenian brotherhood, 'the Cuban avengers,' the Garibaldi fraternity, the Amalgamation of Freedmen (colored, of course)." Companies of Black Philadelphians stepping down Lombard Street, led by Octavius Catto, the handsome, mustachioed captain of the beloved local Negro league baseball team, the Pythians. Or White men clutching flame-throwing "flambeau torches," lighting up New Orleans's river wards. Or brass bands of farm girls in red capes, honking their way through Galesburg, Illinois. It all fit together into a public politics that was colorful and garish, accessible and insistent, tapped out to the rhythm of hard-soled boots on cobblestones.[13]

"It may be," the correspondent warned, "that in some places there will be rioting." But more often Americans campaigned with a gambler's fixation. "The European traveler," riding on an American train, "looks up amazed when somebody comes round, who formally asks him for which candidate he votes." It turned out to be "a common pastime, half jest, half earnest, for a tram full of people thus thrown by chance together to test public opinion" by taking a straw poll of how each rider planned to vote in an upcoming election.[14]

A tourist had to look around and ask themselves: Were they riding on a Republican train or a Democratic one?

Most Americans could tell, at a glance, how their fellow passengers would vote. Race, class, region, religion, occupation, ethnicity, even a style of hat or preference for whiskey or beer all indicated Republican or Democrat. This was true of women as well as men, first-time "virgin voters" as well as old soldiers. As a broad generalization, Republicans often included rural evangelical Yankees, upwardly mobile professionals, Protestant immigrants, skilled laborers, and African Americans. For their part, Democrats attracted many urban workers, Catholic immigrants, many Southerners, and small farmers in the lower North. Republicans tended to support an active federal government, while Democrats denounced "centralism," but mostly, each side just opposed whatever the other side stood for.

Citizens had been showing off their partisan affiliations, flamboyantly playing that "great American game" for decades. Over the course of the nineteenth century, a diverse nation, with few shared holidays or folk festivals, united around a new democratic folk culture. It was the first truly national popular culture in America, engaging and enraging citizens from Maine to California.

And it was building momentum. From the rise of common-man Jacksonian democracy in the 1820s through the Log Cabin and Hard Cider 1840 presidential campaign, Americans mostly demonstrated by rallying around some external totem, raising Liberty poles, pushing wheeled log cabins, or lighting massive bonfires assembled by children. Their processions could be striking, but often had a ragtag quality, a variegated gathering of homemade costumes and homesewn banners. On the eve of the Civil War, the Republicans introduced an explosive new model: militaristic marching companies of young men called Wide Awakes, wearing black, shimmering uniforms, bearing torches, and parading at night. Soon all parties chose this style as the predominant way to campaign. Such clubs could fill Union Square with twenty thousand torches or pour more marchers through some small Wisconsin town than the residents would see in a lifetime. The shift signaled a deepening engagement in politics. Wrapped in identical uniforms, stomping forward through darkened streets and squares, political parties signaled a kind of communal momentum, individuals losing themselves in "this forward moving flood."[15]

Donnelly stood as a perfect symbol of this campaign culture precisely because of the ragged looseness of his ideas. His "soft brain" could never keep to the issue at hand; his sickening verbosity fit well into a political culture that refused to distinguish between politics and entertainment. Donnelly's speeches veered from progress, to partisanship, to pterodactyls, which is exactly how Americans played their game in the late 1860s. Political culture and popular culture overlapped, strengthening each other, and what seemed like daftness to some was actually Donnelly skillfully walking that line.

The men and women who lectured and hollered at the center of these political events were the chief celebrities of their day. Their names fill ordinary people's diaries, and political cartoonists expected readers to recognize their faces, unlabeled, in comics. Dakota cowboys, meeting the much-caricatured Senator Roscoe Conkling, told him that they would rather shake his hand than see Barnum's circus. When the humorist Don Piatt visited an exposition of wax figures of famous Americans in London, he ignored the generals, explorers, and inventors and complained that the show lacked the most "popular and eminent men" in the country, specifically, politicians like "Pig-Iron Kelley."[16]

And once, when Donnelly found himself lost at night in a raging storm, he knocked on a farmhouse door and asked the owner if he could borrow a lantern. The Minnesotan gruffly dismissed the request . . . until he realized that it was *Ignatius Donnelly* asking to borrow his lantern. Donnelly walked home with lantern-light illuminating his path. "So fame is worth something," he wrote in his diary.[17]

And fame came from speechifying. Stump speakers and campaign hollerers were the ubiquitous talking heads of their day. American citizens were connoisseurs of their every gesture and flourish. Rhetoric was taught in school or studied in night courses, where pupils practiced the science of "charismatic movements"—dramatic gestures that look stiff to modern eyes but struck nineteenth-century crowds as bold and decisive. Spectators reviewed speakers they saw, focusing on the specifics of their (unamplified) voice, build, and stage presence. And because it was often considered inappropriate for candidates for higher office—especially the presidency—to campaign on their own behalf, Americans devised an elaborate system of proxy stumpers, each shouting for someone farther up the party food chain. Everyone seemed to be practicing their speech, joked a female comedian in Louisiana: young voters could hardly drink in a saloon without enduring "this shelling of 'principles' and 'platforms' and this thundering bombardment of eloquence."[18]

European immigrants noted this speechifying culture in letters home. One Swede observed: "The Americans are from childhood, and through their very upbringing, practiced speakers; they express themselves very well, energetically," while a dour Norwegian complained about the "bombastic, terribly long speeches." But both agreed that Americans were trained and zealous talkers.[19]

Sometimes all this talk could devolve into stupid shouting or atrocious violence. Some speakers were torn down from rostrums; others kept a hand on their bowie knife while shouting into hostile crowds. Nevertheless, citizens expected public political discussions. Newly empowered Black men and women adapted the habit quickly in the 1860s, bringing long-practiced sermonizing skills to a "speech-making mania," debating the politics of Reconstruction. Frances Ellen Watkins Harper, a Black abolitionist, born free in Baltimore, set out throughout the South in the 1860s, finding crowds of freed slaves "eager to hear, ready to listen." She even speechified on the railroads. When passengers, White and Black, learned that she was a lecturer, she was drawn into heated debates about the future of her people. She found the "congregation of listeners in the cars" to be some of her best audiences. She even had "a rather exciting time" arguing with a former slave dealer about the meaning of race.[20]

More and more, in the postwar years, political speechifying blended with Americans' new fascination with moving, infuriating, or hilarious talks. Though the nation had long enjoyed a culture of instructive lyceum lectures, after the war they became a lot more fun. Much of the shift was due to an odd little man named James Redpath, a former abolitionist who had fought with John Brown in Kansas, and who devoted himself to the task of enlivening American public speaking. After the war, Redpath organized tours of politicians, comedians, mad scientists, and suffragists, winning them huge sums, so long as they could give a lively talk. He forbade reading from prepared text (considering it the equivalent of "making love to a woman by writing my opinion of her and reading it to her"), and promoted heavy-hitting comedians who did not shy away from politics. Even Frederick Douglass, who speechified consistently from the 1840s through the 1890s, found that after the war audiences no longer wanted "to hear statesmanlike addresses, which are usually rather heavy for the stomachs."[21]

Crowds wanted something looser, funnier, sexier, and angrier than the sermons of an earlier era. The poised orations of Daniel Webster, Henry Clay, and other prewar statesmen were out. Americans wanted speechifiers who could heat a one-thousand-person tent with emotion. They expected charisma and wit and the hottest-burning fuel of the era: political outrage.

A long-building political culture was hitting some kind of high gear in those post–Civil War years. America's enlivened speaking culture combined with campaigns that promised the thrill of barely contained competition. It all promoted the kind of aggressive campaigners who were "ready to break their opponents' heads, or to have their own heads broken, for the sake of 'the party.'"[22]

NO SPEAKER, AN impressed journalist wrote, "broke so many skulls in so short a time as did Judge Kelley." In the postwar years, few politicians used public speaking to achieve such fame and notoriety. Known for his rumbling bass, Will supposedly joked (in a newspaper quote that sounds suspiciously unlike him) that he had won office not "for me political ability," but "on account of me magnificent voice."[23]

Kelley's reliance on his speaking skills made him emblematic of his political era. It was a tool that he honed at the very start of his long career, back in 1835, when as a gangling twenty-one-year-old he climbed, uninvited, onto a Boston stage, while a skeptical crowd grumbled "Who is he?"[24]

He was a poor boy from Philadelphia, whose father had died when he was two years old. The first thing Will could remember was seeing his family's possessions auctioned on the Northern Liberties sidewalk to pay their debts. He spent his childhood playing in those filthy streets. Another early memory, which would come to mean more to Will over his life, was his close friendship with African American children, especially Robert Bridges Forten, son of one of Black Philadelphia's most prominent families. At that age, the racial and class divides between the two men mattered less, though they would guide Will's politics decades later.[25]

By the time he was eleven, Will was out of school, working as a "printer's devil" for the *Philadelphia Inquirer*. Most of his tasks were lowly—fetching ink, fetching type, fetching ale—but one sparked a lifelong passion. A copyeditor assigned him to read articles aloud with "such distinctness as would satisfy a careful proof-reader." The job trained his voice and introduced him to news and politics and history, launching an "intellectual awakening" in the skinny boy.[26]

But reading aloud could never pay his family's debts, so Will took up his father's trade, apprenticing as a jeweler and watchmaker. The work of gilding America was dangerous, exposing young Will to intense heat, toxic metals, and his mentor's wrath and leaving him with a permanent scar on his right eyelid. But he also found his lifelong mission. The frustration of crafting baubles for the rich nurtured a commitment to protecting working people. Will wrote that, starting his evening shifts, "I never lighted my lamp for night-work without feeling that humanity was outraged" by the toil of a majority for a minority. For the rest of his life, this conviction would guide Kelley's seemingly unpredictable politics, joining his support for industrial laborers, freed slaves, women's rights, and many other causes that were often at odds. "I stand resolutely," Kelley would declare, for "that class to which I belong by birth and early training, the working class."[27]

Typically for Kelley, his outrage came right on time. In northern cities in the 1820s and '30s, working-class radicals were cohering into a pro-labor wing of the Democratic Party, often called "Locofocos." Convinced that America's new wealth grew from workers' stolen labor, these radicals pushed against what they saw as moneyed privilege, fighting to limit the workday to twelve hours—or even a radical ten. Many admired the common-born president Andrew Jackson and his furious war on America's banking elite (and ignored, or supported, Jackson's brutal ethnic cleansing of Native Americans). A few even saw an inherent link between their struggles and the oppression of enslaved African Americans, offering a rare bridge between the politics of working-class Whites and Blacks, so often set against each other in American history.[28]

Kelley entered politics at a rare moment when it was possible to be a poor apprentice and find a booming political voice, to imagine a coalition of White and Black labor, and to be a radical Democrat while hating slavery. At nineteen he met his hero, Andrew Jackson, and shook his hand. But Will's radical views got him blacklisted in Philadelphia, the home of America's conservative banking establishment.

So he began his skull breaking in Boston. Standing in the crowd at Faneuil Hall in 1835, listening to speaker after speaker try to articulate Democratic points, young Will knew he could do better. He had been reading out loud for a decade, training his voice and sharpening his rhetoric, and something compelled him to take the stage. The crowd was still jeering "Who is he?" when Kelley launched into his first political speech, an opening detonation in a barely interrupted series of speeches that would run for the next fifty-five years. "Who am I?" young Will asked as he paced the stage with long-legged strides. "I will tell you who I am directly. I am an American citizen, a man who can earn his living by the sweat of his brow and the cunning of his good right hand—one who has come to this cradled temple of liberty to pledge himself to stem the tide of time on board the good ship Democracy, with her to swim or with her gloriously to sink."[29]

He had made a name. He found benefactors, allies, grown politicians who would call him up onstage. George Bancroft, the eminent historian and radical Democrat, invited Will to use his private library, launching Will's reliance on data in his speechifying. But all those statistics never cooled his heat. Will became a kind of hype-man for drier politicians, stalking rostrums, "firing enthusiasm into the hearts of sluggish and doubtful voters," his magnificent voice filling the air around the Massachusetts statehouse. The influential *Democratic Review* expressed amazement at his "tall and vigorous frame," his "expressive and mobile play of features," and his "voice of unusual depth and power." In an era when public speeches were often inaudible, Kelley could make every word heard.[30] The chicken bones and cabbages that crowds hurled at mediocre speakers never seemed to sail Will's way.

He kept talking. Rising as a Democrat, he returned to Philly to win election as a judge. For the rest of his life, people who respected him (or wished to mock him before the nickname "Pig Iron Kelley" came along), referred to Will as "Judge Kelley." He found huge support, especially over the Schuylkill River in West Philadelphia, a sparsely settled section of market gardens, mechanics' shops, modest laborers' homes, grand estates, and a growing Black community. Will benefited from the growth as well, buying up real estate. One fawning newspaper profile described him as "a man who literally hammered his way up in life," finding prosperity while attacking whatever "social tyranny or political injustice seek to bar man's progress to a pure democracy."[31]

As he rose in politics, Will grew more eccentric. Many of his later quirks showed themselves as he established himself in Philadelphia politics in his thirties and forties. He went to bed each night with a quid of tobacco in his mouth. He rose each dawn for invigorating ice baths, his angular body crammed into a claw-footed tub. And his mind began to work differently from other men's. His speeches, initially driven by romantic populism alone, filled up with data. He packed the numerous books he published with labor statistics and tables on slavery. It could make for challenging reading, but when delivered aloud with his cemetery roar, Will's evidence fired audiences. If Donnelly was soft-brained, Kelley's brain was like a series of steel wires: tight, logical, self-contained, the mind of a watchmaker's son driven by an intricate inner mechanism, ticking away at its own persistent rhythm.[32]

But even as he rose, it got harder and harder for Will to survive as a working-class, antislavery Democrat. Over the course of the late 1840s and '50s, the Democratic Party contorted into a tool of uncompromising proslavery politics. Will would always maintain that he did not leave the party, "it left me." At the same time, tensions simmered between the small group of Philadelphians who supported abolition and the workers who voted Democratic and could be violently hostile to the antislavery cause.

Drifting farther into antislavery politics, Judge Kelley began hanging around Unitarian services and Quaker meetinghouses. There he met Carrie. The orphaned daughter of Philadelphia Quaker royalty, Caroline Bartram Bonsall had short black hair and wide, expectant blue eyes. She must have looked doll-like next to the scruffy, scarred Will Kelley, with his shabby clothes and graveyard grumble. But Carrie had already known pain in her life, held strong antislavery convictions, and would prove to be a shrewd politician. And in nineteenth-century America, where courtships often depended on partisan sympathies, they were a good match politically. Will and Carrie married in 1854 and moved into the Elms.[33]

That mansion sat on the fringes of the expanding West Philadelphia, at Forty-First Street and Parrish Street. When Will designed it, the land was mostly country, with wild turkeys ambling by its front door. The villa he built announced his newfound status with its three sweeping stories, its two dozen rooms of walnut finishings, its grand front porch, its encircling flower gardens. Kelley had been born into poverty, but had shouted his way to wealth. Will and Carrie kept dogs and goats, and set about filling the Elms with children.[34]

But the gorgeous villa was home to tragedy after tragedy. Kelley children seemed to come into the world and leave it suddenly. Carrie Kelley was pregnant six times in those years, twice with twins, but only three of her eight children lived to adulthood. She must have carried an unbearable weight, losing little girl after little girl, some in infancy and others unexpectedly in childhood. Philadelphians had long claimed that Carrie's father's family, the Bonsalls, were cursed. But infant and child mortality had been soaring across the nineteenth century, as mobile, diverse populations packed dense cities with epidemic after epidemic. Finally, in 1859, with one son—two-year-old Willy Jr.—surviving, a daughter came into the Elms. Will and Carrie hoped that little Florence would stay.[35]

Will Kelley found two new loves in the late 1850s. The first was Florie, the forceful little girl who refused to suffer the same fate as her sisters. From a young age, she struggled with scarlet fever, diphtheria, and weakened vision. She spent long days in bed, wearing a heavy green-glass eyeshade to protect her vision. Will and Carrie worried about her constantly. Will wrote from Washington, as smallpox ravaged Philadelphia, "Had the babes been vaccinated I should feel less anxiety." But her disease made her more curious, more inquisitive, more focused on what the adults were talking about. Soon Florie was following her towering Papa from room to room in the Elms, straightening his study and asking about his nonstop work, his constant reading, his ceaseless speech-crafting.[36]

Will's other new love was the Republican Party. He helped organize Pennsylvania's branch of the party in 1855. Kelley was always an impulsive politician—a "moving mass of boiling fluids," as he described himself to Carrie—and he was thrilled to jump into a new movement in that era of political fluidity. And the new party seemed like a perfect compromise to Will, combining hostility to the Slave Power with a more muscular, working-class appeal than the old elitist antislavery societies.[37] At one abolitionist rally in 1859, "Judge Kelley" was chosen to introduce the urbane Republican orator George William Curtis. Aware that angry crowds were gathering outside the hall, Will took the Quaker organizers aside. He showed them the billy club he had brought, for self-defense, hidden up his long sleeve. That night descended into rioting, window breaking, even bottles of acid thrown at the speakers. Will held his own. Afterward, Curtis thanked Kelley for "your skill in controlling a tempest the other evening."[38]

In the 1860 presidential election, Judge Kelley was selected as a member of the committee sent to inform the Republicans' chosen candidate of his nomination (presidents rarely attended conventions in those days). In Springfield, Illinois, Abraham Lincoln picked Will out from the group of Republican dignitaries, asking with a grin, "You are a tall man, Judge, What is your height?" When Will responded that he was six foot three, Lincoln teased: "I beat you. I am six feet four without my high-heeled boots." Will shot back that he was "glad that we have found a candidate for the presidency whom we can look up to, for we have been informed that there were only *little giants* in Illinois"—a reference to Lincoln's Illinois rival, the Democratic "Little Giant" Stephen Douglas. Two lanky, Republican pun-lovers, Lincoln and Kelley would become close friends.[39] Both won office that November, with Lincoln heading to the White House and Will heading to Congress for his first term representing West Philadelphia. Each became notorious: Lincoln for his jokey, colloquial style, Will for making it impossible for representatives to nap through one of his thundering speeches. They spent the war years in close communication. Will wrote to Lincoln with advice on whom to nominate from Pennsylvania, often drawn from Carrie's deep knowledge of Philadelphia families. And he helped direct Lincoln's reelection campaign in his crucial state in 1864. Will could also make life difficult for the president, ending his letters: "Your sometimes troublesome but always devoted friend." But he was always a committed ally, sneaking off from Thanksgiving dinner at the Elms—the house finally filled with "the laughter and shouts of children"—to sit in his study and scribble notes to Lincoln, drawn "under an irresistible impulse to address you."[40]

Then in April 1865, within months of the January evening when Will voted to end slavery, he set out on a favor for his friend in the White House, joining a delegation sent to Fort Sumter to mark the end of the war. "All," Kelley later recalled, seemed "bright and beautiful and cheerful" on their voyage down aboard the USS *Arago*. But on their way back to Washington, Will's ship passed a small boat whose captain shouted: "Why is not your flag at half-mast? Have you not heard of the President's death?"[41]

The ship full of politicians and officers murmured that it could not be true; such a thing had never happened. A president murdered in office, the optimism of their pure democracy curdling so quickly, Kelley's "troublesome" friend dead. "We looked into each other's faces and were silent," Kelley recalled, his uncanny voice quiet for once.[42]

Three hundred miles to the north, that day, six-year-old Florie's grandparents told her the same awful news. Florie always remembered that moment: her grandfather's long face locked in a single expression, her grandmother's serenity shattered, the city around them draped in black, shutters closed, voices hushed. For Florie, this first political memory would bind her to her father. In her telling decades later, an adult Florence Kelley imagined Will learning the news at the same moment that she had. Theirs would be a relationship joined by political passion and personal tragedy, intimately tied to the governing of the nation.

CONGRESSMAN KELLEY'S NONSTOP bass would suit the voluble political culture that emerged after the war, with its speaking tours and its stomping rallies, its emotionalism and its humor. On the soapbox, Will delighted clubs of Union veterans. In Congress, he argued for a Radical Reconstruction with the "breadth and vigor of a thunder-clap." George William Curtis—the stiff abolitionist whom Will had rescued from an antislavery "tempest"— wrote to Kelley in those years, thanking him for his "trenchant and terrible speeches," gushing, "I am moved to admiration in every campaign by the grand blows you deliver."[43]

But in an overheated era, Will's rhetorical blows could elicit the real thing.

In May 1867, two years after Alexander Pope Field pulled a blade on him in the Willard hotel, men were once again drawing weapons to shut Kelley up. It happened in Mobile, Alabama, as he took the stage to speak in favor of the first big step toward expanded voting rights for African Americans. Congress had just passed the First Reconstruction Act, enfranchising freed slaves and poor Whites in the former Confederacy to vote for new representatives, who would craft more democratic state constitutions. It was to be the first election with mass participation by African Americans in US history, but it was all taking place in a violent political climate, with the terroristic Ku Klux Klan on the prowl, and many still carrying pistols left over from the war.

The Republican Party sent hundreds of speakers south in the spring of 1867 to register former slaves to vote. Black ministers, schoolmasters, and Union Army vets traveled throughout the region, stopping at churches and freedmen's schools, encouraging African Americans to participate. Some used educational skits to offer a rapid primer in democratic citizenship; at least one Florida preacher projected magic lantern slideshows. In under a year, they managed to increase the proportion of Black men registered, nationwide, from .5 percent to 80.5 percent.[44]

Will Kelley went south, too, on a "speaking excursion" to make the case for expanded voting rights. Though he represented the Radical Republicans, Kelley seemed willing to speak anywhere, before even the most hostile crowds. When he arrived in Mobile, he found a city crackling with racial tension between freed Black men and Irish immigrants, fighting for work on Mobile's docks. A Democratic agitator, William D'Alton Mann of Michigan, made the mood worse with his aggressive newspaper, the *Mobile Times*. Mann hated the Republican Party and worked to rile his adopted city against Kelley's visit. He claimed that Will had been born an Irish Catholic Democrat and had converted to Protestantism and Republicanism, though Kelley was in fact a Scots-Irish Presbyterian by ancestry. Will believed that Mann, who was rumored to be a Klan member, was using his paper "to effect MY BANISHMENT OR ASSASSINATION."[45]

Kelley came anyway and stayed at the stately Battle House Hotel. If Donnelly was right, and speechifying was powered by good oysters, the Battle House's baked bivalves were just what Kelley needed. He sprang energetically onto the steps of the Old Courthouse at eight P.M. on the night of May 14, before a crowd of four thousand spectators who had assembled to welcome, or banish, him. Behind Kelley stood one hundred prominent local citizens, soldiers, freedmen, Republican activists, and a crew of northern reporters, their backs to the plastered courthouse wall. In front of him stood a mixed audience of newly enfranchised African Americans, curious local Whites, and furious readers of the *Mobile Times*. Many, on all sides, brought their Colts, Remingtons, and Smith & Wessons.

Kelley launched into his speech on the rights of freed slaves, the need for further Reconstruction acts, and hopes for reconciliation between North and South, filling the space around the courthouse with the same thunderclap that he had trained outside the Massachusetts statehouse. As he spoke, a "gang of rowdies" on the fringes of the crowd began to holler "Rotten-egg him," "Put him down." Soon they were pushing toward the stage.[46]

Will challenged his hecklers. The South had a problem with freedom of speech, he said, rattling off a list of outrages and abuses. He launched into a call-and-response with supporters in the crowd, demanding "Were you allowed before the war to read a Northern newspaper?"—the crowd hollering back "*No!*" The rowdies pressed closer still, shouting "Take him down!" "Put him down!" as they neared the Old Courthouse steps.[47]

Will leaned his long frame over the simple wooden speaker's table and shouted, almost in his hecklers' faces: "Nobody had better undertake to put me down. I tell you that you can not put me down. I have the U.S. Army to fall back upon. I am not afraid of being put down."[48]

What happened next unfolded quickly, a "murderous and bloody affair" spinning out in utter confusion. Somewhere in the crowd, Mobile's chief of police confronted the chief heckler. Within seconds, both men had drawn pistols. Someone was yelling "FIRE!" and the shooting started. "The platform was swept by bullets" as Will dove under the speaker's table. A bullet shattered the forehead of the man standing directly behind him. Others returned fire from the stage. Kelley, with his long body folded under the speaker's table, thought of home. Would Carrie be sitting in the Elms when another letter informed her of his fate?[49]

Later, he would be criticized for not having done more to stop the shooting. But, as he told a crowd of supporters, "I have never been a soldier or sought reputation at the cannon's mouth, and freely admit that when bullets were whizzing and pattering against the wall behind me I would have thanked Almighty God for a bullet-proof table under which to creep."[50]

Four thousand Alabamians scattered, some firing into the air as they went. Two local African Americans "periled their lives" to shield Kelley, dragging him off the courthouse steps and hustling him back to the safety of the Battle House Hotel. The shooting slowed, the city quieted. When the military inspected the courthouse wall the next day, they found sixty-five bullet marks in the plaster. The "Kelley Riot" left two dead and twenty seriously wounded.

Kelley made his way back to Philadelphia, speaking in southern towns along the route. The riot was national news, confirming many Northerners' worst fears about the spiraling "outrages" in the South. And Will's solution to being nearly shot for his public speaking? More public speaking. Philadelphia's Republicans welcomed Kelley with a nighttime rally; thousands of marchers waved banners and torches, blared music, and, as Kelley interpreted it, "congratulated me on my seemingly miraculous escape from the murderous mob."[51]

The moderate *New York Times*, reporting on the riot, wondered whether Kelley, though in the right morally, had been wise to debate "the liberty of utterance with every drunkard or fool who chose to challenge it." The answer, for Kelley, was clearly yes. Public utterance was at the center of his definition of democracy.[52]

It can be tempting to see the Mobile riot as an aftershock of the Civil War's earthquake. But this kind of public violence would continue, powered by partisanship, for the next several decades. It was a living, breathing part of America's contentious political life. Neither was it an isolated example of the South's exceptional history of violence—the chief instigator was a Michigan Democrat, the target a Pennsylvania Republican, the gunmen were likely Irish immigrants, and many of the soldiers and journalists were African American freedmen. The Mobile riot said something broader about American democracy, nationwide. Even after Reconstruction was over, public speakers would be shot at, beaten, or otherwise "put down" in partisan feuds and labor unrest. Unlike the mounting conflicts of the 1850s, America was entering a phase of directionless, self-perpetuated political tension and violence. Such energies would take decades to rein in.

CHAPTER THREE

"The Game Going on at Washington"

D ownstream from all those speechifiers lay the nation's swampy capital. The Washington that they flooded into in the late 1860s had long suffered a reputation for sogginess. It was a town with neighborhoods named Swampoodle and Murder Bay, centered on a National Mall fringed by a filthy canal, which stank like "the ghosts of twenty thousand drowned cats." Horace Greeley, the county's most influential journalist, known for his high-reaching rhetoric of national greatness, summed it up: "The rents are high, the food is bad, the dust is disgusting, the mud is deep, the morals are deplorable."[1]

But if Washington seemed like a moral swamp, it was because it lay downstream from America's voters, absorbing whatever political jetsam they launched downriver. The more campaigners who came stomping into D.C., the swampier it got. After the war they poured in, new men bringing new energy, drawn by the promise of pure democracy and the spoils of federal power. Each race added to what one insider called "the drift-wood of party, which has been set afloat towards Washington, by the rising of the democratic tide."[2]

Besides, the cliché of Washington as a dismal swamp elides the miraculous change it was undergoing. That same sogginess turned it into one of the most fertile, exciting cities in the country. The national government, at the end of a nation-building civil war, found itself greatly empowered to fight secession and end slavery, but also to build a bigger, stronger society. The District's sweeping boulevards and hidden alleys quickly filled with adventurers and empire builders, making room for freed slaves and French chefs, disgraced colonels and ambitious prostitutes. The federal government, which in the early Republic had more congressmen than paid staff, grew from about two thousand workers before the Civil War to six thousand in the 1870s, reaching fourteen thousand in the 1880s. Washington's population nearly doubled between 1860 and 1870, growing five times faster than New York City's.[3]

The alert journalist Frank Carpenter documented this encampment becoming a city, "one vast boardinghouse" of men who still spat tobacco, even on the new marble floors. "Carp" could be seen in Washington's Black-owned eating houses and its ethereal hilltop Capitol, a slight man with wild red hair and twinkling gray eyes, interpreting the scene for a nation that sent politicians and taxes to D.C., but would never visit. Washington seemed like "a living curiosity" to Carp. "One feels that this city could easily vanish, and he could wake up to find himself stranded on the empty Potomac flats."[4]

Emerging faster than the grand new architecture, or functioning sewers, Washington society burned bright in those years. New York had finer food, Boston had wittier writers, and San Francisco had superior saloons, but Washington had power. And that power attracted, if not the wealthiest or the wisest, those most burning for place. To move to Washington, wrote the aristocratic Henry Adams, "announced one's self as an adventurer and an office-seeker, a person of deplorably bad judgment."[5]

Among the adventurers, a new society life cohered, in which "politics and reform became the detail, and waltzing the profession." Those waltzers pressed into "moving, jostling, surging" parties, clinking glasses of "Washington punch"—a stimulating blend of whiskey, rum, claret, champagne, sugar, and lemon slices. Far from new arrivals' gossipy hometowns, these soirees helped make Washington the nation's capital of indiscretions. "In no other city," Carp told scandalized readers, "are such affairs carried on more openly."[6]

Ignatius Donnelly, in Washington as a congressman, offered up a savage satire of such parties, eviscerating the sweaty waltzers, the hosts shaking hands in a mechanical "pump handle style," and the defeated suitors eating glumly in the corners. At such gatherings "great clatter, jangle and chatter goes on, a thousand interests, wishes, vanities, mingle together in one stupendous buzz and burr . . . this is a Washington party."[7]

Often, they gossiped about the rise or fall of some campaign chieftain. Soon it was Donnelly himself. The fiery campaigner had grown bitter in Reconstruction Washington, his wide-ranging brain and scalpel wit targeting those around him. In a self-destructive moment, Donnelly picked a fight with the Washburne family, a powerful clan of five brawling brothers who held offices at all levels of the Republican machine, from ambassador to general. In a frothing speech in Congress, he savaged the Washburnes, drawing uproarious laughter from the galleries but repeated calls to order from the Speaker. Back in Minnesota, the *St. Paul Pioneer* condemned Donnelly as "the nastiest and most foul mouthed wretch who ever had a seat in the American Congress."[8]

Donnelly's heated oratory might be fitting on the frontier stump, directed at Democrats, but breached the civility expected of a small-time congressman from a far-flung district. Soon he was drummed out of the Republican Party, the first, but not the last, political movement he would abandon over the next thirty years.

More often, in 1868, crowds chattered about the presidential impeachment. Vice President Andrew Johnson, who became president after Lincoln's murder, quickly found himself in a power struggle with Republican leadership. Johnson was, at best, proof of the promise of American populism, an impoverished tailor who had climbed to the most powerful position in the nation. But he was also resentful, paranoid, and searingly racist. Even generous observers found him to be "always *worse* than you expect." After a complex battle with the Republican Congress, which ended in his impeachment but not conviction, Johnson served out the last few months of his term before the 1868 presidential race. While the impeachment fight provided juicy gossip for "the floating population" of D.C. partygoers, people outside the capital "generally manifest little interest in the game going on at Washington," claimed William Tecumseh Sherman.[9]

Because Johnson never ran for president, his saga remained unconnected to the popular campaign system. The speed with which Americans lost interest in Johnson demonstrated how little presidents would matter in this era, how incidental they could be when untethered from campaigning.

What mattered more was the new social world of chattering parties and soirees, thrown by senators' wives or the emerging class of lobbyists. Professional influencers like Sam Ward, a "dazzling reptile" of a charmer, opened their homes to private gatherings, offering fine French foods that would have made "Andrew Jackson turn over in his grave." Dinners meant course after course of oysters, rabbit buried under flurries of truffles, terrapins stewed in individual silver pans, the tables strewn with rare lilies and gilded pine cones. And, with Washington's old southern aristocrats vanquished, ambitious Yankee politicians' wives began to flaunt their wealth and sophistication in ways they could not have gotten away with back in Maine or Ohio.[10]

These ladies had considerable influence. Like frontier towns with few women, Washington's lack of a permanent female presence (at least among elites) made the few political wives all the more powerful. A class of canny local women emerged as "lady lobbyists," who used social skills and sex appeal to influence politicos in ways that male lobbyists, belching cigar smoke in the Willard Hotel's lobby, never could. "Lady correspondents" reported the news, finding subtle ways to win difficult sources. Elizabeth Chapin, secretary of the Ladies' Press Association and a vocal advocate for Reconstruction, wrote: "No one can deny the unbounded influence of women at the capital . . . The woman who is shrewd—with fair looks and a healthy mind and body, can make a future, that a neophyte dreams not of in her country home."[11]

One woman who was too shrewd for her country home was Harriet Stanwood Blaine, sharp-tongued wife of James G. Blaine. James was a rising star in the Republican Party, nicknamed "the Magnetic Man" for his immense personal charm, which supposedly bordered on psychosexual magnetism. Harriet had her own, subtler appeal: a pointed wit and a sophisticated family back in Maine. She was often miserable in Washington's parlors, chatting with grasping office seekers and dimwitted presidents in support of her husband's career. But she wielded considerable influence in that "great and wicked and corrupt and corruptible city." So despite her misgivings, Harriet packed up the Blaines' large family each January for the train ride south from Augusta, Maine, into another "Washington winter," wincing in anticipation of "company all the time."[12]

On one of those January mornings, as the Blaines' train car rumbled south past Philadelphia, the family's quiet ride was interrupted by a familiar thunderclap voice as the cheery "Judge Kelley" entered the train. Harriet's sharp green lizard eyes narrowed in silent judgment. Will Kelley was just the type of coarse and low-born politico she would have to spend all winter entertaining. At least Kelley wasn't much of a schemer, warmer than most of Washington's snakes. Harriet seemed to view Kelley much as Sidney George Fisher had, as "a man of obscure birth and vulgar manners," but basically honest. But why was he hovering around her family, and what did he have in that large, greasy parcel?[13]

The lanky Kelley inquired, "in his magnificent voice," if the family "were Pennsylvanians enough to love doughnuts," offering up the Amish pastries to James, who had been born in Will's home state. Kelley explained that he had leftovers from his eating-house lunch, much of which he had given to a beggar girl. He could not bring himself to give away the doughnuts, though, "because he had too much respect for them." Will held out the greasy bag, into which the whole Blaine family reluctantly reached. Harriet had to force her seven-year-old daughter, hissing "O take it, take it." Even James "politely took one." The Republican Speaker of the House would not risk offending a quirky but crucial campaigner from the party's most important state over a turned-down pastry. Will stood to move gracefully on, and Harriet found herself "relieved to have him out of the car."[14]

Will Kelley's intrusion pointed to exactly what made Washington society so unusual. In Philadelphia, the Sidney George Fishers could exclude men like Kelley from their notoriously insular high society. But Washington was not a closed system of inherited privilege; it was constantly fed by those campaign warlords who could rally the votes. It didn't matter if Harriet Stanwood Blaine found Kelley coarse, as long as enough people in Pennsylvania's Fourth Congressional District liked his voice.

In fact, Kelley notoriously stood out in Washington society, too passionate about his causes, not interested enough in parties. Carp joked that when Will Kelley "goes into society," he asked politicians' wives for "their opinion of the duty on steel rails." Don Piatt, the humorist, caricatured Kelley locking visitors in his parlor and speechifying at them for hours. He was admired as a powerful legislative presence, but not necessarily a pleasing one in an age of unctuous lobbyists. The *Chicago Tribune* described Will as "a man of tenacity and force, without genius or personal graces . . . he is the most anxious man and the hardest worker in Congress."[15]

Will wrote to Florie that she would prefer the sparkling parties he was constantly being dragged to. He would rather step out into the streets and enjoy a steamy Washington night, where the "galleries are crowded with youth, beauty, fashion and unwashed men of every race." Those were his people. Mostly, he would rather be crafting his next speech, researching policies, and considering how they might affect working people. He had little need for waltzing, so long as he had politics and doughnuts.[16]

Kelley was a best-case example of the new breed of politicians conquering American politics. Low-born but driven politicos seemed to replace the elite antebellum statesmen who had been born to be senators. Carp summed up the cycle of life in Washington, where "every season the people change. Every Congress a new batch of maidens and a new set of hangers-on appear on the national stage. Every four years a new administration turns the social world topsy-turvy, and the old order gives place to the new. Under such conditions anyone can make his way into society."[17]

Not exactly anyone. Most had to earn their way, through trial by campaign combat, for themselves or for someone higher in the party hierarchy. Though laughably far from a meritocracy, the campaign-obsessed culture at least rewarded a skill, preferring the kind of unstoppably social animals who could mesmerize a town square, saloon, or schoolhouse. Ancestry and station still mattered, but the ability to rally voters—whether freed slaves or German immigrants—meant far more after the war. Even the contemptuous Adams came to grudgingly respect these "new Americans" who were creating "a world of their own, a society, a philosophy, a universe" based on gall alone.[18]

The Civil War unleashed some of these energies. In the early years of the nation, congressmen were often aristocratic planters and landowners. Southerners were overrepresented by the three-fifths clause, and slave owners were overrepresented among Southerners. These planters were not milquetoasts; in fact, they spent a huge portion of their time feuding and dueling, but their squabbles over honor were carefully choreographed, rule-bound affairs. With the growing conflict over slavery in the 1850s, northern voters began to select brawlers to stand up to the Slave Power. The war itself added to this stock, mobilizing Union veterans who had proved themselves with a bayonet or saber. Postwar, with the antebellum slave-owning families toppled, these bumptious Northerners provided a new elite, often seen eating fried oysters and drinking Bass ale in the Capitol's subterranean restaurant. Many of them were new to politics, holding no previous office before winning a seat. The proportion of planters fell by more than half, replaced by small-time lawyers (in an era when a degree wasn't required to practice law) along with businessmen and journalists. Pushy, self-made men, climbing up through society by making money or hollering partisan news, were clawing their way into power.[19]

Once these new men won their station, they intended to stay. The prior generation of politicians, between the 1830s and the Civil War, had the lowest rates of incumbency in American history, serving their terms and then returning to their districts. But after the war, men who had fought for their stations, and had no estates to return to, hung around. Their length of service in Congress doubled. The coming decades would see a spike in incumbency rates, not because postwar politicos were of superior quality, but because they just kept running for reelection. (Of course, quality did count for something. Will Kelley would end up serving longer in Congress than anyone else up till then.)[20]

Americans had long used the term *politician* to mean any citizen—elected or not, male or female, young or old—who became intensely interested in politics, but they were beginning to turn the word into shorthand for a professional class, an identity of its own. And it was rarely a compliment.

The sheer work of running a campaign in America's big, loud democracy explains the new attitude. In an intensely capitalistic era, an economic logic was beginning to take over American democracy—a labor theory of campaigning. Henry Wilson, the cobbler-turned-senator, saw this clearly in the optimistic talk of "pure democracy" after the war. Writing in the *Atlantic Monthly*, Wilson worried over a simple mechanical question: Who was "willing to perform the drudgery of a political canvas"? Sure, "the business of self-government is now in the hands of the people," but "government is no holiday affair." Campaigners sending men to Washington, or Albany, or St. Paul, asked the same question: Who would do all the work? As one Tammany Hall ally of the thieving Boss Tweed complained: "To do what we did in bringing out our vote, getting it registered and then polled, required constant and very great as well as expensive labor."[21]

The politicians who made it to Washington, or to state capitals, arrived at the head of a long tail of allies who had done a great deal of (mostly) unpaid labor to get them there. Elected leaders owed immense social debts, and they could pay them, because the ballooning postwar government had so many jobs to give out. Lobbyists who financed an expensive campaign could ask that the newly powerful federal government help their railroad corporation or boot factory. Wilson already worried that corporate lobbies were becoming the new "Slave Power." But even more corrosive to Americans' faith in government was the way victorious politicians gave out federal positions to the men who helped them get elected. Politicians arrived with dangerous debts, and in Washington's abundant jobs and contracts they saw a perfect thank-you gift.

A new marketplace was emerging along the Potomac's mudflats. Each soiree, each "moving, jostling, surging" party, was driven by these exchanges of campaign labor for government reward. Washington ran on these unspoken trades. Money might be the currency in the rest of the nation, but in Washington, favors counted for more, meted out in stump speeches and choice appointments. So when Harriet Blaine politely reached into Will Kelley's greasy bag and selected a doughnut, sugar sticking to her refined fingers, she was calculating the value of campaign prowess that had redefined American democracy.[22]

THERE WAS ONE perfect model of this new campaign economy, glimpsed prominently at waltzes, overheard at dinner parties, seen commanding the Senate floor. A tough in a swallowtail coat, a campaign warrior whose political skills justified bad behavior, an endless font of public feuds and "private" affairs. Even his name—Roscoe Conkling—declared exactly what you should expect of him, somehow aristocratic and bullying at the same time, as percussive and flamboyant as his political style.

It is surprising that he is no longer familiar to most Americans, for his life provided some of the richest melodrama in American history. Since rising on the national scene as a congressman and then a senator from New York—coming up in the same Civil War generation of "noticeable men" that included Kelley and Donnelly—Conkling seemed to demand that everyone commenting on American politics write about him, often using the word *haughty*. Even his biographer agreed, describing him as "not a pleasant man." He had incredible talent and became among the most powerful political bosses in American history, but managed to destroy it all.[23]

As his greatest victim, James Garfield, put it, Conkling was "a singular compound of a very brilliant man and an exceedingly petulant child."[24]

To understand the impact Conkling had, it is necessary to see him. Many felt that he was among "the handsomest men of his time," the epitome of what nineteenth-century Americans considered "manly beauty." Roscoe stood six foot three, erect and broad shouldered, with a head of blond curls and a pointed red-blond beard that proved a gift to cartoonists sketching him as the Lucifer of the Senate. An early advocate of weight training, Conkling boxed and wrestled, bullying fellow senators into "friendly" matches. When home in Utica, he frequently sparred with a professional boxer, who reported that Conkling was fast to strike but also "very quick in getting back his head out of my reach." This insight could sum up his political style as well.[25]

He was also quite particular. He favored tailored cutaway coats, bright ties, and slim, colorful trousers, all designed to accent his muscular frame, making him "the darling of the ladies gallery." He hated his daughter's husband for the crime of appearing in public, once, in dirty overalls, referring to him only as "Mrs. Conkling's son-in-law." Conkling kept others at a distance, recoiling from personal contact. A colleague's foot on his chair could throw him into a daylong rage. He covered all his books with paper to keep their contents secret, and burnt most of his letters. He would not read a newspaper until it was folded, just so, and carefully creased each dollar before placing it in his wallet. When he wanted to summon a page in the Senate, Conkling "would slap his hands above his head as Roman emperors used to do."[26]

But what made Conkling stand out, in the long span of pompous American leaders, was his unremitting aggression. He came to Washington, before the Civil War, because he was a fighter, and spent the next few decades in a succession of personal duels, a career "inspired more by his hates than his loves." He never forgave, and nurtured his grudges so attentively that they became intimate relationships. The earnest New York abolitionist Henry Stanton wrote, on watching Conkling fume about some slight, "my acquaintance with the English language is not sufficient to describe how angry he was."[27]

Not everyone hated Conkling. In fact, a generation of young Republican children, born during Reconstruction, were named for him. Conkling was especially beloved by African Americans. He stood out as an early opponent of slavery; even when other antebellum politicians spoke cautiously about the practice, Conkling denounced it as an "unmixed and unmitigated social, political and moral evil." After the conflict, he attacked the system that counted Black men as three-fifths of a person in congressional appointments, roaring: "If a black man counts at all now he counts as five-fifths of a man. Revolutions have no fractions in their arithmetic." Years after Conkling's downfall, Frederick Douglass still honored him as a sincere "friend to liberty." Well into the twentieth century, when he was often reduced to a preening stock villain in books on boss politics, a generation of African Americans still proudly bore his name.[28]

It was Conkling's combative politics that won him national attention. Raised by wealthy Whigs in upstate New York, Conkling spent his childhood memorizing poetry, but also bare-knuckle boxing. He got his start as a lawyer in booming Utica, notorious for his skill "at bullying witnesses." When a rowdy Democrat heckled Whig political meetings during the 1848 election, Conkling's boss nominated the then nineteen-year-old bruiser to face down the "big bully" on the stump, declaring: "I shall send Mr. Conkling; I think he will make himself heard." He kept making himself heard throughout the heated politics of the 1850s. In response to the brutal beating of Senator Charles Sumner by a South Carolina congressman, in 1856, a speaker at a Utica ward rally declared: "Boys, we must nominate muscle as well as brains for Congress . . . Let's send Conkling. I guess they won't hurt him." His election brought Conkling into a fiercely contested, violent House of Representatives. Southern congressmen certainly didn't hurt Conkling; instead he made use of his "great physical strength and courage" to intimidate the fire-eaters who had been attacking antislavery representatives.[29]

Finally, many Republicans felt, they had a bodyguard to stand up to the Slave Power. Few considered how men chosen for their muscle might behave in peacetime.

Unfortunately, Conkling spent much of his budding career punishing his own party. In the days after the Civil War, as Washington society was just beginning to glitter, some poor fool invited Conkling to the same dinner party as James and Harriet Blaine. There was no way a man like Conkling would do well with the Magnetic Man mesmerizing a roomful of guests. Over dinner, with Conkling's red-blond hair shimmering in the candlelight, and Harriet Blaine's sharp eyes watching closely, someone quoted an obscure line of poetry. A debate emerged about who wrote the lines. Soon Conkling and James Blaine were shouting at each other across the table linen, the guests watching, stunned. Conkling bet a basket of champagne on the argument.

Books were pulled from shelves, and the guests could see that Blaine was right. Harriet must have smiled, for once happy in Washington. It is one of the minor tragedies of history that we cannot see Conkling's face when he learned the news. His opinion of Blaine froze on the spot, beginning a feud that lasted decades and altered the course of American democracy. Two great politicians and brilliant representatives, inheritors of the triumphant Republican Party at the height of its power, and controllers of Reconstruction and the destiny of millions, left that dinner in a furious feud over a line of poetry and a bottle of champagne.[30]

They took their fight to the Capitol. In Congress, Conkling and Blaine picked at each other's nominees and skewered each other's bills. At one point, Conkling held the floor, denouncing Blaine's allies and shouting "I do not yield! I do not yield!" whenever the Magnetic Man tried to interject. Blaine responded with a bitingly sardonic speech, mocking Conkling's "haughty disdain, his grandiloquent swell, his majestic, super-eminent, overpowering, *turkey-gobbler strut.*" It became his unwanted nickname, with men clucking and gobbling behind Turkey Gobbler Conkling's broad back.[31]

In the grand Capitol, where slavery had been abolished less than two years before, in the very room where veterans and freed slaves had cheered, the victors of that moment were now bickering like children. It was already proving hard to live up to the promise of "pure democracy," especially when it promoted men like Roscoe Conkling.

But all the forces that made Conkling a frustrating ally made him a brilliant campaigner, of a type. If Kelley could inspire rallies with deep rumblings of democratic possibilities, and Donnelly could ask a town square to see how daily politics drove the progress of civilization, Conkling was the muscle, called out to crush the opposition in his "sledge-hammer way." The *Atlantic Monthly* wrote that Conkling was undoubtedly "one of the best speakers in the United States," blessed with "considerable power of sarcasm," able to "make any one he dislikes feel very uncomfortable." If heckled, Conkling would draw out the interrupter, with mock interest, asking him to "present his views" until, sensing some flaw in the heckler's stuttered explanations, Conkling would come crashing down from the stage, bellowing "arguments—cogent, pithy, sarcastic—like the fist of a giant upon a mosquito."[32]

And while Kelley was willing to address hostile crowds, knowing that many had revolvers in their pockets, the fussy Conkling could not handle such bumptiousness. Chauncey Depew, a Republican politician and future tycoon, related as much about the 1868 Republican campaign to make Ulysses S. Grant president. Depew set out with Conkling to campaign in upstate New York—often the region that decided national races. But Conkling refused to lecture outside in fairgrounds or town squares, demanding to speak only in opera houses. So, in Lockport, New York, Depew—though usually Conkling's opening act—addressed twenty thousand cheering Republicans, while Conkling gave his practiced oration to a nearly empty hall, save for "a few farmers' wives" who had straggled in to eat their picnic lunches. The furious Conkling never spoke with Depew again.[33]

That 1868 presidential race captured the democratic moment perfectly, teetering between the promise of an expanded democracy and a new campaign economy that promoted men like Conkling. As the race ramped up, the accumulated ambition that had flowed into Washington pumped back upstream. All the prominent political talking heads returned to their districts to stump and speechify: Conkling hammering away in New York, Kelley climbing bandstands across Pennsylvania, and Donnelly sampling Minnesota's finest oysters.

And they had reason to be optimistic. The 1868 campaign was the first nationwide presidential race since the 1860 election, and the first in which large numbers of freed slaves could vote. The Republican Party was running the beloved war hero Grant under the motto "Let Us Have Peace." From one perspective, 1868 was the fruition of the promise of "pure democracy," offering a kind of inclusion across race and class that had never been seen before.

But on the ground, the 1868 campaign demonstrated the lows of the heated political culture. The Democratic Party ran one of the most bitterly racist campaigns in U.S. history. As one Reconstruction-hating Philadelphian wrote in his diary, the Democrats would beat "the Niggers if they don't cheat us in the Returns, or Contest us in Nigger Courts." In Louisiana alone, as many as one thousand African Americans died in political violence. And while Republicans never approached anything like this level of brutality, many still muttered about a second Civil War to exterminate the Democrats. One young Republican veteran in Minnesota warned off a Democratic canvasser with the statement: "I could kill him and all others like him with better grace than I ever shot at a Johnny."[34]

On election day, the Republicans enjoyed their third presidential win in a row, this time with a new southern base. Hundreds of thousands of newly enfranchised African Americans turned out, swinging the election to Grant. Men who were slaves three years earlier were now deciding who would be the president. The freedmen who turned out to hear Kelley speak in Mobile clinched their state for the Republican Party. The 1868 elections had a high turnout, signaling the way broad hopes for democracy and aggressive populist campaigning swirled together in the new era.

Looking back on his time canvassing in upstate New York during that campaign, before Conkling stopped speaking to him, Depew summed up both his former friend and the state of American democracy. Conkling,

Depew mused, "was created by nature for a great career. That he missed it was entirely is own fault . . . The reason was that his wonderful gifts were wholly devoted to partisan discussions."[35]

The same could be said of the whole republic in those years. It showed itself in Washington's splendid growth and in the intentions of the men and women flocking to the capital. The democracy had strength and momentum and mass appeal, bold new hopes and no real enemies. Besides, of course, itself.

The contrasting careers of Conkling, Kelley, and Donnelly after 1868 would highlight Americans' coming difficulty with those "partisan discussions." The three prominent Republicans, enjoying the "wonderful gifts" of the most progressive, most confident, and most dominant political organization in American history, would spend the rest of their careers fighting out their relationship with the party, and the voters, who gave them power. Each would find his own path, running from Conkling's sledgehammer Republicanism to Donnelly's peripatetic third-partyism to Kelley's struggle to live up to his promise to his constituents, and to his daughter.

CHAPTER FOUR

"I Boast of Philadelphia at All Times"

Y ou have no idea how pleased she was at being told that she looked like you," Carrie Kelley wrote to her husband during one winter session of Congress. Mother and daughter had gone out on a social call, bundled against the February cold. In their host's parlor "everyone seemed struck with the resemblance" between seven-year-old Florence and her famous father. Maybe it was their unusual height, or thick bronze hair. Either way, "Florie was highly gratified."[1]

On the other end of the railroad tracks that brought Will Kelley down to Washington, doughnuts and all, were his growing family, his gracious mansion, and one of America's most vibrant political scenes. Philadelphia of the late 1860s and early '70s was the site of personal and political struggle, formative in both Florence's development and America's politics. So when a congressional session was over, Will Kelley would climb aboard a commuter car and rattle his way back up the eastern seaboard, heading home to a growing daughter and an expanding democracy.

In those years, Florence Kelley was no longer a small child, dimly glimpsing at her father's life. She was beginning to see her father as a gateway to a wider world, and to use their relationship to grasp at an identity of her own. When he came home to the Elms, she rarely left his side. For Carrie Kelley, her daughter's growth and her husband's presence held out a shared promise; the two might improve each other and alleviate some of her darkness. Stressing her daughter's resemblance to her father, and reminding Will Kelley of his proud little girl back home, served all of their purposes.

Florence lived an uneven childhood, an odd blend of ease and suffering. She wrote of her girlhood years "as free as sunshine," filling letters to her father with news of romps with Hector, the bounding Newfoundland; capers with her siblings; and a zealous love of firecrackers, their "great blasts" and her narrow escapes after lighting them. When her father was present, he was full of life and information, a towering figure dancing just into the frame to offer strange knowledge or bad jokes. Her mother was unselfish and kind, even if Florie could already detect a matte layer of melancholy beneath her shimmering surface. Looking back, Florence remembered Carrie's palpable "terror of impending loss," a gentle sadness "that she could only partially disguise."[2]

Her mother's grief meant Florie's isolation. Florence was already weakened by bouts of scarlet fever and other ailments that kept her stuck in bed. When epidemics ravaged Philadelphia, Florie endured lengthy quarantines in the Elms. She was the poor little girl, so bored (but so persistent) that when the family physician came for a social call, Florie "waylaid the Dr." and "begged permission to read a little by daylight."[3]

By 1870 Florie was one of four surviving Kelley children, with an older brother, Willy Jr., a bright-eyed kid sister named Anna, and a baby boy named Albert. But Carrie Kelley had already lost so many children; she was not going to take risks. So even though Florie had grown old enough to attend school, Carrie kept her home. Florie was a smart, active, inquisitive girl, "thoughtful beyond her years," and family members worried that she needed more stimulation than life at the Elms could provide. Her aunt Sarah Pugh—a former abolitionist and towering figure in Quaker Philadelphia—saw that Florie was too isolated, writing to Will that she was "so mature in thought that she particularly requires the companionship of children—not to improve her mentally, but to make her keep to childish things and childish ways." Less time alone in bed; more firecrackers.[4]

And so Will Kelley entered Florie's field of vision again, as an educator and a friend. But he did so in his typically atypical way. Florie's first memory of the "strange, incoherent process of my education" began when she was seven years old. Her father presented her with a "terrible little book" about child labor in England. He sat with her, flipping through page after page of terrifying engravings of gray little children bent under heavy loads of bricks. Will lectured Florie about English factories and the enslaved children recently freed in America. In the background, Carrie and her mother shouted that the book was not appropriate for a little girl, but Will was intent on raising a special kind of daughter, one who would learn about the lives of the less fortunate. It was all part, Florence wrote later, of "Father's never failing, flowing interest" in the struggles of working people.[5]

It can be no coincidence, in fact it seems almost predestined, that little Florie would grow into Florence Kelley, Progressive America's loudest opponent of child labor.

But Will Kelley's "never failing, flowing interest" kept him moving across the late 1860s. His own habit of persistent talking took him around the country. When not in Washington, Will was dodging bullets in Reconstruction Alabama, campaigning for Grant, or present at the 1869 ceremony linking the transcontinental railroad across America, watching tycoons drive a golden spike into the ground in Promontory Summit, Utah. His presence there signaled a new era in his politics. As a Pennsylvania congressman and an advocate for American laborers, Kelley began to prioritize expanding America's infrastructure, to create jobs in his steel- and locomotive-manufacturing state.[6]

Throughout his travels, Will wrote home in jokey letters calibrated to match what his children might find interesting. To the ever-curious Florence he wrote from San Francisco, during that western journey in 1869, reporting on the fascinating world of Chinatown. In great detail, Will explained the course of a Chinese banquet, describing the plates of tiny fried fish, green beans showered with crispy pork, braised daikon radishes, and, in the place of butter, little bowls of "a pungent sauce of sooy." We can imagine little Florie, isolated in her family's yawning mansion, poring over her father's letters detailing exotic travels. Along the way, Will picked up a big picture book to encourage Florie's reading, an illustrated guide to California's resources.[7]

On her tenth birthday, in September 1869, Will Kelley gave Florence that book. He had no idea that he was beginning a formative bond, building a dynasty. Florie found a comfy spot on the library rug, stretched out, and pored over the book's contents. Will expected his daughter to flip through the tome, looking at the drawings, but as the September sun streamed through the library's windows, he noticed that Florie was carefully reading the text of each page, studying the kind of statistics that Will was in the habit of reciting at Washington soirees. He must have realized that the key to his isolated daughter's development sat all around him, a love of books and reading and knowledge that the two could share.[8]

Congressman Kelley put aside his own reports from the House Committee on Coinage, Weights, and Measures and joined his daughter on the floor, beginning what Florie would later call "a companionship which has enriched my whole life." The two launched a series of talks that would extend over years, sharing their visions for a "juster, nobler, happier life for all the American people," what Florence called "a leaven" elevating both of their consciousnesses.[9]

And so that grand library became a kind of shared mission, an intellectual challenge that would serve as Florie's denied education and a bond with her ever-moving dad. Reflecting on her mindset, Florence later admitted with typical bluntness: "I was a very lonely child deeply ashamed of having no school experience," and that sumptuous room "goaded" her to improve herself, to turn her father's books into a "huge indigestible intellectual meal." Whenever he was home, her father would join her in reading and debating, or watch in awe as she worked her way, termite-like, through a lifetime's accumulation of knowledge.[10]

The Elms's library shaped Florie's development to the cusp of adulthood. She began by attacking the small novels running along the higher shelves of the room, demolishing the Dickens, swallowing up "Miss Alcott," and giving over most of "the year of my twelfth birthday" to Walter Scott. By her early teens, she was tackling the weighty histories stored on the lower shelves, consuming the life of Madison, the collected speeches of Daniel Webster, the pathbreaking narratives of Francis Parkman and George Bancroft. When Will Kelley was a young speechifier rising in 1830s Boston,

Bancroft had welcomed him into his personal library; now Will's daughter was devouring his books by the pound.[11]

Many of those histories came as gifts from an admiring constituent of Will's, a voter who had planned to send him a fine suit of clothes, but had learned that the Kelley family preferred "food for the mind rather than rairment [sic] for the body." The rumors were true; generations of well-read but disheveled Kelleys would always accept new books.[12]

The sight of Florie making his library her own forced Will to recalibrate his parenting. Their letters show the shift. Before her tenth birthday, Will's notes to Florie read like the efforts of a decent but distant man, struggling to speak the language of a little girl. He focused on bright objects—ponies, clowns, a Chinatown feast. But following that afternoon in the library, Will's letters welcome Florie into his life. They overflow with the concerns that drove his ceaseless work, and the expansive world of American politics. By the early 1870s, Judge Kelley was writing home about speeches he was drafting, patronage in Washington, and the struggle to pass civil rights legislation. Whenever he succeeded in giving a strong speech, or attended a lecture he thought Florie would enjoy, he wrote with pride. When partisan politics stymied his plans, Will complained bitterly about the Democrats.[13]

Such letters, written to another daughter, might suggest that Will Kelley had given up trying to speak her language. But Will understood Florie's hunger for knowledge, her curiosity about what her dad was doing in that big building on the hill. Some nineteenth-century politicians, men like Thomas Hart Benton or Salmon P. Chase, raised educated, worldly daughters because they lacked sons, or in the place of deceased wives. But Kelley had an astute living wife and two sons. He just saw something in Florie that he never saw in Willy Jr., Anna, or Albert. His letters to them, though loving and engaging, rarely touch on politics or public life. Florie certainly felt that they were communicating clearly; she later recalled the "letters adapted to my age and interest" that her father penned on congressional stationery. Rather than losing touch with his growing daughter's interests, Will Kelley began to see that Florie's driving passions were closer to his own than to stories about clowns or ponies.[14]

Judge Kelley actually knew something about mentoring precocious young women. During the Civil War, Will promoted Anna Dickinson, the electrifying twenty-year-old "girl orator" who spoke out against slavery and sexism with incredible verve. Dickinson was a striking force in American speechifying, a combative young woman who shouted down hecklers and stalked the stage at a time when ladies, if they spoke in public at all, were expected to do so while seated. Though she looked like a schoolgirl, when she spoke, her black eyes "blaze with the passions of a prophetess." Kelley connected Dickinson to journalists, booked her to speak at his campaign rallies, and even introduced her to his troublesome friend, President Lincoln (whom she browbeat for not moving quickly enough on abolition). Will had also long admired the suffragist Susan B. Anthony, making his deep voice "the chief channel" for her women's suffrage petitions in Congress. Florence later told Anthony that her father was constantly advising her to follow Anthony's example. A daughter born in 1859 might never expect to vote or hold office, but Florence Kelley was raised to be a politician nonetheless.[15]

Florie's education extended outside the library as well. In 1871 the family suffered yet another tragic loss. Anna, their cheerful six-year-old, passed away. It was their greatest tragedy, a loss that, as Florie later recalled, "robbed the sunshine of its glory." The Kelleys retreated to a cottage in central Pennsylvania, hoping an autumn in the Alleghenies might brighten Carrie Kelley's gloom.[16]

They found themselves within a few miles of the steel town of Altoona. Will Kelley was becoming fixated on Pennsylvania's steel industry. Political opponents had started to mock him as "Pig Iron Kelley," connecting him to the process of molding steel, in an effort to cast Kelley as a single-issue obsessive and a thuggish, lower-class politico. Though the accusations were deeply unfair, Kelley did not seem to mind. In October 1871 he brought twelve-year-old Florie into one of Altoona's steel mills. Florie stood, holding her tall father's hand, staring in frightful suspense as smudged workers poured molten steel into giant molds. She could imagine "no weirder scene" than the blinding glare of liquid ore in the otherwise gloomy factory. What was her father trying to communicate? At a time when she was starting to read the newspapers, beginning to see him mocked as the fanatical "Pig Iron Kelley," Will was showing his daughter the strange, mystical process of making pig iron, and the laboring men who were building America.[17]

Will Kelley had once told his daughter that it was his generation's duty to build a great nation, and her generation's job to see that its wealth was distributed fairly. Standing among the showering sparks of that Altoona steel mill, Florie received one more of the lessons about the world, the nation, and himself, that Will Kelley was passing down to his persistent daughter. Writing to a good friend a half century later, Florence felt that she still could not articulate her father's impact. "I wish I had time and strength to send you a full description of my father's companionship to which he admitted me when I was ten years old . . . to his influence those six years of my early girlhood, I owe everything that I have ever been able to learn to do."[18]

WHILE FLORIE LAY on the library rug reading Parkman's epic histories, the leading lights of Philadelphia's Black community were climbing into carriages and trotting out to the Elms's leafy West Philly lane. There Will and Carrie greeted his childhood playmates who had become prominent activists, preachers, artists, and barbers, and welcomed them for polite social calls that turned into political planning sessions. Will had made himself a kind of national liaison for Black Philadelphia, representing their concerns to Congress and connecting street-level activists to a national Republican network. When guests visited to discuss "the good cause" in the parlor, Florie was across the hall, digesting the library.[19]

The gracious calm of the Elms set it apart from the real Philadelphia. Turning off busy Lancaster Avenue transported visitors back a generation, barely two miles from city hall, but a world away from the dense, bustling, warring population. Reconstruction Philadelphia exhibited the growing contradictions of the nation. It hosted, famously, America's most secluded elite: hidden away in its narrow, rigid grid were old Quaker and Episcopalian families who made Boston's Brahmins seem down-to-earth. But it was also notorious as the home of the aggressive campaign politics that were over-taking American democracy, driven by the tribal passions of working-class immigrants and struggling African Americans crammed dangerously close. There was, by one account, gunfire at every Philadelphia election between 1870 and 1900. Observers from Chicago described the old town as "at once so riotous, so prim, so full of faction and so fond of gossip." Donnelly, returning to visit his mother in "Phillie" in the 1870s, marveled at the unfamiliar metropolis, piled denser than the sparse, formal town of his youth, wondering: "What would Billy Penn say?"[20]

Philadelphia was coming to epitomize the new style of American politics in the early 1870s. As populist machines cranked into ever higher gear, the "respectable classes" retreated, leaving a less-mitigated democracy, capable of welcoming previously unrepresented groups, but also of pitting them against each other. It was all driven by, as Donnelly put it, "the base scramble of low passions."[21]

And Philadelphia's Black population had to scramble like no other—a minority pushing for rights in the heart of the North. Philadelphia was home to one of the nation's oldest and most important African American populations, a layered community of well-off families along Spring Garden Street, middle-class artisans in Kelley's district, and a more impoverished zone in South Philadelphia. But while it was perhaps America's key Black metropolis, African Americans constituted only about 4.5 percent of Philadelphia's population. Though it loomed large in the Black consciousness, it was a community often overwhelmed by hostile White neighbors.[22]

While Kelley could chug down to Washington or out to San Francisco on the nation's growing train network, Black Philadelphians had to fight to ride the horse-drawn streetcars. And though freed slaves in places like Alabama and Florida had voted for president in 1868, Black people in Philadelphia still could not. Southern African Americans won the right to vote as residents of formerly Confederate states that were being reconstructed by the federal government with Black voting rights. But Pennsylvania had, since 1838, denied its Black citizens that same right. It was fair to say that when it came to voting rights, more had changed in Philadelphia, Mississippi, than in Philadelphia, Pennsylvania.[23]

"I boast of Philadelphia at all times," Kelley declared in an address calling for desegregating the streetcars, "but I cannot help seeing that she is immensely hypocritical. I cannot help seeing her weaknesses."[24]

Philadelphia's Black community was also one of the nation's best organized. Before the Civil War, reform societies mixed African American leaders with elite White Quakers and Unitarians to organize events, hold fundraisers, and blend public action with private philanthropy. Their crowning glory was the Institute for Colored Youth, a Quaker-funded project educating those living in the core of "Negro Philadelphia," at Ninth and Bainbridge. Its principal, the dashing Octavius Catto, balanced education and political activism with impressive skills as the Philadelphia Pythians' agile shortstop. Catto was joined by the elegant Isaiah C. Wears, a talented talker who turned his Northern Liberties barbershop, notary office, and real estate business into a political hub. Catto and Wears worked closely with Kelley to fight for desegregated streetcars and for voting rights. Catto's fiancée, Caroline LeCount, fought as well, challenging conductors who tried to remove her from their streetcars, winning a key desegregation case and a one-hundred-dollar settlement, eighty-eight years before Rosa Parks.[25]

Because they could not yet vote for themselves, electing Black congressmen as southern districts were beginning to do, Philadelphia's Black leaders came to rely on Kelley as their voice in Congress. During the war, Kelley helped lead the committee that recruited African American troops to fight for the Union. And he became a regular presence at public rallies of young Black men asserting their new place in American street-corner democracy. As a congressman, he connected Black Philadelphians to the national network of Reconstruction reformers, and attacked the spiraling violence inflicted on Black voters throughout the South. As a Philadelphian, he assailed the city government and state legislature for their backwardness on race, demanding to know why Black men could not ride the streetcars, when "every white strumpet and thief" could.[26]

In exchange, Black Philadelphia worked to keep Kelley in power. Although they could not yet vote for him, African Americans held political fundraisers to buy uniforms and torches for Kelley's campaign rallies or pay for Dickinson's scintillating speeches. The practical questions of running campaigns underpinned all of American political life, even Will's high-reaching rhetoric about "enfranchising *all* citizens."[27]

By the late 1860s, the northern Republican Party was ready to consider enfranchising all *male* citizens, at least. In the years right after the war, many northern states introduced referenda to give the vote to their Black residents. White voters rejected them all, except in Iowa and Minnesota, states with tiny African American populations (.5 percent and .2 percent, respectively). Clearly, even northern Republicans were deeply skeptical of Black voters in their own states. Kelley denounced his own party for "denying the humanity of the great mass of mankind" by ignoring calls for Black voting rights. But after 1868, when Ulysses S. Grant won the presidency because of southern Black voters, the Republican Party embraced the cause, especially in states with larger Black populations like Pennsylvania, New Jersey, and Connecticut. Suddenly, Kelley's wild calls for Black voting rights seemed like more than earnest idealism. They made good partisan sense.[28]

Finally, in December 1868, Kelley surprised Jacob C. White Jr., the Black political organizer, educator, and ballplayer, with whom he had been discussing a constitutional amendment asserting Black voting rights, with a letter beaming: "I am happy to inform you that I introduced just such an amendment this morning." Kelley had just presented the House with a constitutional amendment barring the use of race to limit the right to vote. The cause won the support of White Republicans who were counting potential votes. In New York, Conkling mocked Democratic claims that Black Americans were too uneducated to vote, thundering that if you wanted ignorance, look to Democratic voters. Fearing that they would soon lose their iron grip on the House, Republicans rushed through the amendment. Different formulations were debated, but in the end it was Kelley's demand that it be made illegal to deny voting rights based on "race, color, or previous condition of servitude" that won out. Not a single congressional Democrat voted for it. But early in 1869 the Fifteenth Amendment passed Congress and was ratified just in time for the 1870 midterms.[29]

The moment marked an epochal peak of a half century of widening faith in electoral democracy, whether motivated by faith in humanity or partisan ballot-counting. Few could sense that the victory also teetered on the brink of a coming crash, commencing an equally dramatic half-century decline of faith in the people to govern.

The response to the Fifteenth Amendment was blindly partisan and utterly predictable. The great majority of Whites in both parties still held deeply racist views, but public feelings about Black voting rights had begun to follow party lines. Prior to the Civil War, there were always some Democrats who opposed slavery, and plenty of racist Republicans. But more and more, as Black rights meant Republican votes, partisan biases converged with racial rhetoric. In Republican corners of the North, Blacks and Whites celebrated the Fifteenth Amendment with demonstrations and barbecues. One parade in Manhattan featured "29 young colored girls," costumed as the twenty-nine states that ratified the amendment. And two thousand miles west—in Helena, Montana—the local Republicans fielded a similar demonstration, complete with "29 young Misses," though there were fewer than two hundred African Americans in the state.[30]

In Philadelphia, Judge Kelley won the praise of Republicans and the hatred of Democrats. The suave barber Wears, representative of middle-class Black Philadelphia and known for his speechifying, reminded West Philadelphia's Black voters to support Kelley, who "had always been a champion of the right of suffrage for the colored man," in upcoming elections. When African American marchers poured down Philadelphia's Broad Street to celebrate the Fifteenth Amendment, the Fourteenth Ward Colored Republican Club waved a giant portrait of Will Kelley, labeled "Friend of the Colored Man." Kelley's distinctive face, with his dense beard, low forehead, and protruding ears, was depicted in honor, not caricature, for once.

Yet Democratic Philadelphians, and some of his own White voters, attacked Kelley for his long crusade for Black voting rights. A furious cartoonist denounced the politicians who schemed "to make the Negro the Equal of the Poor White Man," citing Kelley as one of the worst of the race traitors.[31]

And that proud banner, waved by the Fourteenth Ward Colored Republican Club in Philadelphia's Fifteenth Amendment parade? Halfway through the march, a crew of White toughs ambushed the marchers, hurling rotten egg after rotten egg, until "the banner was ruined" and Kelley's proud face dripped with yolk.[32]

Black voters emerged as a key element of the electorate, at least in places like Philly where they had the numbers. There were about five thousand African American voters in Philadelphia in the 1870s, and as reliable Republicans in Pennsylvania, the core of the nationwide Republican Party, they wielded considerable influence. In campaigns that were increasingly focused on turnout of partisan bases, the Republican Party needed Black voters. As a result, an African American Republican machine began to cohere, capable of getting out the vote. While the pre–Civil War Black community was often led by religious leaders and wealthy philanthropists, the new campaign-focused community began to revolve around school-teachers, barbers, and saloon keepers who knew their districts and could get ordinary men to the polls. Black voters had a tradition of voting early in the day—to avoid crowds of drunk and violent White men—and the new African American Republican machine was skilled at getting voters up and out early on October or November mornings.[33]

But almost as soon as an African American machine got going, members of the Black community began debating their fealty to the Republican Party. It was the same question that millions of Americans, of all races, would ask over the next generation, but the fact that African Americans were so tied to the Republican Party caused them to grapple with the challenge of partisanship before it had dawned on many Whites. Few Black men would vote for the racist Democrats, but what was the Republican Party actually doing with all their votes? The nation's most prominent African American leader, Frederick Douglass, dragged Philadelphia's Republican machine into this debate, including his friend Will Kelley.

Douglass wrote to Kelley, in 1871, with a tone of careful inquiry about what Kelley thought about the national Republican machine. After assuring Will that he spoke often with his sons about Kelley's "audacity, nerve and ability," Douglass began to inquire about what the independent-minded congressman made of the hegemonic party. He wondered "can we do any better?" before claiming that, criticisms of President Grant aside, "the case would not be different with any other man." Douglass carefully assured the congressman that he was "a party man," and felt his "highest political duty today is promoting the success of the Republican party." Yet he left a bit of room, stressing how "highly I esteem those who feel bound to throw off the <u>shackles</u> of party," and concluding: "of course this letter is for you and not the public." "Shackles" was a weighty metaphor for a man born in slavery, and Douglass's letter seemed to hint at some undercurrent, perhaps rumors that Kelley, like some Black voters, had doubts about total fealty to the party that controlled the White House, the House, and the Senate.[34]

Douglass dropped the veil when talking to Philadelphia's Black leaders. He told Philadelphia's Black community, in a prominent speech, that enfranchised African Americans should remember to vote "as they pleased. Each man much decide what men and measures will be best." The speech enraged many in Philadelphia's nascent Black Republican machine. Catto was so livid that he refused to respond, but Wears launched into a back-and-forth debate with Douglass in Philly's Black newspapers. Such high-toned rhetoric might work for national celebrities like Douglass, but he didn't have to shuttle men to the polls early on election day, didn't have to vote surrounded by armed Democratic rowdies, didn't have to worry about William "the Squire" McMullen.[35]

PHILADELPHIA MAY HAVE been 4.5 percent African American in 1870, but it was 27 percent foreign-born, many of them impoverished Irish Catholic immigrants who faced their own struggles. It had not been that long since 1844, when nativist Protestant rioters attacked Irish neighborhoods, murdering dozens and burning cathedrals. To this persecuted ethnic minority, often made up of day laborers and domestic servants living in Philly's dingiest alleys, the Democratic Party looked like a rare ally. By the 1870s, a tribal political machine ran many of Philadelphia's poorer wards, led by the canny American-born sons of famine immigrants. Like Philadelphia's African American Republicans, Irish Democrats saw a political party as one of the few institutions that could help overcome ethnic discrimination and Gilded Age capitalism. And like the Washington politicos who made up for lack of social standing with pure aggression, these hard-driving campaigners replaced the old aristocrats who wanted little to do with men like William McMullen.

Before he became Democratic boss of the Fourth Ward, McMullen was just another South Philly troublemaker, a thick-necked gang leader with a chin-patch beard and a pitiless stare. But before that, he was a scared child of Irish immigrants, growing up in a back-alley slum at Seventh and Bainbridge. By seventeen, McMullen had fought to defend his neighborhood in the 1844 anti-immigrant riots, but also participated in the racist pogroms that targeted nearby African Americans. McMullen survived all this violence unscathed, giving rise to the rumors that guns mysteriously jammed when fired at his chest, because McMullen was "protected by the Evil One."[36]

Protected or not, by the time he reached voting age, McMullen had formed an embattled belief that life meant war for his tribe against Protestants above and African Americans below. He entered adulthood as a crude bully but also as a shrewd leader, simultaneously the voice of one of the nation's most targeted immigrant communities and also the ringleader of one of country's most violent White supremacist movements. His motto—"Always Get Even"—summed up his worldview.[37]

At first, politics seemed a little dry, a little indirect, for the rambunctious young McMullen. Instead, he joined one of Philadelphia's volunteer fire companies, organizations that teetered between public service and public menace. McMullen chose the Moyamensing Fire Company, a famous South Philly Irish Catholic crew recognizable for having their firehouse number, 27, tattooed on their hands. Sometimes the Moyas put out fires, sometimes they fought other firehouses, engaging in melees with hundreds of men, armed with revolvers, knives, axes, and wrenches. In one instance, Moyas ambushed a native-born Protestant company heading to a blaze, blasting its crew with shotguns loaded with cut-up pennies and dumping their lifeless engine into the Delaware River.[38]

Companies like the Moyas—which fought fires and picked fights, but also helped elect Democrat aldermen—made sense in the blended political culture of mid-nineteenth-century America. They existed along the same (albeit more violent) lines as the African American organizations that fought slavery, gathered the faithful to pray, and raised money for friendly politicians. In a time when politics was distinctly unprofessional, with high turnover and elite leadership, these mixed organizations ran communities like Philadelphia.

But in the post–Civil War years, politics began to show itself as a rewarding pursuit of its own, attractive to strivers like McMullen. Philadelphia's city fathers were finally able, in 1871, to replace volunteer firefighters with a professional force, a move the Democratic McMullen felt "our party cannot afford." With his power source threatened, McMullen saw another path to influence, opening a saloon and political headquarters on the border between his Irish ward and "Negro Philadelphia," dangerously close to the Institute for Colored Youth.[39]

Such saloons were emerging as centers for on-the-ground politics in those years, creating a working-class, fraternal environment where canvassers could "treat" potential voters to a glass of lager, a five-cent cigar, and a free lunch of pretzels, bologna, and pickled eggs—all while lecturing them on the coming election. A few years later, Rudyard Kipling observed that such saloon politicians knew the electorate better than anyone and could look across their bar and select "a block of men who will vote for or against anything." McMullen's saloon became a new seat of power, with the perfect backroom to plot campaigns, or assassinations. Soon the club helped win "the Squire" a seat as alderman.[40]

Just as Kelley served as a liaison between Black Philadelphia and the federal government, Alderman McMullen operated as a link between Philadelphia's underworld and the elite Democrats. The party had its working-class immigrant wing, but also attracted wealthier populations through its hostility to centralized government, taxes, high tariffs, and meddlesome social legislation. Often, McMullen ended up supplying the muscle for those Democrats who would not fight for themselves.

He spent much of his time as alderman patrolling the notorious Moyamensing prison, pardoning promising inmates in exchange for doing campaign work. He practiced the art of "colonizing," sending crews to cities like New York or Baltimore to swing elections. When a federal revenue agent started nosing around the illegal liquor stills that supplied Philadelphia's saloons with cheap whiskey, McMullen's associates ambushed the inspector and shot him. The Squire got the culprits freed quickly. And when Philadelphia's Democrats needed to be sure that their allies across the state voted correctly, McMullen's Moyas went to Harrisburg. They were observed in the statehouse, arms menacingly folded across their chests, exposing their number 27 tattoos, standing as silent threats to any Pennsylvania Democrats who might vote wrong. Such traveling thugs were influencing politics nationwide, becoming the violent equivalent of speechifiers like Kelley, Donnelly, and Dickinson, traversing ever-darker political circuits.[41]

Though much of the violence of this era had to do with conflicts over race, men like McMullen proved quite capable of killing each other over a host of political issues.

In exchange for his services, elite Philadelphia Democrats feted McMullen, granting him entry into a new world. At one 1869 ball, for instance, they awarded the Squire a diamond breast pin worth $2,500 and a tobacco box inlaid with gold and yet more diamonds. McMullen's services were obviously valuable.[42]

The Squire's closest ally was one of the most powerful men in the country, Congressman Samuel J. Randall. Randall was the fast-talking, aggressive representative of many portions of Philadelphia that Kelley did not represent, known for his sarcastic, high, scratchy voice and personal incorruptibility. But Randall's power in Washington was underwritten by his relationship with McMullen, who kept Philadelphia's votes and gossip flooding down to D.C. McMullen's personal letters to Randall are funny, warm, and shockingly misspelled, but they demonstrate, in codes and veiled references, a political conspiracy bordering on organized crime, working to steal elections, squelch rivals, and intimidate federal monitors. Chief among their concerns was the suppression of the thousands of Black voters who stood poised to remake Philly's electoral map in 1870. In the words of one of Randall's correspondents, "if it were not for the Negroes we would have everything our way."[43]

All these trends—the shuttering of the fire companies that pointed McMullen to politics, the enfranchisement of Black Philadelphians, and the Democratic Party's willingness to fight dirty—converged at Philadelphia's municipal election, on October 10, 1871. The year before—the first election after the passage of the Fifteenth Amendment—federal troops had protected Black Philadelphians at the polls. McMullen had been out on election day nonetheless, intimidating Black voters by demanding that they shake his hand if they wanted to vote in his ward. But in October 1871, the city exploded. Though McMullen claimed he spent the day getting "blowers back in their wholes [sic]" (i.e., convincing hotheads to go home), his Moyas unleashed devastating violence on Black Republicans. Several Black voters were shot, and one was killed by a fireman's axe.[44]

And that afternoon, Octavius Catto, leader of the movement for Black voting rights, principal of the Institute for Colored Youth, friend of Kelley, and symbol of the promise of Black Philadelphia, found himself walking down South Street. He passed two rough-looking White men who eyed him warily. Black voters were right, Whites did get worse over the course of an election day. The nimble shortstop had a revolver on him, but no bullets. It didn't matter, because as Catto walked on down South Street past the men, one turned, pulled a revolver, cocked it with a hand bearing a "27" tattoo, and shot Octavius Catto dead.[45]

Catto's murder took place at a turning point. The immediate postwar possibilities of "pure democracy" began to recede, or show themselves to be the fictions they were all along. Prominent, optimistic figures, like Philly's Black activists, or Dickinson, or Donnelly, began to show less interest in the grand possibilities of politics. Philadelphia's Black community kept voting, but more and more it was led by machine politicians, like the saloon keeper Gil Ball. Ball knew how to get drinkers to the polls, using his saloon to organize campaigns. He resembled a Black version of McMullen. Ball and the Squire were even friends, somehow, comparing notes about the same campaign tricks applied to rival populations.[46]

The late 1860s and early '70s showed how much public life had changed. Mid-nineteenth-century Americans, both in cities like Philly and in small towns across the nation, layered their politics in with other diverse concerns. The churches, reform societies, educational lectures, and other associations that blended politics with the rest of public life often mixed elite and laboring Americans. Even those antebellum fire companies often joined middle- and working-class men for fraternal bonding across classes.[47] But as the Gilded Age dawned, such diverse institutions fell away, replaced by a politics of tribal machines and men who "Always Got Even." Elites retreated, asking men like McMullen do their dirty work. Those politicians who won office stayed for decades, and those voters who joined political clubs lingered longer at the bar.

And what of Will Kelley, where was he when his friend Octavius Catto was gunned down in early October 1871? Kelley was standing, holding Florie's hand, facing the blast of that Altoona steel mill. It was not Kelley's fault that his beloved daughter Anna had died in the fall of 1871, or that the Kelleys retreated to central Pennsylvania to grieve while Black Philadelphia was battling to vote. But nonetheless, his presence in a steel mill, and absence from the polling place, presaged the next step in his wandering political journey.

Kelley was not just mourning in Altoona. He was obsessing. He was bringing Florie to learn how pig iron was made. He was penning articles on the promise of industrialization, published when he was supposed to be mourning with Carrie. It is no coincidence that Florence's memories of her education revolved around her father's growing passion for industrial conditions, child labor, and the resources of the nation. Will Kelley was shifting from his postwar focus on racial equality to a new fascination with industrial growth and the laboring men and women whom it might help.[48]

A gift Kelley sent to the Institute for Colored Youth a few months after Catto's assassination sums up his shift. Instead of his usual focus on voting as "the entering wedge" of racial equality, Kelley sent Fanny Jackson Coppin, the school's new principal, a copy of his speeches on "the industries of the Country, of agriculture; the finances, railroads, + e." Fanny thanked him for the book, assuring Kelley that it would be useful, because young African Americans, "belonging so largely to the laboring class," should understand the nation's industrial growth "for the safety of their interests and of their rights." She may have been pandering to a powerful White supporter. It's hard to imagine that a community that had just seen several members gunned down while trying to vote could really care too much about the copper resources of the Rocky Mountains.[49]

Douglass may have spoken too soon when he wrote that Kelley was one of the few leaders "of whom I have no doubt or fear," a crusader "who has never failed me or my people."[50]

CHAPTER FIVE

"Swallow It Down"

I n that same October, as Florie and Will stared into the blaze of an Altoona steel mill, and a Moya's pistol sparked the round that killed Octavius Catto, other fires were raging. Huge blazes consumed swaths of the Midwest. One devoured Chicago. That city had ballooned from thirty thousand to three hundred thousand in a generation, filling up with cheap wooden buildings to house its laborers. When all that kindling caught, on October 8, 1871, the resulting "Great Chicago Fire" left a third of the city homeless.

To build Chicago, lumbermen clear-cut vast forests in the upper Midwest. On that same October day, the scrub they left behind went up in flames. Though lesser known than Chicago's catastrophe, the "Peshtigo fire" became the deadliest in recorded history, killing roughly two thousand in Wisconsin and Michigan.[1]

The fires of progress were burning the old order down.

Nor could the firemen be trusted. William M. Tweed, in New York, came up like Squire McMullen, an impoverished boy who rose through the ranks of urban fire companies into Democratic politics. By the early 1870s, he was boss of New York's Tammany Hall. Exploiting the new campaign economy that traded government rewards for political labor, Tweed stole tens of millions from the city's construction projects. In October 1871, he was arrested.

That same month, the cartoonist Thomas Nast satirized men like Tweed, sketching an obese, cocky politico with a moneybag for a head, above the taunting caption: "Well, what are you going to do about it?"[2]

Americans were beginning to ask themselves that same question, *What were they going to do about it?* The fires that scorched the Midwest, and the scandals of men like Tweed, all resulted from the incredible changes of the nineteenth century, the social and economic revolutions that disrupted ordinary people's lives. Some sought protection in political parties. Others looked for easy scapegoats, blaming corrupt politicians or Black Reconstruction. They created a cycle of rage, a self-perpetuating bad mood that simultaneously pushed citizens farther into partisanship while undermining their faith in democracy.

Even Will Kelley felt the bind, choosing to desert some of his closest allies and venture off in an uncharted direction.

Many associate this emerging Gilded Age with impersonal forces, history-class abstractions like Industrialization, Urbanization, and Immigration. But such terms elide how intimate the era's disruptions felt. Millions moved, chasing booms and fleeing busts, across oceans or frontiers. In one Wisconsin county, 89 percent of the teen males present in 1860 had left by 1870, and 90 percent of those present in 1870 were gone by 1880. America's wanderers left behind family and community, sleeping among strangers, dining in boardinghouses, giving birth in freight cars. And the work took its toll. Laborers lost fingers, toes, or lives to the new economy. The chances that a working-age man would die accidentally rose by two-thirds between 1850 and 1880. During these years, the death rate and infant mortality climbed, while the height of the average American fell.[3]

But it wasn't all bad. Especially in the early Gilded Age, a dynamic economy freed strivers from old restraints. Plowmen struck oil; grocers became tycoons. Many entered the exploding upper-middle class, able to afford beef at every meal, vacations for their families, brownstones in well-to-do new neighborhoods. Others went further, announcing their new wealth with diamond stickpins, vast plumages of ostrich feathers, and Gothic palaces looming over New York or Chicago.

It was this freedom from limitations, this giddy disregard for good taste, that led Mark Twain and Charles Dudley Warner to call their era "the

Gilded Age" in their 1873 novel. Twain and Warner borrowed Shakespeare's reference in *King John* to a man who would "gild refined gold" itself. They were not implying—as later generations looking back through the prism of the Progressive Era would assume—a gilded patina covering up internal national rot. Instead, Twain and Warner used Shakespeare's image of gilded gold to capture a society so relentlessly over-the-top that even solid gold got an extra shine.[4]

While booms severed old restraints, busts left Americans dangling. Millions found this out in 1873, when the nation's much-hyped railroad bubble burst, beginning the "Long Depression" of the 1870s. Over the next three years half of America's railroad companies entered receivership. Without trains to build, steel output (Kelley's baby) fell by nearly half, while miners experienced a new phenomenon in the age of wage labor: mass unemployment. By the end of the decade, nearly a third of the nation's workforce had, at some point, been out of work for one hundred days. And money fled from much of rural America, congealing in a few eastern financial centers.[5]

For the next half century, until 1929, the term *Great Depression* meant the cataclysm of the 1870s.

This dark and dreary Gilded Age has become a stereotype, but what is often missed is that the Americans who lived through these years were hardly passive actors, waiting to lose their fingers in cranking factories. Instead, many reacted, looking to the largest, most accessible social institutions for protection. And no institutions were as popular or welcoming as political parties, hungry for new supporters. More Americans voted for the Republicans and Democrats in presidential elections in the 1870s than joined the Methodist or Catholic churches, America's biggest denominations (and this count does not include all the deeply partisan women and the boys under twenty-one who could not cast votes for their favored parties). Few put faith in respectable reform organizations, and while scholars have focused on the radical solutions of the era, socialism, anarchism, and trade unionism attracted only small minorities. Far more citizens looked the shorter distance to the two big national parties, beckoning from saloons and town squares.[6]

Party affiliation offered identity to displaced people who had little else. The future Tammany Hall boss Richard Croker would brag that his political machine welcomed "the untrained friendless man," asking, "Who else would do it if we did not?" Ignored by elites, abused by their employers, impoverished migrants were treated as if they had "no value to any one until they get a vote." But Croker's machine welcomed them. Tammany, its defenders argued, "is a great digestive apparatus," turning strangers into citizens.[7]

Persecuted minorities, like Philly's Black Republicans and Irish Democrats, needed this inclusion the most, but disruption was a nation-wide force, and middle- and working-class Americans, urban and rural, relied on their parties. "A man had to cling to something," recalled the historian Walter Weyl, and in the depths of the Gilded Age, "the tempta-tion to cling to party became ruthless."[8]

Many anxious Americans found solace, belonging, even joy in their political parties. Young men marching in torchlit processions won a feeling of fraternity with each parade. Women shouting for their party from the sidelines surprised themselves with how "strongminded" they could be. Newly enfranchised African Americans earned a palpable sense of agency by stump speaking for the Republican Party. Membership in a party, Jane Addams discovered when she studied Chicago's juvenile criminals, offered the same sense of loyalty and belonging that children's street gangs had.[9]

In an age of ruthless individualism, in an economy that atomized workers, in a society that trumpeted success as proof of personal Darwinian superiority, the parties offered a countervailing sense of community.

As Americans looked to parties for protection, they abandoned the political fluidity that proponents of pure democracy had hoped the war might bring. By the 1870s, attitudes toward parties hardened into outlandish stereotypes. To Republicans, the Democrats were the "stupider" party: rangy, shady criminals, half Ku Kluxer, half Irish rioter, characterized by Roscoe Conkling as "thugs and shoulder-hitters . . . the carriers of dirks and bludgeons, the fraternity of the hells and the slums." Democrats coun-tered that the Republican Party was a national Goliath, made up of moral-istic crooks who clucked about equal rights while perpetrating what the Democratic *Chicago Times* called "*too much devouring.*" Neither stereotype reflected the millions of citizens who found meaning among the Republicans or Democrats, but they served as campaigners and sold newspapers.[10]

Life within a party could be just as constraining. John Sobieski, an idealistic Polish immigrant and Union Army vet, found this out when he entered Minnesota's Republican politics. Sobieski used his seat in the state legislature to call for women's suffrage, Black voting rights, and his chief cause: Prohibition. Soon, a prominent St. Paul Republican invited Sobieski to dinner. In his grand library, the politico gave young Sobieski some advice. "Identify yourself with the Republican party." Memorize the platform. Leave social issues to the ministers. Most important, the older man instructed, match your views to the "average intelligence and morality" of the population. Sobieski's host sounds like Ignatius Donnelly claiming that a leader should never reach "a higher moral standard than their constituency." The mass of voters should determine good and bad, not Sobieski's busy conscience.[11]

And if his party were to advocate some cause Sobieski could not endorse? The politico had a simple answer for the young legislator: "Swallow it down."

In a shaken time, many felt forced to choose between the protection of rigid political parties and the appalling emptiness of life outside those great machines.

The 1872 presidential election displayed just how powerful those machines could be. A movement of high-minded ex-Republicans, unhappy with President Grant, started calling themselves the Liberal Republican Party and nominated Horace Greeley to run against the incumbent. As editor of the *New York Tribune*, Greeley had been the "self-made chief editor in the United States," operating as the crusading, liberal conscience for the nation for decades. Lacking any clear contender of their own, the Democrats nominated Greeley as well. But his moralism was no match for the Republicans' steamroller. Twenty-three-year-old Jacob Riis—future author of *How the Other Half Lives*—recalled being dragged into a Republican rally in Pittsburgh in 1872. Though just a bystander, Riis watched in shock as "a marching band of uniformed shouters for Grant had cut right through the crowd. As it passed I felt myself suddenly seized . . . An oil cloth cape was thrown over my head, a campaign cap jammed after, and I found myself marching away with a torch on my shoulder to the tune of a brass band just ahead."[12]

Grant's juggernaut stomped poor idealistic Greeley, winning the Republicans' fourth presidential victory in a row. Millions did legitimately prefer Grant, but Riis's sense of political compulsion captured what it felt like to stand in the way of a mass of marching partisans.

This new tone infuriated old elites, who felt that they were losing power with each campaign. The massive working-class electorate could always outmarch and outvote them. When the slippery politician Benjamin Butler ran a race for governor of Massachusetts, in 1871, with "no end of brass bands, and with great processionings and multitudinous hand-shakings," it highlighted just how outnumbered the Boston establishment had become. As Butler riled crowds of thirty thousand, the *Atlantic Monthly* griped that such showy populism made his name "a synonym for everything that is bad in American politics."[13] Soon, the old upper classes were dismissing all politics as disreputable. Many came from northeastern families who had been on the vanguard of abolition, but by the 1870s their optimism curdled. Politics was no longer an "occupation for a gentleman" but mostly "a matter of bar-rooms, ballot-box-stuffing, rolls of dirty bills." These gentlemen often linked mass politics and dirt, in an age starting to care a great deal about cleanliness. "Vulgar" was another common barb. The conservative editor of the *New York Tribune*, Whitelaw Reid, told the graduates of Dartmouth College in 1873 that politics was "a vulgar struggle of vulgar men through vulgar means."[14]

The respectable should have little to do with politics. Stick to business and law, the church and the university, leave the town square and the saloon to the Ben Butlers, Squire McMullens, and Pig Iron Kelleys. It became a boastful catchphrase in American high society: "A Gentlemen Never Votes."[15]

There were plenty of vulgar men to complain about in the pages of the *Atlantic Monthly*. Every day in the early 1870s, it seemed, newspaper readers were confronted with some fresh scandal. There was the Tweed affair, the Grant administration's seemingly endless swindles, and the "rings" of corrupt officials profiting off everything from whiskey taxes to Indian treaties to post office jobs. Railroad corporations—the largest businesses in the nation—brought in four hundred million dollars a year, transporting 150 million annual passengers in a nation of 39 million. They had money to burn, bribing leaders in both parties. Some of their corruption was pathet-ically petty. In Iowa, one unemployed wanderer complained that "all prom-inent politicians" made winning a free pass from the railroad their "main object in life."[16]

By 1874, grousing about Tweed or Grant grew into a generalized frus-tration with "all prominent politicians." It was a far cry from the days when Americans used the term to refer to anyone interested in politics. Now anger at politicians "rendered the name obnoxious," according to one Scranton letter writer, turning the word into "an epithet" in the mouths of an anxious public. In lurid denunciations, prominent figures like the famed humorist James Russell Lowell portrayed politicians as "fleshflies that fatten on the sores of our body-politic and plant there the eggs of their disgustful and infectious progeny." The social and economic earthquake of the early Gilded Age pushed Americans into stronger partisanship while also increasing their anger at the leaders who were failing to help them. Many looked to politics as a refuge, even as they looked on politicians with disgust.[17]

The shift was clear in America's raucous political cartoons. In ante-bellum images, cartoonists drew politicians to look like everyone else. During the burst of optimism in the middle to late 1860s, some even substituted the gowned Goddess of Liberty for mortal politicians to repre-sent the federal government. But in the 1870s, politicians deformed into obese, ostentatious, scheming politicos, almost a different species. Especially in the hallucinogenic visions of Nast and Joseph Keppler, elected leaders appeared as vultures, jackals, or rats. And in 1874 Nast hit on the perfect metaphor for the bumbling, stomping, blustering Republican politicians who ran the nation: a big, clumsy elephant.[18]

Nast's elephant was in trouble. The congressional election in 1874 became one of the most significant in American history, as Democrats called on discontented voters to throw the bums out. Jettisoning their old image as the party of slavery and secession, a revitalized Democratic Party ran against the post–Civil War Republican establishment. It attacked that once-triumphant party as a fossil, in this age of dinosaur discovery, no more relevant than "extinct monsters whose bones are gathered for geological museums." Democrats especially appealed to young voters who came of age after the Civil War. Painting a dark picture of a Republican order dominated by centralizing bureaucrats, crooked tax collectors, meddlesome reformers, and African American officeholders, Democrats declared it time "for the young men of the country to act."[19]

Roscoe Conkling complained about the sweeping negativity of the Democrats' campaign. In a furious Brooklyn address in 1874, he argued that Democratic propaganda implied that every American politician, "from the President down, every candidate for public station, is a vulgar trickster." They seemed to believe that the nation "had fallen on the most depraved and venal era of the republic, if not of the world." "The Outs" of the era of Pure Democracy—be they Democrats, or old aristocrats, or ex-Confederates—seemed willing to undermine all faith in representative government to claw their way back into power.[20]

And it worked. In 1874 the Democratic Party won the largest congressional landslide up to that point in American history. The party, out of power in any branch of federal government since 1860, swung ninety-four House seats. It won big among young voters in the populous lower North, swinging New York, Ohio, and even Kelley's Pennsylvania delegation (although he kept his iron hold on Pennsylvania's Fourth District). After 1874 American democracy's midcentury experiment with political independence was over, replaced by two nationally competitive partisan machines. Democrats and Republicans, even as they attacked politicians, demanded unflinching loyalty to the party.[21]

Reconstruction was the first victim of this "depraved and venal era." Newly confident southern Democrats launched campaigns of political terrorism at the polling place. To John Roy Lynch, a former slave who had won office as congressman from Mississippi, the 1874 Democratic landslide felt "like a clap of thunder from a clear sky." White supremacists attacked Black voters with renewed aggression, using organizations like the Red Shirts or the White Leagues to intimidate and murder African Americans in Louisiana, South Carolina, and Mississippi.[22]

But it took more than racist southern Democrats to kill Reconstruction. As long as the project had the support of the northern majority it was federal policy, but by the mid-1870s, many White Northerners were done. Yankee voters who had supported Reconstruction in 1866 or 1870 soured after the Fifteenth Amendment.[23] They were distracted by conflicts closer to home over the depression, money, and immigration. And the political negativity of the 1870s made it easier to give up on a project as optimistic as Reconstruction. In a republic that many believed was "venal and depraved," talk of pure democracy sounded naive.

In the words of John Young, the freed slave and pyrotechnic Republican speechifier from South Carolina, by the mid-1870s freed peoples' old allies in the North "just sat back and allowed de white men of de southern states to skin us out of our rights."[24]

Due to the odd alliances of that era, the corrupt Republican establishment was also the most faithful defender of Reconstruction. Those who saw themselves as subversive critics of the powers that be lined up against both the Grant administration and the African Americans it supported, as relics of a bygone era and a bloated machine. This created a strange alliance, between Black politicians struggling to hold on to hard-won rights, tied to some of the Republican Party's "harshest, strictest, most narrow-minded political bosses," and men like Conkling, crooked as he was, who fought to defend Black political rights throughout the 1870s.[25]

His loyalty to Black politicians set up a striking scene in the Senate in 1875. At the beginning of the session, Blanche Bruce was to be inducted as a junior senator from Mississippi. Born into slavery, Bruce was the first Black man ever elected to the Senate in U.S. history, having won Jefferson Davis's old seat. The dapper, solidly built Bruce arrived at the capitol, anxious for the ceremony. Traditionally, junior senators were escorted to their seat by the senior member from their state. But when Bruce entered the Senate chambers, Mississippi's senior senator hid his face behind a newspaper, refusing to acknowledge Bruce.

Bruce stood awkwardly at the back of the world's foremost deliberative body, digesting this slight, when he felt a firm grasp on his arm. Turning, Bruce saw a copper-bearded, smartly dressed Adonis looming over him. "Mr. Bruce, Permit me. My name is Conkling," the senator from New York offered. The two walked arm in arm into the chamber (despite Conkling's notorious hatred of physical contact). Senator Bruce claimed his seat.[26]

Bruce considered it "the first token of friendship" he felt in Washington, in the waning light of Reconstruction. Later, he would name his son Roscoe Conkling Bruce.

Reconstruction was dying in the mid-1870s, a casualty not just of resurgent racism but of declining faith in the capabilities of American politics. One cannot understand what happened to Black political rights without grasping a larger fight raging over democracy. As a project, Reconstruction had always advanced along two parallel tracks: as a campaign for racial justice, and as the peak expression of mid-nineteenth-century American faith in a populist democracy. But Americans' view of representative self-government darkened in the 1870s, driven by social disruptions and class resentment. Projects like Reconstruction were vulnerable targets.

The parties were building a "mighty wall of political prejudice," tragically separating former allies. The alliances of the age created an artificial divide between orthodox Republicans, who supported Reconstruction, and independent-minded reformers, furious with the devouring elephant. This growing barrier would prove too high for even lanky Will Kelley to surmount.[27]

WHILE BLANCHE BRUCE was embracing partisanship in the very name of his son, Will Kelley was distancing himself from his party in talks and letters to his daughter. As rigid partisanship and individual conscience came into conflict, Kelley felt the squeeze. Always a vanguard politician, who hated men who lead "from the back of their heads," Will had been quick in his embrace of pure democracy, but would be equally quick to explore new crusades in the 1870s. In his fight to maintain independence for his reverberating political voice, Kelley would take his boldest stands and make his gravest betrayals.[28]

It began in the late summer of 1872, as the presidential campaign was in full swing. When he should have been out firing up Republican crowds, Kelley was far west, trotting a horse along the ridges and canyons of Southern California. After daily rides, Will would rejoin Carrie and Florie and Albert in the sumptuous parlors of Los Angeles's Pico House Hotel and read and laugh and eat. Doctors had recommended the trip to cure Will's worsening coughing fits, but in a campaign system where congressmen were expected to shout for their party's nominee, his presence 2,700 miles west of his crucial state sent a message.[29]

Kelley's health provided half an excuse to dodge some of the 1872 race, Florie's education the rest. The family went west, in part, to offer her some sense of the world beyond the Elms. They marveled at the Rockies, watched Chinese ceremonies for the dead, and stuffed themselves until—in Florie's words—"Papa has gained five and a half pounds. Bertie, one, Mama would not be weighed, and I have gained ten." Florie was growing. In photographs the thirteen-year-old—soft chin, pale lace dress, hair pulled demurely back—still looks like the girl who cleaned her father's study, but she was gaining in strength and substance. "Papa thinks," she wrote to her grandparents, that their western travels were "worth very nearly a whole years school to me and I am very nearly of his opinions." Her "very nearly" sums up her bond to her father and his opinions, and her persistent craving for more than even California could offer.[30]

But for Will, there could be no avoiding American politics. In their flailing campaign against Grant in 1872, Democrats unearthed a tasty scandal. A number of congressmen had accepted stock from a company called Credit Mobilier in exchange for helping the Union Pacific's railroad conquer the continent. Kelley's name was on the list. Many were stunned. Will Kelley might be an oddball or an obsessive, but he was usually seen as an honest man—more likely to lecture on the genius of the age of rail than to profit from it. Letters of support poured into the Elms; colleagues who had witnessed Kelley expel "would-be bribers" from his offices by force could not believe the charges. It does seem that Kelley had received some stock, but thought that it was the appreciation on shares he had committed to buy earlier, guiltier of gullibility than of guile. Either way, the charges stung the Kelleys—with Will's heavy-browed face caricatured in political cartoons, and Carrie refusing to "go into society" for months.[31]

Embarrassed by the scandal, and shocked by the 1873 depression, Kelley reminded voters of his working-class roots. He pointedly insisted that the only time he had personally profited from American industry was back when he toiled as an indentured jeweler's apprentice. The moment offered Kelley an opportunity to assure the public that he was one of the few politicians who cared about the unemployed, and also that he disapproved of his party's handling of the crisis. Kelley had spent years debating the "shackles of party" with Frederick Douglass and writing to the women's suffrage activist Elizabeth Cady Stanton that he felt "solitary and alone" among the Republicans. He was the man, after all, who had left the Democratic Party over slavery, who had never believed that an American could truly "express their political views by naming a party." And he was coming to see the Grant administration as the root cause of mass unemployment and national suffering. Even as Americans were tightening their partisanship in the mid-1870s, Kelley was contemplating a bolt.[32]

A fight over money offered Kelley the chance he needed. During the Civil War, the U.S. government had printed "greenbacks," a paper currency not backed by gold, to help pay for the conflict. They had hung around after. But with the Democratic landslide of 1874, congressional Republicans used their last few months in office, in early 1875, to push through a radical belt-tightening. Believing that too much "soft money" had caused the Panic of 1873, lame-duck Republicans passed the Specie Resumption Act, to drain those greenbacks out of the economy. To some, it was common sense. To others, the move affirmed the growing stereotype of the Republicans as the party of the bankers—gobbling up money in the midst of a depression.[33]

To Kelley, his party's Specie Resumption Act was "cruel and infamous," an insult to those scrounging for funds in the greatest depression of their lifetime. It proved, he told the *New York Times*, the suspicion that the leadership of the Republican Party was acting to "concentrate in the hands of a few people all the property in the United States." Florie, at fifteen, was politically astute enough to know how her father would feel about such an act. Responding to a probing letter from her, Will wrote, "You are right in thinking, that I am disgusted with the result of the financial question." Grant's efforts to justify the Republican's lame-duck policy only meant that "my disgust is intensified."[34]

It would be a breaking point. What was this party, this hungry, clumsy elephant, anyway? How had it wandered from its old roots as the party of antislavery, majority rule, and pure democracy?

But Judge Kelley's stand for the working classes got tangled up in another brewing conflict. Those same Republicans who were pushing through monetary legislation before the Democrats took Congress tried one final stab at Reconstruction. In February, they passed the Civil Rights Act of 1875, a bold drive for equal treatment for all citizens, regardless of race, in public accommodations and transportation. It would be the last significant attempt at legislating civil rights for nearly a century. The vote was telling. It won strong support from those old Civil War Republicans who had lost their seats to Democrats in the coming Congress, but politicians reelected for another term were less supportive. Kelley voted for the bill, but wrote Florie after the vote, expressing curious ambivalence about a cause he would have trumpeted a few years before. He was happy, for once, to see that the Capitol's "galleries are being cleared" with the end of the session. "The atmosphere," Kelley cryptically warned his daughter, "has been shifting for days."[35]

It was Will Kelley who was shifting. Still furious with Grant's Republicans, he struggled to find a way to make his stand for working people and tell the nation what he thought was happening to the once-great party. Reconstruction became his strange scapegoat. Ten years earlier, he bled for the cause; now, Kelley had come to view further efforts at Reconstruction as a moral shield obscuring the Grant administration's "cruel" suffocation of the struggling economy. Kelley set out on a trip south that spring and came north with a startling conclusion.

Reconstruction was done. Not because it was dead, strangled by White Leagues and Red Shirts and widespread terrorism, but because it had succeeded. Newspapers began to carry perplexing reports that radical Will Kelley, of all people, was claiming that the South was now in a "settled condition" and that he regretted supporting the Civil Rights Act "more than any vote he has given." If Kelley saw a problem, it was not "the Ku-Klux that was ruining the South," as a Galveston paper put it, but the administration's monetary policies. Democrats cheered Kelley's move as sign of a "growing revolt"; a Georgia paper that had denounced Kelley for years smiled, "we like Kelley's pluck." Reconstruction must really be done if it had been abandoned by "even such a determined Republican politician as the Hon. William D. Kelley."[36]

Others were devastated. Responding to a disappointed letter writer, Kelley publicly affirmed that the strange quotes attributed to him were "substantially correct." "My convictions have been modified," Kelley now insisted. The problem in the South was the depression and a lack of money caused by Grant's policies. And besides, Kelley told reporters, the federal government could not force change on a region that did not want it: "No measure of force will reduce such a community to order." This from a man who, eight years prior, taunted a crowd of angry men in Mobile: "You can not put me down. I have the U.S. Army to fall back upon."[37]

Frustrated radicals could only point to that moment in 1867, when Kelley "refugeed under a table" as the bullets struck African American Republicans standing by his side, and warn that when "a new crop of Southern outrages" killed Black voters in the coming 1876 presidential campaign, the North should "remember the testimony of Judge Kelley."[38]

To be clear, Kelley never abandoned his belief that African Americans were due equal political rights, nor did he stop mentioning southern outrages in rousing campaign-season orations. He merely reshuffled his priorities, shouting about income inequality and monetary policy, and letting Black rights fall out of sight. For a generation, Kelley had achieved a rare feat in American political history, fighting to better the lives of African Americans and working-class White people at the same time. In 1875 he felt, rightly or wrongly, forced to choose.

It was the greatest betrayal of Will Kelley's long career. He left behind all the African Americans who voted for him and bled for him, studied his speeches, and donated to his reelection campaigns. At least when he left the Democrats, it had been because a new, proslavery element had seized control of his once-beloved party. It had left him. But twenty years later, Kelley abandoned Reconstruction, not because of any real change in an issue he had committed himself to, but because he was done with that issue. Within months, mobs in Clinton, Mississippi, would massacre dozens of African Americans; the next year more would die in Hamburg, South Carolina. Nothing was finished, except Kelley's interest. Reconstruction died, in large part, because men like Kelley let it.

But in the partisan climate of the 1870s, Kelley's faithlessness to African Americans confirmed his unique independence. He would not swallow

Republican orthodoxy. One admiring letter writer congratulated Kelley for his willingness to ignore "that stumbling block of commonplace politicians—consistency." "Gentlemen seek to convict me of inconsistency," Kelley roared, but it was actually his "duty to my manhood" to question his party. "I owe a duty to the Republican party," Kelley announced, but he could only "perform it, so far as I can conscientiously." Otherwise, Will would follow his beliefs into "what affiliation it may."[39]

This juxtaposition of "consistency" and "conscience," partisan loyalty versus independent thought, would bind the coming generation in knots.

Most people thought that Will Kelley was a good man. An honest politician, a devoted father. Most people thought that Roscoe Conkling was a bad man, a haughty senator with a closet full of scandals. But when it came to Reconstruction in 1875, Kelley was declaring the site of the greatest political violence in American history "settled," while Conkling was escorting the formerly enslaved Blanche Bruce to his seat in the nation's Senate. Kelley's boiling conscience was of no use to Black men anxiously voting early on election day. Here was the selling point of partisanship for disrupted and vulnerable populations. Many needed the loyalty of Conkling more than the "conscience" of Kelley.

Will's betrayal was also part of a complex political pivot. His real problem with Reconstruction was the Grant administration, and his real problem with the Grant administration was its "cruel and infamous" economic policies. Halting such policies, Kelley seemed to calculate, would require a cross-sectional alliance, North and South. Kelley began to build alliances in the South, attending agricultural fairs in Georgia, allying with southern green-backers, and promoting the industrial possibilities of that section. Always right on time, Kelley was pushing the Republican Party to move from race to class, just as Reconstruction gave way to the Gilded Age. Kelley's turn, in mid-1875, provides as good a demarcation between the two historical periods as any.[40]

Admiring constituents cheered Will's fight against "this concentration of power and wealth." A fan from North Jersey wrote to Kelley that the congressman's new focus on money was "like the clanging of an alarm bell . . . For 10 years past I have eschewed politics—scarcely even voting. I feel summoned again." This writer had ignored the battles over race and

Reconstruction, but felt compelled by the money question. Many voices agreed, especially ones important to Judge Kelley's political future. His West Philly district was filling up with the modest row houses of skilled White workers, just the type who were flirting with the Democrats. Will could appeal to them by warning about "the grave danger which overhangs our financial future." And the chief obstacle to addressing that "grave danger" was his own party, boasting about civil rights while overseeing an economic catastrophe.[41]

Kelley emerged, in mid-1875, with a new political momentum. July found him standing before a crowd of unemployed ironworkers in Youngstown, Ohio. The men in shirtsleeves and overalls were mostly Republicans, but Kelley repeatedly stressed that he was not speaking in the "interests of any party." Instead he made use of his crowd-pleasing call-and-response technique, his scarecrow frame dancing across the rostrum as his deep voice demanded: "Have you suffered a reduction of wages?" ("*Yes!*") "Are you all employed?" ("*No!*") Then Pig Iron Kelley unfolded a "tragic farce" of the history of money in America. When greenbacks had circulated freely, "there was work for everybody," but since the Grant administration began to contract the currency, "our mills, furnaces, and factories are idle; and there are more hard-laboring men living in want than ever before in the United States."[42]

Reaching the peak of his oratorical powers, Kelley shrugged off criticisms that his views made him a radical fomenting a revolution against the rich. Struggling workers would not sit idly by forever, he warned. Repurposing his earlier argument that African Americans who were denied the vote would eventually "rebel against a tyrant who will not listen to their voice," Kelley told the cheering Ohio ironworkers that if nothing was done to help them, "labor would take capital by the throat, and that the scenes of the French Revolution would be re-enacted."[43]

To wealthy Americans, reading coverage of the speech in their parlors, it seemed that their growing fears of class conflict now had a voice in Congress. Pig Iron Kelley was calling for revolution.

The response was swift. Party-line Republicans and "hard money" Democrats agreed that "Pig Iron Kelley is a lunatic," that "God never made a bigger fool," that this "false teacher of political economy was miseducating the consuming millions." Not only was Kelley's rhetoric dangerous, but it seemed popular. "He has," spat the increasingly conservative *New York Tribune*, "got the ear of the country," especially laborers who were "not educated enough to see the folly and immorality of this kind of lunatic." Thomas Nast sketched a striking cartoon in which Kelley, looking dashing and devious, unleashed a murderous jack-in-the-box costumed as a French radical, waving a saber and snarling: "Greenbacks or Death!"[44]

But Nast's cartoon proved that Kelley's pivot had worked. Whereas during the Credit Mobilier scandal he was caricatured as just another thieving politico, by 1875 Kelley was a romantic if dangerous leader taking a stand.

All the elements of the disrupted 1870s came together in Will Kelley's bold stand for, of all things, the driest of monetary reforms. Here was the unemployed workforce, the anti-establishment rage, the fear of social collapse, the death of Reconstruction, and the shrinking sphere of acceptable political views. The problem was that, while Kelley toyed with freedom from his party, he had no clear path elsewhere. He was either dangerously behind the times, expecting the political flexibility he had enjoyed in the 1850s, or strikingly ahead of them, acting like a twentieth-century independent. But in his own era, Kelley was, in the words of one St. Louis paper, one of the "blundering builders of a political Babel," expecting diverse options in a system with only one right answer: Republican or Democrat.[45]

And so he pursued two paths, toying with third parties and with political independence. Will flirted with the newly formed Greenback Party, headlining their convention in Detroit. Speaking without notes, Will gave an impassioned address, growing "carried away by the attention and applause of his audience," until the mostly working-class crowds were hypnotized by "the reverberating cadences of Judge Kelley's sonorous periods." His address left the usually opinionated Greenbackers "hushed to absolute silence . . . We can neither reproduce the language, nor describe the effect. It was simply irresistible."[46]

Kelley went further still, traveling to Ohio to campaign *against* the Republican candidate for governor, Rutherford B. Hayes, in favor of a pro-greenback Democrat. His efforts to change the minds of laborers "who had never voted for a Democrat" pushed at the very boundaries of the partisan political system, especially in Ohio, a decisive state and President Grant's birthplace. In a probing back-and-forth interview with the *Cincinnati Gazette*, Kelley dodged the partisan consequences of his actions, stating that he hoped only that "the defenders of the greenback win," without explicitly admitting that this would mean a Republican loss.[47]

And this evasion cut to the core of Kelley's 1870s maneuvers and the struggles of millions of voters. His problem, an Atlanta paper wrote with biting clarity, was that Kelley "is a Republican congressman. He has been a Republican ever since there was a Republican party." Unless he was willing to leave that party, all of his speechifying meant nothing. Curious interviewers who visited the Kelley family at the Elms agreed. Expecting to find a frothing radical, they reported that this revolutionary lived "in a handsome and spacious three-story villa, surrounded by trim lawns and pretty flower-gardens, situated in a half-rural suburb." Pig Iron Kelley was not a bomb thrower but an "agreeable and pleasant gentleman, ready to talk and rather desirous of being reported. Like other men of one idea, he is an egotist, and believes that sooner or later everyone is bound to accept his views."[48]

As long as he sat among the Elms's flower gardens, kept in power by the Republican voters of his Republican district in a Republican state, all his talk about duty and conscience meant little.

WILL KELLEY WAS not alone in wondering what life looked like outside the two political parties. Most Americans' lives sat more squarely in their parties than ever before. More people lived in Kelley's West Philadelphia district, for instance, than had voted for the Greenback Party nationwide. But on the peripheries of geography and class, oddballs and idealogues were looking for other options, a "ragtag and bobtail" element who wanted to be neither Republicans nor Democrats.[49]

Among elites in the Northeast, the "gentleman never votes" dissatisfaction with vulgar politics offered one opening. Some journalists who previously talked about printing "neutral" newspapers began to throw around the word *independent* in the 1870s. Writing with palpable frustration in the *New York Tribune* in 1875, one Connecticut independent hoped to carve out some space for "the intelligent, conscientious voter" amid a partisan political system that had become "the devil's best weapon, the country's worst enemy."[50]

One day, the writer predicted, Americans would thank independents "for saving the country, if it is saved, from the pit which partisanship is digging for it."[51]

On the other periphery, out on the ragged edges of the Midwest, wilder voices called for freedom from party. The Yankees and Scandinavians who settled this region brought high expectations for American democracy with them. Few were happy to see Republicans and Democrats sell off whole states to the railroads. The Greenbackers were most popular out there, in the same region where the Prohibitionist John Sobieski was warned to swallow the Republican platform. But how to escape one crooked party without falling into the other? James Witham, an impoverished young wanderer in Iowa, puzzled over life outside both parties, wondering whether it was wiser to try to reform the parties from within or "get on the outside and fight?"[52]

Some were already on the outside. On the Minnesota prairie, past the scorched remnants of the Peshtigo fire, one familiar voice predicted a coming revolution. Ignatius Donnelly, exiled from Washington and the Republican Party, farmed and fumed. Still fueled by oysters and caffeine, Donnelly was angrier than ever, and his sharp tongue captured the political rage of the mid-1870s. "I do not come around cringing & whining & asking for office," he warned. "Those who don't like me can lump me."[53]

Republicans, Donnelly shouted in speeches and scrawled in diary entries, were a "genus of shysters and scallewags—small, mean tricky little wire pullers." While Kelley artfully measured his rhetoric about the Republican Party, unwilling to leave it completely, Donnelly wrote with lurid fury. The Republican Party was dead. What was left were merely parasitic politicians, "eating their way into a dead whale, climbing in and about the stinking carcass." Or, when he was feeling more generous, the Republican Party was like the human tailbone, a vestigial remnant that once had purpose but "can't even wag now."[54]

"Not a single issue," Donnelly raged in his diary, "which agitated us in the past remains today alive—slavery—reconstruction—rebellion—impartial suffrage—have all perished." That even "impartial suffrage" was a dead issue captured how far the nation was drifting.[55]

But where to go, outside the two parties? Where could Kelley pivot, what movement might have room for a man like Donnelly? "I feel like a political 'What is it,'" Donnelly complained in his diary.[56]

Yet, like the Connecticut writer imagining independents lifting the nation out of the pit of partisanship, Donnelly felt certain that a reckoning was coming. The parties were, he mused as he looked out over his Minnesota farmstead, like a colony of gophers, chattering and shortsighted, with no idea that a break-team's plow was bearing down on them, "tearing up the sod."[57]

CHAPTER SIX

"If Anybody Says Election to Me, I Want to Fight"

F lorie moved so slowly through the fair that her friends stopped going
with her. Nearly every day in the summer of 1876, she walked the few
blocks from the Elms to the sprawling grounds of the World's Fair. She
wanted to study every innovation, observe every culture. This was the same
girl, after all, who read *The Resources of California* cover to cover on her tenth
birthday. Now, at sixteen, she was out among the millions who flocked to
the Centennial Exposition, looking studious with her plaited hair and dark,
inquiring eyes. Like the other fairgoers, she gawked and snacked, but
unlike them, she related what she saw back to her father, "Centennial
Kelley," congressional advocate for the World's Fair in her backyard.[1]

Some ten million visitors wandered the grounds that summer, an
incredible draw in a nation of roughly forty-five million. Acres of exhibit
space, and miles of bunting, all declared an optimistic vision of the nation's
progress from 1776 into the next century. The fair envisioned a wondrous
future of telephones and typewriters, hamburger steaks and syrupy soda
water. All it would take was wires and fuel, ground beef and cheap sugar,
to make this promise a reality.[2]

"Centennial Kelley" had helped find the funding for the fair and locate
it just north of the Elms. As with Black voting rights and women's suffrage,
Kelley's rumble became the voice of the project in Congress, drafting bills

and lecturing colleagues. He also used the Centennial to reach his daughter. Together, father and daughter became exposition connoisseurs, studying past events, ranking the industrial nations, and planning to attend fairs in Europe. Florence even wrote an article on the topic, her first publication in a prolific half-century career. Will enthusiastically implored her to print it "over your full name." Maybe there could be two Centennial Kelleys.[3]

But as she made her way from display to display, Florence realized that she could never replicate her father. The bow-tied exhibitors who showcased the marvels of technology had little interest in speaking with a woman, outside of the jewelry section. Florie said that, in response to her questions, a lecturer "usually stares surprisedly at me, as though wondering what a girl of sixteen can possibly want to know, and answers in monosyllables with a bored air." Florie was a ferocious questioner. Later in life she could leave talkers like Teddy Roosevelt and W. E. B. Du Bois reeling from her barrages of "How many? How much? How will you get it? How will you enforce it?" The World's Fair exhibitors had no idea what they were up against.[4]

Will wasn't much help. By the summer of 1876, he had moved on to the one event in American culture louder than the fair. Florie complained that he was "too absorbed in the excitement" of the 1876 presidential race "to spend strength visiting the Exposition" with her. The message was clear—the only thing more important than their shared bond was a campaign running hot.[5]

And that campaign ran red-hot, inducing the most popular engagement in American history. Often overlooked for the 1877 Compromise that followed, 1876 drew the highest voter turnout in any presidential election: 82 percent of eligible voters. To get millions to the polls, two warring parties organized the showiest campaign ever, set to brass bands, fed on barbecue and clambakes, illuminated by fireworks. If the Centennial Exposition imagined an optimistic American future, the election exposed nineteenth-century American reality, displaying both its astounding popular participation and its previously concealed tensions.[6]

Ultimately, the 1876 election would show that the same forces that made the political culture so popular could be its undoing. The centennial election would expose just how tenuous some Americans' commitment to democracy could be.

America's biggest elections—with turnouts of over 80 percent—in 1840, 1860, and 1876, all shared certain traits. Each took place three years after an economic panic, in 1837, 1857, and 1873, just long enough for the political system to digest public anger, often mobilized by the opposition party. (Franklin Roosevelt's landslide victory in 1932 also came three years after a crash.) In 1876, the gnawing depression created a centennial campaign of incredible enthusiasm. The young were especially invested—the passing of Civil War issues and the destabilizing 1873 depression charged their generation with new momentum. Sixteen-year-old factory workers turned out for flag raisings in New Haven, twentysomething immigrants traipsed across Nebraska homesteads electioneering. The press ginned up the enthusiasm, reminding first-timers to be as careful with their virgin votes "as a good wife is of her virtue." "*Fresh* and unwearied *young* men" were amplifying already heated campaigns into something unprecedented.[7]

The renewed partisanship of the 1870s helped mobilize youthful enthusiasm. The Democrats, dismissed by many Republicans as "a festering corpse of a dead party," were reanimated, having won Congress in 1874 by wielding public anger against the Republican establishment. Dejected White Southerners, who had sat out elections since the war, were ready to participate, joined by a revitalized northern wing in key states like New York, Ohio, New Jersey, and Connecticut. Their official platform, in 1876, began almost every paragraph with the imperative verb *Reform*. Republicans, maddeningly, made use of the same antipolitician rhetoric. Now that the Grant administration was leaving office and the Democrats owned Congress, Republicans swore *they* were the party of clean government, and the Democrats were the crooked establishment. Political rage was proving to be a weapon anyone could wield.[8]

As Americans braced for the toughest campaign since 1860, many in both parties sensed that the legacy of the last two decades of politics hung in the balance.

Not that the candidates were particularly exciting. The Democrats chose Samuel Tilden, a cunning New York politician with a huge fortune and reformist bent. He had won national fame by bringing down Boss Tweed, helping to clean up his own party and "strike the roots of its growth into fresh soils." In 1876 he could present himself as a reformer battling corruption, an opponent of the Republican "centralism," and an enemy of Reconstruction. Yet he was also notoriously odd, a small and scrunch-faced hypochondriac, hidden away in his Manhattan mansion, rumored to subsist on a secret diet and require daily enemas.[9]

Who could replace Grant atop the wobbling Republican elephant? The candidate would have to simultaneously sound like a reformer while still commanding the allegiance of the Republican machine. The party's flamboyantly feuding chieftains, Conkling and Blaine, reminded voters of why people hated the Republicans. Instead, they settled on the dull, safe, lavishly bearded governor of Ohio, Rutherford B. Hayes. Hayes, Henry Adams observed, was "obnoxious to no one." He targeted the standard Republican villains—southern Democrats and northern Catholics, running against "the Pope and Jeff Davis"—and promised to clean up the civil service. Hayes also hoped to move his party away from its dependence on Black Southern voters. Like comfort food to respectable White voters in the rural North, Hayes could reassure Republicans who were concerned about the direction of their party, but unwilling to try anything else.[10]

Strangely, one of the voices shouting loudest for Hayes, once he won the nomination, was Will Kelley. Just the year before, Kelley had campaigned against Hayes's bid for governor of Ohio, scandalously backing the pro-greenback Democrat instead. But in the summer of 1876, Kelley barnstormed the nation, telling crowds of Ohio workers and Indiana miners to vote for Hayes. The difference between Kelley's anti-Hayes political independence of 1875 and his support for Hayes in 1876 may come down to the fact that Congressman Kelley was up for reelection. Political independence was, in the 1870s, an off-year pursuit. Will did not abandon any of his issues; in fact, he spoke frequently about currency reform and workers' rights, but he wrapped them in the uniform of an orthodox Republican.

Even such boring candidates could not dull a vibrant campaign. The 1876 campaign was marked by an exuberant flood of stuff, a tide of torches and uniforms and badges and banners. Just as the new economy could turn Texas cattle into World's Fair hamburgers, it could transform the material of American democracy into mass-produced, consumer-oriented trinkets. Drinkers toasted Republicans with enormous "Hayes and Wheeler" beer mugs, campaign clubs argued over which new torch design to order, and children wore scarlet "Tilden and Hendricks" scarves to school. Since the birth of popular politics in the 1830s, campaign objects had been made individually, or by families, or by local manufacturers. But in 1876 a national consumer culture sold an incredible variety of campaign paraphernalia. Fireworks companies churned out tons of merchandise, often marketing to both parties. Depictions of rallies from that campaign suggest a growing uniformity, as if a nation of partisans all shopped at the same store.[11]

This was the promise of partisanship, after all. Life might be uneven and unequal, but during campaigns, Americans wrapped themselves in the same uniforms, lit the same torches, and argued over the same candidates.

Under those uniforms were millions of individuals. Getting them all to march in the same direction required immense labor. A typical rally included dozens of companies, each with dozens of members, most of whom gathered dozens of times. Politics meant event planning. But it also meant canvassing street corners, "treating" whole barrooms, sweet-talking "handsome and intelligent young ladies," buttonholing immigrants, and convincing parents to let their children stay out late. Someone had to find matching uniforms, hogsheads of whiskey, barrels of fireworks, clams by the thousand, oxen and firewood and pistols and torch oil.[12]

Money helped. Cash had played an auxiliary role in American elections for decades—what insiders called "irrigating a district"—but as big campaigns demanded more effort, they needed more funds. The massive and merchandized 1876 campaign marked a turning point, allegedly costing six times more than the previous presidential campaign in 1872, the largest increase in the era. The true cost of these elections is incalculable, as the great majority of the labor was voluntary, but the growing need for cash was startling. An Ohio representative told a congressional investigation that holding his seat, over the 1870s, went from costing him a few hundred dollars a race to well over three thousand. "I spent money around saloons, for bands, and for political meetings," he confessed, and for the vote itself: "I hired men to hold tickets."[13]

Holding those tickets was the key to all of American democracy. Back then, elections took place in town squares, saloons, or schoolhouses where voters placed tickets listing their chosen party and its slate of candidates in a wooden or glass ballot box. Unless a voter scratched out some candidates and wrote in other names, almost everyone voted straight party. Those ballots were printed by partisan newspapers and distributed by activists. Election days gathered the voters of a community (usually White, always male) for an incredible celebration of public citizenship, augmented with singing and shouting, drumming and drinking. Women traditionally stayed indoors on election days, underlining their disenfranchisement. But for men "it is fun to see," one Norwegian immigrant wrote home from Chicago, "almost everyone stops work that day and goes out to *vote*, either before or after stopping at a bar."[14]

Such a loose system of voting, monitored by two hostile parties rather than a neutral government, encouraged bad behavior. Partisans clutching sheaves of ballots pursued voters "like a cat chasing a mouse," lobbying, lecturing, hectoring. A persistent minority sold their votes for a glass of beer, two dollars, a sack of flour, or a pork-chop sandwich. Campaigners color-coded their ballots, but this led to fraudulent ballots printed in the opposition's color to trick illiterate voters. (There were no standard colors associated with Republicans or Democrats until color television settled on red and blue a century later.)[15]

Tellingly, over the course of the century Americans shifted the terminology for those activists handing out ballots. Where once men "peddled" tickets, by the mid–Gilded Age, they "hustled" them.[16]

Worse still, parties ran the system of "challenging" voters' eligibility in an age without clear registrations, posting "bad men at the ballot box" to point out who should not vote, or intimidate those who looked like they might "vote wrong." As one Republican politician put it, rallies were fun, but "the real, substantial warfare must be at the polls." Some challengers flashed a revolver or jabbed a voter with a shoemaker's awl. Occasionally, such confrontations devolved into "shoulder-hitting" or "knock-downs," assassinations or riots. Such violence reached a peak in the South in 1876, as a resurgent Democratic Party unleashed brutal violence on Black voters. Americans invented the word *bulldoze* that year, a grim reference to the terroristic use of a "dose" of the bullwhip to intimidate a would-be voter.[17]

But dirty tricks, and explicit violence, accounted for a minority of the hundreds of millions of ballots cast over this era. Far more citizens turned out, thrilled to participate in what was still a rare privilege in the world: choosing one's leaders. Even those millions of women banned from voting could not look away; often they spent an excruciating day pacing their homes, waiting to hear from a husband or father. The ballot peddlers themselves were mostly volunteers, ordinary men working the polls out of partisanship and ambition. Generations of American politicians got their start on an election day in their late teens, peddling tickets, coaxing the lukewarm to the polls, or bullying opposition voters at the ballot box. Even the notorious election day booze was, according to one Boston politico, poured strategically, to ensure that "men kept sober enough to vote for the designated candidate."[18]

Statistics bear out this insistence that men mostly voted because they wanted to. In the 1840s and '50s, half of those who cast ballots in nonsouthern elections had been "core voters," likely to participate no matter what. In 1876 that number jumped to two-thirds. Likewise, "marginal voters," who would participate only when cajoled or coerced, fell by 10 percent over that same period. Despite depictions of Gilded Age politics as mechanistic or meaningless, more and more Americans were choosing to involve themselves.[19]

Just as the 1874 congressional election signaled a return of two tightly competitive parties, 1876 marked an ascent to a peak of popular participation, by choice, with no parallel in the history of American democracy.

Over six months in 1876, some 10 million visitors made their way to the Centennial Exposition in Philadelphia. But on November 7 alone, almost as many Americans—8.5 million—turned out to vote. This massive public involvement represented a 10 percent jump in turnout over the previous presidential race, in 1872. Across the nation, men put on their finest hats, brushed out their election-day beards, procured a ballot for their party, and joined in the chief democratic rite of their society. On the sidelines, millions more watched closely, participants in the ritual, if not the vote. Driven by an odd combination of faith in, and fury with, their system, a record number of citizens participated. Afterward, they rejoined their communities to await the results of this centennial election.

And then time stopped.

Preliminary reports from eastern states suggested that the Democrats had won. Even Hayes went to bed thinking he had just lost the presidency. But the nation awoke to confusing news. After midnight, Dan Sickles—a hot-tempered congressman and former Union Army general famous for murdering his wife's lover—happened by the deserted Republican headquarters in Manhattan. Doing some quick calculations, Sickles saw an astounding possibility. Tilden had clearly won the popular vote, but he lacked the electoral votes needed. Sickles rushed out telegraphs to the four contested states—Florida, South Carolina, Louisiana, and Oregon—ordering Republicans there to "hold your state." The following day, President Grant dispatched the Republican party's toughest fighters to keep Louisiana in their grasp, selecting the fiery former general John "Blackjack" Logan, and Will "Pig Iron" Kelley to lead the charge in New Orleans. They launched months of complex wrangling for those states' electors, battling over the single vote that would give Tilden or Hayes the presidency.[20]

As the politicians fought, most of the nation watched, stunned. The nineteenth-century political clock was profoundly cyclical, a steady repetition of campaign and election, summed up by the Iowa canvasser who said: "We work through one campaign, take a bath, and start in on the next." But without a clear result, nothing could move forward. The post-election "jollification" celebrations that Americans so enjoyed had to be halted. Children usually burnt towering post-election bonfires, but in 1876 they stood by. One town in Maine told of an excruciating bind: its Democratic and Republican boys had assembled rival pyres on prominent hills. Now they waited, teased by the dry autumn kindling, for news from Washington about which to light.[21]

Out in Nebraska, the Republican Grierson family learned the news at the dinner table. Alice Grierson had watched her sixteen-year-old son Robert morosely lower the family's flag outside to half-mast, thinking the Democrats had won. When they heard that Hayes might still be president, Alice's son "jumped up from his supper with a screech (Edith, Harry and George following suit), rushed out to his flag and hoisted it to the top of the pole, where it remained all night, and still floats."[22]

The whole nation felt as if it were floating that fall and winter of 1876–77, watching their democracy fluttering between cause and effect, campaign and administration. As the politicians and lawyers bickered over a single electoral vote, citizens reported the nearly physical toll of the news. Elizabeth Cady Stanton, zealous to see the "corrupt Republican party" lose, claimed: "I have not breathed freely in two weeks." William Dean Howells, editor of the *Atlantic Monthly* and a die-hard Republican, wrote to his father that, after a day of frantically following post-election updates, "I felt sore from head to foot, as if the conflicting reports had all taken effect on my body like blows."[23]

One Virginia woman wrote that after weeks of trying to keep up, she had simply canceled her newspaper subscriptions. She was done learning about it. "If anybody says election to me, I want to fight. Ignorance is bliss now."[24]

The machinations of the months after November 1876 are too complex to detail here, but it is safe to say that they brought out the worst in many. In Louisiana, the head of the electoral commission tried to sell his state's votes to both parties. Will Kelley wrote to Florie, from New Orleans, about the "exciting occasion," but also warned the press about the brutal bull-dozing of Black voters in the state. Democrats, for their part, fumed as they watched their first popular vote victory since 1856 evaporate. George McClellan, former Union Army general and Democratic candidate for president in 1864, talked about raising an army to help seat Tilden. But Tilden, for all his political skill, was not about to take such a dramatic stand, even as the presidency slipped from his fingers. A friend joked that a man who required an enema "every morning to get passage" was not the type to launch a revolution. Conkling, always the bully, teased Tilden for following the "good-boy principle of submission."[25]

The petty politicking exposed all the flaws in America's system of selecting its leaders. The *Atlantic Monthly* pointed to the absurdity of a populist democracy squabbling over a few electoral college votes, writing (140 years ago), "The electoral colleges no longer serve a useful purpose. An aristocracy of electors . . . has no place in our republican system." The people were competent to choose their leaders, the magazine argued, and "they will demand the privilege before long."[26]

Finally, in March 1877, the nation had its president. A special electoral commission, with a Republican edge of a single vote, gave the presidency to Rutherford B. Hayes. He was the first man to win the office but lose the popular vote since John Quincy Adams had in 1824. Looking back on those months, Conkling told a crowd that, though "lasting harm threatened the well-being of the nation," the election was over, "the danger is now safely overpassed."[27]

Just before the election was resolved, a small group of negotiators had met at Washington's Wormley Hotel. The landmark, owned by the African American businessman James Wormley, was Conkling's flashy residence when in Washington. But the negotiators were less flamboyant. They quietly discussed the possibility of a bargain, in which the presidency would go the Republican Hayes, who would then withdraw federal troops from the South, ending Reconstruction as a chip for the Democrats. Hayes had nothing to do with the meeting, and it's unclear what role this discussion played in the outcome. (At most, it probably forestalled the threat of an annoying Democratic filibuster.) When the electoral commission made Hayes president, it was the result of public partisanship—the Republican majority on the electoral commission—more than private dealmaking.[28]

But the notorious bargain at the Wormley hotel has taken on inflated meaning over the years. There is a popular myth about what happened in 1877, an image of the presidency and Reconstruction traded away in a smoke-filled room. It is a distortion. The idea of a bargain, made by a few scheming politicos, is just too conspiratorial; it lets too many off the hook. Reconstruction was killed by political violence in the South and by the millions of White voters nationwide who gave up on it. The Democrats won by large majorities in 1876 and 1874, promising to end the federal project.[29] At the same time, large numbers of Republicans were done with Reconstruction. In addition, if there had been no compromise, and the will of the majority inaugurated the openly racist and anti-Reconstruction Democrat Samuel Tilden, the assault on Black rights would surely have been even more severe. With the Republican Party still in control of the executive branch, it could at least offer important patronage to African American leaders. But most of all, the story of a fateful bargain in 1877 fits too neatly into the antipolitician narrative of the age, blaming the end of Reconstruction on a small ring, rather than the millions of voters who chose, in public, to give up on Black civil and political rights.[30]

Reconstruction was not bargained away by a few but abandoned by a majority.

The distinction mattered little, of course, to African Americans watching their political rights crumble. Hayes did remove federal troops, and attempted to reposition the southern Republican Party with a Whiter base. Frederick Douglass begged him not to, telling Hayes that, in purely practical terms, there just weren't enough White Southerners willing to vote Republican. Others, like the Louisiana African American leader Henry Adams, wrote to the new president that "the colored people of the South had been debarred from . . . the right to vote hold office and the privilege of education." Without federal support, Adams warned, more and more would be "oppressed, murdered, and disenfranchised on account of our race and color." Such appeals no longer moved men like Hayes.[31]

The disastrous centennial election opened another wound. In 1876 two reform politicians ran hugely excited campaigns, firing hopes that the democracy might move out of this dark phase and drawing an astounding level of popular engagement. None of it mattered. The excruciating resolution made a mockery of all those hopes and all those votes. The crowds of excited young men who had the bad fortune to cast their virgin votes in 1876, a Milwaukee paper reported, "have all felt quite disheartened since the election." And while anger at politics had previously focused on Bad Men—the bosses and "rings" fleecing the nation—1876's failure of vote and count pointed a finger squarely at democracy itself. The problem was not just one of parasitic leaders but something broader and more systemic, condemning campaigns and elections as much as officials and agencies. That election, supposed to mark the proud centennial of American democracy, opened a wound that would fester for decades. "The danger," despite Conkling's 1877 assurance, had not been "safely overpassed."[32]

SAFETY WAS ON the minds of many that year, especially those with something to lose. The election coincided with a moment of panic for America's elites. An emerging alliance of genteel old families and rising urban professionals felt squeezed between the "dangerously rich and the dangerously poor." Above, they saw aggressive, uncultured men building enormous fortunes. Below, they feared tramps and criminals, made desperate by years of depression. The Chicago mayor and publisher Joseph Medill warned that idle men lurked in "the lumberyards, vacant buildings, sheds, railroad depots and all public places." It was becoming "dangerous to venture out after dark," and stories spread of gentlemen being "'held up' on some of the leading streets." The well-to-do, in cities like Chicago and Philadelphia, ordered pocket revolvers with names like "Banker's Pal" and "Tramps' Terror."[33]

Something bigger than the odd holdup scared this class. Over the last decade, well-to-do Americans developed a sense that their civilization was being dragged down into revolution, that the odd riot signaled a prelude to a larger insurrection. Few could forget the draft riots of the Civil War, when a "ragged, coatless, heterogeneously weaponed army" seized much of Manhattan, killing hundreds. Though most of its victims were African Americans, New York's first families recalled hiding in darkened mansions, clutching revolvers, the business-friendly *New York Times* offices guarded by Gatling gun. Herman Melville depicted the rebellion as a Hobbesian social collapse, in which "all civil charms . . . like a dream dissolve / And man rebounds whole aeons back in nature."[34]

The 1870s were no calmer. Racist pogroms tore apart southern cities, and ethnic and class tensions caused riots in Manhattan in 1870, 1871, and 1874. Across the Atlantic, Paris exploded in 1871, as the revolutionary Paris Commune seized control of the city, before being brutally put down by the French state, which massacred twenty thousand. Americans frightened themselves with predictions of their own coming commune, "morbidly sensitive," the *Washington Post* wrote, to anything that sounded like revolution. Then, in the spring of 1877, one hundred thousand railroad workers struck around the United States, protesting the wage cuts that had shrunk their earnings by nearly one-quarter since 1873. The movement was crushed by state militias and federal troops, killing about one hundred strikers. Fearing communes abroad and strikers at home, the wealthy began to talk about the coming fall of civilization, pointing to various barbarians at various gates.[35]

In this climate of class anxiety, 1876–77 was a very bad time for an election to go wrong. The centennial celebrations encouraged easy nostalgia for a golden past, while fears of popular uprising foretold a barbarous future. In between, the big, messy 1876 election offered a concrete target for elites' fluttering anxieties. The sound of campaign clubs stomping by their brownstones scared the American bourgeoisie, increasingly fearful of the masses gathered in the streets. The defeat of the popular vote damaged reverence for the power of the ballot. Postwar, Conkling had declared: "The will of the majority must be the only king; the ballot-box must be the only throne." But eleven years later, that sovereign looked impotent.[36]

Thus 1876 marked a stark turning point. A strain of elite writers came out of the other end with a revolutionary new political philosophy: America's experiment in popular self-government had failed. Equality was a myth, voting rights were a waste, and the majority was usually wrong. Their most aggressive proponent, the historian Francis Parkman, declared that democracy had proved itself to be a grand swindle, the inexorable "transfer of power from superior to inferior types of men."[37]

Of course, this was not the first time wealthy Americans warned that democracy would end in mob rule. This was nearly the consensus of the founding generation. But from the Jacksonian 1830s on, mainstream culture accepted the fundamental principles of majority rule. By the late 1870s, this consensus was beginning to unravel. Jonathan Baxter Harrison, the minister and writer who hoped for "pure democracy" after the Civil War, wrote in 1878: "Thirty or forty years ago it was considered the rankest heresy to doubt that a government based on universal suffrage was the wisest and best that could be devised." By the 1870s, "expressions of doubt and distrust in regard to universal suffrage are heard constantly in conversation, and in all parts of the country." The problem was not a ring or a leader or a party, or an ostensibly unqualified race of voters, but a systemic "defect in the character or actions of the whole people."[38]

Harvard professors and *Atlantic Monthly* contributors did not set out, in the 1870s, to attack "the whole people." Many thought of themselves as humanists and reformers, abolitionists and liberals. But they belonged, by class, to the old intellectual elite and hated to see their university chairs and church pulpits overshadowed, in postwar America, by railroad tycoons or party bosses. It was easy, in that centennial year, to wax nostalgically about the "purer days of the Republic," when Americans were, supposedly, better "able to make a democracy succeed." Howells juxtaposed Alexis de Tocqueville's famous visit to America's "Utopia forty years ago" with a modern nation of conniving bosses, despotic railroads, and sheeplike voters. Few acknowledged that the founding generation expressed profound hostility to democracy or that the "utopia" of the 1830s was riven by ugly Jacksonian politics.[39]

If one man captured their darkening tone, it was James Russell Lowell. In the 1840s, Lowell became famous for his plainspoken Yankee humor, using the pseudonym Hosea Biglow to satirize the Mexican-American War. With his dense beard and threadbare peacoat, worn through the coldest Massachusetts winters, Lowell looked the part of an individualistic Yankee intellectual. But by the 1870s, Lowell was souring. His silly persona, Hosea Biglow, was quoted back at him by ordinary people, winning fame that his own careful poetry never would. Lowell spent years in Europe, seeking cultivated minds, but found himself forced to explain American political scandals to French high society. On returning to Massachusetts, in the midst of the 1874 campaign, the poet was shocked by the jocular horse-race mentality of a campaign in high gear. "Instead of wrath" at the state of American politics, Lowell glowered, "I found banter."[40]

And so Lowell published two fierce poems to mark the centennial. In "World's Fair," Lowell imagined the Goddess Columbia "puzzled what she should display / Of true home-make on her Centennial Day." Examining America's corrupt civil service, stolen elections, and crooked bosses, the Goddess shed "spiteful tears / At such advance in one poor hundred years." In the second poem, Lowell assailed a nation that expected entertainment, not morality, from political life, a land of schemers and relativists "whose fibre grows too soft for honest wrath."[41]

But the wrath came for Lowell instead. Popular audiences mocked his aristocratic pretensions, fresh from Europe. Mainstream Republicans rolled their eyes at those sighing nostalgists, who "pathetically whine about 'good old days.'" It did not help that, after the 1876 election, Lowell's support for Hayes won him an appointment as minister to Spain, a position that paid twelve thousand dollars a year. Was there any difference between his new office and the ballot peddler whose election-day labor was rewarded with a city job sweeping streets? In letters to friends, Lowell began to argue that democracy was "no more sacred than monarchy." Juxtaposing mass democracy to individual humanism, Lowell now declared, "It is Man who is sacred." The arch editor E. L. Godkin wrote that Lowell pined for "an earlier republic of the mind" and could never be comfortable "in a republic in which the multitude told the legislators what to do."[42]

Lowell's wrath was warm, at least. The bushy-bearded humorist still had profound faith in "Man," and his plain New England dialect allowed his elitism some cover. Lowell's fellow Bostonian, Francis Parkman, articulated a colder, purer fury. No writer better expressed the doubts that many well-to-do were developing with democracy. Parkman was among the most popular historians of the era, a gifted scholar who explored earthy topics like the Oregon Trail. Florie read his books in the Elms's library. But Parkman, like Lowell, had spent years in Europe, watching American democracy from afar, as well as the devastation of the Paris Commune. He was developing unpopular opinions. In his youth Parkman had been strikingly handsome, with a forthright jaw, a cocky smirk, and a swoosh of thick chestnut hair. But by the 1870s, he had tamed that mane into a tight side part, and his proud chin seemed to grow in each picture, like a man clenching his jaw, struggling to keep his views to himself.[43]

In 1878 Parkman published what can only be termed a screed in the august *North American Review*, with the bold title "The Failure of Universal Suffrage." It represents the best articulation of the kind of antidemocratic wrath bubbling among America's elites. In it, Parkman fundamentally rejected the premise of popular government. He began by mocking Americans' self-congratulatory insistence that democracy is superior to monarchy. By the 1870s, such puffery was, to Parkman, merely "hooting and throwing stones at the ghost of dead and buried privilege." "The present danger is not above," Parkman warned his readers, "but beneath."[44]

"The real tyrant" threatening American good government—in Parkman's view—"is organized ignorance, led by unscrupulous craft, and marching amid the applause of fools, under the flag of equal rights." With each phrase, Parkman stabbed at a different threat: the "organized ignorance" of political parties, the "unscrupulous craft" of manipulative politicians, the "applause of fools" emanating from the popular press. Part of the danger, Parkman went on, was the declining quality of America's voters, the "muddy tide of ignorance," the "invasion of peasants," the "hordes of native and foreign barbarians, all armed with the ballot . . . whose ears are open to the promptings of every rascally agitator."[45]

But while Parkman indulged bitter prejudice against the new immigrants, he went further than simple bigotry. The problem was deeper, more fundamental: "The flattering illusion that one man is essentially about as good as another." Equality, paired with majority rule, was destroying the nation. Nothing was more harmful than the deluded belief that "everybody has a right to form his own opinion." Such nonsense, in tandem with a democratic system won by simple, stupid numbers, meant that the "weakest and most worthless was a match, by his vote, for the wisest and best."[46]

The problem, at bottom, Parkman decided, was voting. In a letter to a former abolitionist, Thomas Wentworth Higginson, Parkman warned that the right to vote was now "a peril to civilization." Whereas little more than a decade before, activists talked about a future of "impartial suffrage," Parkman now wrote, "Promiscuous suffrage is the deepest source of our present political evils." The years in between had proved that democracy was a mass delusion, a national superstition. Any reasonable man would prefer good government, without the right to vote, to what Parkman called the mindless "privilege of dropping a piece of paper into a box."[47]

In a nation governed by the twin forces of equality and majority, the act of voting "becomes a public pest."[48]

Parkman had unclenched his jaw, and what came out was more revolutionary than anything Will Kelley shouted for. True, the notion of genuine equality was constantly under siege for minority populations. John C. Calhoun had gone so far as to reject the Declaration of Independence's assertion that all men are created equal, to justify slavery back in 1848. But Parkman was not questioning the citizenship of a vulnerable minority, he was attacking the wisdom of the majority—White as well as Black, Protestant as well as Catholic, native-born as well as immigrant—who had the vote and did not deserve it.

Around the country, a small class of readers embraced Parkman's revolutionary wrath. Some justified Parkman's fury as necessary "to give offense" and rouse the "gentleman who did not vote." One Texas paper sniped that, after a decade of trying to force equal suffrage on the South, it was Northerners who were finally "sick of it." And Denver's *Rocky Mountain News*, often at war with that boomtown's saloonkeepers and ward leaders, declared Parkman's views "as true as gospel." "The shadow of the commune has fallen upon the land," the *Rocky Mountain News* warned, because unlike the French radicals with their barricades and guillotines, all America's proletariat needed to destroy civilization was the ballot.[49]

It was necessary, then, well-to-do readers of men like Parkman argued, to purify "promiscuous suffrage." Getting rid of suffrage entirely, wrote Harrison, would bring about devastating "social convulsion," but "the subjects of voting can be much reduced." Cities passed laws designed to mean fewer elections, longer tenures, more at-large representatives not beholden to a particular ward, and replaced elected judges with appointed ones. Howells trumpeted the growing movement to limit voters' involvement in the administration of the state as a bold effort to "evolve order out of chaos, government out of anarchy."[50]

Substantial men wrote letters to newspapers proposing suffrage-restriction schemes of their own devising, like tinkerers seeking patents. Why not extend each presidential term to eight years? It would mean less conflict for "a nervous and excitable people like ourselves." Or perhaps, the father of a fourteen-year-old suggested, double the votes a man could cast every twenty-one years, so that a citizen with forty-two years of wisdom could cast two ballots, a sixty-three-year-old would get three. The young could not entirely be trusted. And immigrants? They should spend twenty-one years in the United States before getting to vote at all.[51]

New York State attempted the boldest stroke. Even before the 1876 election, the then governor Samuel Tilden convened a bipartisan panel to consider ways to address the governing of cities in the state. He packed it with worthies hostile to the unruly masses, men like Simon Sterne, a lawyer and economist who opined that "our better class voters, in our larger cities, are as much disenfranchised . . . as any plantation negro was anterior to 1860." Working together, elites in both parties were ready to jettison the unsavory voters from the other's ranks. In 1877 the Tilden commission revealed its recommendations to dramatically slash suffrage for urban voters. In cities, only men who owned $500 in property, or paid $250 in rent, would have the right to vote in crucial board of finance elections. The proposed rules would drag voting rights back three-quarters of a century, to the standards of New York's 1801 constitution. This counterrevolution would disenfranchise 69 percent of the voters in New York City. Only after rallies by working-class voters, ready to violently defend the ballot, was the Tilden commission's proposal voted down.[52]

It was exactly as Parkman would have predicted. For a nation in thrall to the ballot box, there was no way to exterminate "the public pest" democratically.

Huge majorities still loved their democracy, regardless of what the *North American Review* said. Most of America's eight thousand newspapers ignored views like Parkman's; most of its 8.5 million voters remained true to their suffrage. Both parties were still driven by a deep faith in torches and bunting and the promise of the next election. But 1876–77 exposed a growing sense that politics, campaigns, and elections would not settle the issues of nineteenth-century life, the way many had believed in 1865 or even 1870. Instead, the term that kept cropping up—replacing *settle* or *cure*, *rebirth* or *reconstruct*—was *convulse*. "Elections mean periodical convulsions," one writer observed, nation-shaking events "when business is interrupted, the public press monopolized, and the whole community plunged into a furious canvass." The millions who turned to party politics, seeking protection from the disruption in their lives, found that politics only disrupted them further.[53]

No other nation had anything like the campaign culture in America, where "every four years the whole country is convulsed," the *Atlantic Monthly* wrote. "The political crisis through which the United States passes once in every four years has not its parallel in any other civilized country."[54]

Somehow, the nation that hosted the wondrous Centennial Exposition could not govern itself. America had freed its slaves. It had enfranchised its laboring classes. It had built a massive industrial economy. And yet political life felt perpetually unsettled. The promise of "pure democracy"—the hope that fewer restraints meant more participation and better leadership—rang hollow in 1876–77.

Yet, "if you despair of democracy," asked one British observer watching Americans' mounting political gloom, "whither will you flee?"[55]

PART TWO

THE LAW OF EVERYTHING IS COMPETITION, 1877–1890

=

CHAPTER SEVEN

"Bother Politics!"

S treetcar Number 126 wobbled its way up Lancaster Avenue into West Philadelphia. Though it was one of those miserable late November nights, rain melting into snow, fall melting into winter, William Darrah Kelley Jr. stood outside, on the rear platform of the horse-drawn vehicle. It was nearly one A.M., time for Florie's brother to get back to the Elms. He looked like a man who would rather be left alone. Willy Jr. shared his father's heavy brow, but instead of a thick mane of shag and scruff, the twenty-two-year-old ruthlessly slicked down a center part and, in most photographs, wore a resting expression of smug distrust. Despite the weather, he chose to stand outside the glow of the car, listening to the horses' tread and avoiding the growing commotion within.[1]

Through the back window, Willy watched as the men squabbled. While the streetcar rolled past the new row houses sprouting up near the Elms, an argument inside was growing heated. A motley group was shouting about politics. When the horses stopped at Thirty-Third and Lancaster, one man broke from the group and stomped out the back exit. John H. Brown, a thirty-eight-year-old African American barber, seemed to be drunk that evening. He joined Willy on the back platform, wobbling and boisterous, and demanded that the younger man give his opinion on the political argument going on inside.[2]

Willy Jr. seems to have been a difficult fellow. One of Florie's friends later described him mercilessly as "a pill, a cad, everything dreadful," and alluded to his reputation for "dissipation." His father sometimes voiced disappointment as well. He criticized Willy for the grades he earned at the University of Pennsylvania, and "doing himself injustice in not maintaining among his fellows the marks nature assigned to him"—not living up to his intellectual inheritance as a Kelley. For a time, Florie, though four years his junior, was put in charge of his tutoring. He was, in 1877, a young lawyer and an active alumnus in his fraternity, and training to join a local militia. It is entirely possible that he was as responsible for the trouble as Brown.[3]

We do not know exactly what Brown asked; we do not know exactly how Willy answered. Perhaps the men had recognized Will Jr. and were shouting over his dad's controversial politics, so Brown tumbled out the back exit to make the son answer for the father. Or maybe Brown just wanted to draw someone else into the late-night debate. We know that Will Jr. refused to speak with the drunken man. Maybe he did so with contempt, or maybe Brown merely took it that way. Either way, as the car stood in the damp November night, Brown dug into his pocket, produced a small pistol, and shot Willy in the face.[4]

Newspapers as far away as Idaho soon reported that Pig Iron Kelley's son had been "shot by a negro and will not survive." The reports, like earlier claims that Judge Kelley had been stabbed to death, or shot, or died of cancer, were mistaken. The pocket pistol Brown used was probably like the "Tramps' Terror," one of the many small-caliber revolvers that proliferated in the 1870s. The small bullet entered Willy Jr.'s right cheek, cracked his jaw, and embedded in his neck. He was rushed to the hospital, where doctors found remarkably little damage, reporting that "fears of a fatal result are not entertained." Brown hopped off the back of the car and ran into the night, but was arrested before the morning papers were printing. Judge Kelley visited his son, Brown pled guilty, and the affair mostly melted into the late November fog.[5]

Florie's snide friend later wrote that Willy had once been "shot at in the street cars in Phila. by a labouring man," adding, "for a good reason I doubt not."[6]

On one level, Willy's shooting at the end of 1877 meant nothing. A drunk man, a loaded pistol, a perceived offense: it was just how people usually got shot. Yet it did fit into the catastrophizing narrative of the late 1870s. That William Darrah Kelley Jr.—lawyer, graduate of the University of Pennsylvania, Delta Psi member, son of the area's most prominent politician—could be shot in the night by a barber confirmed everything the well-to-do were warning of. This was why elites didn't talk politics on streetcars. Maybe civilization really was imperiled, at least for those trembling at the top of it.

The fact that Brown was a Black man, a well-respected member of West Philadelphia's African American community (that often gave its votes to Congressman Kelley), was both random and meaningful. In the late 1870s Philadelphia's streetcars were barely desegregated, and the city had no Black police officers. Octavius Catto had been gunned down not long before. It was not a bad idea to bring some protection on the cars.

If there was meaning in the late-night altercation, it was the way politics just kept demanding more and more of public life. A dozen years after Judge Kelley was slashed at the Willard Hotel, a decade after he was shot at in Mobile, six years after Catto's assassination, and even after the centennial, the 1876 election, and the boiling of elite wrath, politics continued to convulse American life. If British journalists had found it cute that partisans would poll trains, pre-election, to see who planned to vote how, it looked more ominous on a midnight streetcar, with alcohol and firearms involved. It looked inescapable, insistent, a darkening compulsion. Even after the Compromise of 1877—the demarcation used by textbooks and history surveys to divide heated Reconstruction politics from deadening Gilded Age machinery—men were still drawing pistols from their pockets.

Willy Jr. was not shot at for his idealistic speechifying, like his father had been in Mobile in 1867. Willy was shot—a decade later—for *not* talking politics.

And yet what was most remarkable was how unremarkable the shooting seemed. Surely it meant a great deal to Willy, who bore the physical and psychological impact for the rest of his life. The incident must have altered Brown's life as well. But the Kelleys were used to political violence and wrote little about it. The newspapers lost interest, too; one man harming another over politics was beyond routine. It was just another spasm in the ongoing convulsions shaking American public life, a cause for momentary rage and dread and little more.

If the arc of American democracy from 1865 to 1877 tightened from the possibilities of Pure Democracy to the clenched jaw of Honest Wrath, the next phase calcified into something at once convulsive and cynical. The system was overheating and standing still, attracting great interest but offering little change. Campaigns could shake popular culture, reformers could condemn social ills, men could shoot each other on midnight streetcars, all of it met with shrugs and redoubled partisanship. By the end of this phase, large numbers would offhandedly reference the failure of self-government as an agreed-on fact, all while still turning out to march, holler, and vote.

The central issue of Gilded Age life seemed, at the time, to be neither class, nor race, nor industrialization, nor immigration. It was the political system itself, the way its combination of excitement and inertia made addressing any of those other issues impossible. Modern readers immediately associate the Gilded Age with income inequality, but that is partly because we read this history backward through the prism of the Progressive Era that followed, a time when the inequities of the late nineteenth century were finally laid bare. But reading mainstream voices from well into the 1880s, it is striking how muffled and indirect debate over crucial questions of American life could be, compared with the constant, fraught, public bickering over politics.[7] In their newspapers, their letters, and their streetcars, arguments over the direction of democracy shouted down so much else. The chief battle of this era was not between parties over policy but between party loyalists and reformers over whether this popular but stalled democracy should be changed at all. Politics was strangling governance.

It all fit into the growing class conflict splintering American life. As a new economy disrupted the social order, America's vast middle classes would weigh who offered them more protection, the parties or their detractors. And as a long as politics was dangerously interesting, engrossing enough to make men shoot each other, reform would be, wrote a primer for young Americans, "the dream of weak and amiable men." Bosses, millionaires, and lobbyists did their part to keep politics from tackling "the real issues," but so did the millions who voted for convulsion and against reform. The arc of this second phase had to track from wrath to cynicism to boredom before a change could come.[8]

FLORIE WAS NOT waiting at the Elms when her bandaged brother came home. In fact, the Elms no longer was home. Florence Kelley was one of the small but growing number of young women to enroll in college, traveling up to Ithaca to attend Cornell University's new experiment in coeducation. She had been pining for this for years, ever since the "lonely morning" when she had found a crumpled brochure announcing Cornell's program in the waste bin of her father's study. She begged her parents to let her attend. Carrie's mournful anxieties could not keep her daughter at home forever. Florie, like her ever-moving father, needed more than that glowing library or trips to California or daily visits to the World's Fair could offer. She had written to her father of her hopes that the Centennial Exposition would "fill a vacancy which I have begun to feel." But it was not enough. During the summer of 1876, as the booming campaign shook the nation, Florie passed her entrance exam. Perhaps Cornell, or something beyond, could fill that vacancy.[9]

Florence was stepping out of the cool shadows of the Elms, coming into focus as an exceptional young woman. The future dean of Bryn Mawr College shared a meal with Florie in those years, and noted "Miss Kelley . . . amounts to more than any of the Cornell men and girls." And though she seemed more and more like her father every day—a tall, agile, opinionated orator with a "deep, organ voice" (and ink smudges on her sleeves)— Florence was also preparing to leave him behind. Her path to independence pointed her away from the Elms, away from her father, and away from the political world in which she had been raised.[10]

Her journey began at exactly the moment when her father fell under new pressures. For years he had operated outside the laws of political gravity, but he was finally being dragged down to reality. Politics threatened to break his independent spirit, just as his daughter was asserting hers.

Cornell introduced Florie to a world she never knew existed. Her class of seventy women entered the new university in its third year of coeducation. Cornell was not the first university to admit women—Oberlin had done so back in 1837—but it was part of an early wave and among the most prestigious. This was the bold adolescence of American education. A tiny system of elite, often religious, colleges expanded into a world of research-based, socially engaged, land grant universities, attracting a widening swath of the upper-middle classes. And women played a surprisingly important role. By 1880 young ladies made up one-third of the college population in America. What they would do after school remained an unanswered question.[11]

It was an incredible opportunity for Florie, allowing her to study Greek and German, history and social science. "If I only *could* describe my Latin classes to you!!!!" she enthused to Carrie. "They are alternately delightful, and mortifying beyond measure." Free of the muffled protections of life as a sickly girl trapped in the Elms, she now had a group of friends—fun, warm, opinionated women and men. They lived together in Sage Hall, a yawning, under-heated brick edifice at Cornell, its empty halls slowly filling with inquiring minds and debating voices. The students gathered around dining tables and crackling fireplaces, sharing meals and reveling in the aimless arguments, or headed out to explore Ithaca's frozen gorges. For a girl who had spent much of her seventeen years alone in bed, or smiling at her melancholy mother, or trailing her distracted father, these friendships were a revelation.[12]

She even enjoyed a relationship with an older woman. Margaret Hicks was an open, charismatic student with a passion for architecture, and past experience with other women at Cornell. She and Florie devoted a huge portion of the next few years to each other. Florence skipped dances with the boys of Cornell, but spent endless hours reading in bed with Margaret. Florie introduced her to her family, and Will and Margaret bonded over their shared love of architecture. Although Florie's and Margaret's letters do not reveal whether their connection was sexual, it was undeniably intimate. We cannot understand its exact nature, or what it said about Florie's sexual identity as she would have interpreted it in her own time. But it was clearly a thrilling bond and brought Florence a stimulation no other relationship had.[13]

Florence Kelley's personality began to show itself as well. She was no longer a moon reflecting her father's brilliance, but generated her own "white heat," as one admirer wrote. In her letters, Florie needed italics, underlinings, and strings of exclamation marks to express herself. She wrote about literature and reform, but also about fashion and entertainment, offering self-deprecating jokes or lighthearted asides. Her growing circle of friends commented on her pretty, cunning, mobile face, the way she could express disgust or affection with an arched eyebrow or a trembling lip. She began to stand out as a figure of unusual intellectual abilities, and a devastating orator in English, German, or ancient Greek.[14]

But a prickly brilliance was also beginning to show. When Florie was near, her friends learned to avoid speaking with the kind of mawkish sentimentalism Victorians often used, aware of the torrent of pointed questions she could unleash. Florence celebrated her acceptance into an advanced course at Cornell, for instance, bragging that she was finally "relieved of the burden of the stupids." Like her father, Florie sometimes indulged traits that might, in others, be frustrating, difficult, or imperious. But the Kelleys were so confidently themselves, so unconcerned about how they seemed, that father and daughter usually pulled it off.[15]

The one subject her friends never seemed to broach was politics. For the first time in her life, the election cycle did not define her calendar, party newspapers did not litter tables and ottomans. In her freshman year at Cornell, when her famous father was down in Louisiana fighting over that state's crucial electoral votes in the 1876 election, Florie tried to tell her friends about it. She was wounded to realize that no one wanted to hear her read aloud from Judge Kelley's letters. Her notes to her father expressed embarrassment at the unworldliness of her life. Although Florie's letters to her mother were chatty, to Will she apologized that her coursework would "strike you as very school-girl-y." The outside world, with politics at its spine, hardly mattered at Cornell. "No one," Florie wrote, "read a daily paper, or subscribed for a monthly or a quarterly. Our current gossip was Froude's life of Carlyle. We read only bound volumes."[16]

This pointed absence of politics said something important about the world she was entering. It is true that most of her friends were young women, and though plenty of American women hungrily devoured partisan newspapers, their interest was less obligatory than men's. But class distinctions explain much as well. Florie was surrounded by the daughters of executives and sons of brokers, exactly the kind of families who looked at America's ceaseless campaign convulsions and exclaimed the new, dismissive expression: "Bother politics!"

Pig Iron Kelley's daughter could not entirely abandon the world of politics. At Cornell she helped found the Social Science Club, gathering students and professors to discuss how the emerging fields of sociology, political science, and economics could answer "all live questions social, moral and political." She was the club's only female member, and often its loudest voice. Sometimes the group worried the fringes of partisan politics, like one "very heated argument over Kearneyism." Denis Kearney was a xenophobic California rabble-rouser, famous for his brutal slogan, "The Chinese Must Go." In the 1870s, even Kearney drew on antipolitician rage, calling on San Francisco crowds to "shoot down" politicians who disappointed them. After debating his politics, Florie bragged to her father that "you would have been very much pleased, I think, with the rational tone of the whole performance."[17]

Even the club's debates signaled how significantly Florie's experiences differed from her father's education a half century before. While Will Kelley had grown up laboring and apprenticing, Florie enjoyed all the privileges he had won for her. While Will's education came from working as a printer's devil, Florie could debate the foremost scholars at a cutting-edge university. While his first speech was an unsolicited harangue before a Boston crowd, Florie gave her first oration before professors of rhetoric, in classical Greek. As a young man, Will had put his faith in the Democratic Party, while his daughter was coming to trust the studies of ethnographers and political scientists. As a child of wealth, and as a woman, she was encouraged to look beyond the political parties.

Still, the data-mad Will would have loved to study social science had he grown up in another age and another class. Though they saw the world through different frames, Will and Florie cared about many of the same social, moral, and political questions. They took different tools to the same problems, with Florie building on "Father's years of effort to enlist me permanently on behalf of the less fortunate."[18]

Back in Philadelphia, Will Kelley was struggling in that lifelong effort. By the fall of 1878, he was sixty-four years old, still vigorous and lithe, but increasingly ill. Four decades of unamplified speechifying had worn down Will's magnificent voice. His love of chewing tobacco and cigar smoke wasn't helping. Will's coughing fits grew worse, and abscesses in his throat sometimes forced him to cancel lectures. He blamed it on a congenital "catarrh" and suffered from a "daily effusion of blood from my throat." Will sought out a quack treatment, regularly inhaling "Dr. Starkey's Oxygenated Vapors" from an odd tin contraption with a long glass tube. He never stopped working, but grew easily irritated with those around him—his piercing blue eyes ringed by furious red rims. Florie worried to Carrie, "I am exceedingly sorry that Papa is overworking so for many reasons. I'm afraid too that he is likely to have a very hard winter."[19]

In 1878 Will was having a very hard fall. After winning nine congressional races over eighteen years, he was finally at risk of losing the Republican nomination. For once, he faced a "red hot opponent." Kelley's independence made him vulnerable, dangerously out of step with the struggle being fought over American democracy. He was an odd man out in a narrowing political world, neither a machine politician doling out patronage, nor a blue-blooded reformer dismissing the "ignorant proletariat," nor a bomb thrower hoping to demolish the party system. Too independent to be a boss, too populist to be a reformer, too institutionalist to be a radical, Kelley just didn't fit.[20]

Will's young challenger was John E. Reyburn, the mustachioed scion of a wealthy lightning rod manufacturing family. From his post in Pennsylvania's state senate, where he was denounced as "venal and disgraceful," Reyburn spent heavily to organize a "sledge-hammer-like opposition" against Kelley. He made a persuasive case against Judge Kelley in the language of the campaign economy: Pig Iron Kelley just didn't pay.[21]

Kelley was not a machine politician. During all his years in office, he flatly refused, a fellow congressman admired, to "go to Congress as an errand-boy." This sounds admirable, but for a politician reliant on a large network of campaigners to get his ballots in boxes, it was a major weakness. The party workers who actually ran his campaigns had been growing frustrated for years. They complained to reporters that Kelley "did not recognize them" in the street and "snubbed 'the boys' when they would visit

Washington." He offered no offices as rewards to his canvassers. Kelley had become so distant from the necessities of politics, it was accused, that "his friends were compelled to go down into their own jackets" to pay the one-hundred-dollar fee to get his name on the ballot.[22]

At least as upsetting to the men weighing the Republican nomination was the fact that Kelley was an unreliable partisan. Why back a man who was constantly being nominated by the Greenback Party, who criticized Republican policy, and who picked fights with Republican presidents? Hadn't he always pushed things too far? Hadn't he obsessed about Black voting rights when few Whites wanted them? Hadn't he given interminable speeches on monetary policy when hardly anyone could follow his calculations? Hadn't he always acted like a statesman, when the times called for a boss?

Several newspapers chose exactly the same language to explain his biggest flaw. Will Kelley had become "ENTIRELY TOO INDEPENDENT."[23]

To convince the machine that he valued their labor, Kelley was forced, one paper wrote, to "undertake a personal canvass—a thing distasteful to him." He would need to duck under the striped awnings of Republican clubs along Lancaster Avenue or Chestnut Street and pay his respects to the workers who ran the machine. It's funny to imagine Kelley, expounding to a saloon full of nodding b'hoys about monetary policy, tax schedules, or iron deposits. Kelley was not a stiff—in fact he was often passionate and charismatic—but he was simply not trading in the currency most politicians valued. Machines increasingly avoided ideological arguments over legislation, especially in reliable districts. Politics and governance were diverging, and Will was fixated on the losing side.[24]

But Kelley still had thousands of admirers nationwide. Friends wrote from Kentucky and Illinois, furious with the "soreheads and hostels in his district," certain that "no other man can hold his place." Electors agreed. On September 12, after a heated contest, Philadelphia's Republicans gave 55 percent of their votes, and their tenth consecutive nomination, to Kelley. Even the conservative *North American*, which often attacked Kelley's "idiosyncrasies," acknowledged that not to nominate him would "deprive the party of one of the most able men in the House, and it would have been peculiarly ungrateful."[25]

The contest marked a change in Will. Somewhere in the midst of the hot fight for his seat, Kelley made peace with his party. He had spent the past several years struggling to maintain his conscience without entirely leaving the organization he had helped found. In a sign of his shift, Kelley turned down a request to help stump for Kentucky Greenbacker Colonel Blanton Duncan, writing to Duncan: "You mistake my party relations. I am a republican in good standing dissenting from my party on one point and endeavoring to induce it to accept the faith as it is in me." Kelley claimed that his position was "recognized and tolerated." This was quite a step down from his dramatic promise to follow his conscience into "what affiliation it may" a few years before.

After his victory over Reyburn, Will invited a group of prominent Philadelphia Republicans to the Elms. In the parlor where he once promised his support to Reconstruction, Kelley committed himself wholeheartedly to the Republican Party. Whatever he said in that conversation, the *North American* felt that a chastened Kelley placed himself "in a better attitude toward the party than he has occupied for some time."[26]

What this would mean for his famous conscience, his resistance to patronage, his radical views, and his "duty to his manhood" was unclear. In the late 1870s, there were limits on even Will Kelley's independence.

Will's close call highlighted how the political system had changed. He was still one of the nation's most impressive speakers, and perhaps its most ardent and committed legislator, but such abilities did not matter as much as they once had. Interpersonal campaign savvy—management and delegation, loyalty and subtlety—mattered more than ability to write legislation or speak in Congress. These were the social skills of the saloon or the soiree that Kelley had never truly mastered. Without them, he would be increasingly boxed in by the emerging order.

Just as Kelley compromised his "duty to his manhood," his daughter was envisioning a future path for herself "if I ever, in the slow years, *do* grow into womanhood." The politics dividing Americans were also opening a fissure in the Kelley family. She could hardly know it, but Florie was venturing off on a journey, often lonely, that would take her away from her father, from the Elms, and from American politics.[27]

CHAPTER EIGHT

"When a Man Works in Politics, He Should Get Something Out of It"

T he nostrils of the most powerful man in America quivered as he spoke. His single auburn curl bobbed on his forehead, his eyebrows narrowed, his muscular frame stiffened. As Roscoe Conkling unfolded the layers of sarcasm and scorn in his latest speech, his deliberate diction built momentum, a massive fist cocked to come crashing down. And then he paused, returned to his gilt-edged pages, and scribbled some notes. Across from Conkling, his audience of one beamed in admiration.[1]

Lawrence worked as a low-level employee for the New York State Republican committee. We do not know his full name, but we know that he worshipped Conkling. When the senator had an oration to prepare, he spent months speechifying in Lawrence's face. Sometimes Lord Roscoe would summon Lawrence to his grand home in Utica. There, below the elk antlers and oil portraits of Conkling's forebears, Conkling would make speeches at him till morning, treating the receptive clerk like "a target or a listening post."[2]

The two were crafting what would become Conkling's most famous speech, a weapon meant for one man. George William Curtis, editor of *Harper's Weekly*, had earned Conkling's hatred. With his sad eyes and drooping sideburns, his urbane prose and his staunch morality, Curtis represented exactly the kind of respectable reformer unhappy with the direction of American politics. Before the war, Curtis was the abolitionist whom Will Kelley had defended, armed with a billy club, from a furious proslavery "tempest," who admired "the grand blows" Kelley delivered in Congress. Now Curtis hoped to help the reformist Hayes administration tackle the Boss Power, just as they had once tackled the Slave Power. Curtis was trying to do his part, by attempting to wrest the New York State Republican Party from Conkling's clutches.[3]

But every time *Harper's Weekly* published a pro-reform editorial, or printed one of Thomas Nast's biting cartoons, Conkling summoned Lawrence. Together they sharpened his gilded attack. Conkling hoped to skewer not just Curtis but the very notion that politics needed reform.

Curtis, Conkling, and Lawrence represented three perspectives on American democracy at a crossroads. Elites like Curtis came across as hostile to mass politics, often accused of doubting the very notion of popular self-government. Political practitioners like Conkling defended the system, insisting that voting majorities could never be wrong. And in between were millions of men and women like Lawrence, working people trapped in a tug-of-war. Many of them were repelled by reformers and politicians alike, forced to choose between the former's condescension and the latter's manipulation. In the short term, the Conklings would prove more compelling, using the Gilded Age class war to foment a forceful backlash against reform.[4]

Curtis walked into Conkling's trap. The men intent on reforming American democracy were rarely capable of the "broad-shouldered brutality" it took to run a Gilded Age political machine. At a Democratic New York State convention in 1870, some cheeky friend of Boss Tweed had even picked the reformist Samuel Tilden's pocket. And when New York's Republicans gathered in Rochester in September 1877, Curtis practically demanded that his pocket be picked. He began the session by proposing a loyalty oath to the new president. Rutherford Hayes, despite having lost the popular vote in the 1876 election, was intent on cleaning up his party. Curtis wanted Republicans to affirm that his mandate was "as clear and perfect as that of George Washington."[5]

In response, Conkling's men filled the three-thousand-seat auditorium with hissing and booing. Finally, on the last night of the convention, Lord Roscoe himself stalked onto the podium. He took his mark, not at center stage between the elaborate floral arrangements, but off to the side, aligned with Curtis's seat in the audience. He posed his muscular frame, one foot forward, one foot back. Then, slowly and carefully, his anger "cold, rich, musical, his invective a trifle elephantine but crushing," Conkling began to hurl his speech down in Curtis's face, as direct and pointed, wrote the *New York Times*, "as a boy throws a stone."[6]

"We are Republicans," Conkling asserted, "not representatives of an Administration party, nor of an anti-Administration party. Administrations do not make parties. Parties make administrations. Parties go before administrations, and live after them. The people make parties. The people made the Republican party." It was a sacred conduit for millions of individual voices. No president had the right to reform it, unless they could do so at the ballot box. And Hayes had failed to do that.[7]

As far as Conkling was concerned, there would be no loyalty oath.

"Parties are not built up by deportment, or by ladies' magazines," Conkling went on. Power was not won through lectures on morality. It could never be earned by "these oracular censors so busy of late in brandishing the rod over me and every other Republican in this state . . . in newspapers and elsewhere, cracking their whips and playing school." At a time when rigid partisanship signaled masculinity, the men claiming to clean up American popular democracy, were, in Conkling's view, not real men at all.[8]

Reformers like Curtis, Conkling sneered, were merely "carpet knights"—an antiquated insult for lords who had won their titles through service in court, rather than glory in battle. If you had not triumphed in the central contest of American political life, if you had not won an election, you had no claim to authority. In a culture obsessed with campaigning, carpet knights were worse than Democrats. Democrats at least honored the rules of winner-take-all democracy. Reformers like Curtis and Hayes, Conkling accused, were trying to circumvent the chief battle of American life, working to restrain a democracy that they could never succeed in at the polling place.[9]

"When Dr. Johnson defined patriotism as the last refuge of a scoundrel," Conkling pronounced, "he was unconscious of the then undeveloped capabilities and uses of the word 'Reform.'"[10]

Conkling spoke his speech, never shouting, never halting, in a kind of pointed trance, all aimed down at Curtis's sad face. When Curtis moved to interrupt, Conkling warned that "nothing but the proprieties of the occasion restrain me" from handling Curtis "as I feel at liberty to do in the walks of private life." Before delivering his attack, Conkling had given newspapers a draft of his address. Afterward, editors remarked that he had delivered ten newspaper columns worth of text word for word, exactly as they appeared in the script he had painstakingly prepared with Lawrence.[11]

Throughout the speech, Curtis sputtered in his chair, exclaiming "Remarkable!" "Extraordinary!" "What an exhibition!" "Bad temper!" "Very bad temper!" Afterward, he described the assault as "the saddest sight I ever knew . . . that man glaring at me in a fury of hate." Taking the high road, Curtis claimed to pity Conkling, stating, "I had not thought him great, but I had not suspected how small he was."[12]

The papers were divided. The working-class New York press admired the way Conkling "carried the day by sheer force of eloquence and animal magnetism." The papers read by the better sort, like the *New York Times*, claimed shock. Was this the direction American democracy was heading? Where had the statesmen of the Civil War era gone? Calling Conkling "a maniac," the *Times* scolded, "he abused Mr. Curtis like a fish-wife."[13]

History textbooks often mention Conkling's "carpet knight" speech, usually to demonstrate the pettiness of Gilded Age politics. But Conkling's speech represented something bigger than a personal spat. It contained a thesis statement, an articulation of the fight raging over the system governing American life. It synthesized themes—party over person, campaigning over governing, masculine loyalty over prim morality—that defined politics. Conkling offered a backlash to reform's "rancid canting self-righteousness," meant to appeal to majorities in the working and middle classes who saw themselves as manly combatants in the partisan fight. If Francis Parkman's "Failure of Universal Suffrage" exposed how little faith some had in the "public pest," Conkling shouted a rejoinder, declaring his high faith in masses of voters above morals or ethics.[14]

In this fight, politics was *the issue*. Americans argued over many conflicts during this era, but no ideological question loomed as large as the fight over democracy itself. The split divided American society—not just Republicans against Democrats, or North against South, or Labor against Capital—but between supporters of popular politics and those who wanted to revise its fundamentals. That is why Conkling accused Curtis of being worse than a Democrat. Crushing reform even took precedence over partisan victory. As one political independent observed, whenever the two parties were confronted with reform, they "let go of each others' hair" to turn on the reformer who, like a bystander trying to break up a "domestic unpleasantness," draws the wrath of both husband and wife.[15]

One line in Conkling's harangue marked the ground over which this battle would be fought. Conkling huffed that reformers seemed to think that it was "corrupt and bad for men in office to take part in politics." If he was going to defend one thing, as a boss, it was the campaign economy that joined running for office and running the government, using appointed positions as a reward for campaign labor. Such patronage was no side issue; it powered the massively popular political culture of the era. And reformers hoped to shut off the tap of rewards-for-labor, believing that cleaning up the civil service might finally separate politics from government.[16]

Patronage had been a regular part of American politics going back to Jefferson. With each new election the victors tended to award government offices to friends who got them there. But as campaigns dominated public life in the postwar era, and the size of government exploded, such jobs became a powerful fuel keeping millions of unpaid citizens working. Those lucky enough to get a government job were expected to pay a portion of their salary—usually between 2 and 7 percent—back to the party. These "assessments" financed further campaigns. But only a small portion of the millions of political participants would ever win an appointment. Far more simply liked the possibility of getting something out of politics. They considered this transaction a legitimate exchange of labor, no different from getting paid to make steel or sell pickles. It offered a simple, concrete answer for the murkiest question present in American democracy: Why bother participating? As the loudmouth Tammany district boss George Washington Plunkitt put it, Republicans and Democrats might disagree on everything else, "but we agree on the main proposition that when a man works in politics, he should get something out of it."[17]

Often, what a man got out of politics was a job running the local post office. No institution played a greater role in making the power of the federal government tangible, providing a circulatory system feeding nineteenth-century America. Post offices distributed mail, but also dispensed hundreds of millions of newspapers, becoming the key nexus of personal, political, and economic information. And with roughly fifty thousand post office jobs to be delegated (about 250 per congressman), they outnumbered all other federal positions combined. Winning a coveted postmaster job meant a generous federal stipend, plus profits from selling stamps, shipping materials, and (of course) liquor. Total incomes averaged between eight hundred and one thousand dollars a year, twice what coal miners made, and four times more than a schoolteacher.[18]

Such patronage built empires. More important than the money, to political parties, friendly postmasters could insert campaign literature into people's mail, limit rivals' access to newspapers, or conveniently lose important messages. Canvassers fought bitterly to win each post. One comedian joked about "that unutterable lust which takes possession of the average American citizen when he casts covetous eyes upon a post office." When a local office seeker felt his campaign efforts merited a job in the village post office, "there follows a social and political convulsion, before which Congressmen and Cabinet officers go down like broken reeds, and whole populations hunt their cyclone pits for refuge."[19]

In all seriousness, a Democratic congressman concurred. Cabinet nominations might matter in Washington, but in most of the rural nation, "the fate of the party and the Administration lies in the crossroads post offices."[20]

This patronage was not some crooked gig for the lucky few. Because positions were earned through campaign labor, they connected to the experiences of millions. Corruption was intimately bound up with mass culture. Patronage touched the lives of an incredible spectrum of Americans, from Washington politicos to lowly street sweepers. The very halls of Congress showed the impact. The women who mopped the floors and emptied the spittoons often won their jobs through "sweeping and scrubbing patronage," built on the campaign work of a relative. One father of an aspiring female clerk wrote the Treasury Department: "I think I have done enough for the cause and for yourself to give her a place."[21]

Fifteen hundred miles west of the capitol's spittoons, a moon-faced, sandy-haired Swedish immigrant named Rolf Johnson joined in the same exchange. Ever since arriving in Nebraska, twenty-year-old Rolf had grumbled about the native-born "ring" that ran Phelps County. During the 1876 election, Rolf and a group of Swedish immigrants ran an aggressive campaign to unseat the "Phelps County Ring," electioneering from homestead to homestead, dragging Swedes to the polls. Soon Rolf was rewarded, given jobs as assistant postmaster, county clerk, clerk of the District Court, and even clerk of the next election, although he was not yet old enough to vote. To Rolf, this did not look like corruption; it looked like a public trust, earned through hard political labor in the system that ran America's government.[22]

Administering all this patronage occupied many politicians' labors, making them middle managers between street-level campaigners and federal authorities. William "the Squire" McMullen—the South Philadelphia ward boss who ran the Moyas fire company and did so much to suppress Black voters in his district—spent most of his time lobbying for spoils. McMullen regularly wrote the Pennsylvania congressman and Speaker of the House Samuel J. Randall, identifying deserving appointees in their district. His misspelled, sometimes solicitous, sometimes threatening letters offer a window into how public politics turned into private gain. He pointed Randall toward useful allies, often based on his wife's knowledge of the community. But when McMullen felt neglected by federal power, he warned Randall that those in "charge of distributing publick Patronage must be compelled to look closer to home." That one of the most powerful men in the country often collaborated with a local ward boss, born into Irish Philadelphia's impoverished "alley people," spoke to how widespread and grassroots nineteenth-century democracy could be, even at its most crooked.[23]

Perhaps more than anyone else, African Americans relied on patronage as Reconstruction slipped from their fingers. On the federal level, Republican congressmen could still find jobs for African Americans even as voting itself became difficult. Those jobs built the bedrock of Washington's middle-class Black community. But these officeholders understood that such positions were not charity; instead, they were intended as a trade for on-the-ground campaign labor. At one point, the African American congressman John Roy Lynch warned President Grant about a Mississippi postmaster who, though appointed by Republicans, refused to campaign for the party. Lynch acknowledged that the appointee was "a good, capable, and efficient postmaster" but must be replaced. "What I have against him," he informed the president, "is solely on account of politics . . . politically he is worthless. From a party point of view he is no good." Lynch was an impressive man, born a slave, one of the youngest politicians to rise in his state, and a leader in the fight for Black voting rights. But he was not above the rules of patronage. Why employ a postmaster who would not campaign?[24]

Nonetheless, African Americans were slighted even when it came to patronage. Out of tens of thousands of positions, there were only forty-three Black postmasters during all of Reconstruction.[25]

African American activists usually endorsed patronage as a necessary evil. Here was a population that truly needed to "get something" out of politics. The Reverend Henry McNeal Turner pointedly told Black Republicans, in 1878, that they should be "getting more for your political services . . . with all of your speaking, organizing, parading the streets, ballyhooing, holding mass meetings, voting, and sometimes fighting, what do you get?" Isaiah C. Wears, who used his North Philadelphia barbershop to build a respectable political machine in the years after Octavius Catto's death and Will Kelley's betrayal, saw patronage as the best resource available. When activists finally won a few places for Black policemen on the Philadelphia force, Wears chose a barber's metaphor, declaring, "I do not thank the Republican party for any privileges. For myself, I only use it as a tool. It is a knife which has the sharpest edge and does my cutting."[26]

Wears's clear-eyed realism captures the open exchange of the campaign economy driven by practical politics. High-reaching rhetoric of pure democracy was fine for 1865, but by 1880, the best Wears could hope for was a sharp tool to slice something useful off for his constituents.

For their part, reformers like Curtis were driving at a fundamental reenvisioning of American democracy when they attacked patronage.

Though cloaked in the unsexy Victorian language of "Civil Service reform," they were pushing for revolutionary change. Many identified themselves with classical liberalism, attacking the growth of the federal government since the Civil War. Such liberals were often Republicans by heritage, but by the 1870s believed that the bloated elephant needed a diet. They argued that Reconstruction was complete and that high protective tariffs meddled in free market capitalism. But the issue that most motivated liberals was fury at the way federal power propped up the worst aspects of public politics. If liberals could reduce patronage, and with it the incentive for all that hard campaign labor, they might calm the convulsion of American politics.[27]

The new president Hayes picked the New York Custom House to make a stand against patronage. The domed and spired Wall Street edifice stood at the center of the nation's finances, and also Roscoe Conkling's empire. More than half of all federal revenues were made through import fees at this time, and most came in through the New York Custom House. It paid for much of the spoils in New York State, siphoned off by Conkling's minions. Conkling "joked" (though it is hard to see how this was anything other than a statement of fact) that the federal building was "*my* Custom-House." So President Hayes chose to make wresting control of the Custom House "the first and most important step in the effort to reform the civil service."[28]

For this mission, Hayes selected a perfect embodiment of the "Best Men" that reformers were always talking about. Theodore Roosevelt Sr.—"Thee" to his intimates—was born into one of Manhattan's oldest, wealthiest families. Respected for his philanthropic work and public rectitude, the bearded, leonine Thee was well known around Manhattan. He was loved particularly fiercely by his own teenage son, the sickly but energetic Theodore Roosevelt Jr.—called "Teedie"—who considered his father "the best man I ever knew."[29]

Poor Thee, selected for his quiet dignity, had no idea about the fight he would be dragged into. Conkling ran the Senate committee responsible for confirming Hayes's nominee. In committee, and in the press, he savaged Theodore Sr. He scoffed that Hayes would like to fill political offices "by nothing less than divine selection." After days of personal attacks, and a six-hour harangue in committee, Theodore Sr.'s nomination was rejected.

Victorious, the pro-Conkling *New York Sun* fawned that when other politicians "hesitated to assert their manhood," Lord Roscoe gave "voice to the sentiment of the millions of voters" who preferred patronage to reform.[30]

Like Curtis, Thee tried to take the high road. He wrote to Teedie, then at Harvard, that "the machine politicians have shown their colors," but nonetheless "a great weight was taken off my shoulders." He put on a brave face, even as the stress of his very public rejection coincided with bouts of painful stomach cramps, doubling over his large frame. Thee cheerily reasoned that the job "would have practically kept me in the city almost all the time in the summer and that would be no joke." Here he summed up why reform failed. The men who lived by the campaign economy, who outmaneuvered dilettantes like Thee, and who saw each appointment as "their bread and butter"—they had no Long Island summer homes to distract them.[31]

Despite his cheer, just two days after his rejection by the Senate, Thee collapsed in awful pain. His bowel cancer progressed quickly and painfully. Within two months, Thee was dead.

Conkling's defense of patronage did not kill Theodore Sr. That tumor had already been lingering in his bowels. But the extreme stress of his public nomination fight probably accelerated it. Devastated by his father's death, young Theodore Jr. reassessed his path forward in life. Previously, Teedie felt called to a future as a scientist and natural historian. But the painful loss of his father, in the midst of the humiliating nomination fight, pointed Theodore Jr. in new directions.[32]

Before he died, Theodore Sr. wrote to his son, worried about the future of American democracy. Reform seemed to lose at every turn, outweighed by sheer numbers willing to join in a crooked system. "I fear for your future," Thee wrote. "We cannot stand so corrupt a government for any length of time."[33]

THE FIGHT OVER democracy was a fight over class, a terrain in which men like Curtis and Theodore Sr. were ill-equipped. Conkling was, to be fair, born to wealth and privilege as well, but since his early role as antislavery muscle, he had crafted a populist appeal. The crumbling of the old class structure powered this feud. When Americans think of the Gilded Age today, they tend to imagine extremes of wealth and poverty, a nation of millionaires and tenement dwellers. But in reality, what was happening in the middle would determine the future of democracy.

Prior to the 1870s, America enjoyed a large bulk at the center of its class structure, a mass of common men and women divided by hazy boundaries. Except for the very poor or very rich—who controlled far less wealth than European aristocrats—America's vast middling classes enjoyed unusual social mobility. Gross inequities existed in terms of race and gender, but flexibility ruled the experiences of the majority. Later signifiers of class meant less. Men who worked hard labor might end up as judges or congressmen; urban neighborhoods mixed the wealthy and the poor; and an unsystematic education network blurred class lines.[34]

But around the time of the 1873 depression, America's middling classes began to experience what the historian Robert Wiebe called "a general splintering process." As the radical economist Henry George put it, in his groundbreaking 1879 work *Progress and Poverty*, the socioeconomic revolutions of the era were not lifting up the entire fabric of American society. Instead, "it is as though an immense wedge were being forced, not underneath society, but through society. Those who are above the point of separation are elevated, but those who are below are crushed down."[35]

This wedge split the old middle. We tend to think of Gilded Age America in terms of a contest between the haves and the have-nots, but the bigger story was the widening chasm between the have-mores and the have-lesses. For the latter, employers began to abandon apprenticeship, long the route to advancement for unskilled workers. Bosses invested in machinery and hired unskilled laborers, whom they had little interest in promoting. At the same time, above the wedge, skilled workers saw dramatic jumps in their incomes. A booming upper-middle class emerged, from clerks and typists to lawyers and executives. In the 1880s, while working men donned blue denim shirts, one in five urban White men would clip on disposable white shirt collars at the start of the day to signal just how clean their new jobs were. Wage earners were separating "blue collar" from "white collar."[36]

The participatory political system had long prospered in the hazy middle, blurring class divides in marching clubs and campaign rallies. It was the small population of elites who sat on the sidelines. But as the wedge of income inequality splintered the old middle classes, the feuding party men and reformers both scrambled to claim majority opinion.

Reformers looked down the economic ladder and claimed to speak for the rising middle. As Parkman put it, respectable voters were trapped between "an ignorant proletariat and a half-taught plutocracy. Between lie the classes, happily still numerous and strong, in whom rests our salvation." The vicious defender of White Anglo-Saxon Protestant America, Josiah Strong, warned against "the two extremes of society—the dangerously rich and the dangerously poor." Men like Parkman and Strong were calculating that the wedge of economic division struck the class structure low enough to leave a large alliance of middle- and upper-class Americans to retake control of American democracy. Below that point they saw only vulgar politicians and filthy tramps, violent radicals, uneducable Catholic or Jewish immigrants, African Americans, and other populations hardly deserving of the ballot.[37]

On the other side, many politicians depicted would-be reformers as a tiny splinter of the elite. They used the language of weightlessness, contrasting "that Rainbow-Hued Reform Bubble" to the steady, manly masses. Party apologists exaggerated how high the wedge struck America's class structure, figuring that it was splitting the down-to-earth majority from a few untethered aristocrats. Conkling famously dismissed New York reformers as about "three hundred persons," so convinced of their own purity that they saw themselves as above America, looking down from "the milky way," lifting "their skirts very carefully for fear even the heavens might stain them."[38]

Relying on crude stereotypes and childish name-calling, the defenders of politics made heavy use of class and gender biases in their attacks on reform. When the well-to-do lectured about morality in politics, they were dismissed as sentimentalists who would be better off running Vassar College. When they joined the scrum on election day, they were mocked as dandies who "put on their neckties before they went to vote." Too often, a Milwaukee newspaperman wrote, the self-impressed "Best Man" was actually an "anaemic, prim, old maidish, statistical person, whose manner is marked by an acid propriety, whose conversation is heavy with figures and Latin derivatives, who has no more blood in his veins than a shad, whose dissertations make his hearers feel as if somebody were putting snow down their backs."[39]

The Hayes administration practically begged to be laughed at. At a time when mugs of foamy lager signaled working-class fellowship, President Hayes's teetotaling wife, Lucy, forbade alcohol from the White House, instead serving lemonade (except to the Russian delegation, who alone merited wine). For entertainment, the spindly, bespectacled, German-born secretary of the interior, Carl Schurz, offered piano recitals. Conkling, always a beacon of maturity and civility, mocked "Ruther-fraud" Hayes's administration and his "snivel-service reforms." When Schurz came to speak to Congress, Conkling loudly crumpled newspapers to throw off the reformer's address.[40]

Conkling successfully smeared reformers as effete dilettantes, but his own private life supported the image of politicians as vulgar sinners. Over the late 1870s, Conkling carried on a shockingly public affair with Kate Chase, the brilliant, beautiful daughter of the prominent antislavery politician and Supreme Court justice Salmon Chase. Kate was considered one of the most striking women in Washington, commented on for her "saucy" nose, her "well-formed" figure, and her "imperial" posture. She was the only other person in Washington as frequently described as "haughty" as Roscoe himself. She was also an experienced political operator, who managed her father's campaigns, handled his correspondence, and represented him in society.[41]

Kate and Roscoe seem to have begun their affair in the midst of the 1876–77 contested election fight, with Kate visiting Roscoe's chambers in the Wormley Hotel, just a few floors above the smoke-filled room where the supposed Compromise of 1877 was brokered. Kate attended his speeches in the Senate, sitting in the ladies' gallery prominently wearing jewelry Conkling had given her. It was as if, one gossip writer put it, the two haughty political celebrities had "snapped their fingers contemptuously in the face of public opinion, as if to say, 'We are too lofty to be affected by aught you can say of us.'"[42]

Kate Chase's furious husband, the messily alcoholic Rhode Island senator William Sprague IV, finally confronted the pair in the summer of

1879. The illicit couple were staying together in Newport at "Canonchet," the Spragues' sixty-four-room, multitowered fantasia of a mansion. Sprague, supposedly out of town, returned with a shotgun. The accounts of their showdown differ, but each include juicy and humiliating details— Kate's son watching his father load his shotgun, Conkling escaping out a window, an armed Sprague pursuing him into town, Sprague confronting Conkling in the middle of the resort's shopping district. Newspapers were soon reporting the alleged exchange between two sitting senators, the unctuous Conkling trying to calm Sprague, the furious Sprague warning: "I want this distinctly understood. Go away from here at once. You say you are not armed. Then go, for, by God, if you don't I'll blow your brains out; and further, never cross my path again. If you do, be armed. I shall be armed, and if you cross my way I shall kill you."[43]

What was true, and what was merely good newspaper copy, is hard to tell. But whatever the reality, Conkling's name became synonymous not just with bare-knuckle politics but with immoral seductions. The father of the future actor "Fatty" Arbuckle insisted on naming his son Roscoe Conkling Arbuckle, later in the 1880s, because he doubted his boy's paternity. Conkling's scandal exposed exactly what reformers had been warning about, the bad men running American democracy. President Hayes glowed about the "exposure of Conkling's rottenness," happy, for once, in his besieged presidency.[44]

The politicians and reformers fighting over American democracy were really at war over two conflicting definitions of political authority. For the defenders of nineteenth-century politics, authority had to be earned through victory at the ballot box. No other currency mattered. Even cash had less significance than the votes of the majority—Conkling hoarded power, but did not enrich himself significantly. Around 1879, Americans started calling this route to power "practical politics." The term described the "smart dealings" and dirty tricks of canny men who snatched as much power as the voters would give. It fit with the confiscatory economy of the age, that encouraged the same unrestrained devouring that robber barons were displaying in business. "The law of everything," Conkling summed up, "is competition."[45]

It was quite a comedown from 1865's "pure democracy" to 1879's "practical politics."

Those hoping to reform democracy saw an entirely different path to authority, not seized by the cunning but granted to the deserving. Reformers harked back to the old Jeffersonian notion of a "natural aristocracy," believing that morality, education, and respectability should determine who would lead. Government should be run by "the Best Men." (It was merely a coincidence that those best men all happened to attend the same schools, clubs, and galas.) Power should be granted by superiority, not won through popularity.

In between the practical politicians and reformers, some sought to explain what was happening. One rising Republican star, James Garfield of Ohio, tried to connect the dots. The famously sweet-tempered Garfield agreed with reformers' criticisms, but also recognized that practical politicians had majority opinion on their side. The problem was the public itself. "Congress," Garfield wrote, "comes much nearer to the daily life of the people than ever before." Whatever was good or bad in politicians' behavior grew organically from "the firesides of the people, on the corners of the streets, and in the caucuses and conventions of political parties." There was bad behavior, but it was no conspiracy. The American people themselves "are responsible for the character of their Congress. If that body be ignorant, reckless, and corrupt, it is because the people tolerate ignorance, recklessness, and corruption."[46]

Here was the problem that reformers had not grappled with. Most had treated civil service reform as an easy, mechanical fix. They talked about reform, Theodore Roosevelt Jr. later wrote, "as if it were some concrete substance, like cake, which could be handed out at will." End "the spoils system," and "the best men" would naturally rise to the top. But the whole of politics was too enmeshed; reformers could not remove one slice at a time. From Boss Conkling to his clerk Lawrence, from the South Philadelphia machine to the Phelps County Ring, from the Capitol's cleaning ladies to the Speaker of the House, the system that powered public, partisan, passionate campaigning would require a broader, cultural solution.[47]

CHAPTER NINE

"Where Do All These Cranks Come From?"

Washington's bedbugs grew fat on American democracy. The city had a notorious pest problem, supporting an industry of discreet exterminators. The ceaseless flow of office seekers and election contesters tossing and turning in the city's boardinghouses offered up tides of fresh blood. Fourteen thousand federal jobs, fifty thousand post offices, and ten million voters made fitting bait. And when practical politicians left town, more bugs hitched a ride in their carpetbags, heading down to Georgia or up to Minnesota.[1]

The same tincture of transience and intimacy, participation and power, that made Washington heaven for bedbugs (and the capital of Gilded Age "indiscretions") also welcomed a peculiar population of visionaries and oddballs. Among the pests filtering into 1880s Washington were some truly dangerous creatures.

Charles Guiteau was one of these, hardly noticed until he became a national scourge. Small and scrawny, with the close-cropped hair of a convict, and a disconcerting habit of cocking his head to one side while avoiding eye contact, Guiteau was probably afflicted with a serious mental illness. But his condition made him a casualty of his shaken era. He bounced around the country, drifting and scheming, dodging debts, and communing directly with God. A free-love cult in upstate New York kicked him out (the women spurned him, calling him "Charles Gitout"). His brother warned that he was "capable of any folly, stupidity, or rascality." Yet in the disrupted nineteenth century, Guiteau just kept circulating, drawn to crowds and attention and the will of God.[2]

America's pyrotechnic politics caught Guiteau's eye. The nation was in the midst of the 1880 presidential election. It was, by Gilded Age standards, one of the calmer ones. The Democrats ran respected war hero Winfield Scott Hancock, and the Republicans ran respected war hero James Garfield. "Gaffy" was a big, friendly man, known for his piercing blue eyes and his physical affection, often seen strolling arm in arm with his friend James G. Blaine. Garfield gave a good speech, and walked a careful line between partisanship and reform.

To many in 1880, Hancock and Garfield seemed hard to distinguish. One woman in Maine chuckled at the crowds of confused young marchers hollering "Hurrah for Han-field." But even the calm race felt like a "deluge," the magazine *Puck* complained. There was "no limit to the campaign," *Puck* wrote. "The voter cannot get away from the political struggle by refusing to read his newspaper." Throw down that gossip-sheet, and the very walls of the nation were slathered with partisan broadsides.[3]

In the end, Garfield won, claiming the closest popular vote victory in American history. Eight years before, President Grant had won reelection in 1872 by 763,729 votes; in 1880 Garfield triumphed by just a few thousand votes. Such narrow margins—and a turnout of 78 percent—highlight why canvassers fought so aggressively for each vote, and why their labor was so generously rewarded.

A committed Republican and an awed admirer of Conkling (of course), Guiteau believed that it was his labor that won the day. The deluge captured Guiteau's attention-seeking mania. During the 1880 race, he spent weeks crafting a Republican address, then weaseled his way onto a stage during a late-night Manhattan rally. There he stumbled, muttered, and fled, complaining about the glare of the torches in the audience. A nineteenth-century speechifier who couldn't handle torches had better find another hobby. But when Garfield won, Guiteau knew "I was on my way to the white house."[4]

He joined the tide pouring into post-inauguration Washington, seeking appointments and feeding bedbugs. Lines of office seekers stretched out of the White House, down the lawn, and along Pennsylvania Avenue. Garfield complained that he had been elected to grapple with "the fundamental principles of government, and here I am considering all day whether A or B shall be appointed to this or that office." But 4.4 million voters had been convinced to vote for him, and their convincers needed rewarding. Garfield's frustration shows how distant presidents could be from the realities of practical politics. Election day no longer concluded a campaign—the spoils system extended the political calendar into a permanent cycle of running and rewarding.[5]

Somewhere in those crowds was Guiteau. He pestered Garfield, his wife, Lucretia, James Blaine, and other key Republicans, demanding a consulship. Preferably in Vienna, though he might settle for Paris. He hung around the opulent Riggs House hotel, ambushing Republicans and demanding his reward.[6]

And at this fraught moment, Guiteau was further agitated. Lord Roscoe felt sidelined by the new president. Senator Conkling saw Garfield as a rival in the Republican Party and a puppet of Blaine, whom Conkling had despised ever since their bet over poetry and champagne. After an elaborate fight over federal appointees, Conkling made his stand. He flamboyantly resigned from his position as senator from New York in protest. At this time, senators were not directly elected, but chosen by their state legislatures. Conkling demanded that the New York legislature reappoint him, to prove his popularity over Garfield. But many were tired of his games. President Garfield privately hoped that if the legislature had "sense and pluck they can end his hateful career." The New York legislature chose to leave Conkling hanging, his drama having achieved nothing by the loss of his own career.[7]

Guiteau watched his hero's maneuver in awe. Just two days after Conkling resigned, Guiteau concluded that the Republic would be better off "if the President was out of the way." Visiting a sporting goods store, Guiteau bought the largest pistol he saw.[8]

On the morning of July 2, 1881, Harriet Blaine watched her husband, James, set out to accompany President Garfield to Washington's train station. Within a few hours, the Blaines' newfangled telephone rang. The call, Harriet wrote, "will never pass from my memory." A man had ambushed Garfield and Blaine in the train station and fired two rounds into the president's back.[9]

Fighting her way to the White House, Harriet found Washington's streets packed and wild. Soon she learned that the president was alive. He persisted, in indescribable pain, for seventy-nine days, pawed over, and infected, by doctors. Finally, in September, Gaffy died, leaving the practical politician Chester A. Arthur as president. The whole excruciating affair left Harriet embittered, writing, "You can't imagine anything so vile as Washington. It seems like a weed by the wayside, covered with dust, too ugly for notice."[10]

A president had been gunned down in the nation's capital for the second time in just sixteen years. Boys born the day of Lincoln's assassination were still too young to vote when the next president fell. A crime that had never happened in the nation's first eight decades now seemed to be a regular occurrence. The assassination demoralized a population already shaken by the uproar over the 1876 election. And it confirmed the sense that something was broken in American public life.

Usually, Garfield's assassination is attributed to the monstrous actions of the unstable Guiteau. Sometimes the machinations of Conkling and the simmering war within the Republican Party are cited, with students quizzed on the distinction between Stalwarts and Half-Breeds (basically, Republican practical politicians and party reformers). But the assassination was bigger, growing directly from the central question roiling Gilded Age life. Garfield was killed in a fight over patronage, and patronage grew out of the colossal demands of campaigning. It was a political assassination, not a freak of insanity. How could America control the runaway campaign culture designed to agitate, but could have such deadly consequences? How could it rein in those encouraged to participate? Garfield's death was inherently political, a consequence of the forces inciting and obstructing American democracy.

Guiteau himself attested to this. When arrested, police found a note in his pocket describing his labor in the 1880 canvass. The assassination, he scribbled, "was a political necessity."[11]

Guiteau's revolver was also a starter pistol, sparking a stampede. A new species of "cranks" suddenly seemed to swarm Washington. The term was novel, but "the whole English speaking world has instinctively grasped" the reference to misfits like Guiteau. Over the next few months, Washington police arrested dozens of madmen, from White House fence jumpers to a man—armed with four pistols, two knives, and a bottle of chloroform—who attacked the doctor testifying in Guiteau's insanity trial. The capital's bartenders agreed that such maniacs were becoming a fact of life—their city had become "a paradise for curious characters." The intensity of American politics was making the capitol a "Mecca for the pilgrimage of many a visionary mind," attracting "the insanity of the entire country."[12]

Fear of "cranks" hitched around, becoming a kind of national catch-phrase, until the Los Angeles Times wondered, "Where do all these cranks come from?" But as the term proliferated, its meaning widened to include a huge swath of eccentrics. Guiteau fit the definition, but so did Thomas Edison, and Sitting Bull. Unlike today, cranks were not grumps; rather, they suffered from an excessive, eccentric optimism. A crank, explained the humorist Robert Burdette, "turns something, it makes the wheels go round, it insures progress. True, it turns the same wheel all the time, and it can't do anything else." The phenomenon captured the proliferating stories of solitary enthusiasts, loudly advocating a single sweeping plan to fix a broken society. Some wanted to kill the president; others believed that they could reform gender relations, or revolutionize capitalism, or prove that Hebrew-speaking giants lived in the center of the earth. The press mixed up the dogmatic, the demented, and the dangerous. Each was a crank, wrote the Chicago Tribune, "a fool of one idea."[13]

And such cranks arrived right on time, in a Gilded Age political culture that fired enthusiasm but made change impossible. The disruptions of the old order freed unrestrained energies. The Morning Oregonian explained that "in the traditional slow-coach age the crank was a rarity." America had always had "maniacs in painful plenty," but they tended to stay put, anchored by family and tradition. Now, the crumbling of old social and political bonds was letting them loose. A booming political culture encouraged speechifiers and demagogues, rewarding the "egotism which is at the bottom of much of the crankiness." Partisan newspapers' "intemperate abuse of public men" fostered a climate of hostility and extremism. Cranks were the logical result of a culture that was both overheating and standing still, that prized politics but had little interest in governance, that demanded participation but rarely looked beyond the next race. It reminded the

Augusta Chronicle of "a locomotive that has run off the track, turned upside down with the cow-catcher buried in a stump and the wheels making a thousand revolutions a minute."[14]

Attacking cranks was also a useful political tool. As the revolutionary possibilities of the postwar era settled into the cynical machine politics of the 1880s, practical politicians and mainstream journalists had an epithet to limit the horizons of public discourse. The term *race crank* was hurled at anyone, Black or White, who focused inordinately on racial issues, be they defending Black voting rights or excessively preaching White supremacy. Socialists, anarchists, and third-party voters were easily dismissed as "cranks—crack-brained, semi-idiotic." Even the mild George William Curtis, already skewered so mercilessly by Conkling, was mocked as a crank who "imagines that by softly stroking his side whiskers he can purify the Republican party."[15]

Some embraced the mantle of "crank." Out on his failing Minnesota farm, Donnelly was already on the fringes. In the early 1880s, Donnelly felt defeated on all fronts. He had been barred from the Republican Party and lost congressional races running with the Democratic, Greenback, and Workingmen's parties. He watched with impotent fury as Garfield, who entered Congress in the same class as Donnelly (and was "13 days younger than I am"), won the presidency. Apocalyptic grasshopper plagues devoured his crops. His hair grew gray, his vision worsened, his teeth fell out. And his money evaporated. "I get the blues sometimes," the formerly exuberant speechifier wrote in his diary. "I ought to win something sometime . . . my life has been a failure and a mistake."[16]

And then, Donnelly started writing his books. Everyone had long agreed that he had a burning eloquence, better suited for public entertainment than public governance. In 1882 Donnelly published *Atlantis: The Antediluvian World*, blending mythology, pseudoscience, and his sickening verbosity to speculate about the lost city. Readers devoured it. *Atlantis* went through twenty-three editions in America and twenty-six in England by 1890 and helped reignite popular interest in the subject. From there, Donnelly published a series of works of crankish nonsense—one speculating about the origins of the planet, another "proving" that Shakespeare did not write his works, and a work of dystopian science fiction brimming with anti-Semitism, which sold seven hundred thousand copies. Through it all, he was publicly and frequently identified as "the Prince of Cranks."[17]

And like so many of his fellows, it was Donnelly's fury at "the dirty cess-pool of politics" that propelled him in new directions.[18]

Others made themselves cranks by delving further into politics. To most Americans in the late nineteenth century, few causes were crankier than women's suffrage. It is hard for twenty-first-century Americans to appreciate just how unlikely the cause looked in 1880, lazily caricatured as a small movement of humorless women and emasculated men. And after the setbacks of the postwar era—the failure of the Republican Party to include women in the Fifteenth Amendment, the defeat of a suffrage amendment in Kansas, and the fracture of the movement itself—women's suffrage embraced some of the trappings of crankishness. Susan B. Anthony joined the national speaking circuit. Individuals like Victoria Woodhull and Belva Lockwood prominently showed up on election days, attempting to vote, or even ran for president. The National Council of Women felt it necessary to defensively remind readers that, throughout history, "cranks" were responsible for "all the great reforms which have improved the world."[19]

The cool, forthright suffragist organizer Carrie Chapman Catt confessed to Anthony that, in the current climate, their movement had "not a ghost of a show for success." The cause of women's suffrage, Catt warned, could be compared with Prohibition, "always remembering ours is the more unpopular." *More* unpopular than Prohibition: "Ours is a cold, lonesome little movement, which will make our hearts ache." Partisanship, Catt argued, defined the limits on acceptable change. "Men have been accustomed to take new ideas only when accompanied by party leadership with brass bands and huzzahs." In the Gilded Age, anyone outside the booming campaign culture looked like a crank.[20]

IF ONE MAN epitomized the ranty, cheery crank, it was William Kelley. What had he been, over all his crusades, but a proto-crank, always fighting for a burning cause, always pushing just beyond the boundaries of propriety? From workers' rights to antislavery to Black voting rights to monetary reform, Kelley brought a warm monomania to each cause. More than any other politician of his era, he would identify a blockage in society and doggedly hunt a way around it. He would research and lobby and lecture, proposing earnest ameliorative legislation. What the public chuckled at about Judge Kelley, what made him awkward company in Washington society, was his ceaseless, unabashed crankery. Will was, a Colorado paper joked, "a man whose whole soul is wrapped up in pig iron."[21]

But by the 1880s, Kelley's crankishness had been worn down. His famous free-spiritedness had meant partisan fight after fight, abandoning Reconstruction, battling over money, and nearly losing his seat for being "too independent." The renomination fight in 1878 further trimmed his wings. By 1880, all his passion and energy, his sheaves of data, his dancing frame and his booming voice, all pursued one remaining issue as the central cause of American political life. Kelley became America's foremost tariff crank.

The tariff is boring. It sounds like a joke of an issue, dreamed up to mock a dull age. Especially for Kelley, scarred veteran of the fights over race, class, and democracy, it seems particularly dry. But Will had a talent for picking the dividing lines in nineteenth-century American life. And during the Industrial Revolution, America's high tariffs—designed to protect manufacturers from overseas competition with fees on imported products— were the cause of bar fights and family feuds.

Supporters, most of them Republicans, honored the high tariff as the root of all prosperity. Free trade opponents, Democrats especially, compared their fight to lower tariff rates to the war against slavery. Rudyard Kipling, making his way across America in the 1880s, joked that in every saloon he visited someone was always making a speech about the tariff, "which he does not understand, but which he conceives to be the bulwark of the country or else the surest power for its destruction."[22]

Few understood the economics of the tariff, but most appreciated its politics. With Reconstruction dead, little ideology held the parties together. The one line that gave the system coherence was the fact that most Republicans wanted high tariff rates, and most Democrats wanted lower ones. Both made class-focused arguments. Republicans reasoned that the tariff kept working men employed and sustained the American family. Democrats claimed that tariffs kept prices high and forced women to find jobs. America's high tariffs accumulated into a huge federal surplus and paid for the majority of government expenses, including generous pensions to (mostly Republican) Union veterans and their widows. The tariff was also seen as a diplomatic tool in America's bid to unseat Britain as the world's chief economy. Finally, the tariff earned the Republicans a kind of "political rent"—a crowd-pleasing, vote-getting issue that underwrote less popular policies. In a growth-mad and class-obsessed time, the tariff melded industrialization, income inequality, partisanship, gender politics, foreign policy, and Civil War memory into a single tangible political plank.[23]

And the human embodiment of that tariff, in most American minds, was the grizzled but graceful Will Kelley. Frank Carpenter joked that he "thinks tariff, talks tariff, and writes tariff every hour of the day." Opponents agreed. A Democratic paper in Wisconsin claimed that Will was using the tariff to mastermind a grand corruption scheme, raising money to buy elections and send more Republican "ignoramuses to congress who will vote under the gag of party for any bill that Pig Iron Kelley may concoct." Kelley had passionately backed high tariffs since the 1857 panic, but as his other causes fell away, he became a true crank in the late 1870s and early 1880s. He expressed a rare faith in the power of protection to aid both manufacturers and working people alike, believing that the tariff might lift all boats.[24]

Over the late 1870s and '80s, the Elms received letters from producers of everything from underwear to Gatling guns, all hoping for favorable tariff rates. Will went so far as to defend the presence of "alkalange" in the tariff schedules, despite the fact no such substance existed—it was merely a printer's error that Kelley refused to remove. He even waded into the furious legal battle over whether tomatoes should be counted as a fruit or a vegetable. Will Kelley became a trumpet for industrialization. It was one of the reasons he had hung on to his congressional seat for so long, the way he won support from both laborers and manufacturers in Pennsylvania, the nation's chief industrial state.[25]

Nowhere did the tariff matter more. Pennsylvania led the nation in the production of steel and train cars. It had more coal miners than the rest of the nation combined. The state developed a strange coalition to keep the tariff high. Will used his position as chairman of the House's all-powerful Ways and Means Committee to defend the tariff, joined by a surprising ally. Samuel J. Randall, Democratic congressman and former Speaker of the House, differed with most of his party in his love for high tariffs. Kelley and Randall worked across party lines to keep tariffs high for Pennsylvania.[26]

In 1883 Kelley and Randall made a furious defense of high tariffs against rising resentment and an incoming Democratic House. The two lobbied and schemed all winter to pass a compromise bill. They made an odd couple: Randall's high, scratchy voice spitting out sharpened sarcasm while Kelley's bassoon pounded out earnest low notes, Will tall and dancing while Randall stood solid and glowering. With each day that winter, Will grew thinner and coughed more, but by spring they passed their greatest achievement, the so-called Mongrel Tariff of 1883.[27]

Few saw the tragedy of Kelley's alliance with Randall. Randall was the congressman on the receiving end of all those needy, misspelled letters from William "the Squire" McMullen. Randall held his seat, in large part, because of the boss of South Philadelphia. Because on election days the Squire and his Moyas were out, dragging White Democrats to the polls and keeping Black Republicans away. Because a Moya had shot Octavius Catto in the back. McMullen had orchestrated the most brutal Black voter suppression north of the Mason-Dixon. And now Will Kelley—who had hosted Black Philadelphia's leading lights in his parlor, whose face had been emblazoned on the banners of African American marchers as they cele-brated the Fifteenth Amendment, who had been sliced and shot at for Black voting rights—was now an ally of Squire McMullen and the men with the number 27 tattooed on their hands.

The *Harper's Weekly* editor Henry Loomis Nelson later recalled an odd scene from those cranky days of the early 1880s. He boarded a Pennsylvania train car and found himself seated next to Congressman William Kelley. But Will had no doughnuts this time. Instead he was grumpy. In low, confidential tones, Will told his seatmate that he had just endured a hot, bumpy, miserable ride from Harrisburg. There he had sat his state's Republican legislators down and explained why they had better not gerry-mander Randall's district away from him. Keep it Democratic, Will had argued, keep Randall in power, keep the tariff-defending Democrat in

Congress. "They actually did not know that Mr. Randall in the House is as valuable to us as ten Republicans," Will grumbled. Of course, preserving those boundaries not only kept Randall in the House; it kept Squire McMullen in power, and put thousands of Black voters at risk. It was no longer clear, by 1883, what exactly was valuable to Pig Iron Kelley.[28]

A political system where a former radical lobbied to maintain the power of a violent boss, where an assassin shot down a president expecting partisan reward, where no reform could succeed without brass bands—it was enough to make anyone a crank.

CHAPTER TEN

"Now We Shall Have the Worst Again"

I n the summer of 1881, amid Washington's "paradise for curious characters," a group of suffragists gathered for an evening convention. True to
form, there were no brass bands, no huzzahs, just earnest orations presided
over by "the Major," the erect and martial Susan B. Anthony. The Honorable
Judge Kelley was listed as the main draw. In the audience sat his twenty-
two-year-old daughter. But as the evening wore on, Will did not arrive.
Florie's dark eyes searched the hall, her long frame strained to spot her
father. On the rostrum Anthony's anxiety showed. The convention
conflicted with a Ways and Means subcommittee meeting on industrial
acids, and Will chose to tinker with the tariff. Finally, when it became clear
that he would not appear, Anthony announced his absence, declaring it "a
new and painful illustration of the lack of respect for the vote even among
men who are convinced advocates of suffrage."[1]

Kelley, Anthony jabbed, clearly cared less about voting rights than he
did about "the tariff on vinegar."[2]

Florie walked away furious—"my heart in my shoes"—returning to
Judge Kelley's boardinghouse. She worried about her father, imagining
his frustrations that "after a quarter century's active allegiance to a cause
still sufficiently unpopular, he was ridiculed by the great leader whom he
counted a friend." But the next morning, Florie found she had little to

worry about. Between daughter and father on the breakfast table sat the morning paper. Florie had avoided it for hours, having "not courage to open it myself." But Will blithely rustled it open. Then he began to chuckle. Reading Anthony's barb, Will exclaimed: "The good old Major! I'm afraid I deserved that!"[3]

In 1881 Florie still took her father's side in most questions, especially political ones. That would change. Within a few years, Florie made herself an independent force, not merely reacting to the world her father presented to her. She would emerge as a scholar and a renegade, setting off on a mission that would take her far from home. It all coincided with the crank years of American democracy, when many searched for alternative paths around the blockage at the center of public life.

Her first steps took her to Washington, that "Mecca for the pilgrimage of many a visionary mind." Florie's senior thesis at Cornell required research at the Library of Congress. She bunked with her father in the opulent Riggs House hotel, where Guiteau lurked that same summer. Father brought his daughter to the society parties at which he so often stumbled, and she charmed Washington just as she had charmed Cornell. Her manner—playful but intense—stunned many. She could go from singing and chatting with the young people to carefully "discussing remedies for labor troubles with some old friend of her father's."[4]

It was all a bit intimidating, a fawning journalist wrote, noting that in Washington "the young girls in society were just a little afraid of her; the young men were not entirely at ease in her presence, and old legislators were very careful about statistics when talking to her." The writer went on, tapping into a deep vein of sexism, that "if Miss Florence had been an old maid or indifferent looking, no one would have been surprised at her taking to such an outlandish thing as politico-economics, but she was a young, sweet, and pretty girl with whom it was impossible to associate any masculine tendencies."[5]

But her presence in Congress was even more striking. Florie followed her father's passion for the tariff and studied it as closely as he did. She would prepare statistics for him and accompany him to hearings in that big building on the hill. She stood out in the ladies' gallery, her dark eyebrows knit, her intense gaze set on the proceedings, her lips practically mouthing the statistics her father's voice was reciting on the floor. Watching her carefully, observers noted the way Florie seemed poised to break into her father's addresses and "call him to account for any lapses he might make."[6]

When she wasn't at Washington parties intimidating the other guests, Florie was sitting in the Library of Congress's grand hall, analyzing state health reports and Blackstone's legal code. She was piecing together an impressive work of original scholarship, a history of working children's legal status in the industrializing world. It was a topic her father had introduced her to in the Elms library, but now she was making it her own. She traced a narrative of growing government power over children, shifting from "absolute ownership of the father" to faith in a protective state. Her project perfectly mapped the changes she would make in her own life.[7]

Florie emerged as an able researcher and clear-eyed writer. By 1882 her thesis was complete; Florie had something to say. With Will's help she began to publish. Her thesis and other articles on working women appeared in the *International Review*. Tackling a subject few journalists knew much about, Florie's writing began to draw notice in newspapers. But often it was refracted through the prism of her famous father. Journalists reporting on Florie's work fondly recalled meeting her when she had been just a "bright-eyed little daughter of 8 years," playing at the Elms. One congressman congratulated Will "on the possession of a daughter who could write the article he had read in the *International Review*."[8]

She had to fight to be more than just her father's possession. She applied to enter the University of Pennsylvania for graduate study. The male-only school, just a mile from her home, simply ignored her request. When Will pushed his friends on Penn's board of trustees, Florie's application was rejected. One trustee wrote that he could think of nothing "more abhorrent" than men and women studying together.[9]

But just as she began to appear in the press calling for educational opportunities for women, random chance threw Florie onto a new path. Willy Jr., her troublesome brother who had gotten himself shot in the face a few years prior, suddenly went blind. His recent injury may have caused his condition, though gossipers claimed it was syphilis. Either way, his doctors recommended an immediate rest cure in Europe. It was an emergency, and Florie was the only relative free to accompany him. She dropped her studies, her writings, and her fight with the University of Pennsylvania and acted the dutiful sister, sailing with her blind brother for southern France. It was not the path she'd planned for herself.[10]

Her loving family soon followed. Her mother, Carrie, and younger brother, Albert, relieved her of the burden of Willy Jr.'s care. The family seemed to flourish abroad. Carrie—always so attuned to her daughter's health—wrote proudly to Will that Florie looked "wonderfully well . . . I never saw her more blossoming. Her color, eyes, teeth and hair are beautiful." True to Kelley form, Florie's coat and hat were shabby, but none of that detracted from her glow. Carrie benefited from time away from her tragic memories of the Elms as well; her daughter could not recall a time "when Mother was so rigorously, cheerfully, muscularly well!" By mid-1883, Will wrapped up his battle for the "Mongrel Tariff" and joined the family in England.[11]

With Will and Florie reunited, they naturally set out on one of their father-daughter fact-finding tours. Traveling across industrial parts of the English Midlands, the two cranks studied "unrestrained capitalism" at its very heart. In the "Black Country," Will and Florie met hungry laborers hauling coal carts from the mouths of dark pits and visited chain-makers' cottages where women sweated onto their anvils. But unlike their visit to Altoona's steel mills a decade before, father and daughter went looking for different lessons on this trip. Will sought evidence of American superiority, turning every instance of English suffering under free trade into a defense of America's protective tariff. The increasingly radical Florie went searching for ways around America's blockages, hunting out answers to her growing concerns about class, gender, and politics. Still, the pair relished their trip together. Florie "enjoys Will's fun intensely," observed Carrie. It would be one of their last happy times together.[12]

Florie found answers. For one thing, she learned that, while sexism still barred women's paths in Europe, there were openings for her not available in America. In Paris she noted how much finer she would find French society if she were a man, but also felt that "I can get more here than anywhere else, but only for the persistent asking." Her persistence pointed her toward the University of Zurich. The Swiss school would accept women for graduate degrees. Florie took a train into the mountains, writing to her new correspondent, Susan B. Anthony, that she would accept "from this little Swiss canton instructions which the University of my own state, would on principle refuse me." "If," she added sharply, "it had such instruction to bestow."[13]

Zurich might seem like the last place a burgeoning critic of capitalism would go. No nineteenth-century city was more orderly, more bourgeois, more restrained. But the Swiss financial capital attracted Florie with the promise of an education, charmed her with its lakeside ease, and radicalized her. Florie rented rooms with a "pretty outlook" on the lake and the Alps hovering beyond. She began to explore the winding stone streets, the impressive opera house, and the city's giddy nightlife of balls and concerts. And she delved into courses at the university, studying German, government, politics, and modern history. She was often the only woman in her classes.[14]

Though the city's dominant culture was wealthy, it was also the home of a burgeoning revolutionary underground. Because of its liberal policies, the university attracted foreigners, particularly women and Jews from Russia, barred from educational opportunities in that repressive empire. Political exiles from Austria, France, and Italy all flooded in as well. Florie mixed with this diverse cohort, discussing "the labor question" and trading books. One Russian Jewish medical student named Lazare Wischnewetzky— "well-bred" and impeccably mannered—snuck Florie rare books on political economy from a private library he had access to. His name, often misspelled, began to appear regularly in Florie's letters to Will and Carrie, along with the "pleasant conviction" that his "acquaintance we shall value increasingly as the year wears on."[15]

But even more enticing than dark-eyed medical students was the world of meetings, debates, and pamphlets roiling the radical Swiss subculture. Florie had known about socialism for years, ever since a visitor to the Elms, friends with both Will Kelley and Karl Marx, brought her communist pamphlets with flaming red covers. Learning of socialism, Florie wrote, was like learning that her abolitionist great-aunt boycotted sugar during slavery—a revelatory personal answer to a gnawing systemic problem. In Zurich, educated but frustrated, Florie's "mind was tinder awaiting a match."[16]

The spark came at her first socialist meeting, in the worn old room above a proper Swiss eating house, smelling of fried potatoes and broiled sausages. Florie joined the young students and the weathered laborers, feeling such excitement that she clutched the sides of her chair, trembling: "Here was I in the World of the Future!" Unlike America's cyclical democracy, socialism promised a Future, an inevitable revolution to come.[17]

Her first meeting addressed, fittingly, the problem of high tariffs, specifically in Bismarck's Germany. Probably no one in the meeting hall guessed that they were joined by the daughter of the architect of America's even higher tariffs. Florie had accepted much of her father's protectionist rhetoric, and prepared some of his arguments, but in that airless second-floor meeting hall she saw that, from the perspective of an international movement, high tariffs in one nation merely hurt the laborers in another. Her father's effort to protect America's working men and women further "crowded down" lives overseas.[18]

Though she studied the labor question in the heart of Europe, Florie never took her eyes off America. She began to reflect on her childhood rides through Philadelphia, on the "pastyfaced little working children in jail-like textile mills in Manayunk," and the growing "oppression of the recently emancipated Negro, by disenfranchisement and lynching" rising in the 1880s. Florie wrote about her concerns to her father, observing the way the wedge of the modern economy splintered the old harmony between labor and capital. Whereas Will's faith in protection depended on the notion that a strong economy benefited all, Florie was coming to accept the Marxian view that labor conflict was inevitable.[19]

Still the proud father, Will read her letters aloud in Congress. His voice now speaking for his daughter, Congressman Kelley quoted letters from "a young lady, now in Europe, who bears my name," admiring the "conclusions of this young but profound student of political science." Going further, he introduced eight-hour-day legislation in Washington and federal territories. Moving left with his daughter, at least rhetorically,

Will rumbled that if socialism means "the desire to achieve the best possible conditions for our laborers . . . I declare myself a socialist."[20]

Soon Florie's letters from Zurich found influential readers, including Susan B. Anthony. In early 1884, "the Major" wrote to Florie, asking her to stir her father to push harder for women's suffrage.[21] Florie wrote back with a sharp and observant letter, expressing a newly independent voice. Yes, of course, Florie wished "profoundly for the franchise for every woman in America" and felt "humiliated that my country does not confer upon me a responsibility to which I feel myself adequate, just as I am mortified that the Universities of America are closed to me." But Florie also defended her father, pointing to his lifetime of "labor for enabling all American working people, whether men or women, to emancipate themselves."[22]

The problem was not Will Kelley, Florie argued, but American voters. "Unhappily," Florie informed Anthony, "my father stands far in advance of his constituency upon this question. Neither the men nor the women of Pennsylvania support him to any helpful extent in carrying forward liberal measures for the Emancipation of Women."

Will was a politician, one who had already tested his voters' tolerance. Florie was beginning to see the limits on American electoral politics as a solution to social problems, looking beyond the campaign convulsions that ordered Will Kelley's and Susan B. Anthony's worlds, imagining a future unchecked by constituents.

Florie's frequent appearance in American papers made her a target. In 1884 the *New York Tribune* interviewed American women studying abroad, including Florie, who opined that American women's "position in respect to educational advantages is painfully like that of the negro at the close of the war." Her radicalism was making enemies. A vicious writer in the *Washington Post* spat out a deeply personal attack on "Congressman Kelley's daughter, Florence." Why was Florie wasting her time studying political science at all, the writer demanded? "As Pennsylvania shuts her courts and her caucuses on her, why doesn't she come here and be a nice little doctor"—a profession slightly more open to women. "Miss Florence" would never be "one of the boys" who run political machines, so who cared if she had a Swiss degree in politics?[23]

"As long as she can't vote," the writer taunted, "her father's hostler [stable keeper] can contribute more to the success of pig iron and practical politics than a dozen pretty girl graduates from political science classes." The harshest aspect of the attack was that, from the perspective of the all-consuming American political system, the writer was right. For all her education, wit, and worldliness, Florie could contribute little when it came time to campaign among the hostlers and the practical politicians.[24]

"PRETTY GIRL GRADUATES" might not have the vote, but in 1884 they were transfixed by the tawdry mess of a presidential campaign just like every-body else. Charlotte Conant, a student in western Massachusetts, wrote to her Republican father as she watched the race unfold. At the start, she was optimistic. In school they had studied "political machinery," and Charlotte pronounced: "The organization seems to be very just and fair." She begged her father to explain the inner workings of a campaign, peppered him with questions about what actually went on in political headquarters, assessed the quality of torchlight processions she had attended, and asked him to send campaign badges for her school friends to wear.[25]

By the end of that brutal race, however, Charlotte had turned a corner: "It had been a low sort of campaign." She hoped that the "election will be all over." And yet, like millions, she could not look away. Despite her disappointment with the race, she promised her father, one week before the 1884 election, that "next Wednesday I shall be early at the telephone to hear the news."[26]

For all the cranks looking for ways around the obstructions of American politics, millions more stood at the center, shaken by yet another convul-sion. And for all the criticisms of this very criticizable campaign, most did not turn away. Instead of following the cranks, America waded deeper into the race that many agreed was the "dirtiest, most disgusting and disgraceful our nation has ever known."[27]

For once, all that ugliness was partly the candidates' fault. The two previous presidential elections, in 1876 and 1880, showed that reformers like Hayes and Tilden, and nice guys like Garfield and Hancock, could sit atop dirty campaigns. But 1884 introduced a kind of personal mudslinging not seen for generations. The Republicans began the ugliness by nominating James G. Blaine, the most divisive man in their party (Conkling having retired). To many, Blaine was the exemplar of Republican statesmanship, known both as the enchanting "Magnetic Man" and as the "Plumed Knight" forever riding to his party's rescue. But to the growing population of reform-minded Republicans, Blaine looked like the definition of a "flashy, ambitious and selfish" politico, as William Dean Howells described him. This made him a good fit for his era, but bad publicity for a party promising to reform itself. Many pointed to rumors about Blaine's corruption stretching back to the Credit Mobilier scandal in 1872. One elderly letter writer, worrying about what had become of the Republican Party of his youth, considered Blaine's nomination "the negation of political virtue and the death of Republicanism."[28]

The punchy, florid Democratic magazine *Puck*, whose gaudy cartoons made even Thomas Nast's pale in comparison, depicted Blaine disrobing before his party, his monumental nude body tattooed with the names of all his scandals. "Mulligan Letters" across his belly, "N. Pacific Bonds" on his forearm, "Anti Chinese Demagoguism" scrawled down his shin.[29]

A small number of very vocal Republicans, the kind of squeaky-clean reformers who sided with George William Curtis, announced that they would rather vote for a Democrat than support Blaine's corruption. The press mocked them as "Mugwumps"—from an old Algonquian word meaning "war leader" or, in this case, a self-important bigmouth. Theirs was the first prominent break in the ironclad partisanship that had stifled American democracy for a generation. But such virtuous independents were outnumbered. Comedians joked that most men would vote for the devil if their party nominated him. Charlotte Conant simply asked her father to provide rejoinders for all the accusations against Blaine, wondering, "How can I show that none of the charges of corruption in politics against him have been proved?"[30]

On the other side, the Democrats were running a new, enticing figure. The New York governor Grover Cleveland did not act like a practical politician. Instead, he somehow accomplished the trick of being a career politician who seemed more like a well-fed businessman. He certainly didn't look like a tricky little wire-puller: Cleveland was monumental, over 275 pounds, with mitts for hands. His campaign surrogates bragged about the size of his neck; his nephews called him "Uncle Jumbo." He was a man most comfortable in hotel lobbies and chophouses. Cleveland's politics were conservative about the government's role in the economy, supportive of civil service reform, and active in their faith in executive power. There was something about his bland sturdiness that appealed to voters who wanted quiet politics for once. He was, at bottom, the opposite of a crank.[31]

But then the news of his "illicit connection" began to spread. Cleveland, it seemed, had fathered a child a decade ago with a widow in Buffalo named Maria Halpin. Hiding behind his image of bland rectitude, Cleveland openly admitted that he and Maria Halpin had a brief relationship—neither was married at the time—and claimed to have paid child support. Halpin asserted that she had been sexually assaulted by Cleveland and harassed by his goons ever since. The truth is unknowable, although Halpin's account is supported by an affidavit from a decade before the 1884 campaign. The scandal made Cleveland even more of a classic Victorian Man—hearty, conservative, and hiding a terrible secret.[32]

Republicans crowed. Already the party more willing to trumpet its Christian purity, they made Cleveland's sex life the center of their attacks. The *Congregationalist* newspaper denounced Cleveland's sins as "peculiarly demoralizing," even for a politician. Pointing to the first-time voters who admired Cleveland, the paper worried that young men would use his sins to "justify their own vicious courses."[33]

The differing Democratic and Republican responses to the scandal showed the alternate realities partisanship could generate. To Democrats, Cleveland's response was refreshingly forthright in an age of moral posturing. To Republicans, he was at best a libertine, at worst a rapist.

Forcing voters to choose between Cleveland's sexual crimes and Blaine's financial ones, the 1884 race seemed to affirm all the vulgarity that reformers had been denouncing. And though presidents usually remained above the fray, both candidates' personal reputations were in the gutter in 1884. The increasingly freethinking Howells equivocated that he would rather vote "for a man *accused* of bribery" (Blaine) than "a man *guilty* of what society sends a woman to hell for" (Cleveland). And he joked, to his buddy Mark Twain, that he wished he could vote for Maria Halpin. "She's the one who ought to be elected."[34]

The striking thing about all these scandals was how little impact they had. Sure, citizens gossiped and joked, but neither man's moral stains mattered once the regular campaign ramped up. The on-the-ground race in 1884 was as big and baroque as any in American history. Seizing on Blaine's nickname, "the Plumed Knight," the Republican Party chose a medieval theme, turning out marching companies wearing knight's helmets, colorful tunics, and waving torches shaped like battle axes. Fireworks reached a new scale in 1884; depictions of midnight marches show faux-knights marching through smoke-hazed streets, explosions overhead, their visors down and their torch-axes aloft. Real weapons supplemented the tin axes: to help monitor a particularly rough race in Cincinnati, the Republican National Committee shipped six hundred British bulldog revolvers to hastily deputized poll watchers. No financial misdeed, no sex scandal, could derail the two parties once campaigning got going.[35]

A new generation of immigrants had no idea how to interpret this loud, cynical democracy. Migration from Europe was up in the 1880s, and by 1890 America reached a still-unprecedented peak proportion of foreign-born citizens of 14.8 percent. Many wrote home trying to explain their new nation's contradictions. A Swedish railroad hand wrote from Illinois, impressed by the fantastic costumes of the midnight rallies he watched. Unlike in "old Sweden," where the lower classes showed "extreme indifference to all matters of state," in America "both the millionaire and the poor working man . . . all work with both hands and feet to get the party they belong to on top." But did it mean anything? A recent Dutch immigrant, the twenty-one-year-old Edward Bok, spent the 1884 race asking around his Brooklyn neighborhood, trying to figure out what differentiated the parties. He could hardly get a straight answer. Voters and marchers seemed indifferent about platforms and policies. "America," Bok later wrote, "fell short on the moment of most significance to me: that of my first vote!"[36]

Perhaps no one felt the growing darkness of American politics, and the thrilling dumbness of a campaign running hot, more acutely than Harriet Blaine. Over the years she had gone from an aloof judger of Reconstruction-era soirees (and reluctant eater of Will Kelley's doughnuts) to a pained spouse, watching her husband's "fiery ordeal." There was a time when a younger Harriet delighted in the political scrum. After the Republican victory in 1880 she lay in bed with James for hours, joyfully picking out Garfield's cabinet from among their friends. But Garfield's shooting, and the months she spent at his bedside, left a dim view of all Washington. She complained that the "election of a President every four years makes life very short." Her husband's nomination in 1884 dragged Harriet into the mud as well. Democrats, grasping for a titillating scandal in response to Cleveland's, argued that Harriet was six months pregnant when she married James.[37]

To Harriet, election night, 1884, was "all a horror to me." Inside the Blaines' towering brick fortress in Dupont Circle, Harriet, James, and the campaign staff felt "absolutely certain of the election." But then the nerve-trying reports began to come in, Harriet wrote: "the click-click of the telegraph, the shouting through the telephone in response to its never-to-be-satisfied demand, and the unceasing murmur of men's voices, coming up through the night to my room." Each new report threw her into nervous sweating and panicked chills. That night, like the morning she had learned that Gaffy had been shot, would "never go out of my memory."[38]

It is no surprise that, after years in the center of convulsion after convulsion, Harriet wrote, "I am so deeply disgusted with American politics, our whole system of popular government, with its fever, its passion, excitement, disappointment, and bitter reaction."[39]

Losing feels that way. But for Democrats, 1884 felt incredible. Grover Cleveland had been elected, the first Democratic president since 1856. Though today we might confuse Cleveland with the other silly-named presidents of his era, he was no Rutherford Hayes. His rise signaled a massive change in American politics. Between Lincoln and Roosevelt, he was America's most powerful executive. The vote was inconceivably close. Where Garfield won the popular vote in 1880 by a few thousand voters, Cleveland won New York State's electoral votes (and thus the election) by just 1,047 ballots. Barely one thousand men in New York State decided the race. There were probably one thousand Manhattan Mugwumps who switched from the Republicans to the Democrats in 1884, showing that independent bolters could determine the course of the nation.

There were also more than one thousand voters in Oneida County— Conkling's home district. Roscoe Conkling, still furious about his old feud with Blaine, refused to campaign for the Republicans. He joked that, though a lawyer, he would not "engage in criminal practice" of representing such a crook. Blaine lost Oneida, and with it New York, and with it the nation. All, perhaps, because of his old feud with Conkling over a line of poetry and a basket of champagne.[40]

The escalating suppression of Black voters in the South denied the Republicans far more than one thousand votes. The result was cyclical: the rise of a Democrat president meant less patronage to African Americans, which would further weaken Black campaign organizations and make it easier to steal votes from an already disenfranchised community. The forces of White supremacy could operate with even more impunity. Teachers in African American communities saw the future clearly, immediately assessing the threat to their schools. In Kansas, a Black man was shot dead in the street for "hurrahing" Blaine and the Republican Party. (He managed to shoot his assailant before dying.) Howells, the former abolitionist, predicted a future of "cold weather for people of our politics" to his father, foreseeing that the 1884 election meant "a great cycle has come to a close; the rule of the best in politics for a quarter of century is ended. Now we shall have the worst again."[41]

Washington's bedbugs would drink Democratic blood for a while. But they thrived on either party. The biggest takeaway from 1884 was how almost nothing could dim popular engagement, neither scandal nor disgust. "The vital, potent political forces still gather under the old ensigns," the reformist *Atlantic Monthly* was forced to admit, "although it would be hard for any one to say just what those ensigns now signify."[42]

Henry Adams, descendant of two presidents, put it best. Forget the cranks on the margins, the socialists in their meeting rooms. In the center of American society, "we are here plunged in politics funnier than words can express. The public is angry and abusive. Every one takes part. We are all doing our best, and swearing at each other like demons." Yet "the amusing thing is that no one talks about real interests. By common consent they agree to let these alone. We are afraid to discuss them. Instead of this the press is engaged in a most amusing dispute whether Mr. Cleveland had an illegitimate child."[43]

Those who claimed that democracy had failed were not quite right. Rather, to most Americans, failure didn't matter. They would play a broken game. The best anyone could hope for, Adams wrote ruefully, was that "a great political revolution seems impending. Yet, when I am not angry, I can do nothing but laugh."

−CHAPTER ELEVEN−

"A Young Lady, Now in Europe, Who Bears My Name"

The whole system is rotten from top to bottom. As rotten as rotten can be." Somewhere in the North Pacific, a loud American voice was expounding on the failure of democracy, a Western twang filling the dining mess of the SS *City of Peking*. Around him stood a mixed crowd—Americans, Brits, Japanese, and Indians—spending the "infinite monotony of a twenty days' voyage" from Yokohama to San Francisco, comparing their frustrations with their respective governments. Now the Americans had the floor, but the famously proud people sounded surprisingly bleak.[1]

One of the men in the crowd was Rudyard Kipling, the Indian-born English writer, already famous at twenty-three for his rhymes of adventure, manhood, and imperialist racism. He was traveling east to America, a nation he disdained. Kipling saw the U.S. as a cautionary example of the consequences of unrestrained freedom, swaggering and barbaric and self-impressed. Usually, he rolled his eyes at the way Americans "prostitute and pervert the English language." But onboard the *City of Peking*, he was impressed by the fluency with which members of the crowd were denigrating their own government.[2]

"They call us a Republic. We may be. I don't think it," contended a traveler from San Francisco, shaking his head. Despite Americans' dislike of English monarchy, "I know, and so does every man who had thought about it, that the Queen doesn't cost you one-half what our system of pure democracy costs us."[3]

"Politics in America?" the Californian went on. "There aren't any. The whole question of the day is spoils." All that money attracted the worst men to office. "No one," he declared, "but a low-down man will run for Congress and the Senate."[4]

An Englishman leaned over to Kipling and whispered in his ear: "If I weren't among Americans, I should say we were consorting with Russians."[5]

But the Americans went on. Their nation's problems were bigger than their borders; they pointed to the failure of the premise of democracy itself. Self-government was a swindle. "The more power you give the people, the more trouble they will give." One grizzled Yankee attested: "I have been three times round the world and resided in most countries on the Continent, that there was never people yet could govern themselves."[6]

The European nations passing democratic reforms were heading toward the same rapids that were sinking the American republic. Britain's respectable class would find itself in the same position as America's. "With us our better classes are corrupt and our lower classes are lawless. There are millions of useful, law-abiding citizens, and they are very sick of this thing." Britain should be wary of expanding suffrage to men without property. "When you reach our level,—every man with a vote and the right to sell it; the right to nominate fellows of his own kidney to swamp out better men,—you'll be what we are now—rotten, rotten, rotten!"[7]

For decades, Americans had been bragging that they were the greatest country on earth, the Californian declared. "No one cares to contradict us but ourselves; and we are now wondering whether we are what we claim to be."[8]

If there was ever a "bottom" to Americans' faith in their own democracy, a low point of confidence in the system, it came in the mid- to late 1880s.[9] Even in the stormy North Pacific, the rhetoric of failure was louder than the waves hammering the hull, a morose consensus shared by the middle-class Americans traveling back from Japan. The nation that the *City of Peking* was sailing toward contained sixty million people, with sixty million different views, but a kind of shrugging negativity about politics dominated public talk. Unlike the fierce rage of the 1870s, the failure of democracy was discussed as a widely agreed-on fact. Disillusionment did not mean disengagement—during these years citizens still zealously participated in huge numbers—but it did mean a resigned cynicism toward America's defining system.

Yet it was also in these depths of the political pessimism in the 1880s that we can first detect the outlines of a submerged new order, slowly rising to the surface. The political changes that would revolutionize American democratic life found their earliest expression in the crooked, booming, resigned High Gilded Age of the 1880s.

In the strangely twinned bond between the Kelley family and their government, this era marked an unforeseen crisis of family as well. But while attitudes toward democracy were dulled and cynical, feelings among the Kelleys ran dangerously hot.

Moving west to east across the nation Kipling was sailing toward, this shrugging cynicism showed itself again and again, marking an incredible change since the postwar era. In California, where in 1865 a congressman could believe "the one question of the age is *settled*," the *Los Angeles Times* now wrote that Americans' criticisms of politics were so widely shared that "there is little use in throwing stones at a dead dog. The evils that I speak of are well known to every citizen."[10]

In Kansas, where women's suffrage had been on the ballot in 1867, a combative practical politician could now explain that there was no hope for political reform in America. The *St. Louis Sunday Post-Dispatch* interviewed the Republican senator John Ingalls, an aggressive partisan with a habit of saying things that, the *Post-Dispatch* cautioned, may be "misleading, inconsistent and wrong, but they have always been vigorous and epigrammatic." Senator Ingalls brushed aside the notion of political reform. "There has not been an absolutely fair, free and impartial expression of the deliberate will of the people in any presidential election since the foundation of the Government," Ingalls argued, adding, "I doubt if there ever will be." There could be no restraints on the runaway race for power. "Force will coerce the timid, demagogueism will guile the credulous, fraud will rob the weak." Ingalls explained that there was no other way: brutal political warfare was inevitable. "Government is force. Politics is a battle for supremacy. Parties are the armies . . . In war it is lawful to deceive the adversary, to purchase mercenaries, to mutilate, to kill."[11]

Martial metaphors had long heated politics, but there was something in Ingalls's calls to rob, mutilate, and kill that captured the sense that American democracy was beyond a cease-fire.

Farther east, in the southern states where African Americans had built political organizations from scratch in the 1860s, hopes were crumbling. The end of Reconstruction did not immediately lead to the Jim Crow era of mass disenfranchisement. Instead, the 1880s existed as a murky twilight, with White supremacist Democrats encroaching and Black leaders painstakingly holding on to what they could. Lynchings were on the rise, nearly 40 percent higher than at the beginning of the decade. But there were still Black men, some of them former slaves, elected to Congress for a decade after the end of Reconstruction. Much of what they managed to salvage came not from voters supporting them from Mississippi or South Carolina but from careful dealings with White politicians in Washington, working with Republican friends to preserve diminishing power.

And in Pennsylvania, where Will Kelley once hoped citizens could come to express their views without resorting to "naming a party," attitudes toward democracy seemed both heated and frozen. Frederic Howe, an inquisitive young man in Meadville, Pennsylvania, paid keen attention to his town's strange attitude toward politics. On the one hand, elections were fervent and partisanship determined even which children he could play with as a boy. But at the same time, those alliances seemed to feed an alien occupation. "The thing that rules the state," Howe later reflected, "was like a nervous system of the human body. It had filaments in every township and every village. And the antennae responded intelligently, not to the will of the people, but to the will of something quite outside my scheme of things."[12]

In Howe's Pennsylvania, that nervous system was the Pennsylvania Republican machine, the largest and most powerful political structure in the country, dwarfing even Tammany Hall. It was run by Matthew Quay, a clever, quiet politician (and a recognized member of the Lenape Indian tribe), whose presence loomed over Howe's hometown. In Meadville, "few persons questioned the right" of Quay's cartel to dominate political life. "It did not seem improper." Most of Howe's elders remained faithful to Boss Quay. "He was a good organizer. He kept his word, rewarded his friends, and punished his enemies. That was political morality enough for

Meadville." Another rising boss, Mark Hanna of Ohio, summed up the politics of Pennsylvania as "corrupt and contented."[13]

When the *City of Peking* finally landed in America, Kipling found exactly the rot he was prepared to see. Moving east across the continent, Kipling only furthered his disdain for American men, his love of American women (he married one soon after), and his general sense that the nation represented a de-evolution from a higher European civilization.

Kipling loved imperialism, but he also loved the jungle. Wild, messy Gilded Age America somehow appealed to something in him. The nation's politics, in particular, embodied everything that made America unique, thrilling, and frustrating, unmoored and unrestrained, a study of human nature allowed too much freedom.

Kipling made his way east, chatting with journalists and writers and prominent locals from San Francisco to Chicago to Buffalo. Whenever he asked about the origins of some important politico, the answer came back: "Well, you see, he began by keeping a saloon." He began to make a study of saloon-democracy, noting the way crafty men with little else built empires by "keeping a liquor saloon and judiciously dispensing drinks." Like many tourists, he saw only the broadest stereotypes: bars full of "strong, coarse, lustful men," obese, bejeweled, swearing, smoking. Kipling met few voters and did not enjoy the compelling fun of a campaign or the unity that partisanship could offer the disrupted. Mostly, he aped what he had heard from the middle-class men in the middle of the Pacific— democracy was rotten. It had eaten away at America and would soon corrode Britain.[14]

America digested the famous writer and expelled him out its other end. By the time he set sail from New Jersey for Liverpool, Kipling had made a tourist's broad survey of the problems with American democracy. What he heard, although he did not recognize it, was a version of Francis Parkman's "Failure of Universal Suffrage" or James Russell Lowell's "honest wrath." In the late 1870s, the failure of democracy, equality, and majority rule had been an elite view. It hadn't penetrated the breadth of America's newspapers or millions of party members. But by the late 1880s, Kipling found that middle-class Americans, the kind living moderately above the class-splitting wedge, sounded more and more like Parkman from 1878. As an American bourgeoisie cohered, it accepted many of the sentiments of the gentlemen who did not vote. Something was spreading.

And it seemed unstoppable. E. L. Godkin, the disdainful editor of the *Nation* magazine, put it well, writing that "no government has ever come upon the world from which there seemed so little prospect of escape. It has, in spite of its imperfections and oddities, something of the majesty of doom." Pure democracy was no longer a thrilling experiment, Godkin wrote: "I have pretty much given it up as a contribution to the world's moral progress."[15]

JUDGE KELLEY HEADED east across the Atlantic in those years as well, but he did so in a desperate hurry. Will rushed aboard a Europe-bound ship in the summer of 1884 in response to a jarring letter from Florie. His wife, Carrie, who was with her in Switzerland, already knew what the note said. After years of receiving upsetting dispatches on Will's latest scrape, Carrie felt that Florie's news "cannot fail to give him shock." Will rushed to Switzerland to meet the man Florie had suddenly announced she would marry. Florie's note worried that her news would "bring you surprise and pain."[16]

"You were right," Will wrote back. In a letter that reached Florie before he could, Will tried to articulate precisely what hurt him about her announcement. He claimed to be particularly wounded, not that she chose to marry a man he did not know, half the world away, but that for the first time in their close relationship, neither my "advice nor consent have been invited." Struggling, for once, to keep his booming voice quiet, Will promised, "I will not thrust either upon you."[17]

Florie's decision marked a turn in those years, a willingness to make sudden changes. She was developing a confident spontaneity, inherited from her father, that "moving mass of boiling fluids." In the mid-1880s, Florie began a radical self-revision. In an age when frustrations with democracy led to shrugging stasis in America, Florie began to experiment and attack, developing new identities and crushing out old ones. She would be many things in these years, sometimes bold, sometimes cruel, but Florence Kelley was not one to shrug.[18]

Lazare Wischnewetzky was nearly as adamant, particularly in his courtship of Florie. At first, he was one among many admirers. A fawning newspaper article claimed that when she arrived at the University of Zurich, "every masculine student at once fell in love with her." Lazare came on particularly strong, bringing her obscure books and radical pamphlets, a gentlemanly presence with noble manners and seemingly ceaseless knowledge. He came from a wealthy Jewish family in Taganrog, a town in southern Russia experiencing waves of anti-Semitic pogroms and restrictive laws in the 1880s. This, along with his socialist politics, explained why he was studying in Zurich. Lazare was built along large lines, with a powerful jaw, full dark hair, and a physicality that looks by turns awkward, cocky, and looming in successive photographs. In her letters, Florie depicts Lazare as impressive or knowledgeable, but never funny or warm.[19]

Florie's views on her personal life were unusually shielded in these years. Fortunately, Carrie Kelley was staying in Switzerland and watched her daughter's courtship unfold. Initially, Carrie liked Lazare, describing him to Will Jr. as "an upright man, a gentleman in every sense of the word, and his affection for Florrie is as sincere and deeply-*rooted* as any that ever existed in the heart of a man. He is frank and truthful, and has no hidden motive. He is not looking for money or influence—has enough of both!" Carrie sought his opinion on medical questions, writing that she had "a great deal of faith in his judgment."[20]

But as Carrie watched her daughter, she saw signs. Sometimes, Florie complained about Lazare's intensity, the way "her adorer consumes rather more time than she thinks he is entitled to, but he does not see things precisely in that light." He was clearly in love with her, though perhaps too much. Florie told Lazare, early in their courtship, that she could never marry him, claiming that the idea of settling down in Europe was "utterly preposterous."[21]

And yet, in the spring of 1884, Florie announced that she would wed Lazare. Carrie told Will "I have never felt quite right" about that strange, sudden turn, "but I did not oppose it too much, because she would have been so unhappy." Soon after, Carrie's letters to Will, which were well preserved from the 1850s until the 1890s, disappear. They seem to have been deliberately destroyed.[22]

When Will arrived in Switzerland, the family spent an awkward summer in their rooms overlooking Lake Zurich and the mountains beyond, struggling to bond with Lazare. They resigned themselves to the idea of Florie making a permanent life in Europe. It must have felt like a terrible loss. Will was back in America, though—battling through the year's sleazy presidential campaign—on October 14, 1884, when his only surviving daughter married Lazare at a spare civil ceremony.

Florie was already a minor political celebrity in America, delighting editors as an attractive, well-connected source of quotable radicalism. News of her sudden marriage hinted at buried drama. Will had struggled to keep Florie's engagement out of the papers, rushing to Europe without telling anyone, "to make our friends believe I have been consulted." But he could not shield his daughter. Gossip columns erroneously reported that she had married a mysterious Russian duke or "some sort of a scion of Polish royalty." None seem to have realized that Lazare was, at least by background, Jewish, at a time of rising anti-Semitism in America. Other reporters picked up on Will's unhappiness, declaring that when he learned of Florie's plans to marry, "her father was very angry at first." One columnist merely joked that the always bold Florence was "brave enough to change the name of Kelley for that of Wischnewetzky."[23]

Florie and Lazare's married life was less exciting. The pair spent much of their time together operating as a radical translating team, Lazare rendering Russian Marxist tracts into German, and Florie translating them from German to English. They settled into a quiet routine, studying, visiting public reading rooms, coffeehouses, or the opera, and spending much time at home. "We are happier together in our nook," Florie wrote. Within a month or two of their marriage, she was pregnant.[24]

Most Victorian women greeted pregnancy as a fundamental shift toward a maternal identity in all aspects of life. But Florie saw motherhood as something exciting she did along the way toward her greater passions. She claimed to feel "not the slightest anxiety" about giving birth, and continued to work at her translating. A photograph of her during her pregnancy shows those familiar dark inquiring eyes and full mouth, but also a bit of gauntness around her cheekbones, and a new air of authority as well. One can sense her growing gravitas, her room-filling charisma, the reason that "young men were not entirely at ease in her presence."[25]

As she was growing a new life, over the winter and spring of 1885, Florie dramatically reshaped her old existence. Perhaps it was marriage and impending motherhood, or her new socialist dogmas, or a longer evolution that had been brewing since childhood. Whatever the source, Florie went to intellectual war with capitalism, democracy, and her family's complicity in both. It all began with a little book.

Before her marriage, in 1883, when Will and Florie traveled across England studying industrial conditions, they collaborated on a series of letters on working-class struggles, combining Florie's knowledge of social science with Will's protectionist hostility to English free trade. Will helped Florie shape those letters into a little book, and Houghton Mifflin agreed to publish it on "most favorable terms." It was to be the signal achievement in the intellectual bond they had nurtured since Florie was a little girl. Some, like the journalist Frank Carpenter, anticipated it eagerly. But Houghton Mifflin held the book for nearly a year, wanting it to coincide with the 1884 election. In the meantime, Florie changed immensely.[26]

By the time the book was due to be published during the raging 1884 race, Florie was a Marxist with little faith in either protection or democracy. "I outgrew it," she wrote to her friend May Lewis, a suffrage and labor activist from Altoona, Pennsylvania. Florie worried that the book "could be used for advocating Mr. Blaine and Protection and I believe in neither." Even though portions of the book were already being printed, Florie sent a curt telegram to her father insisting: "STOP PUBLICATION. FLORENCE KELLEY WISCHNEWETZKY." An angry publisher pulled the book and made Florie pay the costs. But the greater damage was done to her relationship with her father.[27]

Will, Florie accused, "wanted the book for campaign purposes and has made my suppression of it—in spite of my elaborate explanations that I could not publish what I no longer believe—the cause of profound unhappiness." Perhaps Florie was right, and Will's history of prioritizing campaigning over everything else in his life made him blind to how much Florie had changed. Or maybe he was still angry with Florie about her sudden marriage.[28]

Soon a larger scandal erupted. The American press began to print baseless claims that Florie's "Russian Nihilist" husband "forbade me," in Florie's words, "to publish the poor little worthless book for fear of the Russian authorities." Carpenter implied that Florie's recent marriage to "the Russian nobleman with the unpronounceable name" had scuttled the project, which Will Kelley had hoped would be the capstone of his career and a foundation of his daughter's. Florie would visit the English-language newspaper rooms in Zurich and Heidelberg, now visibly pregnant, and spend the morning reading falsehoods about herself in various American publications. Will waded into the mess, trying to keep Florie out of the scandal sheets and pointing an angry finger at Houghton Mifflin. The newspapers continued to print the gossip, now adding that Florie's marriage to Lazare was failing and that she was causing "great sorrow to Judge Kelley."[29]

The fight over the little book exposed Florie's growing disillusionment with America. To her, it felt like the whole American "scandal-press" was pouring "cruel miserable slander" down on her. Florie lashed out. Her dawning socialism mingled with her frustrations with the press, with Houghton Mifflin, with the University of Pennsylvania, and with her father. Soon it grew into a rejection of America altogether and predictions of its impending demise. Over the second trimester of her pregnancy, in the spring of 1885, Florie spelled out her fury in a series of letters to her friend May Lewis. Every paper she read "brings tidings of the coming revolution which you, who are living among the volcanoes, probably do not recognize as such."[30]

What Florie saw was the incapability of democracy to solve class problems. She grumbled about the women's suffrage movement's fixation on the "wretchedly narrow horizon" of winning the ballot. Middle-class women's focus on electoral democracy was, to Florie, merely a way of taking "refuge behind the ballot . . . to escape the Labor question." Unable to see beyond their campaign obsessions, Americans fixated on the next vote, the next canvass, the next scandal. Even radical suffragists were tragically myopic. The only solution, short of class revolution, would be "getting rid of our fourth years' meaningless turmoil"—ending presidential campaigns. But worse than a few women's suffrage activists, Florie blamed the millions of workingmen who had been tricked into partisanship, and the politicians who deceived them. "Ordinary, non-socialized workers let themselves be hoodwinked by Free-Trade and Protection professional politicians," Florie condemned. Politicians like her father.[31]

Florie knew that she was rejecting something personal. She did not shy from attacking her father, the man who had raised her as a thinker and reader and arguer. He made his fame profiteering from America's crooked politics, Florie wrote to May Lewis, tricking workers into thinking he could help them, when only revolution could do that. Even his pose as a workingman was a sham. "My father," Florie wrote, "would never have become a member of Congress if he had stuck to his printing or his diamond settling; but he abandoned his craft and became a lawyer ie entered the privileged class."[32]

Florie's view of her brother Willy Jr. was no gentler. Willy, she wrote, was busily exploiting those same privileges, having recovered from his blindness and become Philadelphia's assistant city solicitor and an active Republican stump speaker. "Not in a thousand years" could Willy have achieved this, Florie accused, "without the paternal name and fame." Even her family's wealth and comfort came from "embarrassed land" that Will had bought with money he earned as a lawyer, a career almost as parasitic as that of a politician. On that "embarrassed land" sat the Elms, leafy, quiet, and cool, a home she was leaving behind.[33]

Very late in her pregnancy, as she made her increasingly uncomfortable way to the English reading rooms, Florie came to a kind of furious clarity. She received a letter from her father, fewer and farther between in those days, applauding Willy's "success as a political speaker before masses of work men." Will Kelley was proud of his son for once. In his spare time, her father bragged, Willy was going to the city armory, to practice "riot drill" with fellow middle-class Philadelphians. As income inequality grew, as the wedge pressed the working classes ever downward, riots became a perennial fear of propertied urban society. Bourgeois Americans reacted by joining militias, building city armories, and banning armed public marches by workers. Now a Kelley, part of a lineage supposedly devoted to helping working people, was training with a rifle and bayonet "to shoot down workmen in the expected riots."[34]

Reading Will's letter, Florie felt a "realizing sense of the mortal conflict that is inherent in the nature of the two classes." That same conflict was inherent in her family as well. Since seeing her father's handwriting, once a source of wisdom, Florie wrote, "I have had no peace of mind."[35]

Later that same month, Florie's contractions started. It was an easy birth, and Florie and Lazare were thrilled to meet Nikolai Wischnewetzky. He had, even from the youngest photographs, his mother's searching eyes and full, resolved mouth. Florie doted on "Ko," dismissing the nurse Lazare hired and pushing him over Zurich's bumpy cobblestones in "a funny arc of a baby coach" made of wicker, with red curtains and a leather roof. She fed him a Nestle's formula, that new Swiss invention, and dressed him in woolen diapers. Though she would not let motherhood interfere with the rest of her goals, Florie loved Ko immensely, reporting the thrill she felt when, if tired or hungry, he called out for his "mama."[36]

As Florie settled into the life she had made for herself in Switzerland, she began to broadcast her confrontational new views. While pregnant, she undertook to translate Friedrich Engels's *The Condition of the Working Class in England*. Engels had become, after Marx's 1883 death, the central force guiding international socialism, and his breakthrough 1845 work had never been made available in English. Florie saw an opportunity to publicize this work and to print a rejoinder to the "poor little worthless book"— also on the English working classes—that she had so painfully outgrown. Working diligently, Florie completed her translation while eight months pregnant. It is still considered the best English-language version. She began to correspond with Engels, a witty, jovial polymath, editing the work and considering how to grow socialism in the English-speaking world. In her letters, Florie began to express her new, unvarnished views on American democracy. As Florie, just twenty-six years old, wrote to the elder statesman of the growing international movement, she began to mix incisive, systemic criticism with a glowing personal anger.[37]

She focused on the failure of American workers to move beyond practical politics, clinging to "the old parties" instead. She pointed to the 1884 presidential campaign as proof that "the masses, themselves, are in a state of confusion incredible if it were not proved at every election." The recent presidential campaign "turned upon no principle whatsoever. The sole question was, 'who is the least of a rascal?' That was all the enlightenment that the whole struggle between the old parties offered." Those old parties worked assiduously, Florie accused, to keep voters thinking small. "The Free Trade-Protectionist ding-dong has been clanged and droned into the workingmen's ears for generations," Florie wrote. "Workingmen take up the chorus."[38]

Florie offered a strong answer for the perennial question asked of the era—"Why no socialism in America?" A worldview that was burgeoning across Europe was barely known in the United States. The comparative wealth of American laborers has long offered some explanation—the German thinker Werner Sombart blamed too much "roast beef and apple pie." But the popularity of the two political parties offered working-class Americans a stake in the political system. Their intimate bond to the Democratic or Republican parties pointed many away from the cause of socialist revolution.

Though neither protection nor free trade held out much promise for struggling American laborers, Florie's condescension was palpable. Those workers (and family members) who disagreed with her revolutionary views were suffering from "confusion." She dismissed the two largest political organizations in American life—powerful institutions with millions of members and a palpable physical presence in nearly all communities—as the antiquated "old parties."[39]

Florie's rage at her father's role in this fraud was obvious. No American figure had so energetically promoted protectionism as a solution to working people's problems, and here his daughter was badmouthing this project to the head of international socialism. Clearly referring to her statistics-crank of a dad, Florie complained about the way certain American politicians relied on "skillful perversions" of labor data to convince workingmen that America's tariffs were working. In an 1886 letter she specifically attacked Will's career, writing to Engels about the misguided workers in Pennsylvania "electing for the fourteenth time to the twenty-eight consecutive year of service, as their representative in Congress my Father whose sole wisdom is praise of American protective tariff." Florie criticized those same voters for also electing her brutish brother Willy as assistant city-solicitor, though he "is among the first at the shooting down 'rioters' in every disturbance."[40]

Persistent, vocal, unrestrained Florence Kelley could never have kept these political views from affecting her personal relationships. Few of her letters to her family from this era survive—conveniently absent, like her mother's views on her marriage—but it is clear that she was growing estranged. Sometime after Ko's birth, Florie stopped writing home. For nearly two years, she did not communicate directly with her parents, formerly the most important people in her world. "Affectionate intercourse," Will wrote, had ceased "between our poor daughter and us."[41]

Will and Carrie had parented eight children. Three were still alive. Of them, they had a single grandson, living in Switzerland, of whom they heard nothing. The pain must have been excruciating.

Florie did more than neglect her brother Willy. Outraged by his membership in a militia, she sent him a furious letter, criticizing him with "demented" language that Willy thought would have been inappropriate "addressed to a dog." Willy Jr. complained to Carrie about his sister's "nihilist views." He claimed to be shocked by her aggression, writing "she is a savage as the Tartar"—an ignorant reference to her Russian Jewish husband. Perhaps more accurately, Willy Jr. sensed a "terrible anger" in her, "in insult to her right self." He believed that her "letters are her cries of pain," but wondered "has it not been self-inflicted? She has disregarded the happiness of all who love her."[42]

What was Florie doing? Why was she lashing out, specifically and articulately, at the foundations of her former identity? Was Lazare poisoning her against her family? Or was she going through a late adolescence, rejecting, in her twenties, the basis of a childhood she felt ready to leave behind? Maybe she carried legitimate anger at her unusual childhood—her mother's overprotection, her father's political obsession, her nation's failings?

It is too easy to attribute her turn to the men in her life, jumping from father figure to father figure. Will Kelley, Lazare Wischnewetzky, and Friedrich Engels were all handsome, looming, bearded intellectuals. (Engels's cascading beard was truly extravagant.) But to do so denies Florie the credit she deserves. Florence Kelley was responsible for her own politics and the new worldview she shaped in those years.

Florie's rebellion was striking because it affirmed the fundamental values she had been raised to hold dear. Even in her bitterness, she was not rejecting her father's views, but clutching them so tightly that his efforts looked partial. Florie had organized her life around the principle of protecting working people, around the lessons from Will that started with that grim book in the Elms library when she was seven. This was not the usual contrarian rebellion of one generation denouncing its elders. Florie expressed her fury with her family, and with American politics, because they seemed insufficiently committed to working men and women. To Florie, the political institutions designed to uphold America's highest values—"the old parties," the "fourth years' meaningless turmoil," the "American scandal-press," and "refuge behind the ballot"—were all evidence of systemic failure. Taken together, she sounds like Parkman condemning "organized ignorance, led by unscrupulous craft, and marching amid the applause of fools, under the flag of equal rights."[43]

But more than anyone, Florence Kelley sounds like Will Kelley. Even at her angriest, Florie demonstrated the depth of her intellectual connection to her father. She held fast to his mission while rejecting his mechanisms. American journalists who read her work in those years could not help but see the parallels, noting the way Florie's "mind has something of the strong pig-iron cast which distinguishes her father." Florie was Will intensified: iron refined into steel.[44]

And she was not alone. A generation rising in the late 1880s would push back against the sense that American politics would always be irredeemably rotten. The sharp-eyed reform writer John Jay Chapman reflected, a decade later, on the slow process by which the younger generation began to scorn their fathers' politics. Many came to view their fathers as unthinking, tribal, cowardly partisans who could be "whistled back to support iniquity by an appeal to party loyalty." Men who acted as though "they must daub themselves with party names or they would catch cold." The criticism is hardly fair for a father like Will Kelley, who so often wrestled with the strictures of partisan loyalty. But otherwise, Chapman might as well have been quoting from Florie's letters to Engels.[45]

By the fall of 1886, Florie's time in Europe was over. Another ship crossed the ocean, and Florence, Lazare, and Ko landed in New York City. Florie was carrying her second child as well. They did not plan to stay in America for long, but her pregnancy, Lazare's failure to find work, and political entanglements kept the growing family in Manhattan. For a full year there, she did not contact her parents.

When the young family sailed into New York, their ship cruised past the new Statue of Liberty, its luminous not-yet-green copper gleaming over the harbor. Congressman Kelley had, naturally, been invited to that dedication ceremony. The statue had, in a way, followed Florie for years: she had first seen it as merely a disembodied torch-clutching arm, mounted at the 1876 Centennial Exposition. Then, she was just a precocious girl, realizing how much she would have to fight to get her questions answered. Now, she was returning to America a decade later with her own answers, witnessing the Gilded Age's heavy-handed metaphors—a torch passed to her generation as Will Kelley's began to retire. The Kelleys were always right on time—Jacksonian in the 1830s, abolitionist in the 1860s, feuding about the direction of the nation in the 1880s. Passing that torch was an awkward process, riven with hostilities, particularly in a democracy where torchlight meant so much.

– CHAPTER TWELVE –

"Reformers Who Eat Roast Beef"

T he snow was already falling when Roscoe Conkling left for his Wall Street office on March 12, 1888. Out of politics since 1881, Lord Roscoe was a private citizen again, ever since his self-destruction in a feud with President Garfield. Then came Guiteau, the excruciating death of a president, the nation's accusing fingers pointed at Roscoe's rhetoric. So Conkling burnt his correspondence, returned to private practice, and avoided the public. He wandered incessantly around empty stretches of upper Manhattan, shunning public transportation, the recognition of strangers, and the specter of another Guiteau coming after him.[1]

Conkling flourished as a corporate lawyer. He represented Joseph Pulitzer and numerous steamship and railroad corporations. In his most influential case—*San Mateo County v. Southern Pacific Railroad Company*—Roscoe convinced the Supreme Court that the Fourteenth Amendment had meant to include corporations as people, arguing that he was one of the congressmen in the room when that amendment was written. As much as any partisan battle, Conkling's argument for corporate personhood would shape America's political future.[2]

And then, around midnight on March 12, 1888, the snows began. A balmy spring turned cold, the wind picked up, and the East Coast was hit with one of the greatest blizzards in its history. From Boston to

Washington, snow fell hard and fast, depositing twenty inches in some places, nearly sixty in others. Winds gusted to eighty miles an hour, piling huge drifts of fifty feet or more. Manhattan closed down. Photographs show a city abandoned halfway through construction, crackling webs of icy telegram wires, snow drifts rising higher than the elevated tracks, the new Brooklyn Bridge standing like some frozen monolith. The *Times* screamed: "NEW-YORK HELPLESS IN A TORNADO OF WIND AND SNOW."[3]

But Conkling would not be helpless. A man who had dominated the politics of that era—who could intimidate Slave Power bullies, crush Democrats, sabotage Republicans, stomp out reformers, and fire a madman with enough outrage to gun down a president—was also the kind of man who walked to work in a blizzard. Yet by the end of a full day of heavy snow, he was faced with a daunting walk back to his opulent rooms in the Hoffman House hotel, at Twenty-Fourth and Broadway. Conkling set out through a lonely metropolis in a swirl of snow and wind, groping his way blindly north.[4]

His six foot three inches of boxer's muscle were hardly enough—snow accumulated to his armpits, slammed him back, and encrusted his mighty copper beard. He thought of Russian novels, of peasants grimly traipsing across trackless steppes. But he was crossing Union Square, the center of America's largest city. Where vendors once sold sausages and lemonade, where uniformed partisans waved torches in campaign rallies, now there was nothing but howling wind and blowing snow. Conkling ground to a halt in the middle of the park, incapable of moving on. He swayed blindly, a lonely silhouette buffeted by the ceaseless blizzard at the heart of American public life. "I came as near giving right up and sinking down there to die as a man can and not do it."[5]

Eventually he found a last reserve and pushed on. By the time he collapsed into the warm glow of the New York Club at Twenty-Fifth and Broadway, Conkling's fastidious clothing was encrusted with ice, and the gentlemen of the club could hardly believe he had walked up from Wall Street.

For a week or two Conkling seemed to have recovered, but then he fell gravely ill. Doctors believed that an abscess had formed between his ear and his brain, caused by exposure and exertion in the storm. He hovered—like Garfield—in prolonged, excruciating pain. He paced wildly, cursing and hallucinating. It took several Hoffman House porters to hold him down for doctor's investigations. To his friend, the politician and financier August Belmont, Conkling described his days of "darkness and disorder," of "limitless agony."[6]

And then, on April 18, 1888, Roscoe Conkling died. The African American press honored him as a protector who never abandoned the fight. His enemies still hated him enough to publish denunciations of a dead man seven years out of politics. The *New York Herald* commemorated the passing of a crucial but corrosive presence. "His controversies made history," the *Herald* wrote. "We have lost the most aggressive leader in American politics." That aggression had made him the most dominant politician from the most dominant party during its most dominant phase. It also sank his career and ultimately took his life. "Roscoe is finished," the statesman John Hay had written when Conkling blew up his career. His fall amounted to a suicide, "the logical result of the personality of Conkling and the workings of the Boss system."[7]

Conkling's death also signaled how that system had changed. The sledgehammer bosses of the 1860s and '70s, who dominated politics with aggression and braggadocio, were dying out. The flamboyant Lord Roscoes and vengeful Squire McMullens were evolving into quiet, clever executives, running their machines like businesses, not armies. "The boss is a product of natural selection," the *Atlantic Monthly* reasoned, and the big old dinosaurs were being outcompeted by nimble mammals, men who understood "the arts of management." Men who could keep their mouths shut. The Boston boss Martin "the Mahatma" Lomasney ruled under the motto "Never write if you can speak, never speak if you can nod, never nod if you can wink." These bosses found in self-restraint a power those raging old warriors never appreciated.[8]

But they were *bosses* nonetheless, labor contractors who managed the campaign economy. There was no better metaphor. In an industrial age, bosses were political foremen who kept the machine running. The next question, then, for those cool, cunning new executives, was whether their machines needed to be so noisy. Conkling's death signaled an end to something. The Blizzard of March 1888 felt blinding, but it came very late in winter, and a thaw was on its way.

OVERLOOKING THE SPOT in Union Square where Conkling contemplated sinking down into the snow, another dinosaur was making his last stand. James Russell Lowell, the democratic-skeptic poet who imagined the Goddess of Columbia's "spiteful tears" at the Centennial Exposition, gave a landmark speech as Conkling was dying. Lowell had grown into an elder laureate, his clothes still threadbare, his poet's beard ennobled with wobbly tusks of mustache. And his views had evolved beyond "honest wrath." In the last phase of a long career, Lowell took the stage in Steinway Hall on Union Square, stared out at 2,500 well-to-do Manhattanites lit by seven hundred flickering gaslights, and explained how to save democracy.

"It is admitted on all hands," Lowell declared, that American politics "have been growing worse for the last twenty years." Partisanship, patronage, and a cynical press were to blame, but so was the "splendid complacency" of the wealthy who had left politics to the lower classes. But their abstaining hadn't solved America's problems. Respectable Americans must reengage politics on a practical level, Lowell proclaimed. This meant more than giving sermons and writing articles; it meant delving into the mechanisms of democracy. If politicians had become "majority manufacturers" whose "tricks of management are more and more superseding the science of government," the solution had to be equally mechanistic. "If the parties," Lowell told his audience, "will not look after their own drainage and ventilation, there must be people who will do it for them."[9]

Lowell predicted that this would be the greatest crusade in American history. In 1861, he reminded his audience, the Union fought "to prevent half their country being taken from them." But the corruption of democracy was "slowly and surely filching from us the whole of our country." The battle for political reform was, to Lowell, a cause more crucial than crushing secession or ending slavery. In the 1860s "they emancipated the negro; and we mean"—Lowell declared without shame or irony—"to emancipate the respectable white man."[10]

The *Atlantic Monthly* thrilled to Lowell's new momentum. Yes, huge numbers still turned out for partisan rallies, burning with "undiminished zeal for racket and rocket," but an "emancipation from conventional ideas of what politics means" was underway. Both Lowell's and his reviewer's use of the term *emancipate* points to their sweeping hopes for major change. Many sensed that, bad as democracy looked, it was on the verge of something transformative. Hopeful reformers in Chicago's eminent Sunset Club declared that a political system "is already far advanced towards reform when its failure is acknowledged." All that grumpiness about democracy signaled a turning point.[11]

Elite reformers, the persona comic Mr. Dooley joked, had long tried "to get into office on a flyin' machine." But the odds were better for the man who "tunnels through." Between 1886 and 1890, political reform began to abandon the "flying machine" approach of stern lectures about good and evil. A new generation started to tunnel through. They began to consider the mechanisms by which "majority manufacturers" had won control. If people wanted good politicians, a Prohibition activist declared, it was not enough to point to the sins of bad men in Congress. "They must provide machinery for electing" better men. Focusing on the tricks of management would also obscure the goal of suppressing popular participation. Bold disenfranchisements like the Tilden Amendment of 1877—which would have stolen the vote of 69 percent of New Yorkers—would always fail. Instead, respectable reform shifted its focus from who should vote to how.[12]

Over these same years, money had played an increasing role in politics. Even as gentlemen refused to vote, they threw their cash around. In a society with few checks on wealth, businesses could easily buy favors, and politicians were happy to benefit from—or extort—the wealthy. Matt Quay, the quiet, cool Pennsylvania boss who replaced Conkling as the most powerful man in America, famously called politics the "art of taking money from the few and the votes from the many under pretext of protecting one from the other." After President Garfield's patronage-inspired assassination, Congress passed the Pendleton Civil Service Act, which effectively ended the practice of "assessments," where parties raised election funds by demanding a cut of office seekers' salaries. In its place, men who already had money stepped in to bankroll campaigns. Tycoons astutely played all sides, like the financier Jay Gould, who declared that, as he bribed his way across America, "I was a Republican in Republican districts, a Democrat in Democratic districts." But the "emancipation" of the 1880s saw a shift from nose-holding businessmen offering secret bribes to a wave of young elites publicly reengaging electoral democracy. In addition to the rise of money-in-politics, reformers were proposing a rise of the moneyed-in-politics.[13]

"The respectable white man" was changing as well. As they refocused on political mechanisms, elite reformers began to ally with a wider swath of the upper-middle classes. The aristocratic reformers who spoke Latin and lived on named estates had been easy to dismiss. By the late 1880s, reformers deliberately widened their definition of "respectable" to include what one Chicago group referred to as "business and professional men of all classes." Reform needed this swath of white-collar brainworkers: men in mustaches and top hats who dined on roast beef at businessmen's eating houses; women in the sleek new fashions of the 1880s, who asserted their class identity by buying a piano or planning a summer vacation. It was a population that would vote for "prosperity" above all other causes. The Republican Party had made an appeal to this demographic with their "top hat" campaign in 1888, when marchers wielded torches shaped like that most dignified of headgear. After all, this population hungered for respectability, and their votes would expand reform from a tiny sliver of elites to the much larger bloc of Americans rising above the wedge of Gilded Age income inequality.[14]

For much of the 1800s, American politics had meant an alliance of the laboring and middle classes—which often alienated the very wealthy. But by the 1880s, a new white-collar coalition of the upper and upper-middle classes—with the working classes on the sidelines—would redefine democracy.

To appeal to these "intelligent and business classes," reformers shifted their metaphors. Instead of references to classical literary figures, activists began citing "the science of government," the new cult of efficiency, and the arts of business, management, and engineering.

One figure who would artfully appeal to this broad upper-middle class got a rocky start. In 1882 a young man burst into New York's Morton Hall Republican club with such verve that it appeared "as if he had been ejected by a catapult." The roughly dressed practical politicians stared on as the grinning youth pulled off his overcoat, revealing full dinner dress, elegant gloves, and pince-nez glasses suspended by a silk cord. Theodore Roosevelt Jr. seemed more like a caricature of an effete reformer than a streetwise politico. "He looked like a dude," one said disapprovingly of the twenty-four-year-old. But within a few years, "Teedie" Roosevelt would make himself the physical manifestation of the new, more muscular vision of reform.[15]

Theodore Jr.'s daughter once joked that her dad wanted to be "the bride at every wedding, and the corpse at every funeral." It is important to rein in his irrepressible drive to make himself the center of every story. Later tellings of this era portray Roosevelt as the chief savior of American democracy. But really, his role was to provide substance to the new vision to reform, tacking back from elitist moralism and appealing to a class of newly upper-middle-class voters. Roosevelt was not an innovator but more of an early adopter. Over his life, Teddy would make a great show of throwing himself into manly, dangerous occupations foreign to his patrician upbringing. But before he became a cowboy, a soldier, a hunter, or an explorer, Roosevelt fought to "hold my own in the rough and tumble," by making himself something men of his class traditionally shunned: a politician.[16]

It happened soon after the death of his father. Before Theodore Sr.'s public savaging by Conkling and tragic death, young Teedie had wanted to become a scientist. But afterward he "began to take an interest in politics," compelled to prove himself in the bare-knuckle combat where his father had faltered. Starting in 1880, Theodore Jr. began asking around elite social clubs about how to enter New York's Republican machine. The fellows laughed at him. They warned him that he would find himself surrounded "by saloon-keepers, horse-car conductors, and the like," men who "would be rough and brutal and unpleasant to deal with." Rough and brutal was exactly what Theodore was looking for. So he sought out a local political club, declaring: "I intended to be one of the governing class"—at a rare moment in human history when the governing class and the moneyed class were two distinct entities.[17]

His incorrigible confidence won admirers. As a speaker, Roosevelt never developed great oratorical skills, but he was probably the most vigorous

On the evening of January 31, 1865, the House of Representatives passed the Thirteenth Amendment to the Constitution, banning slavery. Though not identified, one of those bearded, seated men may be William Kelley, describing the momentous events to his wife and daughter.

Congressman William Darrah Kelley, also known as "Pig Iron Kelley," "Judge Kelley," "Centennial Kelley," "the Father of the House," and Florie Kelley's Papa. Taken ca. 1860–1875, when Kelley was somewhere between forty-six and sixty-one.

Photograph of Florence Kelley, taken during her intellectual awakening in her early twenties, either while she was attending Cornell or when she was intimidating congressmen, debutantes, and cranks in Washington, ca. 1879–1883.

Wide Awake campaign club and rival Douglas campaign club, as depicted by a French cartoonist struck by the vibrant politics of the 1860 presidential election.

Child-size campaign cape from the 1880 presidential campaign, showing the proliferation of the Wide Awakes' style of caped, torch-bearing marching clubs across American democracy, to even the littlest of partisans.

A rare, casual photograph of a partisan marching club, in this case California Republican campaigners supporting Henry Markham in the 1890 gubernatorial race.

Though less common than male campaign clubs, women's clubs did march in partisan rallies, like these Republican "Ladies of Wataga (Illinois) for McKinley," from the 1896 presidential campaign.

Thomas Nast's 1869 Thanksgiving cartoon demonstrates the peak of faith in the promise of "Pure Democracy." Shortly after the passage of the Fifteenth Amendment, which used Will Kelley's text to make it illegal to deny citizens the right to vote based on race, Nast envisioned a diverse, peaceful nation, joining Black, White, Asian, and Latino figures around the centerpiece of "universal suffrage." Such triumphant faith in Pure Democracy would not last long after 1869.

Former slaves voting in their first election, in New Orleans in 1867. After centuries of slavery, and just one year after the brutal massacre of dozens of African American activists in New Orleans, this moment surely felt promising to the voters, hangers-on, and boys and girls present. Over the next few years, Louisiana would elect 210 African American officeholders, including the first Black governor in U.S. history.

FRANK LESLIE'S ILLUSTRATED NEWSPAPER

No. 891—Vol. XXXV.] NEW YORK, OCTOBER 26, 1872. [Price, 10 Cents. $4 00 Yearly. 13 Weeks, $1 05.

NEW YORK REPEATERS DRIVING BUCKALEW VOTERS FROM THE POLLS.

POLICEMEN ARRESTING CITIZENS FOR CHALLENGING THE VOTES OF NEGRO REPEATERS.

THE ARRIVAL OF THE NEW YORK REPEATERS, ENGAGED BY THE HARTRANFT PARTY, AT THE RAILROAD DEPOT, WEST PHILADELPHIA.

THE PHILADELPHIA ELECTION FRAUD.—From Sketches by Albert Berghaus.—See Page 102.

By the early 1870s, faith in democracy began to crumble, as close, high-turnout elections drew out the worst in many. This print of election day outrages in Philadelphia includes New York thugs imported to attack reform voters (top left), Philadelphia police arresting racist vote challengers (top right), and the arrival of reinforcements from New York to swing the 1872 Pennsylvania gubernatorial election.

TAKING VOTES IN A RAILWAY CAR

Despite the increasing frustrations, Americans refused to give up on their electoral system, instead betting on outcomes and conducting straw polls on train cars on election day, as in this 1872 print.

"KEEP COOL!" TEN DAYS AFTER THE ELECTION.

Thomas Nast captured the national mood in this cartoon published shortly after the contested 1876 election, while the nation read conflicting newspaper reports, worried about another civil war, and wished they too had a "Polar Refrigerator" to cool their anxieties.

IRON AND BLOOD—THIS "DON'T SCARE WORTH A CENT."

In 1875 Will Kelley's working-class politics, support for an expanded money supply, and ferocious speechifying led conservatives to depict him as a radical French revolutionary calling for Greenbacks or the guillotine. Kelley's warnings that Labor would eventually rise up against inequality echoed his earlier argument that African Americans were entitled to fight for rights denied to them. But in the narrowing political world of the mid-1870s, such rhetoric sounded dangerous to many in both political parties.

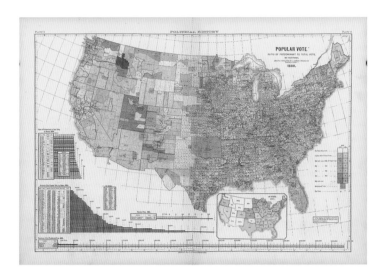

This map of the 1880 presidential election is the first to depict county-level results, revealing the depths of partisan division in the closest popular vote election in U.S. history. Advances in cartography, printing, and statistics made clear that, while the previous generation had been defined by a war between the states, democracy now meant war within nearly every state.

By the 1889 centennial of the U.S. Constitution, Americans had gone from hope, to rage, to disillusionment with what had become of their democracy. This *Puck* cartoon depicts the thuggish bosses of the 1880s sneering at upright Benjamin Franklin and George Washington ("You didn't even tell a lie"), while a pinheaded High Society snob, a slick lobbyist, and a sleazy journalist all help highlight how far America had fallen, in the cartoonist's view, from the 1780s to the 1880s.

This cartoon depicts the haughty, conceited boss Roscoe Conkling finally bursting his own bubble in his feud with President James Garfield. Though labeled "A Harmless Explosion" in this May 1881 satire, in July an infuriated supporter of Conkling's would fatally shoot President Garfield.

A HARMLESS EXPLOSION.

Exploding politicians was clearly a common desire in the 1880s, although this optimistic cartoon promising that the ballot box would blow up bosses seems to misunderstand the relationship between bosses and popular politics. By the 1880s, many were coming to see how the ballots of millions sustained the power of America's worst bosses.

AMERICAN INVENTION FOR BLOWING UP BOSSES.

Newlyweds Florence Kelley and Lazare Wischnewetzky pose in Switzerland, ca. 1885. Lazare displays some of the self-assurance, and contempt, that he would bring to their relationship. Florie, pregnant with Ko and embroiled in widening feuds with her father, her brother, the American press, and the premise of democracy, appears slightly gaunter, though no less formidable, than in earlier portraits.

Nicholas "Ko" Kelley, age six, 1892. By this age Ko had lived in Switzerland and New York City, and was spending most of his time among his mother's friends in Chicago, alternating between the Lloyd's Wayside mansion and a dingy apartment near the Hull House settlement.

By the 1896 election, depicted in this print, torchlit campaigns were losing influence, denounced for their cost, noise, and the way they dangerously excited the working classes. Yet in this election, which bridged the campaign styles of the nineteenth and twentieth centuries, various clubs of ragged marchers, as well as a company in white uniforms wielding ax torches, can still be seen enjoying themselves.

This rare photograph of a Republican campaign headquarters in 1896 displays several key elements of that turning-point election, including the crucial role of African American campaigners, the increasingly bureaucratic style of political organizations (compared with the marchers in the street shown above), and the inflated importance of an individual candidate—in this case William McKinley, looming over the rank-and-file canvassers who would elect him.

In the 1896 race, apocalyptic cartoonists drew a connection between James Garfield's mad assassin, Charles Guiteau, and John Peter Altgeld, the radical Illinois governor (who hired Florence Kelley as a factory inspector). The comparison was unfair and baseless, other than a slight physical resemblance, but it drew out the paranoia brewing in the 1890s.

Florence Kelley, third from the left, at age fifty-five in 1914, roughly the same age as her father when he voted to end slavery. Florie is pictured here with a number of other female factory inspectors, and looks commanding even among this impressive crew.

George P. Holt, the former Wide Awake marcher from the 1860 campaign, pictured in New Hampshire in 1914. By then his uniform had come to seem painfully "old fogey," but his torch staff still bore the markings from every presidential campaign he used it in, from 1860 through 1904.

By the 1908 presidential election, campaigning had calmed dramatically, to the point that phonographs repeating speeches of the candidates replaced soapbox speechifying at some penny arcades. Note that the automaton of William Howard Taft is laughably skinny to represent the 340-pound president.

The 1898 Gillespie voting machine was one of many innovations designed to "protect mechanically the voter from rascaldom," hoping that technology might fix what was broken in American democracy.

Beginning in the early twentieth century, depictions of voters shifted from masses of fighting, shouting, anonymous men to individual citizens pondering their consciences, often while stroking their chins. Over the years since 1865, ballot boxes had gone from a Thanksgiving feast, to a bomb used to blow up politicians, to a remote, emotionless machine.

hand-shaker in American politics. At one later event, Teddy reputedly shook the hands of 8,500 well-wishers. In the 1880s he campaigned zealously and rose quickly, winning a seat in the state assembly and then a position as minority leader, then fighting to prevent Blaine's nomination in 1884, before running for New York mayor in 1886, and winning a key position as Federal Civil Service commissioner in 1888.[18]

Anyone who looked beyond the dinner dress and flashing glasses saw a man carefully calibrating his class appeal. Roosevelt fought against the corruption of individual tycoons and crooked judges, but never against capitalism itself. Running for mayor of New York in 1886, and finding himself trailing the radical economist Henry George (who had first pointed to the "immense wedge" splitting America's class structure), Roosevelt insisted that poverty was as inevitable as "some people being shorter, or more near-sighted, or physically weaker than others." His voters were doing well for themselves; Roosevelt would not undermine their success.[19]

And crucially, unlike many wealthy reformers, Roosevelt constantly stressed his partisan commitments, announcing regularly "I am a Republican, plain and simple." When his party nominated James G. Blaine in 1884, Roosevelt muttered bitterly to his sister about how the choice "speaks badly for the intelligence of the mass of my party." But instead of bolting, Roosevelt stayed, understanding the fundamental importance of partisan identity to his voters. Articles heralding Roosevelt as the young prophet, come to liberate the upper-middle classes, made this point, stressing his willingness to "go to our legislative halls" and make reform from within the lion's den of the party system. This mattered a great deal to lifelong Republicans justifying their continued partisanship. The *New York Times* promised Republicans that Roosevelt's faith in reform-from-within the party would be "to the satisfaction of you all." "Gentlemen," the article heralded: "Behold your Daniel."[20]

But even as he made himself the symbol of reform, Roosevelt worked to distance himself from the discredited old Mugwumps. He ranted regularly about "the 'silk stocking' reformer type" and mocked elite editors' "snobbish worship of anything clothed in wealth." This class of snooty parlor reformers made all anticorruption look bad, and even worse, they lost elections. Roosevelt was careful to distance himself from both their elitism and their "inefficiency." "My business," he declared in his autobiography, was to blend high morals with low politics, to "combine decency and efficiency: to be a thoroughly practical man of high ideals who did his best to reduce those ideals to actual practice."[21]

Americans, Teddy claimed, want "reformers who ate roast beef."[22]

Roosevelt attacked the old model of reform so vigorously that he ended up endorsing the greatest villain in his life. In his autobiography, Roosevelt repeated a quote he believed came from the witty Speaker of the House, Tom Reed, that "when Dr. Johnson defined patriotism as the last refuge of a scoundrel he was ignorant of the infinite possibilities contained in the word reform." This was in keeping with his political project. But it was actually Roscoe Conkling, his father's fatal tormentor, who had uttered those words in his famous "carpet knight" speech.[23]

The real culprit in American politics, young Theodore asserted again and again, was a mentality shared by both inefficient reformers and immoral campaigners. It was the angry shrug, the belief that all politics was corrupt. Such blanket criticisms hampered reform, keeping good men away and allowing bad men to justify their conduct. The constant obituaries declaring the death of democracy made its resuscitation harder. Among his fellow Republicans, Roosevelt saw this in the 1884 presidential campaign, shocked by the mass of partisans who acknowledged Blaine's corruption but supported him anyway, not seeing him as "any worse than the rest of them." Among reformers of his class, Roosevelt railed against the "indiscriminate, abusive criticism" of politicians. In a book of essays on practical politics published in 1888, Roosevelt denounced the typical voter's "all politicians are crooks" attitude, which makes it "impossible to rouse him to make an effort either for a good man or against a scoundrel. Nothing helps dishonest politicians as much." If Roosevelt was visionary about one thing, it was the way constant negative political talk made reform harder.[24]

It's difficult to see the indomitable Theodore Roosevelt as an emblem of restraint. It's hard to believe that a man so compulsively interesting was pushing toward a political system focused on the dull tasks that Lowell called "drainage and ventilation." But over the 1880s, that was exactly the direction Roosevelt was moving, pushing back against satisfying but inefficient rage. All his verve provided a cover for what was really a project of reining in those "rough and tumble" forces he claimed to admire. A growing number of well-to-do Americans were following Roosevelt and Lowell, acknowledging that politics would not be fixed with outrage. It could only be reformed if the system could be made dull enough that all the fun of "racket and rocket" fell away. Few could see, in 1888, the revolution, building among America's bourgeoisie, for boring politics.

IN THOSE BLINDING, blizzard years of the late 1880s, as the "business and intelligent classes" were reengaging American politics, the men and women falling below the Gilded Age wedge began to look for other options. Though often overlooked, 1886 to 1888 saw an incredible birth of communal solutions to the isolating era. In the Midwest, preachers like Maria Woolford joined huge crowds in trance-like, evangelical prayer. Further west, the explosively popular Ghost Dance offered laboring Native Americans a shared vision of a reincarnated future. And in the heartland of American labor—miners and steelworkers in Pennsylvania or Ohio, farmers and lumbermen in Kansas or Minnesota—a small minority began to unite against both the exploitative economy and the parties that were failing to protect them. Certainly, the great majority remained committed Republicans and Democrats, but the first wobbles of iron partisanship were starting to show themselves. In the same years that the well-to-do veered back toward party politics, some blue-collar voters veered away.

Working-class Americans were becoming more articulate about income inequality in these years and less pacified by the assurances that a growing economy would eventually aid them. One Scandinavian immigrant living in the Dakota territory, R. D. Støve, wrote in 1888 about his dawning awareness that "our money is disproportionately in the hands of the few." He had long known about inequality, but was shocked to learn that just five thousand people possessed half the wealth in America. "I had never dreamt that it was so wild." Støve wondered: "What has allowed so much wealth to accumulate in so few hands in the course of approximately twenty years?"[25]

To some, the answer seemed obvious. It was the political parties. They had claimed to protect ordinary Americans, but really they sold power to the wealthy. In the southwest, young, struggling Texans felt less tied to Confederate roots and the Democratic "big bugs" who owned massive ranches. In the upper Midwest, new immigrants with few memories of the Civil War felt slim ties to the old Republican Party. In Wisconsin, anti-tariff workingmen denounced what they called "The Rape of the Party," blaming politicians for siding with capital against labor. Even purported allies like William Kelley were really working for big business, they accused, a fact that "is slowly dawning upon the average-minded man of that party. This complaint is heard everywhere."[26]

Over the late 1880s, a great wobbling away from partisanship began, especially in the western states. Places like Kansas, Nebraska, and Minnesota—which had each voted more than three-fifths Republican in 1880—could not muster majorities for that party a dozen years later. Instead, these voters showed a greater willingness to experiment with third parties, backing experimental movements at four times the rate of mid-Atlantic voters. The men toying with political alternatives were still a minority, but workers and farmers were showing more flexibility than at any time since the fluid days after the Civil War. When that old crank Ignatius Donnelly gave stump speeches for third parties in Minnesota in 1886, he found that almost all his converts were aggrieved Republicans. He also found that, to campaign safely among hostile Republicans, he had to bring his two sons and three loaded revolvers. From the rostrum, Donnelly would make it clear that "I was armed & Stan and Ig stood behind me armed also."[27]

The sad truth was that, however unhelpful the parties looked, there was no viable alternative, especially for Yankees raised to hate the Democrats, or White Texans who could never imagine voting Republican. Kelley had proved this the hard way. That old question—"Whither will you flee?"—was a familiar refrain among the disgruntled. But in these same years, some began to toy with another option. What if no political party could provide refuge? What if a communal organization, in the weeds just beyond the grass flattened by the political parties, might be more helpful?[28]

One of the most popular options proved to be the Knights of Labor. The movement, organized by tailors in Philadelphia after the war, found new recruits in the 1880s. They pushed for an eight-hour workday and accepted a wide swath of the diverse working people of the near Midwest.

Popular among Catholics and White immigrants, with room for women and African Americans in its northern branches, it acted as a proto-union that supported miners, railroad laborers, and steelworkers, especially in interior lower northern states like Pennsylvania, Ohio, New York, Indiana, and Illinois. Essentially, it connected to exactly the class of men to whom Kelley spent the 1870s speechifying. But by the mid-1880s, the Republican Party held less promise for men and women who knew that neither the tariff nor the greenback would save them.

To laborers looking for an advocate, the Knights of Labor looked like a viable alternative, not yet corrupted like the parties but still widespread and social. In 1880 the Knights of Labor had about twenty-eight thousand members, but by 1884 that number had exploded to one hundred thousand. At its peak in 1886, nearly eight hundred thousand Americans joined. In lodges from New Jersey to Missouri, working people saluted each other with glass beer steins embossed with the Knight's trademark image: a worker clutching his hammer shaking hands with a knight in shining armor. Perhaps there was a world of fraternal membership and public influence outside the two parties.[29]

But the boom didn't last. The movement was never built to sustain hundreds of thousands of members, and it crumpled quickly over the late 1880s. Its dramatic failure showed just how much power the two political parties really had. Other organizations could win hundreds of thousands, but could not keep them. The Republican and Democratic parties had the internal structure—the "nervous system" as Frederic Howe put it—to keep millions turning out over decades. Still, the fact that so many laborers joined, even temporarily, showed the hunger for something like the Knights of Labor—a public organization and shared identity that was not a political party. And the fact that the movement was most popular among the classes with the highest turnouts—skilled laboring men in the settled lower North—showed the capacity for real change incubating in the late 1880s.[30]

Farther west, the Farmers' Alliance played a similar role, searching for communal answers to the isolating anxieties of farm mortgages, failed crops, and exploitative railroads. One Farmers' Alliance activist, Luna Kellie, kept an enlightening diary of her evolving thinking on the matter. Luna grew up in a family of itinerant farm laborers and homesteaded in

Nebraska with her husband, J. T. They struggled to make a profit, to heat their home, to fend off ravenous swarms of grasshoppers, and to feed their growing family. It looked like the Farmers' Alliance might offer the aid and community she sought. But as she began to work in the organization, Luna came to believe that struggling farm women like herself needed more than a community. By the late 1880s, she was convinced that they needed a vote.

Since her childhood, Luna had assumed that partisanship would solve her problems. She was raised in a strict Republican household and worshipped Abraham Lincoln, but also believed that a woman's political place was on the sidelines. Wild campaigns were meant for men alone: "No good woman," Luna wrote, "would or could go to the polls to vote in that drunken, fighting, smoking outfit."[31]

But as she saw the way that Gilded Age inequality imposed itself on apolitical wives and mothers, and the utter failure of the Republican Party to offer help, Luna rethought her assumptions. Campaigns were so ugly, and Republicans so central to their ugliness, that women could no longer put their faith in the party of Lincoln. That party avoided legislation that might help farmers, Luna felt; instead, they just "kept fighting the war over and over." Likewise, Republicans helped make election days a vulgar spectacle. Raised to believe that Democrats alone ruined America's public politics, she was shocked to learn that "there is just as much yes more republican whiskey furnished at the polls."[32]

Slowly, Luna broke with her inherited faith in a political party and its old limits. First, she argued that politics would have to clean itself up "before you can ask or expect a woman to vote." But she began to see a solution in women's suffrage. The political system could not cure itself; it would take, according to Luna, fundamental change in voting to tackle all the other policies that might help farmers. Until democracy itself was changed, she told her husband, "there was very little use of thinking of any other reform."[33]

The Knights of Labor steelworkers and Farmers' Alliance homesteaders were expressing the inverse of what newly prosperous "business classes" were saying. They were losing faith in party politics just as the well-to-do were giving them another chance. But Luna Kellie and Teddy Roosevelt shared a renewed faith in reform. Luna hoped for bold political change after generations of complacent Republicanism. Teddy saw muscular reform as a way around the old, elite retreat from practical politics. Both were veering from the stereotypical politics of their elders. After a decade of increasing cynicism, something seemed to be shaking loose in the late 1880s. It would take a decade to show itself, but diverse Americans were poised to reconsider who exactly made up "the governing class."

CHAPTER THIRTEEN

"A Man Who Has Been Through as Much as I Have"

I n the same formative winter of 1887–88, a strange couple checked into an anonymous Manhattan hotel. The woman was unremarkable, a sad-eyed, dark-haired older lady in damask skirts. But the man was so tall and skinny that he looked like "a skeleton in skin," dancing under a head of thick iron-gray hair. With his grizzled beard, furrowed brow, and multiple scars, his worn overcoat and battered hat, he seemed like some "hale old sea captain." But he spoke with an unmistakable thunderclap voice. The pair signed the guest book under false names, but anyone who had seen a political cartoon for the last thirty years would immediately recognize Pig Iron Kelley.[1]

Will and Carrie were in New York on a thrilling mission. "A peace or truce has been patched up," Will beamed: after two years, they would see their daughter. Who initiated this reconciliation has been lost to history, but soon Will and Carrie were traveling up to visit Florie's dismal little flat in the heavily German Yorkville section. And meeting their grandchildren! A new flood of letters began to pour back and forth, Florie writing cheerily about motherhood and her struggles to find time to work with "my small animals"—two-year-old Ko, one-year-old Margaret, and newborn John— "squealing at the top of their lungs." Much of the venom of her Swiss letters had evaporated. Even during the March 1888 blizzard that sank Roscoe

Conkling, when Florie was trapped for days in her flat with her large family and little food, she wrote cheerily to her parents. Lazare was there, too, gloomy and unwell. But that was not what mattered. What mattered, Will explained in elated letters to family, was that "affectionate intercourse had been resumed."[2]

Sounding like a protective father who had been wounded too often, however, Will urged friends to "abstain from giving publicity" to their reunion. He hoped to quietly knit his famous family back together and "prevent those creatures who live by publishing and aggravating the sorrows and miseries of families from rehashing the slanders poor Florence and her husband have been made to read."[3]

This reconciliation, and Florie's love for "the chicks," brought incredible joy to her life. Things were far worse with Lazare. He found little work as a doctor in America, and was constantly irritable and unwell. The couple was forced to borrow money from friends, and then from Will and Carrie. Florie lavished some of it on Riesling and opera tickets for herself. But in a rare acknowledgment, Carrie referred to Florie and Lazare's financial embarrassments and general sense that "life was gloomy." The growing family was forced to relocate frequently, to smaller and smaller apartments around the city. Lazare suffered from painful rheumatic fever, sleeplessness, and even "violent deliriums." He felt trapped in America and forbade the speaking of English in their flat. He grumbled about Florie's efforts to save money and spent Will and Carrie's generosity on spa treatments for his rheumatism. At first, Florie wrote sadly about "my poor martyr." But she was also taking care of three children, recovering from three pregnancies in just three years, and working to rebuild her career in America. Soon Lazare was taking cures at foreign spas, and Florie and "the chicks" were returning to the inviting embrace of the Elms for extended stays.[4]

Florie was charting a new path forward in politics as well. She was growing distant from Marxism in America. She found the German socialists to be clannish and the native-born radicals ill-informed. Florie had essentially earned a graduate degree in radical labor theory, advised by Engels himself, and looked down at the undergraduate opinions of East Side pontificators. She had less confidence in the transformative promise of Revolution, seeing a growing meaning in concrete, incremental change.

Florie cheered on Henry George's insurgent run for mayor of New York (against Theodore Roosevelt). And working with the New York activist Ida Van Etten, she achieved a rare coup, successfully lobbying the legislature to empower some female factory inspectors. Gilded Age women faced abysmal conditions and frequent sexual harassment in industrial shops; Florie hoped inspectors might curb the worst abuses. Nationwide newspapers were once again reporting that Pig Iron Kelley's amazing daughter had "inherited her father's ability."[5]

Florie and Will avoided discussing their old passion for politics, but she did hint at opening a door to that formative bond. Trapped in her flat during the blizzard of 1888, she wondered if Will might take a vacation around Easter, suggesting that he could use a break "after the wear and tear of this most annoying session" in Congress. Instead of dismissing all of American democracy, she was clearly watching the goings-on in the big building on the hill once again.[6]

Down in that big building that winter, another session of Congress was opening. In those years, each new session was heralded, wrote one journalist, in the same spirit "in which the Romans flocked to the frays of the circus." Crowds packed Pennsylvania Avenue, glamorous ladies in svelte sealskin coats and "suave, oil-tongued" lobbyists, their salt-and-pepper beards trimmed, their fingers manicured. Rising young congressmen strutted with chests swelled past the elegant railroad lawyers, the crafty female lobbyists, and the nattier journalists.[7]

But at the center of this scene sat "the Father of the House," Congressman William Darrah Kelley. After three decades in that chamber, seventy-four-year-old Will had become a kind of living monument in the House of Representatives. He had seen hundreds of bright young politicians rise and fall. He had seen slavery die. He had seen Reconstruction strangled. He had seen Republicans fight Democrats, Greenbackers fight Gold Bugs, Stalwarts fight Half-Breeds. He had administered the oath of office to five Speakers of the House. With the opening of each new Congress, Will sat calm amid the pageantry, in his ragged coat and artless hat, "laboring under no very intense excitement," a journalist observed. "He is quite cool and comfortable, thank you. He sits in the same place that he has occupied lo these many years."[8]

This was literally true. After so many sessions, Will Kelley had been awarded his own honorary seat in Congress, marked with his dog-eared hat when seat assignments were being made. He sat there for years, paring apples, scribbling notes to Carrie, interrupting proceedings with his jarring "Mr. Speak-*arr*—Mr. Speak-*arr*." Scorned as a radical race traitor in the 1860s, a wild-eyed communist in the 1870s, and a tariff crank in the early 1880s, by the late 1880s Will was treasured as an artifact of the world he had survived. "In the last two years his bushy gray hair has whitened considerably, the furrows in his fine old face have visibly deepened," wrote one journalist. But the Father of the House still won elections, still swore in Speakers, still jumped to his feet with considerable grace to make some statistical correction. Chuckling at his graying beard, Will admitted his age but bragged: "I am well for a man who has been through as much as I have. I once was shot and once more had sixty shots fired at me." That he survived this long was truly miraculous.[9]

He may have been too confident. Despite his physical grace and unstoppable energy, ill health had always loomed over Will Kelley. Florie later wrote that he suffered from a "nervous excitability which distressed him throughout his long life," which he blamed on a childhood of hard labor. His persistent cough rattled through all of Florie's memories of him, stretching back to her first letter hoping that "YOUR COUG-H HAZ LEFT YOU." A life lived in smoke-filled rooms, not to mention the plug of tobacco he habitually fell asleep chewing each night, surely did not help. In 1883, after a hard congressional fight, Will had been diagnosed with cancer of the mouth. It had been removed by a surgeon. Afterward, Will seemed revitalized. He swore off tobacco and began to drink copious quantities of champagne, for his health.[10]

Soon he was promising reporters that he would stand as a candidate for Pennsylvania's Fourth District "until I am a sufferer from paralysis or lunacy."[11]

As late as 1886, Will was still picking fights. At an event at West Point, he learned that a "stylish rig" parked nearby contained the man who had once conspired to have him killed. William D'Alton Mann, the former editor of the Alabama newspaper who spurred rioters to shoot Kelley down in Reconstruction-era Mobile, was attending the same event. Again and again, lanky, aging Will Kelley crossed the field to confront Mann, who whipped his horses and rode to a new spot as Kelley approached. "I scattered him every time," the congressman bragged to the press, as combative then as when, in 1867, he had warned an armed and angry crowd, "You can not put me down."[12]

But a man can fight only so many battles. In December 1889, when Will swore in the fifty-first Congress, he was clearly flagging. He was its oldest member by far, the only one who could remember the full arc of popular politics, from Jackson to Lincoln to the present. His stretched and worn frame showed fatigue. He still burned with a "determination to do his share of the labors," but struggled physically. The proprietor of the Riggs House, unable to bear the sight of this once-graceful man struggling up the stairs, gave Will an opulent first-floor suite that otherwise would have been beyond his means.[13]

And then, a few days before Christmas, 1889, Will Kelley dined with Congressman Charles O'Neill, the second-oldest member of the House. O'Neill had been with Kelley a quarter century before, when Alexander Pope Fields attacked him at the Willard Hotel. It was O'Neill who had helped tear Fields away from Kelley. At dinner in the Riggs House, Will confessed to his old friend that he was growing weaker each day, that he was too unwell to ride the train to the Elms for the holiday. Will's sonorous voice halted for long intervals, even as his watery blue eyes shone with information. "How difficult I am finding it to talk much," Will told O'Neill. "My dear, long-time friend, I want to tell you that I am a dead man."[14]

The news spread as 1890 began. Congressman William Darrah Kelley had cancer of the jaw, tongue, and throat. One of the nation's most famed voices could hardly whisper. He was trapped at the Riggs House, demanding to attend congressional sessions but kept at rest by his friends. The Riggs lobby filled with well-wishers, prevented from seeing Will but chuckling over tales of his "picturesque individuality." It was in death, comedians had observed in the 1880s, that society finally appreciates a crank. Hundreds of newspapers from Philly to Idaho tracked his condition daily, printing headlines like "JUDGE KELLEY SINKING" as their concerns grew. The *Atchison Daily Globe* had the bad taste to joke that the old tariff defender's cancer might be fought off by the "High protection."[15]

Attended by Carrie, who had already sat beside so much death in her life, and joined by his sons, Will fought for days. But by January 9 he was delirious and then unconscious. At six twenty P.M., Will Kelley's mobile frame stilled, his perpetual speechifying hushed, his long life finally ceased.

No one knows how Florie heard the news. Her last letter to him, sent as he was flagging in mid-December, was warm and solicitous, smiling "the chicks are well and jolly and rosy." But she did worry about the sudden drop-off in his letters, writing, "I feel very anxious about you" and demanding "a triweekly bulletin." She signed her last contribution to their long, flowing current of missives: "With a longing to hear that you are feeling better, I am Your Loving Daughter Florence." Within a month, she was on a southbound train, heading to Philadelphia to meet her father's northbound casket.[16]

The memorials, wakes, and toasts began immediately. Congress held a mournful ceremony. Will's personal seat was draped with black silk and piled with white roses. In Philadelphia, clubs and saloons held wake after wake, culminating in a memorial at the Continental Hotel, attended by Republicans, Democrats, and Independents. Philadelphia's "justly ambitious colored element" prominently mourned Will, demanding pride of place in the Continental Hotel's extravagant lobby to honor their man in Congress. Although he had fallen far short of his promises to Black citizens, he had also done more for their community than almost any other White politician. Black Philadelphians staked their claim on the voice that had spoken for them, and African American newspapers from Indiana to Alabama marked his passing.[17]

Thousands of other papers around the country printed glowing obituaries. Punctual Will Kelley had even died at the right moment. The nation was changing dramatically, crossing some invisible boundary into a new political, cultural, and technological era, and many were eager to commemorate Will. He was a safe manifestation of the world that was passing, now that he was no longer a threat.

The memorials and obituaries beamed with affection for Kelley's passionate, aggressive, peculiar career. Writers honored the way Will never hid his humble origins but made labor both his personal habit and his chief constituency. Many depicted his singular appearance, his resonant voice, and his reputation as "a straight-forward man, a hard-hitter in a fight, but with a kindly heart." Will was, the Ohio congressman William McKinley noted, a man forever drawn to bold stands, "always in the very front rank and on the extreme outpost." Frank Carpenter observed that he had won either the admiration or the hatred of every great man since the Civil War. Carp especially mourned that Will never produced an autobiography, owing to some mysterious conflict with his would-be coauthor, "a woman of extraordinary intellectual ability"—his daughter Florence.[18]

Many praised the way Kelley felt "sublime confidence in the soundness of his own opinions" against the currents of the corrupted democracy. He was, Congressman Joseph Cannon declared, "a politician in the best sense of that much-abused word," unmoved by partisanship, unmotivated by spoils. He never worked in "servitude to a political machine," he was not a manipulator of "political arts and management," Congressman William Wilson of West Virginia memorialized; Will could not be confused for a boss. At a moment when even congressmen eulogizing one of their own were forced to acknowledge how much anger Americans felt toward politicians, it was a point of pride that at least one man had behaved like a statesman.[19]

Will Kelley was honored in death for traits that he had been condemned for in life. He stood as one of the few models of independence in a political system defined by dependence. Over his long career he had left the Democrats, feuded with Republicans, and flirted with third parties. Independent conscience beat tribal loyalty each time. What was left unsaid, in glowing obituaries, was the way his fights dragged down his career. Looking back from 1890, few recalled his role in ending slavery, or demanding Black voting rights, or battling for a more just economy. It was no coincidence that he was remembered for the most orthodox party issue he had ever supported—the tariff, a mainstream Republican plank on which he still managed to make his own "extreme outpost." Kelley had fought to remain distant from partisanship and patronage, but only barely succeeded. His commitments to workers, African Americans, women, immigrants, and children were all overshadowed by the one issue where he was in agreement with the machine. In life, he hammered as independent Will Kelley, but in death—and in history—he would be remembered as the tariff-obsessed Pig Iron Kelley.[20]

Perhaps he was a failure. At the end of all his efforts—seventy-five years of life, fifty-five years of speechifying, twenty-eight years in Congress—working people were worse off, tariffs had not helped, women still lacked the vote, and Black rights were evaporating. Will's belief that he could provide a rare bridge between the White and Black working classes, or between labor and capital, crumbled in an age of divisive tribalism. His vision of a majoritarian political system, where masses could demand what they needed at the ballot box, rang hollow. For all of his labors, the 1890s, like the 1860s, could still be described as "terrible times for timid people."[21]

Or maybe he was an uncanny success. Congressman Joseph Cannon—future king of the House—attended Will's burial in Philadelphia's Laurel Hill cemetery. A fellow political animal, he stood over Kelley's grave and thought that, purely in policy terms, "his life was a success." Kelley's chief battles had all been victorious: slavery was ended, African Americans (theoretically) had newfound rights, and the nation's economy had grown enormously, protected by high tariffs. Kelley was on the winning side of nearly every big fight of the second half of the nineteenth century. His papers overflowed with admiring letters from the manufacturers industrializing the economy, the laborers building America, the freedmen grasping for citizenship. From his birth in 1814 to his death in 1890, America had changed dramatically. And each of the revolutions that wrought this new Republic—the rise of democratic politics, the death of slavery, and the industrialization of the economy—had benefited from Will's deep organ voice, shouting for them loud and early.[22]

Both views were true: Will Kelley had succeeded, and he had failed. He was a good man laboring in a flawed system; he was a disappointment to many who needed him. Most important, he was there. There to shake Jackson's hand, to make Lincoln laugh. To demand Black voting rights, to bind the continent with iron rails, to fight his friends over income inequality. To commemorate the nation's first century, to welcome the immigrants who would help build its second. To craft an American economy for both labor and capital. He fought a long life through, doing as much as an individual could do in a system defined by masses.

"It is greatly to his credit that he died a poor man," an obituary noted, reporting on the settling of his estate. The Kelleys were far from poor, except by the demented standards of a Gilded Age Congress of robber barons and railroad attorneys. For years rumors had swirled that Kelley was out of money, that he was selling off volumes from the Elms's library. After his death, his estate was revealed to include $35,894.68 in property, to go to Carrie. This was a large amount, but not for a Gilded Age politician, especially one so intimately tied to so many manufacturers and financiers. Will's political efforts had actually reduced his wealth. All his work promoting West Philadelphia's manufacturing base had filled his section with laborers' modest row houses, until the value of the land he owned plummeted. Turkeys no longer waddled past the Elms. It now sat squarely in a busy city of factories, shops, and saloons.[23]

While tallying his assets, Florie found herself standing with her younger brother Albert in the Elms's library, awash in January sunlight. Albert recalled their Papa's pride, laughing: "Didn't Father once say that you had read all these books?"

When Will's father died, in 1816, John Kelley's property was auctioned on the sidewalk to pay his debts. Two-year-old Will saw his inheritance laid out for sale. The nation's newspapers had just done the same for Florence Kelley, setting out her father's legacy before her eyes. Here his independence, there his betrayals. Here his friends, there his feuds. Here his fight for working people, there his struggles with the political system. It was all on display for her to choose from.

Yet aside from the sharp-eyed Frank Carpenter and a few Philadelphia papers, hardly any obituaries noticed the daughter who had read every book in Judge Kelley's library. For much of the press, Florence was an awkward subject, once a source of great interest, but after her years abroad, her strange marriage, and her falling out with her father, hardly a subject for his eulogy. Many saw Will Kelley's death as the end of an era, commemorating him as last of an extinct breed of statesmen. But the real story was one of succession and continuity, the torch being passed within American history's most unique political dynasty. Will Kelley was gone, but his daughter was ready to continue his fight.

Just as few could see the reforms incubating in the depths of the political blizzard of the 1880s, hardly anyone could guess at the impact Florie Kelley would have. Both she and the nation stood poised for a rebirth in those years.

A few months before Will died, an office seeker wrote him a letter full of flattery. He predicted that Kelley would guide the nation into "the days that are to come, when partisanship and passion have passed away, and the historian shall give an unprejudiced verdict."[24]

He was right about the coming change, the withering of partisanship and the cooling of political passion, but the writer had the wrong Kelley in mind.

PART THREE

NEW WEAPONS OF DEMOCRACY, 1890–1915

CHAPTER FOURTEEN

"Some Change Must Occur Very Soon Now"

The second time Lazare hit her, Florie took the chicks and left. The first time had been on the anniversary of Will's death. Florie cooked a Russian stew, but left out an ingredient to save money. Lazare grew darker than ever before. They argued. He cursed her, hit her, spat in her face, and chased her out of their Fifth Avenue flat and down to Eighth Avenue, screaming in German. Proud, fierce Florence Kelley left with a black eye and three small children repeating the curses they overheard their father shout.[1]

When he did it again, Florie grabbed Ko, Margaret, and John. She packed one trunk with clothes and another with books and toys, and borrowed money for four train tickets to Chicago.[2]

The magnetic forces that drew Kelleys to the right time and place pulled Florie to Chicago two days after Christmas 1891. The thirty-hour journey, with three small children and bruises on her face, must have felt like a dive into darkness. But Illinois had notoriously liberal divorce laws, and Chicago had a reputation as a hotbed of inequity and activism. Florie could not have found a more exciting place to remake herself.

She was not the only one trying new things in the early 1890s. The American people were, William Allen White would reflect, "feeling for new weapons of democracy." No one would realize it for some time, but titanic changes in American politics would come from small decisions made in those years. Somewhere hidden in the early 1890s lies a hinge on which American public life would swing. There were those contemplating the "drainage and ventilation" of party machines, hoping to tighten politics down to a clean and quiet works. Others were considering how to expand democracy's narrow scope to take on more of the social challenges of modern life. There was no plan to move forward, but many hurtled into the 1890s exasperated with democracy as it was. Like Florie, as her train chugged into looming Chicago, they did not know what they would find, but agreed that they must leave the past behind.[3]

Everyone who saw Chicago in those years felt compelled to write about it. Letters home to Lithuania, boosters advertising scams, reports on the conditions of its slaughterhouses. Rudyard Kipling, after his eye-opening voyage across the Pacific, declared Chicago worse than Calcutta, "inhabited by savages . . . crammed with people talking about money and spitting about everywhere." Others were awed. Its population nearly doubled in every census, almost half of its residents foreign-born, until it replaced Philadelphia as the nation's second-largest city in 1890. The value of the goods it produced increased twenty-seven times between 1880 and 1890. Some found Chicago intoxicating and planned never to leave. Others, like Kipling, wrote that having seen Chicago once, "I urgently desire never to see it again."[4]

Chicago also seemed to be the capital of a mounting national instability. It was there, in 1886, that a series of strikes and police riots culminated in a bombing in Haymarket Square that killed seven policemen, punished with death sentences for seven innocent activists. "We had a political execution in Chicago yesterday," William Dean Howells condemned. Lucy Parsons, the African American anarchist widow of one of the executed, walked the streets calling for a "war of extermination" against the rich. The whole nation took notice. Nowhere in America did the wedge of income inequality seem more jagged. When the economy crashed in 1893, Chicago's poor crowded into the jails rather than freeze on the street. Newspapers pointed to a renewed "craze for cranks and crankery," as hungry tramps, utopian theorists, and anxious millionaires all agreed with the Illinois industrialist

George Pullman, who told his wife: "Some change must occur very soon now, but I cannot yet predict what it will be."[5]

It was into this "richest, filthiest, ugliest aggregation of houses, streets and people to be called a city" that Florie arrived just before New Year's, 1891. Within a day, she sought out an organization about which she had heard much, a growing movement that was doing exactly the kind of intimate social work that she had been calling for. Florie climbed the icy porch steps of a large complex of brick buildings on Halsted Street, amid mounds of coal-blackened snow and piles of garbage. A woman with an oddly calm, knowing presence opened the door and introduced herself as Jane Addams, founder of the Hull House settlement. Florie was instantly impressed (but not so struck that she failed to notice the "singularly unattractive" baby in her arms). Addams would become a host, friend, and mentor to Florie over the next "happy, active years" of her tumultuous life.[6]

Inside Hull House, Florie found a busy little universe. College women taught English to Yiddish-speaking mothers, Italian workingmen ate healthful suppers, neighborhood children played, and researchers studied the diverse needs of the communities around them. Addams used Hull House as a physical embodiment of her efforts to fill the gaps in a civil society stripped bare by industrial capitalism. She wrote with startling clarity about the ways that the modern world "can detect only commercial values" in human beings, thinning out the social sphere. She was working to thicken this new urban society with education, play, community. It was a more fully realized version of what political partisanship had once promised.[7]

Florence could have found no better home. She was a trained social researcher, versed in the lives of working women, and adept in German and Russian. She went to work, conducting studies on labor conditions in the neighborhood. The tenements around Hull House looked like homes, but they were also makeshift factories, churning out goods at the atrocious rates demanded by "the sweating system." She diligently mapped the ward, ultimately interviewing over five thousand women from dozens of countries, working in 474 occupations. She calculated that the ward's schools had room for only one-third of its children. The rest often worked ten hours a day, six days a week, for just a few dollars. Outraged, Florie dug deeper.[8]

At the same time, she made herself a presence at Hull House. Florie's intensity complemented Addams's cool. The two made a striking pair, Addams in serene gray, Florie in furious black. Some at Hull House were charmed by Florie's lack of snobbery. One Jewish socialist laborer was stunned that an elite Yankee woman, who was the daughter of "the father of the system of protection in America," would kibitz with him as an equal. Younger residents would wait up for Florie each night and bribe her with hot chocolate to get her talking about her life amid presidents in Washington and revolutionaries in Europe. She spoke with "sparkle and fire" in the vacant Hull House dining hall. But her friends "had to be careful . . . foolish questions, half-baked opinions, sentimental attitudes, met with no mercy."[9]

Others in the community found Florie shocking. She did not behave like a good, Christian college woman. Surrounded by moral, upright, sometimes humorless reformers, Florie seemed "vivid, colorful, rather frightening." She launched a campaign of gentle mockery aimed at Addams, laughing at those who treated "Sister Jane" like a living saint. She even ridiculed their prayer meetings until the residents stopped holding them. Their reminiscences often mention "F.K." with love and affection, but many surely hated her.[10]

Hull House was an ideal home for Florie, but not for Ko, Margaret, and John. Lazare was looking for his children. One wintry day in early 1892, Addams bundled up Florie and her chicks and dragged them to a snow-kissed mansion set on a wooded bluff outside Chicago, looking out over the choppy expanse of Lake Michigan. The spectacular home—called the Wayside—was once an inn. Ushering the little refugees inside, Addams introduce them to two figures who would be a central presence in their lives—the warm, red-haired, blue-eyed Jessie Bross Lloyd and her husband, Henry.

Henry Demarest Lloyd was a gentle but powerful presence, both in the lives of the Kelleys and in the development of American democracy. With his beak nose, heavily lidded eyes, and proud flop of hair, he resembled an insistent owl. In photographs taken across his lifetime, Lloyd always seems poised to interrupt, as if the photographer had just said something sadly misguided. But those who knew and loved him recalled Lloyd as a sensitive man who tempered his brilliance with incredible warmth. Born into New York's "shabby gentility," Lloyd got his start as a classic Mugwump reporter, writing for his wife's father's newspaper, the *Chicago Tribune*. But over the 1870s and '80s, Henry and Jessie's politics grew more and more radical. When Lloyd publicly campaigned to save the accused Haymarket bombers, his Republican father-in-law disinherited him.[11]

Henry was doing more than angering his in-laws; he was on the cutting edge of a movement to revolutionize journalism. For a lifetime, newspapers had been openly partisan rags. There was no expectation of independence, and no financial path toward it either—most of America's fourteen thousand papers were supported by fiercely partisan subscribers or underwritten by the parties themselves. The men and women who wrote for them were a rough, aggressive, ink-smudged guild, producing papers of dense political articles and colorful insults. One Associated Press manager described his profession as "partisan, unscrupulous, dependent, frequently inane." But in the 1890s, the growing consumer market meant that newspapers could be funded by advertisements, not subscriptions. Journalists found themselves beholden to corporations eager to sell to all, rather than subscribers nursing partisan grudges. By 1890 about 25 percent of papers openly declared their political independence, up from 5 percent in 1860. And as newspapers stood alone financially, a new confidence showed among some of their best writers. The word *journalist* entered regular use. "The newspaper thinks more of itself than of its party," the *Washington Post* quietly bragged.[12]

Henry Demarest Lloyd was first among these proud new journalists. No one would call him a "muckraker" yet, but Lloyd was one of the originators of the style of independent, investigative, public-interest reporting. In 1890 he published an anatomy of a labor conflict with the cheeky title *A Strike of Millionaires Against Miners*. Florie read and loved it. A few years later, Lloyd followed up with what remains among the wisest, clearest books ever written on income inequality, *Wealth Against Commonwealth*. In this attack on the Standard Oil Corporation, Lloyd unpacked the way unlimited competition led to monopolies in every industry—"from meat to tombstones"—ultimately undermining capitalism itself. "Liberty produces wealth," Lloyd observed, "and wealth destroys liberty." Though writing about economic inequality, Lloyd kept coming back to the failure of democracy. "We have been fighting fire on the well-worn lines of old-fashioned politics . . . but the flames of a new economic evolution run around us, and we turn to find that competition has killed competition." Those words offered a thesis for what had gone wrong with America's politics, as well as its economy. To save the republic, America needed to restrain excessive competition. After thirty years of "pure democracy" and "practical politics," America needed a *new democracy . . . a new political philosophy.*"[13]

And so Ko, Margaret, and John made their temporary homes with this architect of "the new democracy." Florie missed her chicks "with perennial heartbreak" and visited the Wayside as often as she could. Sometimes she was joined there by Addams; at others, she dined with Booker T. Washington, the Black poet James Corrothers, the feminist writer Charlotte Perkins Gilman, or the "People's Lawyer" Louis Brandeis. The Lloyds were experimenting with new forms of community in the 1890s, and they gathered together a diverse salon of reformers and cranks, artists and nobodies. Tommy Morgan, a railroad repairman and labor activist, found himself a frequent guest in their finely appointed dining hall, with its flocked wallpaper and long white table artfully laid out with lush, curving vines. There he "lost all my feeling of class distinction and antagonism." A French visitor recalled the feast he enjoyed at the Wayside, dining on the Lloyds' famous fish chowder, along with thirty guests, "rich and poor, white and black, gentle and simple, college president and seamstress, artist and mechanic, divine and layman."[14]

Among the guests at the Wayside were a group of politicians who, over their chowder, passionately discussed a key element of the "new democracy"—a viable third party. The Lloyds invited the former Greenback Party congressman (and ally of Will Kelley's) James B. Weaver, the radical labor leader Eugene V. Debs, his equally radical attorney Clarence Darrow, and many other figures who spoke earnestly about the coalescing movement. Sometimes they were joined by a pudgy Minnesotan who commanded the room with his wide-ranging, impassioned talk of a new party, eloquent and soft-brained at the same time. That old "Prince of Cranks," Ignatius Donnelly, was working alongside the Lloyds and many others to get this new "Populist Party" off the ground.

In February 1892, just as the Kelley kids were getting settled at the Wayside, Donnelly told a massive Populist rally in St. Louis: "We meet in the midst of a nation on verge of moral, political, and material ruin.

Corruption dominates the ballot box, the legislatures, the Congress." The parties were busy fighting "a sham battle over the tariff" to distract voters from the corporate takeover of American democracy. (This was exactly the point Florie had made to Engels about her father's protectionism.) The movement called for federal regulation of the railroads, elimination of private banks, more coinage of silver, and such radical stances as an income tax, an eight-hour work day, and the direct election of senators.[15]

Especially on the fringes of the rural west—places like Kansas, Colorado, and Nevada—tribal partisanship had dissipated with the repeated migrations of Yankee Republicans and southern Democrats. Populations mixed, or found themselves battling the same challenges— thieving banks, crooked railroads, useless legislatures—from North Dakota to south Texas. Many came to believe that "we are the worst governed country on the face of the earth." It would feel like "a sacrifice," a Kansas farmer acknowledged, "to fall away from party." But who could ignore "this great coming together of the people"? Who "intended to stand firm to party tho' heavens fall"?[16]

As Howells put it in a letter to his father two days before the 1892 presidential election: "The Republican party is a lie in defamation of its past . . . it is only less corrupt than the scoundrelly democracy. The only live and honest party is the People's Party."[17]

This live and honest movement did surprisingly well as the two main parties wobbled. In the 1892 presidential election, Benjamin Harrison and Grover Cleveland faced off in a lackluster campaign. Henry Adams joked that "one had no friends, the other, only enemies." In a full three-quarters of the states, neither party won a majority of the vote. Across the nation, small third parties held the balance of power. At the same time, control of Congress boomeranged wildly back and forth. In the early 1890s, Democrats and Republicans each briefly won 70 percent of Congress. In this environment, voters were willing to take a chance. The Wayside attendee James B. Weaver ran for president on the Populist ticket in 1892. He won 8.5 percent of the vote and twenty-two electoral votes from western states. More than a million voters (and many more nonvoting women, African Americans, and young people) supported the Populists in the strongest third-party showing since before the Civil War.[18]

The Populists did better than any third party of their era, but were still fundamentally outnumbered by the massive Republican and Democratic parties. In much of the populous East the Populists hardly existed at all—receiving zero votes in Delaware and Louisiana, just forty-four in Vermont, and failing to earn 1 percent of the vote in ten states. One Democratic immigrant, writing home from his Brooklyn apartment decorated with framed prints of Grover Cleveland, dismissed the Populist Party as not even "worth mentioning." Deep down, many Americans just refused to believe that a person could leave their party. Some suspected that this new movement was merely the opposition in disguise. While historians have devoted great efforts to understanding the Populists, it's worth remembering that American voters still preferred the mainstream parties by more than ten to one.[19]

This dismissal did not stop the mainstream press from heralding the Populists as the civilization-destroying "cranks, lunatics and idiots" that Gilded Age elites kept warning about. Somehow, the movement was both nonexistent and an existential threat. The conservative editor E. L. Godkin saw the Populists as a sign that America had grown too large, writing snidely, "We do not want any more States until we can civilize Kansas."[20]

Out in Kansas, one young journalist vented his fury at the uncivilized new party. William Allen White was the combative, self-impressed son of a middle-class Republican editor. At twenty-four he launched his own paper, promising to support Republicans "first, last, and all the time. There will be no bolting, not sulking, no 'holier than thou' business." He began to write furious editorials against Populism. To White, the movement represented the same old cranks and hayseeds who "for twenty years had been the laughingstock of the countryside for its visionary nonsense."[21]

But as he went riding at night, White couldn't help but notice the rural schoolhouses lit by Populist rallies. On one train ride, he fell into conversation with Donnelly and left shocked that such an eloquent man could support the "Popocratic Cranks." As the party grew in Kansas, some readers cautioned the young reporter to temper his tone. Soon Populist marchers were hanging White in effigy, "Silly Willie" painted across his "capricious cartooned posterior." Years later, he reflected that instead of mocking the Populists, he should have noticed their willingness to vote against their fathers. "Kansas politics was reflecting the iridescent colors of the dawn," White observed in his later autobiography. "I saw the gorgeous picture. I wrote about it. But I had no idea of its meaning."[22]

Ko Kelley saw the dawn. He was only six years old, eating his soup at the Wayside while the adults around him talked and joked and argued. But children see the world of adults, and Ko would look back on those years of "ever bubbling fun, humor and wit," delighted to live among the Lloyds' confederation of cranks. "I was blessed," he wrote as an adult, "with the best bringing-up and educating of anybody that I have known," saturated in dinner-table politics of the Lloyds' visionary salons. He would feel lucky to sit next to his mother and take in that "magic compound of informality, decorum, high thinking, and interest in all that was going on."[23]

Ko had his mother's proud mouth, her deep-diving dark eyes. He had his grandfather's low shaggy brow. He reminded her of him, minus some of the combativeness that drove Will Kelley. And Ko was the same age that Florie had been when she stretched out on the rug at the Elms, back in the 1860s, and watched "high thinking" adults debate the future of American democracy. The political flexibility of those years had stiffened, the promising guests at the Elms had wandered off. The fiery young female orator Anna Dickinson was in an insane asylum, the African American political organizer Isaiah Wears was writing books on etiquette, Will Kelley was dead. But Ko was witnessing a new birth, a return to some of the possibility of the 1860s in the 1890s. The arc of American democracy could be strung across the late nineteenth century, from the Elms to the Wayside.

In between, campaign convulsions shook society. Roscoe Conkling had confidently declared that in politics, "the law of everything is competition." But here was Henry Demarest Lloyd, sitting across from Ko Kelley, warning that "competition has killed competition," and building a new structure to restrain it.[24]

CHAPTER FIFTEEN

"The Secret Cause"

A cross Chicago, fortresses were going up. The same year that Hull House opened its doors and the Lloyds started inviting strangers to their Wayside salon, the First Regiment's Armory lowered its portcullis. The prestigious Illinois National Guard regiment, its ranks populated with the sons of prominent families, opened a new armory just off "Millionaires' Row." The famed architect Daniel Burnham designed a massive medieval castle that had no windows on its faceless stone lower stories, but swelled at the top with a broad brick chest of turrets and crenulated rifle-slots. "War is clearly embodied in every line and angle," the *Chicago Tribune* announced. The militia it housed would be called to suppress public disturbances, to pour out into the restive slums to the south and west in the event of a riot or strike. Building a "veritable fortress capable of resisting any attack" sent a clear message to the wards outside the Loop.[1]

Not everyone was working to build a broader social democracy in the 1890s. Public life increasingly scared many Victorians. Francis Willard, head of the powerful Women's Christian Temperance Union, made it her mission "to make the whole world more HOMELIKE," and proposed a cabinet-level "Department of Recreation" to enforce "decency" at public spectacles. A guide to raising young men, published by the *Ladies' Home Journal* in 1893, joked that the best way to raise a decent boy was for the "fellow to be buried when he was fifteen and not dug up again until after he was twenty." It offered tips for keeping one's son at home.[2]

There was also a harsher edge, the implied threat of the First Regiment's armory, the sabers worn by militiamen like Willy Kelley Jr. Cities were training militias, passing vagrancy laws, and restricting public rallies with permitting requirements. And across the nation, strikers were met with truncheons and rifles. The National Guard was called out 328 times between 1886 and 1895. In 1894 an Ohioan named Jacob Coxey led a ragtag assembly of unemployed protestors in the first march on Washington. "Coxey's army," as they were called, were beaten and arrested for trampling on the grass around Capitol Hill. To the well-to-do of the 1890s, public gatherings seemed newly ominous.[3]

This fear of the public combined with the political mission to "emancipate the respectable white man." The boisterous social world that nurtured American democracy was about to come under dramatic assault. Without ever having a coherent goal, well-to-do partisans introduced a set of piecemeal reforms that would reduce what the English thinker James Bryce called "the excessive friction in American politics." Such restrainers were working toward the very opposite of what Hull House and the Wayside salon were attempting. Instead of growing new political communities with a wider sense of social impact, the reformers in the Republican and Democratic parties pushed a narrower interpretation of democracy. They aimed to isolate organizing, campaigning, and voting from the public; in the words of the Republican National Committee chairman James Clarkson, they would move political discussions from "the open field, as in Lincoln's day, to the private home."[4]

Many of these restrainers saw themselves as modern, scientific, progressive thinkers. They looked down on irrational campaign spectacle, condemning the stuff of public politics—the torches, the uniforms, the skyrockets. Some criticized the "lost sobriety" that went along with big public rallies organized by saloonkeepers, others dryly argued that "the torchlight procession is, at the very best, a silly sort of show." These business-minded men made a financial argument, condemning "the money flung away on torches, uniforms and outside demonstrations." But their repeated mentions of "outside demonstrations" and the "open field" hint at their deeper concern. It was the public, not the cost, that these reformers found threatening.[5]

Their first target was the marching club, that basic nucleus of American campaigning since Andrew Jackson. These temporary, local organizations drew together working- and middle-class young partisans for meetings in saloons or barns, gathering to talk politics, drink and smoke, and practice drills. Clubs focused an inordinate amount of time on what uniforms to wear, what torches to wave, what order to march in. Their vibrant rallies did more than excite voters; they asserted the centrality of electoral politics in public life, demanding that entire communities behold their "racket and rocket."[6]

As an alternative, some elite urban reformers had organized what they called Good Government Clubs (mocked as "GooGoos"). They invited "the Best Men" to join. While campaign clubs marched, Good Government Clubs talked, holding meetings and lectures. Its members were the kind of high-minded, bloodless reformers mocked for their "acid propriety," for putting on neckties to go vote, for speaking about politics as if morality mattered. Their clubs existed for deliberation alone; some even forbade their members from running for office with tellingly titled "Chastity Clauses."[7]

By the late 1880s, a larger class of well-to-do partisans debuted their own model, somewhere between chaste GooGoos and promiscuous marching companies. The "intelligent and business classes" wanted to make an impact beyond armchair deliberation, but worried that marching clubs threatened their respectability. "The *better* class of people," the Pennsylvania Democratic reformer Chauncey Black wrote, simply would not join a club. In 1887 the Republican Party found a third way. Hoping to create a "regulator on this machine of politics," they introduced the nationwide Republican League, based in clubhouses in downtown districts. Democrats soon debuted their own permanent clubs to help "bring politics indoors."[8]

By the 1890s, the Republican League maintained meeting halls in business districts in thousands of cities and towns. Chicago's Hamilton Club was typical. Occupying two adjacent buildings downtown on West Madison Street, it represented a political community as experimental as

Hull House. Yet it had more in common with the First Regiment's Armory. The Hamilton Club's 360 prosperous members signed a charter, elected leaders, and discussed club finances. The club's bylaws boasted that its location in a central business district, not a residential neighborhood, meant that few members would "frequent the new rooms in the evening." They would host no "ladies day," no evening balls. The Republican League's new style signaled that its politics would now be "wholly removed from the social field." The Hamilton Club locked its doors early each evening.[9]

African American politicians saw the same splintering of clubs along class lines. In Philadelphia, Gil Ball, the African American ward boss and occasional drinking buddy of Squire McMullen, ran the "Matthew Quay Club" out of his Lombard Street saloon. (The fact that a Black ward boss ran a club named for a Native American party boss hints at the overlooked diversity of nineteenth-century politics.) In addition to coordinating campaigns, Ball's saloon was a noted gathering spot for craps and faro games. And it was a haunt of local criminals—including Ball himself, the perpetrator of at least one stabbing. Meanwhile, up in the middle-class Seventh Ward, the politico, barbershop owner, and realtor Isaiah Wears joined the Citizens Republican Club, which invited urbane African Americans to political meetings but banned drinking, cards, and "unseemly behavior."[10]

Instead of the "silly show" of campaign rallies, permanent clubs began to refocus on "Educational Campaigning." Based on the earnest belief that studying the issues was superior to barroom canvassing or public marching, party restrainers prioritized the writing, printing, and distribution of pamphlets. In the 1888 election, the Republican National Committee set up a Literary Bureau in a Manhattan townhouse, employing seventy-five clerks and printers to churn out tariff pamphlets. In 1892 both parties embraced the model. Inside of buzzing offices, educational campaigning felt like a whirlwind of activity, but out on the street, the 1892 contest was noted "for the utter lack of spirit or enthusiasm on the part of the old parties." Perhaps this technique helped make the Populist campaign for James Weaver more appealing. The *Washington Post* complained about the new style in an 1892 article titled "Why the Campaign Is Quiet," dismayed with a race that "refuses to get noisy or to break out in the gooseflesh of barbecues, torchlight processions, brass bands, joint discussions &c."[11]

The new model of educational campaigning did not replace public rallies. There were still torchlit marches, but they coexisted with several other methods of running a campaign. The rise of educational campaigning did have a few unintended consequences. First, the focus on the written word made politics less accessible to those who were illiterate, non-English speakers, or simply reluctant to study the issues closely. Second, these centralized printing bureaus shifted power from the galaxy of small-town clubs to a few headquarters run by professional politicians in New York and Chicago. Although educational campaigning was introduced as a solution to the cost of torches and uniforms, it ended up being more expensive—all those writers, editors, and printers had to be paid for campaign labor previously done by volunteers. The dull 1892 campaign was nonetheless the first in which both parties' national committees spent over a million dollars. This shift undermined the entire campaign economy, which had been based on recruiting and rewarding voluntary participation.[12]

The third big shift was the introduction of the most revolutionary government form in American history: the secret ballot. For decades, American democracy had been shaped by its strange system of voting, where voters cast a party-printed ballot in public. Supporters and challengers used everything from slogans and bodyguards to shoemakers' awls and brass knuckles to influence the process. The system made election day a communal, social holiday, but also allowed intimidation, inaccuracy, and indecent behavior.

In the late 1880s, activists in Philadelphia, New York, and Boston began to push for a cleaner, saner system. The government could print ballots and administer a process to ensure that they were cast in privacy. Such a system was already in place in Britain, Belgium, Italy, and Australia. It became known as "the Australian ballot." Secret ballots would allow participants to vote their conscience without fear of intimidation. And it would shift much of the effort from party volunteers to government agents. Massachusetts established a secret ballot in 1888, launching a wave of excitement for the "ease and precision" of the new model, and the way it empowered independent voters. The laws spread quickly; between 1888 and 1893, all nonsouthern states adopted secret ballots.[13]

Instead of the surveilled and violent polling places of the past, the solitude of a polling booth and the neutrality of a government ballot must have felt revelatory. One woman admired the way it "requires that each voter, before depositing his ballot, shall shut himself up in a confessional box, and fight the political campaign out all by himself." A fan of the secret ballot in Los Angeles wrote, "The voter, when he enters the booth to mark his ballot, is alone with his conscience." The secret ballot and the privacy of the voting booth briefly freed Americans from the constant imposition of society. During the rest of their lives, they were trapped in a web of social relationships, their inner views limited by their parties, their employers, their neighbors, their families. "But all these restrictions fall away from him during the brief time he occupies the polling booth." If politics could be "removed from the social field," as the new clubs suggested they should be, the secret ballot was a brilliant innovation in pure democracy. However, if Jane Addams and Henry Demarest Lloyd were right to warn about the social isolation of modern life, the man alone in the polling booth was a perfect example of that seclusion.[14]

The government-issued ballot also meant a revolution in political participation. By replacing partisan hustlers and challengers, the new secret ballots increased the power of the government as an institution over its voluntary participants. It empowered party leadership to select which candidates would be on the ballot, making it harder for local candidates and factions to get nominated. All these changes undermined the same campaign economy that educational campaigning and permanent clubs threatened—work once done by volunteers was now the province of professionals. Slowly, the democratic process was lifting away from the public square, into the halls where bureaucrats designed ballots, clerks printed political pamphlets, and clubs met privately.

As with educational campaigning, the all-text government ballots were harder for illiterate and immigrant voters to use. But that was part of the point. Many reformers hoped that, as Francis Willard put it, changes in voting laws would introduce a "safeguard on the ballot-box at the North that would sift out alien illiterates." The Manhattan writer Henry Childs

Merwin warned that reformers "distrust the people" and were "taking power away from the illiterate." The white-bearded Social Gospel preacher Lyman Abbott saw the same scheme. He argued that the secret ballot represented the "increasing tendency to question the practical wisdom or justice of universal suffrage." Outright suppression was difficult, but restrainers could merely undermine the ability or willingness to vote. Abbott explained that the rapid adoption of new voting laws in the 1890s had the "secret cause" of reducing participation.[15]

The well-to-do northern restrainers were cagey about their "secret cause," but the men remaking suffrage in the South were more blunt. Their goal, as one White Virginian wrote, was the "elimination of the negro from the politics of this state." In the decade after Reconstruction's demise, southern politics hovered between two worlds. The near-total suppression of Black voters seen in the twentieth century did not emerge immediately. There had been nearly a million Black voters in the South; they did not all go home in 1877. In safely gerrymandered districts in Mississippi, Alabama, and South Carolina, African American Republicans clung to power and voting rights. In the upper South, states like Virginia and North Carolina, Black voters and working-class Whites built careful, creative coalitions. Voter suppression was endemic, but with the Republican Party and Reconstruction-era state constitutions on their side, many bold African Americans managed to cast their ballots.[16]

Around 1888, southern Democratic elites took a new tack, an extreme contortion of the antipublic attitudes reshaping elections nationwide. Leaders like the Louisiana governor Samuel McErnery warned against an "impersonal mass" of Black voters "hovering over us and threatening our civilization." An 1890 rally of young White men in Mississippi published a broadside titled "A Blast from the Youth," threatening that they would not allow voters to "foist on us again this black and damable machine miscalled a government." Lynchings of African Americans peaked in these years, averaging 127 murders per year between 1891 and 1895, each an atrocious public spectacle and a political threat. Many southern Democrats worried about Republican plans for a Federal Force Bill to monitor elections. So in the late 1880s states moved to suppress Black voters entirely with legal restriction.[17]

States introduced new constitutions, undoing the ones written during Reconstruction. Mississippi moved first, in 1890, just as the rest of the nation was reassessing suffrage as well. The Mississippi laws became a model for other southern states, introducing poll taxes for voting, literacy tests, residency restrictions, and bans on those convicted of a crime (even minor offenses) from voting. Poll taxes had been a common fiscal mechanism across world history, not tied to political rights (*poll* is simply an archaic word for "head," meaning a tax on each individual). But the new laws linked them specifically to voting. Those who didn't want to vote needn't worry about them, but would-be voters had to pay. The effect was another way to separate voting from the rest of life. Soon after the passage of the new state constitution, the number of registered African American voters in Mississippi fell from 147,000 to 9,000.[18]

The new laws drove African Americans from the public scrum of politics, no longer even able to fight for representation. During the wars of Reconstruction, bold African Americans had to confront a violent Democratic Party to vote. Now the power of the whole state, not a party, stood in their way. In Alabama, the sharecropper Ned Cobb recalled how a new state constitution cut his father out of the elections he had once joined at the Chapel Ridge polling place. Cobb never heard his father use the word *disenfranchisement*, but noted the way his dad "just stopped goin' up the Chapel Ridge on voting day; stayed home or went out and done what he wanted to. But he didn't vote no more."[19]

The state constitutions passed in the 1890s did more than close off African Americans from politics. They further separated the region from the rest of the nation. Politics in the Deep South had always been different, stretching back across the 1800s. Suffrage was more limited, turnouts anemic, competitive parties a rarity. But during Reconstruction, Black and White southern voters had made their voices heard in vibrant nationwide elections, attracting politicians like Will Kelley to stump across the section. After 1890, all the South's old abnormalities returned and intensified. Black (and poor White) disenfranchisement furthered these unhealthy trends, making political participation even less central to social life. Turnout and competiveness had been trending downward since 1876, but then they crashed in the 1890s. What was left hardly looked like an election at all. The men reforming the voting laws of Mississippi or Louisiana made a choice: killing Black electoral power, even if it meant choking off public politics in general. Southern politics, always an outlier, became an aberration.

Though different, northern and southern political restraint shared two key traits. Both separated political life from public life, often using the power of the state as a buffer. And both used mechanisms of discouragement, putting the onus on the voter without ever banning participation outright. The Fifteenth Amendment was never revoked, but African American voting became close to impossible in the southern states where most Blacks lived. The *Macon Telegraph* argued, and the *New York Times* affirmatively reprinted, that "if the Australian ballot reduces the negro vote in the South, it is the fault of the negro." If a Black voter could not read the Constitution in Georgia, or an illiterate immigrant could not decipher a printed ballot in Chicago, "the responsibility lies with him."[20]

Something else had happened, only visible in retrospect. So many elements of the political process—the voter "alone with his conscience," the clubmen meeting behind locked doors, the pamphleteer writing tracts in a literary bureau, the sharecropper who knew better than to walk to his polling place, and even the militiaman looking south over Chicago through a rifle slot—had all been sealed away at the same time. Each of these fortresses had a foundation laid between 1887 and 1889, and ramparts visible in the early '90s. It was during the depths of the late 1880s that real change began. Reform—for good or ill—had started before anyone seemed to notice.

MARY BRYAN HAD been asleep when her husband came in and sat down on the edge of their bed. "Mary, I have had a strange experience," he said, beginning to tell her about his speaking engagement the previous evening. "Last night I found that I had power over the audience. I could move them as I chose. I have more than usual power as a speaker. I know it. God grant that I may use it wisely." And with that, William Jennings Bryan began to pray.[21]

Nine years after that night in 1887, Bryan used his power to win the Democratic Party's presidential nomination. His 1896 campaign would become one of the most debated races in American history. Bryan's incredible speaking skills, his progressive views on money and taxation, his appeal to Populists, and his takeover of the Democratic Party all made him a polarizing figure in the gnawing depression of the 1890s. The election is usually explained as a showdown between those below the wedge, putting their faith in Bryan and his plan for silver currency, and those above the wedge, defending America from what they believed was a class uprising of cranks who "hate prosperity." It would be remembered as a culminating battle, the peak of the Gilded Age.[22]

But this is not quite right. What made 1896 significant was not the extremity of its conflict but the way it employed all the new mechanisms that had been introduced to restrain American politics. In addition to educational campaigning, ballot reform, permanent clubs, and Black disenfranchisement, 1896 would add another striking element. That command William Jennings Bryan had told Mary about, his "power over an audience," would fundamentally alter the relationship between candidate and citizen.

Certainly, there were plenty who saw Bryan's nomination as a sign of national Armageddon. But he was no revolutionary. He was merely trying to fix capitalism, claiming, in his famous "Cross of Gold" speech, to represent the crossroads store owners and small-town attorneys. Florie Kelley's friend and babysitter, Henry Demarest Lloyd, dismissed Bryan's plan to coin silver as "the most trifling installment of reform." And yet many wealthy Americans looked down from their new fortresses and saw a Marxist uprising. Theodore Roosevelt was especially hysterical. Working as police commissioner of New York, Teddy denounced Bryan's supporters as "the men who pray for anarchy . . . who want to strike down the well-to-do," who were willing to "sacrifice their own welfare, if only they can make others less happy."[23]

Such a threat, Roosevelt said privately, "can only be suppressed, as the Commune in Paris was suppressed, by taking ten or a dozen of their leaders out . . . and shooting them dead."[24]

In Kansas, that derisive young editor William Allen White looked on with horror. The fanatics who had been hanging "Silly Willie" in effigy had captured a national party. In his later autobiography White reflected on how he "was moved by fear and rage as the story came in," how he saw Bryan as "an incarnation of demagogy, the apotheosis of riot, destruction and carnage . . . It seemed to me that rude hands were trying to tear down the tabernacle of our national life." He published a scathing editorial on the radical tone of politics in his state, titled "What's the Matter with Kansas?" It was snide, hateful, and really very funny, a masterwork of polemical journalism in a snarky era. Reprinted nationwide, White's article earned him praise from prominent Republicans, including his new friend Theodore Roosevelt, and shaped the tone of national hysteria.[25]

Bryan's chief innovation was his approach to the race itself. For once, a presidential candidate campaigned. Making use of his "more than usual power as a speaker," Bryan set out on a ferocious tour. He gave over five hundred speeches in one hundred days, traveling some eighteen thousand miles of railroad and reaching millions across the Midwest. The effect was electric. Even White marveled at the way Bryan "thrilled the nation." Those who saw him kept coming back to that word: he "thrilled" them.[26]

This was something new in American politics. For decades, the thrill of American democracy had been in the marching, the shouting, and the fighting that surrounded voting: the excitement of participation. In 1896 the candidate thrilled the public. He was the subject; they were the object. He was the actor; they were the spectators.

Bryan was toying with a new conception of the presidency. Traditionally, presidential candidates had not campaigned for themselves, and those who had—oddballs and losers like Stephen Douglass and Horace Greeley—lost, and then died. But candidates were gradually demanding more of a stake in governing—a task mostly done by clubby legislatures. Garfield and Blaine had given campaign speeches. Blaine declared that the voters "want a positive, absolute President, not a mere do-nothing." Grover Cleveland made himself the most "positive" president since Lincoln, asking, "What is the use of being elected or re-elected unless you stand for something?" He pushed Congress to reform the tariff and vetoed some five hundred bills, more than all other presidents to that date combined, and only later surpassed by FDR.[27]

The idea of a more powerful executive fit into the vision of a new democracy expressed by America's political restrainers. Some argued that a single bold leader could clear out the corruption of rotten legislatures and vulgar machines. City reformers in New York, Philadelphia, and Chicago found that they achieved real successes only when voters periodically elected an effective reform mayor. Innovative leaders in Toledo, Detroit, and Cleveland launched the first reforms that would become the progressive movement in government. It all grew from that same "alone with his conscience" revolution in voting: a fear of mass, public participation and a faith in the wisdom of a solitary, decisive man. "Personal leadership" was the trick, one writer argued in 1894. "The people will not come out for a principle, but they will for a man."[28]

The man put forward to defeat Bryan's insurgency, William McKinley, was not thrilling, but he too stressed "personal leadership." McKinley was a protectionist Union veteran from Ohio—in other words, a typical Republican candidate. In the face of Bryan's thrilling charisma, McKinley projected stability. Even his frame—five foot seven and over 230 pounds— suggested that he would make no significant movements. White, summoned to meet McKinley after publishing "What's the Matter with Kansas?," found him to be imposing and inaccessible, "a bronze statue" of a man. Yet his role in the campaign was revolutionary in its own way. The year before the election McKinley went on a punishing speaking tour, giving 371 speeches in three hundred cities. And as the Republican nominee in 1896, he sat through the innovative "porch-front campaign," where he greeted half a million supporters who visited his front lawn in Canton, Ohio. This approach offered a plausible deniability Bryan lacked—McKinley was not *campaigning*, merely standing on his porch, his fortress. But the effect was similar. McKinley was the bronze statue that the citizenry came to behold.[29]

In reality, it took huge teams of party professionals (and millions of dollars) to let Bryan and McKinley thrill spectators. As Republican campaign manager, the Ohio boss Mark Hanna ran an impressive Republican machine, shipping hundreds of thousands of visitors to McKinley's porch front as if they were pork bellies. Hanna spent liberally, helping to further shift political participation from voluntary to paid labor. Educational campaigning supplemented personal interaction, especially in an election fought over the arcane details of gold versus silver-and-gold currency. Party pamphleteers tried to explain what Bryan and McKinley were talking about. The Republican Party printed 275 different types of pamphlets in English, German, Italian, Swedish, Greek, Polish, and Yiddish—120 million in all. "The people," one Kansas Republican noted with surprise, seemed willing to "listen to long and tedious discussions with extraordinary patience."[30]

The parties supplemented the lectures, porch-front meetings, and pamphlets with seas of stuff. The 1896 election represented a tipping point in the consumption of political gimmicks. Buttons proliferated, often just barely coherent—like the trend of Republicans wearing little beetle-shaped brass brooches to indicate that they were "Gold Bugs." Democrats wore equally arcane endorsements of Bryan's proposed sixteen-to-one ratio of silver-to-gold currency. "Crosses of Gold" and "Full Dinner Pails" (McKinley's signature phrase) appeared frequently. More than these slogans, Bryan's and McKinley's faces were everywhere—the Democrat's proud nose facing off against the Republican's stern brow. Theodore Roosevelt joked about a campaign that was so pushy and merchandized that Hanna might as well be selling a patent medicine. These objects represented a shift from earlier campaign materials. There were fewer torches, uniforms, and hats—participatory tools that supporters used to *do something*, to become the campaign themselves. Instead, there were the faces of Bryan and McKinley over and over again, doing the work for citizens who simply wore the things.[31]

By beginning the switch from participatory objects to consumable trinkets, the 1896 election further increased campaigns' reliance on money. Led by Hanna, the Republicans raised some $3.5 million, playing on bankers' fears of Bryan. Most of it was spent in doubtful midwestern states, using New York cash to bring Indianans to Canton or distribute buttons across Iowa. Many have argued that this was the moment when corporate financing conquered American democracy. Money played a significant role in the campaign, to be sure, but it filled the growing void left as participatory demonstrations were deliberately restrained. Cash was one campaign tool among many in an evolving political world. After all, the Republicans spent seven times more than the Democrats, and far more than any past election, but the ultimate turnout was exactly the same as the far cheaper 1888 race.

On the eve of election, the old bonds of partisanship seemed to be crumbling. "The independent voter who has been predicting and hoping for a smashing of the old political parties," the *Los Angeles Times* trumpeted, "cannot fail to be satisfied . . . Such a sundering of old political ties has not been seen for decades." With conservative Democrats fleeing their party for the Republicans, and radical Populists voting for Bryan's Democrats, November 1896 promised to be "a good time for the independent voter."[32]

It was a good time for William McKinley. On election day he trounced Bryan, winning 60 percent of the electoral votes and the first clear majority of both the popular vote and the electoral college since 1872. Turnout was a healthy 79.3 percent—high, but nothing unusual for the era. Historians have paid attention to Bryan and the thwarted possibilities of his takeover of a mainstream party, but McKinley *won*, convincing the voter just above the wedge that Bryan threatened his prosperity, his stability, even his dinner. The 1896 election has been cast as a fight for the future of American democracy and capitalism, but it was more of a portal, combining the old campaign convulsions of the nineteenth century with the more restrained, merchandized, managed, candidate-focused races of the twentieth.

The defeated struggled not to blame the voters. Donnelly fell into another of his funks. "Never were the circumstances more favorable for success," Donnelly moaned after watching the results come in by telegraph at the *St. Paul Pioneer Press* offices on election night. "We had a splendid candidate and he made a gigantic campaign; the elements of reform were fairly united; and the depression of business universal, and yet in spite of it all the bankrupt millions voted to keep the yoke on their own necks!" Henry Demarest Lloyd struck a similar but more cautious tone. Maybe campaigning was simply "antiquated and inefficient." Maybe it was not possible to "carry on democracy by means of party government."[33]

The election had a lot in common with the fateful race in 1876. Both were defining moments that have been misremembered. The 1876 election is retold as a story of a backroom compromise, when really it should be remembered for its incredible turnout and the way the popular voice could still be painfully indecisive. Likewise, 1896 is retold as a furious showdown, when really it was a showcase for the "new weapons of democracy" crafted over the 1890s. Both have been memorialized as conspiracies—a backroom compromise in '76, an election bought with corporate money in '96. But both tell a far more complex story of the fundamental challenges of mobilizing, counting, and understanding the will of the people. Together, these elections bookend the rise and fall of the most misunderstood phase in American history, the unleashing and restraining of convulsive, popular energies that would remake democracy.

CHAPTER SIXTEEN

"Investigate, Agitate, Legislate"

G overnor Altgeld made my boy a good birthday present without knowing it!" Florie cheered to Henry Demarest Lloyd on Ko's eighth birthday. The radical Democratic governor had appointed her chief factory inspector of Illinois, entrusting her with the astounding task of monitoring industrial practices in one of the busiest, dirtiest economies in the world. Florie had a staff of eleven, a budget of twenty-eight thousand dollars, and more influence over labor conditions than any other woman alive. Finally, someone would have to answer to her persistent asking.[1]

Not everyone embraced her appointment. The German Republican newspaper *Illinois Staats-Zeitung*, the second largest in Chicago, denounced Florie as "an extremist socialist agitator" and taunted: "Her famous deceased father would have nothing to do with her." Wielding impeccable German and incapable of stepping down from a fight, Florie shot back a letter to the editor, shaming the Republican paper for misrepresenting the memory of William Kelley. "My father was much too courageous a man and too loving a father to let a difference of opinion about questions of political economy tarnish his relationship with one of his children," Florie wrote.[2]

And besides, Florie stressed, she was no partisan. She hated both parties and was hardly "a yes-person." "Nothing political is involved" in her appointment.[3]

In the mid-1890s, for the first time in decades, it was possible to claim that nothing political was involved and not sound ridiculous. Politics felt calmer, if not cleaner. It was as if the 1896 election had lanced some sore. The war with Spain that erupted in 1898 further distracted the public. Americans were eager to argue over new questions about empire and nationalism. Under the surface, though, a shift was taking place. Over the previous decade, a whole suite of restraining mechanisms had begun to calm American politics. Together, they undermined the old political model, but did not yet amount to a coherent new philosophy. One political scientist called the reforms the "contrivance theory of government," and Jane Addams observed that reformers were so obsessed with perfecting political "methods that they fail to consider the final aims." And yet, just as reform sprouted in the dark years of the late 1880s, a new thesis for democracy blossomed in the quiet late '90s.[4]

Florie was at the heart of this revolution in public life, though rarely quiet herself. As reformers restrained the campaign culture that dominated the nineteenth century, activists like Florie began to explore ways to influence the public. Some were political; others relied on private lobbying, or consumer boycotts, or bureaucratic regulations. For generations, Americans—men in particular—had focused strictly on electoral politics as the chief way to change society. But campaigning was becoming just one of many means to an end. Women often led the way; the sexism that kept them out of politics also freed them from the party machines. Florie, in particular, spent the 1890s darting in and out of public life, experimenting with every avenue to reform. She pursued many of the same goals that her father had, but was freed from the partisan system that had enabled and ensnared his career.

It was wrong to claim that there was "nothing political involved" in her work. It's just that what was political was changing.

Jane Addams's nephew, James Weber Linn, spent a good deal of time at Hull House in the '90s and struggled to describe the tall, striking woman with dark braided hair known simply as "F.K." Linn found her fascinating and frightening. "Full of love as she was," he wrote, Florie was nonetheless the "toughest customer in the reform riot, the finest rough-and-tumble fighter for the good life for others, that Hull House ever knew. Any weapon was a good weapon in her hand—evidence, argument, irony or invective." Linn was struck by Florie's "fiercely joyous impatience," the way her mouth curled up in a wicked smile when she was being difficult, the way she "hurled the spears of her thought with such apparent carelessness of what breasts they pieced." Though hardly careless, Florence Kelley did hit, in the 1890s, on her lifelong strategy of employing "any weapon" at her disposal.[5]

Delighted with her new position as Illinois's factory inspector, Kelley spearheaded investigations of labor practices in thousands of workplaces. She made sure that her department's reports were highly readable, "full of indignant satire" for newspapers to quote. Traveling constantly, Florie pursued abusive child labor practices, weighing and measuring young workers to document the atrocious toll industrial labor took on a maturing body. She showed how repetitive, punishing tasks in cutlery factories left teams of boys with the identical deformity to their right shoulder. She documented the "dogs" of southern Illinois glass factories—kids in their early teens whose hard labor in sweltering glass mills rendered them too damaged to continue in that trade as adults. Fighting Illinois's large businesses, its conservative press, and ultimately its Supreme Court, Florie pushed for an eight-hour-day law for female employees. And when Chicago's condescending district attorney refused to pursue a case she brought to him in a tense morning meeting, Florence took the streetcar to Northwestern University and registered for a law degree that afternoon.[6]

This new career agreed with her. To celebrate her job, she took Ko—always her favorite—to the Chicago World's Fair, where she happened upon an acquaintance from her days in New York. He barely recognized her. The gaunt and tired Florie—trapped with Lazare, floundering professionally, struggling to feed three small children—was gone. "I looked so much stronger, healthier and happier," Florie reflected. Frances Perkins, who met her at the end of this period, described Florie as a "handsome woman, although her total inattention to her personal appearance and her method of dress, her unconcern with fashion, often led people to think of her as dowdy." Florie's rumpled clothes connected her back to her father, perpetually too busy steering the nation's economy to buy a new hat. She settled on a personal uniform in the 1890s, putting aside the corsets, puffed sleeves, and feathered hats of the era for simple, robe-like black dresses.

She looked refreshingly austere; a woman unconcerned with frills. In photographs, Florie appears to almost hover above those around her, her black dresses and confident posture lending her a nearly supernatural heft.[7]

She worked so hard that she often missed her chicks, mostly seeing them as three small, slumbering bodies when they were visiting. She won custody from Lazare after an ugly public fight soon after arriving in Chicago. But instead of settling down with them, Florie circulated her children around, boarded first at the Wayside, then in the slums around Hull House, and then with the architect Frank Lloyd Wright's mother. The children often spent their summers at Jessie and Henry Demarest Lloyd's luxurious Rhode Island beach house.

Florie wrote to them often; just like her father before her, she refused to shield them from her work. She detailed the experiences of the glass trade's "dogs" to Ko, who was the same age as those boys, just as Will Kelley had introduced young Florie to children working in English brick factories. The three children were clearly growing up as Kelleys. Their school report cards even noted their classic Kelley dishevelment. Each earned above average grades, except for low marks in "Care of Clothes" and "Care of Room."[8]

Florie also rebuilt her tattered bond with her mother. Carrie came to Chicago and lived with Florie for a period. Albert asked his sister not to allow their mother to be "too much alone and get a chance to brood over the many disappointments of her life." Coming into her own, Florie was also coming out of her destructive, angry phase. She apologized again and again to her mother for "my years of cruel ingratitude." On New Year's Eve 1893, Florie wrote to Carrie of her immense appreciation for "the loving heart that you kept so warm for me when I did not deserve it." Reflecting on her new career, she wrote, "It has been in every way, a good year for me, personally. Good health, good children, good work, good friends, and as much of your presence as it was at all reasonable to ask for. What more could a woman wish, who has survived the illusions of youth without bitterness."[9]

Another illusion of youth—that she could keep her distance from electoral politics—fell away. Her patron, Governor John Peter Altgeld, was up for reelection in 1896, and he had made many enemies in Illinois by pardoning some of the Haymarket bombers. Republican cartoonists seized on the resemblance between the governor and President Garfield's assassin, Charles Guiteau—both bearded, scrawny men with cropped hair— suggesting that a vote for Altgeld was a vote for assassination and anarchy. If he lost his reelection, Florie would surely be replaced. So she began to speak and organize on Altgeld's behalf. With Bryanists seizing control of the Democratic Party, and smaller radical socialist factions pinballing back and forth, Florie had wandered into the most "badly muddled" election in years. She found no easy home in any party. She would never be a Democrat or a Republican, she considered the Populists' focus on silver to be childish, and she even quarreled with the tiny Socialist Labor Party.[10]

One thing was certain. "If the working people allow" Governor Altgeld to be defeated in 1896, Florie swore to Lloyd, "surely they deserve to have no other friend until this generation dies out and another and better one takes its place."[11]

Altgeld's crushing defeat left Florie out of work, but oddly motivated. The huge Republican win in 1896 devastated a generation of Populists, socialists, and radical Democrats. Many gave up on reform or wandered off into crankish causes, or simply died in the years after 1896. But Florence Kelley, more than almost any other figure, came out of 1896 with new momentum. Her first taste of political battle left her grasping for other weapons. Her next crusade meant picking a fight with one of Chicago's most powerful bosses.

Alderman John Powers—nicknamed "Johnny De Pow"—was the very stereotype of the nineteenth-century machine politician. Mustachioed and pop-eyed, he wore diamond brooches across his barrel chest and jeweled rings on his fingers. With constituents, Powers was unctuous and ingratiating, a "consummate slapper of backs" and distributor of cigars. He was a key member of the "Grey Wolves" ring of crooked aldermen, and a notable presence at Chicago's flamboyant First Ward Balls, rubbing elbows with mayors and madams. In the Nineteenth Ward, he wielded his social skills and wealth of political jobs in exchange for votes. In particular, Powers haunted funerals, paying for caskets, supporting widows, and finding jobs for bereaved sons as garbage collectors or street sweepers. Addams calculated that one third of the voters in the Nineteenth Ward, in which Hull

House was located, were at one time or another employed by Chicago's "chief mourner."[12]

But Powers was not doing his job, as Florie and Addams saw it. For all those city positions he disbursed, little work got done. The ward was swimming in garbage; boys and girls played among the corpses of dead horses, left to rot where they fell. Powers used his army of street sweepers as a political weapon, threatening one opponent: "You won't get a can of garbage moved out of your ward till hell freezes over." Powers was also failing to provide education. Florie calculated that there were just 2,579 seats to serve over seven thousand children. And, as her research had rigorously proved, a child denied space in school was often headed for a factory instead.[13]

So Florie and Addams began to organize "indignation meetings" against the Powers machine, at which, the *Chicago Tribune* gleefully reported, "trouble sizzled and boiled for Alderman John Powers in his own bailiwick." Addams and Florie also recruited male candidates to run for office against Powers. But neither Florie nor Addams were practical politicians, and they had come up against a wily enemy who publicly cursed: "Hull House will be driven from the ward." They watched, in three successive elections, as Hull House's chosen candidates backed out of each race, only to take up cushy city jobs that Powers found for them. With neither the right to vote nor the mechanisms of the city at their disposal, Florie and Addams saw that reform would lose as long as it followed the old script of indignant meetings and untested candidates.[14]

Hull House's defeats confirmed Florie's dim view of politics. To her, men like Powers won, and Altgeld lost, because the voters were wrong. Or, at least, "hoodwinked." She often sounds like the despondent Donnelly, disappointed when "the bankrupt millions voted to keep the yoke on their own necks!" Florie complained that workingmen "never read anything but a democratic or republican newspaper" and ignored socialist pamphlets. She also observed a telling gendered distinction: when working with labor unionists, the men became unreliable around age twenty-one, distracted by party politics. Female activists, lacking the vote, remained doggedly committed to their organizing. And when reforms did succeed, Florie wrote, it was often because a cause did not develop into a political issue.

There was more room to change minds on issues that "elections have not hinged upon."[15]

But her defeats drew her farther into the political system. By the late 1890s, the rough-and-tumble fighter in a black dress had become a nationally recognized force. When President McKinley assembled an industrial commission on labor issues, a friend pushed for Florie's inclusion. Without her, Florie's friend joked, the commission would be just another gathering of "innocuous old ladies of the male sex." Florie could bring some fire. McKinley had been Will Kelley's greatest admirer in Congress, taking up his place as America's chief protectionist after Will died. It was McKinley, the bronze statue, who had tearfully honored Will as always "on the extreme outpost" in his congressional memorial. Florie traveled to Washington, where President McKinley spoke lovingly to her about her father. "He actually had tears in his eyes," she wrote to Carrie. She did not win a position—their politics were as far apart as almost any in American life. But the idea that she might have shows how far she had come from her days as a sidelined Swiss socialist in the 1880s. Little by little, Florie was finding her way in a political sphere she so harshly denounced.[16]

The next year, in 1899, Florie saw an even greater prize. The journalist Jacob Riis recommended that his old friend Teddy Roosevelt, now governor of New York, appoint Florie as the state's chief factory inspector. It was an even bigger job than the one in Illinois. "Nothing has seemed to me since I was twenty years old so great an opportunity for social usefulness," Florie gushed. She admired Roosevelt's combative verve and daydreamed about what she could achieve, backed up by "Teddy's fearlessness." Working through Riis and other connections, Florie sent her indignant reports to Roosevelt—exactly the kind of dense, rich material he loved to pore through. She made sure Teddy knew that she was more than a harmless do-gooder: her work in Illinois had taught her the rare confrontation skill of knowing "how to inspect the inspectors!" It was her talents as a questioner, her persistent asking, that made her ideal for the job.[17]

Florie made her pitch and anxiously waited, trusting "to Providence and Teddy's whims."

Teddy decided against her. He told Riis that he had no prejudices against Florie, but that her legacy as an appointee of Altgeld scared the conservative Republican machine on which he relied. New York's all-powerful "Easy Boss" Platt—trained by Conkling himself—would never accept her. Florie accepted yet another defeat gracefully and struck up a habit of letter writing with Teddy. Yet she was furious to learn that the position had gone to an Albany elevator operator whose only experience was years of running Republican campaigns.

After all these efforts, Florie joked to Lloyd: "I am becoming a professional office-seeker." In a nation run by patronage, no one wanted to play at practical politics less than Florie.[18]

One way around these obstructions was the National Consumer League, newly founded by Addams and the veteran reformer Josephine Shaw Lowell. The NCL joined the slew of civic organizations emerging in the Progressive Era, as reformers sought avenues around the electoral system. Founded in 1899, the NCL's goal was to mobilize the nation's consumers, wielding mass buying power as a weapon to improve working conditions. The movement notably shifted activism from the traditionally male sphere of politics to the traditionally female sphere of purchasing goods for the home. The organization choose "Investigate, Agitate, Legislate" as its motto, and the relentless agitator Florence Kelley as its general secretary.

As her first mission, Kelley chose an unlikely target: America's underwear. By inspecting cotton undergarment factories, the NCL identified department stores whose products were produced "under clean and healthful conditions." Marking each pair with a little white ribbon, the NCL hoped to steer consumers away from sweatshop labor. The campaign was a huge success. It also pointed at Florie's drift from socialism to a reformed vision of capitalism—Friedrich Engels would never approve, but Lloyd did. Florie's NCL work marks an important reapplication of her father's refusal to wear foreign manufactured clothing and her antebellum aunt's boycott of sugar produced by slave labor. And it can be seen as a stepping-stone to the New Deal's later National Recovery Act and the Buy American activism of the twentieth century.

With these accessible consumer campaigns, and Florie's ferocious speechifying (she was soon giving over one hundred speeches a year), the movement spread quickly. It was exactly the kind of public activism that appealed to Americans around 1900: not the totalizing campaigns of the nineteenth century, but conscientious, occasional, and nonpartisan. In 1899 the NCL had half a dozen leagues, in 1900 there were thirty, and by 1904 there were over sixty leagues nationwide. But to run the organization, Florie was forced to leave behind the friendships she had built in Chicago and return to New York. It was the end of an era. She had left New York in 1891, bruised and scared. Now she returned to take up a national position, live with friends at the Henry Street Settlement, and build a prominent new career.

During her Chicago interlude, Florie had experimented with many avenues of reform. She had found her greatest influence in government regulation, as Illinois factory inspector, and consumer activism, as secretary of the NCL. And she experienced her greatest defeats in electoral politics, campaigning to reelect Governor Altgeld or unseat Alderman Powers. A decade of life experience confirmed what Florie had muttered about for years: political democracy was unreliable, and there were more efficient ways to influence the public.

Kelley had spent the 1880s preaching about class revolution, and the 1890s worrying about garbage and underwear. Here she tracked another crucial trend—reformers were learning to think smaller. Instead of grappling with electoral politics as the central convulsion dominating public life, activists were putting more energy into small-scale goals, municipal reform, and the "drainage and ventilation" of industrial society. This shift in scale grew from the passing of the Civil War generation, who watched Emancipation attempt to "settle" the one great question of the age, who told themselves that "Pure Democracy" could be an arbiter of national life, and who morphed into the monomaniacal cranks of the 1880s. In an era when the ballot box was the only king, it made sense to be a "fool of one idea." And in a disrupted society, it was comforting to hope for sudden, winner-take-all change.

But by the 1890s this approach looked naive. Lloyd warned against "parlor utopias" and mocked those "throwing up their hats in the air" for silver, or the tariff, or any other cause around which campaigns were organized. Florie Kelley, and the many who followed her, skirted the big, dumb elections that had never again brought about anything like Emancipation. The constant talk of the power of the ballot box had prevented a generation from trying other means to effect their ends. "Under guise of republican freedom," Florie declared, "we have degenerated to a nation of mock citizens." To become real citizens again, she had concluded, Americans had to ask less of politics.[19]

LIKE FLORENCE KELLEY, Lincoln Steffens grew up watching men speechify. A child of privilege, raised in the soaring mansion that would later become the California governor's house, young Lennie wandered Gilded Age Sacramento. He would visit the statehouse to watch the politicians debate. Steffens loved memorizing the rules of the legislature, but even as a boy he noticed that the printed regulations did not seem to be the real force governing politics. Soon a friendly page brought him to the committee rooms and hotel suites where politicians and lobbyists drank, smoked, played poker, and made deals. They assumed Lennie was just another page. At a young age, he watched with disdain as politicians made up their own rules. They were "bad men," Steffens concluded: "how I hated them."[20]

Steffens's childhood taught him two skills that would prove useful later on: puzzling out the real rules to the game, but doing it so unobtrusively that the rule breakers kept talking.

Twenty years later, around 1896, "Lennie" Steffens was a crime reporter, observing the crooks of New York City. He was handsome and self-assured, with a boyish pompadour, a dainty Van Dyke, and a clear, confident gaze. He worked for the *New York Post*, and ran with a crowd of energetic young reformers, including Jacob Riis and Teddy Roosevelt. Showing his legendary resourcefulness, Steffens learned to meet with the famously talkative Roosevelt while he was getting a shave—with a barber's straight razor held to Teddy's face, Steffens could get a word in. His boss at the *Post* was that desiccated old reformer, E. L. Godkin, the last voice of the aristocratic, antidemocratic grumblers of the 1870s. To the young, cocky Steffens, Godkin sounded like a croak from the past, forever crusading "against bad government and bad journalism, which he attributed to bad men. His cure was to throw the rascals out and elect good men." In the strange portal of the mid-1890s between two political universes, Steffens was beginning to wonder what calling a politician a "bad man" really meant.[21]

He was not alone. The changes in journalism that had propelled Lloyd were, in the decade after 1896, seeding a field of energetic young men and women, each trying to write "the new Uncle Tom's Cabin." They hoped to dig into the gritty social inequities of American life and report out to a concerned public. With new magazines piling up middle class parlors, these journalists could afford to pursue independent, in-depth research. In 1906 Roosevelt mockingly compared these obsessive journalists to the "muckraker" in the classic *The Pilgrim's Progress*, "who could look no way but downward" at society's filth, and the term stuck. But in their crucial early phase, no one called them that. And though they are remembered today for tackling the social evils of the meatpacking business and industrial trusts, they first sharpened their knives on politics.[22]

Though they framed their projects as tackling corruption, these journalists were digging into something deeper. To explain how politicians stole and cheated, reporters had to explain why voters let them. To understand corruption, they had to understand democracy. These were nagging questions that had not been well explained in decades of popular politics. Reformers never really understood how politics worked, and practical politicians weren't about to tell them. In the quiet years tucked into the end of the nineteenth century and the dawning of the twentieth, politicos were shockingly forthcoming. One midlevel Tammany boss—George Washington Plunkitt—plopped himself down at a Manhattan shoeshine stand and expounded on a lifetime of dirty tricks to a *New York Evening Post* reporter. Perhaps they sensed that their era was passing and wanted to leave a legacy. In the process, they answered crucial questions about how democracy actually fit into Americans' lives.

Many of these writers are a joy to read, distinguished from the musty old Mugwumps by their wit, humanism, and excoriating self-criticism. Most came from the ranks of what William Allen White called "the conservative plutocratic democracy" and were turning their pens on the political misdeeds of their well-to-do communities. Often they had spent the 1870s and '80s, like Steffens, with a profound antipathy for American politics. Starting adulthood with the assumption that democracy had failed, they had little use for outrage, which seemed self-evident. Instead, they wanted to know why.[23]

To do so, Steffens planned an unprecedented research project for the new *McClure's Magazine*. He would learn, city by city, how political corruption worked. For decades, men of his class had been vigorously condemning politics, but mostly from their drawing rooms. (George William Curtis's column in *Harper's* was actually titled The Easy Chair.) But Steffens set out for the chophouses and billiard halls of Philadelphia, New York, Boston, Chicago, Minneapolis, and St. Louis to learn the unwritten rules to the "great American game." He interviewed men with nicknames like "the Easy Boss" and "the Dying Boss," "the Mahatma" and "the Rascal King," "Hinky Dink Kenna" and "Bathhouse John." And he was good at it. There was something in Steffens's manner that got men talking, as if he already knew the crimes to which they were confessing, like the boy who had figured out the real rules to Sacramento's smoke-filled suites. "He seemed," his friend Frederic Howe said admiringly, "not to be hating any one."[24]

Instead of hating, Steffens was hunting. To the politicians he interviewed, he came across like some kind of corruption aficionado. Finally, someone wanted to understand how they managed the incredible task of getting millions of citizens to vote. Sitting with a Republican boss in Philadelphia on one trip, Steffens offhandedly referred to a trick used by the St. Louis machine. The Philly politico lit up, and the two began excitedly comparing notes, talking like "one artist to another." For his deep interest in the mechanisms of corruption, the Philadelphia boss paid Steffens a huge compliment, calling him "a born crook that's gone straight."[25]

All these quiet conversations were mounting to a "dawning theory." Steffens noticed that the problems in Philadelphia looked like the problems in St. Louis and, for that matter, in rural Pennsylvania or backwoods Missouri. Something larger had to explain it all. Elitism and bigotry had long been the basic explanation, with White Protestant elites blaming working-class ethnic bosses for corruption. But Steffens found that Philly's Republican machine, made up of WASPs from old families, was the dirtiest in America. Likewise, the evils of urban life were not to blame; state machines used the same tricks.[26]

Interview by interview, Steffens slowly concluded that what seemed to be "exceptional, local, and criminal" wrongdoing was inherent to American democracy. Once, he asked a well-connected Manhattan attorney why he kept hearing Wall Street defend Tammany Hall. The lawyer kicked Steffens in the shin, hard, and then asked him why his mouth cried out when his shin hurt. Politics was a holistic system with a single anatomy, like the "nervous system" with "filaments in every township and every village" that Howe observed in his Pennsylvania hometown.[27]

Steffens's "dawning theory" meant rejecting assumptions that went back to the early 1870s, when reformers had argued that individual sinners were corrupting a good system. It was a satisfying narrative for the old American families who had lost control of the political system devised by their ancestors. But the journalists were challenging this. The progressive thinker Herbert Croly wrote that until about 1900 he had believed that greedy men corrupted "an essentially satisfactory political and economic system," but he came to see that the acrimony in American politics was actually "the result of their normal operation."[28]

For a generation, critics of American politics had been attacking widening circles of badness. Starting around 1870, the problem was bad politicians, then bad machines, bad parties, bad campaigns, and finally a bad public. But by 1900, journalists exploring the "normal operation" of democracy looked beyond morality. Their approach became less theological, more sociological. Steffens pointed to the work of child labor reformers like Florie, noting that they were discovering "about children what I was discovering about men: that there are no bad boys and girls, and no good ones either." Teddy Roosevelt, who mocked the muckrakers but befriended and relied on them, had made this point since the 1880s. "Every man who has been in practical politics," Teddy wrote, knows that politicians "are no more all of them bad than they are all of them good."[29]

Instead of condemning, some muckrakers were finding that they liked their subjects. Howe had grown up scorning politicians and earned a PhD from Johns Hopkins, where he was taught that politics should be "the business of a gentleman." But after a period of unemployment, living down-and-out on the Bowery, Howe found the local Tammany politicians shockingly "human, generous, kindly." He liked them "better than the old English worthies whose opinions were quoted with so much veneration in the textbooks." Howe concluded, after a hard winter surviving on free baloney lunches in Bowery saloons, "it was social conditions that were bad rather than people."[30]

In 1900 this lesson was revelatory. Writers were finally able to see what millions of working people had known for decades. Partisan voters were not mesmerized by dark forces, they were making a deliberate choice. Americans' lives were so disrupted and unstable that even the small kindnesses of political machines made a great difference. Steffens noted the little gestures that won voters' trust, the way machine politicians "speak pleasant words, smile friendly smiles, notice the baby, give picnics up the River or the Sound, or a slap on the back." Millions turned out to vote for crooks and demonstrate for demagogues, not because they were fools, but because they got something material or psychological from their participation. It all turned on partisan loyalty, which, in Howe's observation, promised "security in a strange land under strange laws." Politics might be dirty, but they were rational, with voter and politician joined in a social exchange.[31]

The muckrakers were not simply soft-hearted excusers of bosses' bad behavior. Instead, they pointed to a larger culprit undermining American democracy. It was not a few selfish politicians but the great mass of voters whose behavior had to change. This view had been building for years. From the 1860s through the 1890s, voters had determined the "moral standard" of Donnelly's speeches, politicians had been warned to swallow the views of their constituents, and Florence Kelley had reminded Susan B. Anthony that her father's support for suffrage was limited by the voters of Pennsylvania. The muckrakers took this thesis further. Breaking with a lifetime of populist dogma, they concluded that, as White put it, "no one was to blame more than the people themselves."[32]

Steffens organized his 1904 collection of essays *The Shame of the Cities* around this revelation. The book is one of the most influential ever written on American democracy, cited by Theodore Roosevelt, argued over by Tammany politicians, and mentioned in practically every history textbook. But it is tragically misremembered as an easy piece of anti-boss moralism, usually paired with a Thomas Nast drawing from thirty years earlier. In fact, Steffens had little interest in blaming a handful of politicians. He hoped his book would test the depths of Americans' faith in democracy, "to sound for the civic pride of an apparently shameless citizenship." Packaging his work with a scorching, relevant, and very readable introduction and conclusion, Steffens spelled out his dawning theory: "The misgovernment of the American people is misgovernment by the American people."[33]

It was too easy, in a populist democracy, to condemn the men at the top. "You may blame the politicians," Steffens had found, "but not all the classes, not the people." He satirized the way craven politicians played along, begging "Blame us, blame anybody, but praise the people." But the same outraged Americans who attacked bosses sustained their corruption. "The people are not innocent," Steffens nearly shouted at his readers. "That is the only 'news' in all the journalism of these articles."[34]

After Steffens laid out the corruption of seven cities, his conclusion pointed straight at readers in their easy chairs. The simple truth, Steffens wrote, was that politicians were expert readers of public demands, and the public had not demanded good government. Instead, for decades they had been driven by outrage, alternately between political parties, throwing out one set of bums, then the other. Steffens asked: "Do we Americans really want good government? Do we know it when we see it? Are we capable of that sustained good citizenship which alone can make democracy a success?" For too long, American voters had been devoted to "turning the rascals out." But "any people is capable of rising in wrath to overthrow bad rulers . . . With fresh and present outrages to avenge, particular villains to punish, and the mob sense of common anger to excite, it is an emotional gratification to go out with the crowd and 'smash something.'" Everyone knew that Americans were capable of public anger, Steffens wrote, but whether they could "go forth singly also, and, without passion, with nothing but mild approval and dull duty to impel us, vote intelligently to sustain a fairly good municipal government, remains to be shown."[35]

Steffens's book was not one stray jeremiad. A host of thinkers, from Jane Addams to Teddy Roosevelt to Walter Lippmann, agreed "that the trouble lies with the voters themselves." A number made the dubious comparison to lynchings, arguing that Americans expected their democracy to operate like "a species of political lynch law." The parallel was hyperbolic and insensitive, but spoke to muckrakers' willingness to take on the crowd (several of them became prominent antilynching activists). William White chose a slightly gentler metaphor, writing that "the real danger from democracy is that we will get drunk on it." Individually, Americans were good sober citizens, but the nation's political culture had spent decades intoxicating itself. The political scientist James T. Young agreed, blaming "Government by indignation" and warning that "the consumer of political alcohol finds that his system is less and less exhilarated by the accustomed stimulant." By 1900 a lifetime of political outrage was starting to taste like weak whiskey.[36]

Who were "the voters" to which these writers referred? When Francis Parkman condemned the "public pest" in 1878, he shouted at those "beneath" him, blaming impoverished "hordes of native and foreign barbarians . . . the weakest and most worthless." But now, the muckrakers blamed their own well-to-do readers and prosperous families. "We are all involved in this political corruption," Addams reminded her readers, calling it "the penalty of a democracy" to stand indicted for mass bad behavior. It was the broad middle class of men and women living above the wedge who were most complicit. "That was what impressed me most," Howe recalled about the voters he grew up with in Meadville, Pennsylvania, "the kind of people I knew had neglected their duties."[37]

How could these writers be so severe about the voters, but so under-standing about individual politicians, many of them acknowledged crim-inals? Steffens seemed to write more forgivingly about a man who murdered his political rival than about law-abiding voters enraged by the crime. But this contradiction points at the changing vision of politics in the new century, a dawning humane antipopulism. It was empathetic about the actions of individuals, curious about their rational assessment of their needs, but harshly critical about the behavior of groups, especially unre-strained ones "drunk on democracy." To the new class of muckrakers "the mob sense of common anger" could never be trusted. But Man could be. Saving democracy had to be done one by one, as Steffens asked: voters must "go forth singly."

For forty years, Americans had reassured themselves that populist democracy could save them. Back in 1865, when Will Kelley had first called for Black voting rights on the floor of Congress, he had made this argu-ment. The fundamental question of democracy, Will had rumbled, was not the quality of the individual voter, "not whether each man is fitted for the most judicious performance of the functions of citizenship, but whether the state is not safer when she binds all her children to her." Together, "all her children" could achieve what "each man" could not. Life in the nineteenth century might be terrifying for isolated, powerless individuals, but mass democracy offered a refuge. By 1900, however, a new generation was saying just the opposite. When the nation put her faith in all her children, they usually tried to smash something. Humane antipopulism put forth a new vision of democracy, driven by a faith in people, but a skepticism about the People.[38]

The muckrakers' skepticism toward the People flowed in the same direction as political restrainers' fears of the public. Progressives were calling for the same cultural shift as conservatives. Two wings of upper-middle-class life—people who bickered over Christmas dinners and rolled their eyes at each other's views—converged. Restrainers brought the mechanisms, and muckrakers added the motive. Armed with a new vision, reform no longer looked "frightened by democracy," as Addams had warned.[39]

Together they fought to replace partisan tribalism with political individualism. It may seem odd that this individualism emerged during the Progressive Era, a moment of greater acknowledgment of the social influences on life. But politics was often a countervailing force to the rest of society. In the disrupted, atomized Gilded Age, Americans joined mass political parties for protection and community, but in a twentieth century where mass culture was a daily reality, individualism seemed to promise safety.

Instead of outraged masses and opportunistic bosses, the new politics called for conscientious voters and efficient leaders. "Efficiency" emerged as a crucial new value, a brake on the emotionalism of the drunken crowd. It was popular with social-scientific progressives and business-minded conservatives alike; both groups envisioned a modern, rational nation run by bureaucrats. Florie Kelley had long condemned "the inefficiency of representative bodies" and the "incompetence and inefficiency" of bosses like Johnny Powers. Teddy Roosevelt agreed, complaining about the choice between practical politicians (effective but immoral) and Mugwumps (virtuous but useless). He called for a class of manly, skilled, moral administrators. Pushing further, the historian Walter Weyl boldly asked, "Is democracy after all a failure? Is not the bureaucratic efficiency of Prussia as good as the democratic laxness and corruption of Pennsylvania?" In these years fewer and fewer members of Congress came from the ranks of journalism, business, or wealthy old families. More and more were lawyers, heralding a new state run by experts in law.[40]

Buried deep in these quiet years, Florie's wise, owlish friend Henry Demarest Lloyd published a vision of the new social democracy titled *Man, the Social Creator*. The last century had been devoted to politics, Lloyd wrote, but it had only demonstrated the self-perpetuating waste of political outrage. "Government by party is not a means of settling things," Lloyd noted; "it is the best of devices for keeping them unsettled."[41]

Ever since the Civil War, Americans had tried "politics without government." It had failed. Now, in the dawn of a new century, Lloyd predicted: "We are moving toward a government without politics."[42]

IN 1889 A manufacturer of agricultural machinery named Jacob H. Myers invented a mechanical voting device. Myers was a well-to-do Democrat in Rochester, New York, tired of watching upstate Republicans falsify vote counts. Just as the other restraints on popular politics were being built, between 1887 and 1889, Myers designed his voting machine to "protect mechanically the voter from rascaldom." Such a device would never get drunk on democracy. All it did was count, efficiently and dispassionately.[43]

Ten years later, an updated version entered regular use, with a key innovation. At the top of the freestanding voting machine ran a semicircular curtain rod, bearing a green, checkered curtain. To vote, its user stepped up to the machine and pulled a lever that both activated the device and closed the curtain behind him. Locked away from the crowd, "alone with his conscience," the voter moved various switches to select his candidates. Only after completing voting could the user toggle the lever back, which counted his vote, reset the machine, and flung open the fluttering green curtain.[44]

American democracy had been forged, over the nineteenth century, by anxious people seeking safety in numbers. But in the twentieth century many were coming to see danger in those numbers and safety in their solitary consciences. A democracy that had been built in town squares and saloons now required seclusion from the crowd and automation from rascaldom. A public, partisan, passionate political system was being replaced with one that valued privacy, independence, and restraint. And a simple cloth curtain embodied what progressive muckrakers and conservative restrainers, social democrats like Florie and practical reformers like Teddy, were all pushing toward. Lock the lever, pull the curtain, and register your conscience with the machine.

CHAPTER SEVENTEEN

"The Right Not to Vote"

I n 1860 George Holt bought a torch attached to a six-foot wooden staff. He joined the Wide Awakes, the Republican movement that introduced the style of torchlit marches by uniformed young partisans. After marching for Lincoln, Holt marked his torch-staff with bold black ink "1860." Four years later he marched for Lincoln again, and marked his staff with "1864" just below his mark for 1860. Holt marched for Grant in '68 and '72, and Hayes in '76, and Garfield in '80. He marched in 1884 while out in South Dakota, and in 1888 and 1892. Each time he added the year to the tally descending his torch-staff. Holt turned out for McKinley in 1896 and 1900. Then, after an anarchist assassinated McKinley in 1901, Holt marched for his successor—Teddy Roosevelt—when he ran in his own right in 1904. After printing "1904" on the handle, George Holt put his torch away for good. He was done marching.[1]

Holt was a bounder and a striver, five foot four and wiry, a man of the peripatetic nineteenth century. He had been both a prisoner and a constable, a slave overseer and a Union Army soldier. He had served in a fire company and gone out to the future state of "Mt. Taner" to "fight the Indians." And he was a zealous campaigner, marching in every presidential election from 1860 through 1904. After 1904 he lived another fourteen years, through three more presidential elections. He kept active, but never again lit his torch for the Republican Party. George had not gotten too old for campaigning; campaigning had gotten too old for him.[2]

A photograph from 1914 shows Holt standing in his Wide Awakes uniform, holding his torch. One can imagine the impact a thousand George Holts had, marching through his New Hampshire hometown on an autumn night fifty years before. But in the 1914 photograph George stands alone, leaning slightly to one side, a little man with a white mustache and unkempt white hair. There is high grass at his feet, and pine trees sway behind him. He is out in some New Hampshire backyard, demonstrating an old curiosity for the photographer's lens. The era of midnight marches is over. George Holt looks old. His torch looks like an artifact.[3]

Holt wasn't the only partisan who put his torch away. Across the first decade of the twentieth century, men and women mostly stopped turning out for spectacular political displays. The nation still held plenty of parades, but they usually substituted dull patriotism for pointed partisanship. The campaign convulsions that had shaken society quieted. That was the term Americans chose to describe the change, a great *quieting*. In Kansas City in 1900, a reporter noted the "extreme quietness" of the presidential campaign, cheering: "Intemperate disputation and bitter partisanship are happily absent." In Cincinnati in 1904, a comedian joked that he planned to take a rest cure, so he "got a job at campaign headquarters." To the *New York Times* in 1908, "the quietness of the campaign is a relief." But to others, it felt more like a silencing.[4]

Americans offered unsatisfying explanations for what was happening. One man in Connecticut argued that "everybody is busy, by night is tired, and in no mood." But this was the age of the late-night dance hall and the extra-inning baseball game; Americans were turning out for public fun, just not for political fun. Another writer, in New York in 1908, argued that campaigns had quieted because "the money to pay for the shouting and the banners, the torches and the processions, has been lacking . . . every cheer has its price." But those cheers had been volunteered, free of charge, for decades. An editor in 1908 stepped closer to the truth when he expressed disdain for the kinds of people at midnight political rallies. "It is little wonder," he snipped, "that the general public is unwilling longer to be jostled by the crowds in ill-smelling halls in order to hear political harangues."[5]

This was the real explanation. The new "Quiet Campaign Method" deliberately replaced an entire culture of "torchlight processions, spreadeagle oratory, red fire, cannonading, and other spectacular features." Elections should have "more thinking and less shouting," the *Los Angeles Times* proposed. By 1910 the head of the New York Democratic State Committee acknowledged "the passing of old-time campaign methods," but argued that "the new system of campaigning is the better one, red fire and parades don't make votes." The best way to run a campaign was to "get away from the outward and visible sign of political activity." Politics was not going away, but it was certainly going indoors.[6]

The quiet was most jarring on election day. What had previously been a raucous civic holiday for the enfranchised (and an isolating cliffhanger for those barred from voting) felt dry and orderly. Men still voted, and women joined, too, as some states extended suffrage, but the crowds thinned in almost every election from 1900 on. Editorialists debated the merits of not voting, some advocating "the right not to vote" and others attacking the problem of "stay-at-homes." By 1907 an election day editorialist in the *New York Tribune* was asking: "Where were the crowds of yesteryear? By all tradition Broadway should have been filled from curb to curb."[7]

Some Americans embraced "orderly" election days as a sign of their uplifted civilization. "No disturbance occurred," announced the *St. Louis Post-Dispatch* in 1910, reporting "ELECTION QUIETEST IN HISTORY." "Citizens voted without interruption, and repeaters and thugs were not in evidence." Instead of vote challengers who usually "terrorized citizens at elections, Tuesday saw only policemen." No more drunk partisans swaying to the polls, no more rowdy first-timers hollering slogans in the street, no more challengers with revolvers in their coats. In some states, political machines switched from bribing men to vote their ticket to paying potential rivals to just stay home. A voter in Augusta, Georgia, in 1904, smiled: "It was gratifying to see the voting booths free from noisy crowds."[8]

These stay-at-homes were really the human evidence of an unprecedented crash in turnout. In the 1896 presidential election, 79.3 percent of eligible voters participated. From 1896 to 1900, turnout fell 6.1 percent. It crashed another 8 percent by 1904, plunged 6.6 percent in 1912, and crashed a full 12.4 percent by 1920. By 1924 nationwide voter turnout bottomed out at 48.8 percent, nearly one third lower than what it had been in 1896, and below any other presidential election since the rise of popular suffrage in the 1820s. For the first time in the history of American democracy, stay-at-homes made up the majority of eligible voters.[9]

The mechanical voting reforms of the 1890s were having their impact. Turnout crashed everywhere, but it fell twice as much in states that introduced secret ballots which required voters to select individual candidates, rather than voting a straight party ticket. Likewise, many complained that they felt rushed when using the new voting machines, hurried up to the inanimate device and pressured along, as if they worked in a voting factory. Campaigners noticed that voters spent less of their day hanging around the polls singing and drinking and arguing. Instead, many "dash in here and vote quick."

Together, all the reforms built a new culture of efficient and individual voting, which discouraged voters just enough to get many to stay home.[10]

Turnout collapsed unequally across the nation. It was most extreme in the Deep South, where Jim Crow voting laws disenfranchised Black voters, discouraged poor Whites, and enthroned a small, White, wealthy, Democratic electorate. On average, half as many Southerners voted after 1900 as before. In Florida, turnout dropped 52 percent; in South Carolina it fell 65.6 percent between 1880 and 1916. Just 17.5 percent of eligible South Carolinians voted in 1916. In the 1920 election, Jones County, Georgia, registered the lowest turnout in any U.S. county: 2.8 percent.[11]

Nationwide, other populations were hit hard as well. Poorer voters, who had made up much of the active nineteenth-century electorate, fell away. For the first time, after 1900, wealthier people registered higher turnouts. The old "a gentleman never votes" attitude was dead. And young first-time voters stopped turning out in high numbers to cast their "virgin votes." Immigrant participation fell as well, especially among newer immigrant populations coming from eastern and southern Europe, who had less facility with English and less experience with democracy. African American voting rates plummeted, not just in southern states but in places like New Jersey. Urban areas lost turnout. So did areas experimenting with women's suffrage—not surprisingly, new voters were less enmeshed in the political culture that brought so many male citizens to the polls.[12]

Traditionally, political scientists have attributed this crash in turnout to a "realignment" in politics after 1896. The South voted more solidly Democratic, and the North leaned more heavily Republican. Elections grew less competitive, losing the thrilling acrimony that drove participation. But political scientists' abstract realignment was felt by real humans, on the ground. They did not realign as anonymous statistical blocs. Rather, there were fewer Republicans in the South because of Jim Crow voter suppression, and fewer Democrats in the North because of the active discouragement of working-class urban immigrant voters. The public culture of politics drove marginal voters from the polls. The palatable story of an abstract realignment was really a battle over voting rights, fought out with secret ballots, polling booth curtains, and literacy tests.

If we think of nineteenth-century democracy as bigoted and exclusionary—and it undoubtedly was—we too often forget that its twentieth-century replacement meant crashes in participation among poor, young, immigrant, and African American voters. Whatever was hurting turnout hurt it most among those already disadvantaged populations, leaving an electorate that was wealthier, Whiter, older, and more likely to be native-born. The efforts of fifty years of restrainers had succeeded. A new political culture had been born: one that had been cleaned and calmed, stifled and squelched.

In 1913 the white-bearded Progressive preacher Lyman Abbott wrote a book of reminiscences on his long life. Abbott had played a pivotal role in much of this era. He had been an abolitionist and a Social Gospel preacher; it was Abbott who recorded his friend Teddy Roosevelt's use of the phrase "a Bully Pulpit," and Abbott who admitted the "Secret Cause" of the new voting restrictions. In his reminiscences he lingered on his first election, back in 1856, drawing from an old letter he had sent to a cousin. He wrote in thrilling detail about the massive Republican demonstrations in New York City, about getting caught up in a crowd that dragged him along with his feet barely touching the cobblestones. He recalled the balconies thick with Republican ladies waving handkerchiefs, and his struggle for air in a sea of bobbing top hats. Abbott also documented his efforts as a young vote peddler on election day, pressing tickets on Brooklyn Heights voters, and doing battle with Democratic vote peddlers using "fisticuffs," bowie knives, and even a shaker of cayenne pepper.[13]

Then Abbott returned to the present and sighed, "Such was an election in New York City in 1856; such was political campaigning 57 years ago. Reformers have not lived and labored in vain. The conditions which I described to my cousin in 1856 could not be duplicated anywhere in America in 1913."[14]

TO THE WELL-TO-DO, the changing nature of politics felt like the dawning of a new day. Abbott hailed this sudden rebirth, writing: "As sometimes in a year the girl develops into womanhood, as sometimes in a week the skeleton plant bursts into leafage and perhaps into bloom, so a nation, which has been growing silently, suddenly puts forth the evidence of its growth."[15]

In reality, these changes had been incubating for decades, but the early years of the twentieth century felt like a flowering to many prosperous Americans. Men and women who had spent decades despairing for their rotten democracy struggled to come up with the right metaphor. The New York writer John Jay Chapman looked back over the efforts of reformers across his lifetime, arguing, "We have moved forward by jolts, until, like a people emerging from the deep sea, the water looks clearer above our heads and we can almost see the sky." William Allen White chose the new language of biology, writing: "It is as though the social body were the host of a myriad altruistic bacteria . . . The blood of our national life is thick with these germs that are consuming the poison of selfish decay." Whether a girl entering "womanhood," a plant bursting into bloom, a people emerging from the sea, or a beneficial bacterium, a class of reformers cheered a sudden metamorphosis.[16]

Occasionally they acknowledged the class roots of this revolution. It burned the brightest in the new institutions of the well-to-do: college campuses, independent magazines, ladies' clubs, professional associations, reform societies, summer resorts, fraternal clubs, mainline Protestant churches, and Chautauqua lectures. The word *democracy* bounced around lectures by professors, sermons by preachers, and letters to the editor, no longer paired with words like *failure* or *scoundrelly*. One did not have to be progressive to hail this moment; conservatives of the same class were newly motivated, as Chapman put it: "The great pendulum of wealth has swung toward decency, and henceforward the cause of political democracy will have money at its disposal." In attempting to argue that the revolution reached beyond the wealthy, William White inadvertently underlined its limitations, claiming that the new mood "filtered down pretty well toward the bottom of the middle class."[17]

White was perhaps the loudest cheerleader, happy to slam the door on nineteenth-century politics (and his own role as a nasty partisan editor). Still claiming to speak for the decent, respectable middle class, by 1910 he winced, "It is not pleasant to recall American political conditions as they were in the late nineties." So much had changed so quickly. Americans had spent a decade "melting down old heroes and recasting the mold in which heroes were made," tearing down the Gilded Age scoundrels who "had cast themselves in monumental brass." Old dividing lines were being forgotten. White Northerners, for instance, turned their back on the memory of the Civil War and increasingly entertained fictions like the Lost Cause of the Confederacy and lies about Reconstruction. But the biggest change came in how politics worked. White imagined explaining how modern elections worked to the bosses of that bygone era, and the politicos "cackling in derision until they were black in the face."[18]

This new era meant a willingness to abandon the populist precepts of nineteenth-century democracy. By 1901 Woodrow Wilson felt the nation was undergoing a "reaction against democracy. The nineteenth century was above all others a century of democracy," but now Americans were questioning old assumptions. Abbott predicted a country moving "away from government founded on the consent of the governed . . . away from universal suffrage toward limited suffrage . . . and away from political authority resting on the will of majorities." Of course, there was not *less* *democracy* in America after 1900. In many ways, democracy grew more reasonable, more enlightened, and more transparent. The transformation was not a matter of more or less but a redefinition, a change of phase of the same element into new form.[19]

Nonetheless, when Teddy Roosevelt's campaign manager exclaimed, "The people don't know enough to rule . . . the right of the people to rule is bunk," he was dangerously close to the unspoken sentiments of many progressives.[20]

Partisanship began to weaken its grip as well. There were still Democrats and Republicans, and behind the scenes the national parties actually grew stronger as they consolidated their hidden holds on the political process. But in public life a larger cultural shift took place. The tribal, nearly biological view of partisanship, and the demonization of the rival party as "enemies of the human race," weakened. Partisanship shifted from an indication of Gilded Age manhood to a sign of backward-looking pigheadedness—especially, one partisan complained, "with the cultured mob." Political independence looked more like the ability to follow one's own conscience. "Neither party dares," affirmed Chapman, to make political appeals to their supporters "on purely party grounds."[21]

Chapman also noted what really had made the difference: a small chunk of the electorate—5 to 10 percent—who remade their minds each election. "It is encouraging," he wrote, "to find how small a body of men it takes." The base-focused elections of the nineteenth century were no longer useful when a small faction of fence-sitters decided everything. After decades of casting about for a viable third party, nonpartisanship proved to be a better alternative. Let the two parties have their power, but let some portion of voters toggle back and forth between them each election. By 1910 White believed that America was being led by an "undeclared third party" of reform, and pointed out that three consecutive Congresses had passed uniform legislation despite being ruled by different parties.[22]

Abbott marveled at the way these new factions barely even seemed to have names, other than that of their "representative expounder, as Cleveland or Bryan Democracy, or Roosevelt or Taft Republicanism." This was quite a shift from Conkling's insistence, in his "carpet knight" speech three decades prior, that "administrations do not make parties. Parties make administrations. Parties go before administrations, and live after them."[23]

While "the cultured mob" redefined democracy, a broader middle class seemed happy to take a break. In the 1900s a lighter, less combative, and less apocalyptic popular culture bloomed, a nation delighted by ragtime and vaudeville, Gibson Girls and men in straw boaters. The crankish fog of the nineteenth century seemed to burn off with the new day. And as some of the social disruptions that had pushed scared citizens into party membership settled, a confident, stable middle class *needed* politics and parties less. Public life no longer meant political life. It would be odd and rude, after 1900, to quiz a train car full of strangers on how they planned to vote, though one might ask who they liked in the World Series.

A changing press signaled this shift. Newspaper empires like Joseph Pulitzer's *New York World* and William Randolph Hearst's *New York Journal* fought for circulation by stressing sensation. Though both papers were nominally Democratic, they often led with scandal, crime, sex, fashion, and entertainment, not partisan politics. Freed from the control of political parties, the mainstream press found itself dependent on gossip instead. In 1901 people started to talk about "tabloid journalism." Even the look of these papers changed, from the dense blocks of furious political prose to an airier aesthetic with plenty of white space, photographs, and lurid headlines.[24]

At the same time, new associations offered isolated Americans the kind of membership they once found in parties. Workplaces grew from the small shops and lonely fields of the nineteenth century into the large factories and offices of the twentieth. The urban population shot up from 20 percent of the country in 1860 to a majority of the country by 1920. Educational access expanded, linking people together in public schools and universities. Religious affiliation grew over this same period; Americans were not necessarily more devout, but the number of people who joined congregations rose significantly between 1890 and 1916. And a host of new professional and social organizations satisfied the joining instinct. Many of the major institutions of twentieth-century life were founded in these years, including the Rotary Club (1905), the National Audubon Society (1905), the National Association for the Advancement of Colored People (1909), the Boy Scouts of America and the Girl Scouts (1910, 1912), Kiwanis Clubs (1915), and the American Civil Liberties Union (1920). (On a darker note, a reorganized Ku Klux Klan reared its head again in 1915.)[25]

Even bowling leagues—later pointed to by the sociologist Robert Putnam's 2001 work *Bowling Alone* as a sign of Americans' social capital and community health—emerged during this era. There were eight times more bowling teams in America in 1913 than in 1900.[26]

While middle-class Americans were becoming more public in many other ways, they were becoming noticeably private, even secretive, about their politics. The political scientist James T. Young documented a strange shift. For nearly a century, Americans had "exalted politics to what now seems an unnatural position." And yet, by 1900, the "exciting character of political struggles has largely died out." In most bourgeois, twentieth-century families, "politics is rigidly excluded from the home." Young ranked the interests of the average middle-class White father as "1. Business, 2. Family, 3. Church and religious societies, 4. Charitable and benevolent associations, 5. Social organizations, such as clubs, 6. Politics." In an earlier age, the ranking might have had business and family tied for first, and religion and politics as close seconds.[27]

Political enthusiasm had long relied, Chapman once quipped, "upon the dinner-table talk of men who are not in politics at all." In the new century, for many Americans, it was no longer polite to talk politics at the dinner table.[28]

Working-class Americans felt this new distance from political talk most strongly. The thousands of college students and club women who spent the 1900s arguing about democracy were outweighed by the three-fifths of wage earners who made less than ten dollars a week. Millions of miners and factory hands—who would have marched in Democratic parades or drunk in Republican saloons in the 1870s or '80s—found other things to talk about. It was all part of what the historian Robert Wiebe called "the sinking of the lower class" in the twentieth century.[29]

The crash in working-class turnout was especially clear among new immigrants. While the British, Irish, German, and Scandinavian immigrants who predominated in nineteenth-century America eagerly embraced the political system, the newer eastern and southern European arrivals were less engaged. Part of this was an increasingly high bar thrown up by nativists. Several states had previously offered the vote to noncitizen immigrants to attract new settlers, but they all removed that right in the early 1900s, leading up to the federal ban in the xenophobic 1925 immigration act. New laws helped discourage legal voting by immigrants and their families as well. In 1896, 73 percent of eligible foreign-born in New Jersey voted, but twenty years later barely half did. Even their American-born children grew up alienated from voting: in 1916, just one in five New Jerseyites with foreign-born parents voted.[30]

Refuting nasty stereotypes about immigrant voters flooding election places and selling their ballot for a drink, newcomers proved reticent to get involved in political life at all. Rose Cohen, a Jewish woman recently arrived from Belarus, watched the strange rituals of a normal American election day with dread. Observing "the Gentile boys on our block" assembling scrap lumber for an election-night bonfire, Rose "noticed with fear that not a Jew was to be seen on the street." She retreated to her Lower East Side tenement. (Historically, local boys building a bonfire has rarely been viewed as "good for the Jews.") Jewish immigrants found their way into labor movements and socialism far more rapidly than they entered the political parties. Likewise, immigrants who fled the Mexican revolution deliberately avoided American politics, telling interviewers that they considered America a politically neutral destination where "there are no troubles here on account of political questions." While many Irish, German, and Scandinavian immigrants came to America specifically to engage in what looked like the nineteenth century's boldest experiment in liberal democracy, large numbers of twentieth-century immigrants saw the United States as a prosperous haven from the turmoil of the old country.[31]

The same attitude—that politics was bad news—could be heard among native-born working classes. When the sociologists Robert Lynd and Helen Lynd interviewed people in Muncie, Indiana, in the 1920s, they attempted to explain the record low turnouts, especially in a state that had once burned bright each election. Many of their subjects reported that political participation seemed to welcome trouble and might spook employers. One man warned that "timid capital is more afraid of politics than anything else, and when capital becomes frightened badly enough the load falls on the wage-earner." A textile worker in South Carolina echoed the sense that there was something distasteful and risky about political action, telling an interviewer, "Vote[?] No, ma'am, I don't never vote. I don't believe in 'sociation' with folks that hang around the polls."[32]

African American voters shied away from voting as well, even in states with fewer draconian Jim Crow laws. Black political involvement had long relied on support from the Republican Party, but fewer White Republicans cared about these old commitments. In 1900 the party of Lincoln even segregated its convention in Philadelphia, separating its Black delegates under the coded label "Mississippians," regardless of their home state. Theodore Roosevelt—himself a man with belligerent racial beliefs and a southern-born mother who loved the Confederacy—ran "lily white" campaigns in the South. Most White politicians—Democrat or Republican—accepted "the demise of the Fifteenth amendment" and left Black voting rights in the nineteenth century. In the early twentieth century, after the decline of a supportive Republican Party but before the rise of the Great Migration, African Americans found themselves uniquely trapped. Even the proportion of African Americans in the nation dropped—swamped by immigrants from Europe—until they made up less than 10 percent of the total population for the first time in American history.[33]

The most overt example of "the sinking of the lower class" in American politics was the war on the saloon. Those "poor men's clubs" had offered a crucial institution to workingmen (and "disreputable" women). By 1900 there were over 250,000 in America—more saloons per capita than there are Starbucks today. Some were ritzy establishments with cut-glass chandeliers and elaborate cocktails, others were wretched places that served lager in old tomato cans, provided a shared "mustache towel" by the door, and occasionally even featured a "urination trough" right at the bar. But these saloons were also a rare institution where diverse people found camaraderie and entertainment, where the hungry could get a cheap lunch, where the homeless could establish a mailing address, and where ordinary voters could interact with elected officials. Though associated with all the ills of Gilded Age society, saloons were mostly a flimsy response to the ravages of industrial capitalism and income inequality. "At the saloon," one researcher argued, the average laborer "rids himself of the horrible sense of isolation which weighs upon workingmen."[34]

Nothing could be more distasteful to America's respectable Protestant reformers. Across the nineteenth century they had been fighting a moral campaign for Temperance and individual abstention from drinking, but after the 1890s it shifted to the invasive, punitive model of legal Prohibition, targeting the political base of working-class democracy. The newfound Anti-Saloon League made public drinking, not private tippling, its target, declaring saloons "the devil's headquarters on earth." The powerful pressure group openly hoped that closing saloons would kill off the political world they sustained, writing that "local political clubs die young when removed from the bung of the beer keg and the tap of mixed ale." Kill the saloon, and a large chunk of the undeserving electorate would die as well.[35]

Soon, antisaloon activists began to successfully lobby for local prohibitions. Between 1900 and 1919, thirty states passed fifty-two antisaloon referenda. Rural regions of states managed to outvote the urban, working-class, and immigrant areas where saloons predominated. States with large working-class immigrant populations like New York, Pennsylvania, and Illinois hung on to their saloons, but many others shut down a key political institution, and with it the working-class vote in those states plummeted. These victories built upon themselves in a vicious cycle: by closing the chief site of working-class political assembly, states made it more difficult for laborers to resist further prohibitions. Rather than a newly mobilized anti-alcohol vote, what was really happening was the suppression of the votes of saloon supporters. The passage of the Eighteenth Amendment in 1920, prohibiting the sale of alcohol nationwide, represented both the apogee, and the consequence, of the movement to push the working class from politics.[36]

If one moment captured the closing of this era of public drinking and public politicking, it was the death of Chicago's First Ward Ball. Chicago's political machine—the very same "Grey Wolves" who had tangled with Florie Kelley and Jane Addams—held this infamous political fundraiser in a notorious red-light district. Started by prostitutes in the 1880s, the fundraiser was maintained throughout the 1890s by the First Ward's bosses, who offered up wild festivals, serving thirty-five thousand quarts of beer and ten thousand quarts of champagne. The boss Johnny Powers was there, of course, in his diamonds and his funeral suit. Mayor Carter

Harrison attended regularly, socializing with the city's most prominent madams and mobsters. The Ringling Brothers' circus loaned its elephants for the evening. It was all overseen by the flamboyant Alderman "Bathhouse" John Coughlin, decked out in a green tailcoat, lavender trousers, pink gloves, and yellow shoes. Over the years, the ball was also the site of shootings, a bombing, and beatings, some delivered by Coughlin himself.[37]

Each raucous evening culminated with a "Grand March"—a kind of conga line of politicos and prostitutes, crooked cops and elephants, dancing backward and forward, led by the nimble "Bathhouse" John Coughlin.[38]

Across the 1890s and 1900s, the First Ward Ball provided a barely believable caricature of everything reformers hated about politics and urban life. Many dreamed of closing it down. Women's Christian Temperance Union leaders groaned at a system where "the popularity and political strength of the attendees is gauged by the number of empty champagne bottles that cover the tables and floors." Finally, in 1908, reform won. They could not close down the private event, but a coalition of "meddlesome newspapers and reformers" convinced a judge to pull its liquor license.[39]

In 1909 the First Ward's political machine held one last, tragic, painfully sober event. Chicago's respectable press published mocking accounts of "the ball that didn't happen." The *Record-Herald* detailed a brightly lit, nearly empty hall, an outstretched "waste of empty chairs." In the center sat the loyal remnants of the Democratic machine, former ballot hustlers and election challengers, hats in their laps, ringed in by hundreds of uniformed Chicago cops. "If you want to think of something particularly sad," one writer mocked, "think of Billy the Dope, Larry the Lush, Wrecking Crew Jerry, Joe Goose and the rest of the First ward guards, sitting around in a half empty hall, listening patiently to a concert of almost sacred music—and not a drink in sight."[40]

By 1910 there were ninety-three million people living in America—nearly three times as many as during the Civil War. The nation was big and diverse and complex in ways that were unimaginable to those thinking about Pure Democracy back in 1865. It was entirely possible for one population to feel, politically, like a girl entering "womanhood," a plant bursting into bloom, or a people emerging from the sea, while another felt that their chief institutions were being crushed. Meddlesome newspapers may have had fun at their expense, but "Bathhouse John" and "Wrecking Crew Jerry" also represented nodes in a system that, however vulgar and venal, gave voice to millions of otherwise voiceless working people.

Either way, their day was ending. "I'm a good guard," one longtime Democratic lieutenant told a newspaperman at the final First Ward Ball, "but I've played this loyalty stuff to the end of my string." Rising to flee the depressing scene, he offered: "Come on out and we'll get a drink."[41]

BETWEEN 1900 AND 1920 American politics re-formed. A new order emerged that would define the outlines of democracy for much of the coming century. Even the iconography of American politics changed. The nineteenth-century engravings of dense, hectic crowds waving torches or ballots gave way to twentieth-century photographs of orderly voters lined up on election day, or individual conscience-ponderers stroking their chins in the voting booth. Generic depictions of politicians—who had inflated and coarsened from regular men into slavering beasts between 1860 and 1900—softened again.

Even the uniforms got a makeover. From 1860 to 1900, politics meant a young man in a military cape bearing a smoky torch. During the sweltering 1900 Republican convention in Philadelphia (the one in which Black Republicans were segregated as "Mississippians"), the straw boater hat emerged as the symbol of the man in politics. It lasted for the next hundred years, still seen in political cartoons well into the 1990s. The nineteenth century's outfit suggested uniformity and militarism, while a man in a boater looks cool and jaunty, no matter how much he's sweating.

The re-formation of politics went beyond hats and capes. Striking numerical changes proved just how dramatically political power was retracting from public engagement. The number of seats in the House of Representatives had expanded with the growing population since America's founding but froze in 1911, part of a decades-long effort by rural Republicans to disenfranchise growing urban areas. The big building on the hill has had just 435 seats to this day, even as the nation tripled in size. The average district, as of 2020, contains 750,000 people, more than lived in any state in 1790.[42] And these more distant representatives became harder to unseat—the average length of a congressional term doubled. Incumbents held on to their seats with more authority as well: the close races of the nineteenth century, decided on average by a margin of 5 percent, eased into landslides won by an average of 17 percent.[43]

And those incumbents found common ground in the small, clubby House of Representatives. Congressional polarization across parties had climbed to unprecedented peaks in the 1890s, but crashed across the first half of the twentieth century. After a long trough of low polarization from the 1930s through 1970s, the distance between the parties shot up again from the 1980s to today, describing an arcing U-curve of division across the last hundred and forty years.[44] Politicians learned how to get along with each other, and then lost that skill again.

The most radical change happened on the presidential level. Presidential elections had been contested and unpredictable from the 1860s through the 1890s, mostly won by pluralities or even a loss of the popular vote. After 1896 most presidents enjoyed larger majorities, and unprecedented land-slides gave presidents Warren G. Harding, Franklin Delano Roosevelt, Lyndon Johnson, and Richard Nixon previously unimaginable mandates. A world in which Harding could win 60 percent of the popular vote, while Abraham Lincoln earned just 39 percent, suggests a change in the system itself, rather than in the men running it.

Those presidents used their mandates to remake the office. The nineteenth century's odd formula of inactive presidents and lively citizens inverted around 1900. Some warned about the executive "insidiously acquiring a complete mastery over the government," but others found the idea of a single national manager calming. Teddy Roosevelt's forceful personality changed much of this. Though he first entered the White House with President McKinley's assassination, Roosevelt managed to loom larger than past presidents. Teddy's gnashing teeth and glinting glasses could be seen on mountains of political stuff. While nineteenth-century political prints showed a president hemmed in by senators and bosses, depictions of Roosevelt often show him as the single human in the frame, fighting a dragon or taming a lion. He even cut free from party, in 1912, in a way few previous presidents could have managed, running on the Bull Moose ticket. Many came to sound like Jacob Riis, who was mocked for the way he "talks Roosevelt, thinks Roosevelt, dreams Roosevelt." Though no presidents immediately after Roosevelt matched his verve, Teddy obliterated the old model of the virtuous, retiring national grandfather, replacing it with expectations of an active president who made himself the physical embodiment of the government.[45]

In keeping with Roosevelt's grand vision, the class of Americans who talked about reforming democracy aimed bigger. Many Progressives declared that it was time to change the Constitution. The historian Walter Weyl denounced that "stiff, unyielding, and formidable" old document as an "obstacle to a true democracy." The Constitution was like "an old, rambling mansion, which cannot be lighted, and in the dark places of which our enemies secrete themselves." Between 1913 and 1920, it underwent its greatest revision since Reconstruction, with the introduction of four key amendments—establishing a federal income tax, mandating the direct election of senators, prohibiting the sale of alcohol, and giving women the right to vote.[46]

Progressives launched another round of political re-forms, less covert than the mechanical changes of 1887–96, but also aimed at finding new ways around old obstructions. One prominent shaper of the new democracy was a former blacksmith named William U'Ren. He had witnessed political dirty tricks as a young campaigner in Colorado in 1880, and the tinkerer in him wondered why a modern nation "still worked with old tools, with old laws, with constitutions and charters which hindered more than they helped." Why were there no "legislative implements to help the people govern themselves? Why had we no tool makers for democracy?" Diving into politics in Oregon, U'Ren led a crusade for more direct democracy, introducing the tools of ballot initiatives, referendums, and referrals. The so-called Oregon System passed in 1902 and was taken up by dozens of other states. More democratic toolmakers hammered out new implements of "direct democracy": party primaries, ballot initiatives, referenda, recall elections, voter registrations, and the direct election of senators.[47]

In the best cases, these reforms gave the public a voice in processes that had been formerly decided in smoke-filled rooms. In the worst cases, what reformers called "direct democracy" merely empowered well-organized, well-funded special interests to push through causes and candidates that would never win popular support in a general election. One antiprogressive polemicist complained that the new model enthroned a "nuclei of party workers who know what they want. The direct primary . . . creates the illusion" of popular support. Organizations from the Anti-Saloon League to the National Consumer League, from the National Association for the Advancement of Colored People to the Ku Klux Klan managed to wield quiet influence through these new tools.[48]

This era of political reform culminated in granting women the right to vote—the biggest expansion of the electorate in American history. The passage of the Nineteenth Amendment broadened democracy in ways that had seemed impossible to generations of women. The cause that lacked "a ghost of a show for success" in the 1880s was federal law after 1920. And even this triumphant moment grew from the changes in the political system. It took the decline of the age of "brass bands and huzzahs" before male voters would seriously consider the push for women's suffrage.[49]

The movement succeeded by fitting into the changing politics of the early twentieth century. A cause long dominated by well-to-do, otherwise respectable, White ladies adeptly sold itself as a way to strengthen the ascendant middle class. Though the Nineteenth Amendment was intended to enfranchise all women—the movement incorporated an often-ignored diversity—it was deliberately promoted as a way to offset the power of a working-class and increasingly foreign-born male electorate. Most suffrage advocacy focused on middle-class, native-born, Protestant White women for a reason. As one female nurse who had voted in elections in western states put it, "I enter the poll-room just as I do a church . . . you see what it means for the woman to vote? It means a help to her husband. It means the doubling of the respectable vote." For decades women's suffrage activists had to counter claims that women voting would ruin the hypermasculine culture of election day. But in a new political world where the well-to-do were looking for ways to extinguish that old political culture, "doubling the respectable vote" became one of its greatest selling points.[50]

The irony of women's suffrage was that the movement finally won the right to vote at the precise moment in American history when voting was coming to matter less. There could have been no duller introduction into presidential politics than the low-turnout races of 1920 and 1924. Of all the inequities of women's long fight for equal standing in American society, one of the less remarked on is the fact that generations of women missed out on the competitive thrill of nineteenth-century election days and got to play the game only after most of the fun was over.

The new political order was in place by 1920 or so. Even the conservative backlash against progressivism in the 1920s left the political reforms intact. From one angle, the new model meant votes for men and women, free of domineering political machines, campaigns driven by somewhat reasoned debate, which empowered skilled executives and administrators to govern aggressively. From another, the new form of American democracy meant a passive electorate of mostly White, native-born, well-off voters, presided over by an inflated president, a distant Congress, concealed parties, and busy lobbyists. Neither perspective is wrong. And just as the old model had dominated many decades of the nineteenth century, these new standards shaped the broad lines and limits of American politics from 1920 to 1960 to 1980 and beyond.

Restraint defined the change more than any other value. The Supreme Court justice Louis Brandeis (Florie Kelley's friend and ally) argued in 1922 that the chief attribute of a democracy was the way self-government "substitutes self-restraint for external restraint." This was the value that elite critics like Francis Parkman had believed that ordinary Americans lacked, the ability to rein in their worst instincts. But in the twentieth century, Americans made a big show of controlling themselves. "American Cool" emerged as a value acknowledged around the world, a taciturn composure used to promote everything from Hollywood to Coca-Cola. European stereotypes of nineteenth-century Americans usually involved boorish strivers shouting about politics or business; in the twentieth century many embraced the idea of the quiet American, cool, collected, unsophisticated but honest.[51]

There was still plenty of aggression and extremism in American life, but it usually lived outside the party system or under the surface of seemingly unruffled politicians. The extremist political groups of twentieth-century life, from the Ku Klux Klan of the 1920s to the Weathermen of the 1960s, or the militia movement of the 1990s, mostly operated outside the party system. The Klan manipulated public aggression in its startling rise in the 1920s, when nearly three million Americans joined, and it did influence some politicians in states like Indiana, Georgia, and Texas. But even at its height, the movement counted far more opponents than allies, and "respectable" citizens fought hard to restrain it. That herald of the sober new political style—William Allen White himself—ran an anti-Klan campaign for governor of Kansas. Even many who held bigoted views dismissed the movement as coarse and unseemly, a throng of "hooded hoodlums, covered cowards, sheeted jerks," and it crumpled in most of the nation fairly quickly.[52]

Within the party system, plenty of politicians who privately boiled with emotion worked to present a sober, self-contained public image. This is a fair way to describe the first three U.S. presidents born in the twentieth century—John F. Kennedy, Lyndon Johnson, and Richard Nixon, all of whom worked to restrain their private emotions when in the public eye. Even the bosses and machines that still dominated American urban politics kept their heads down, shielding their dirty tricks from public view in ways that Roscoe Conkling or William "the Squire" McMullen had not bothered to. Every so often a Huey Long, Joseph McCarthy, or George Wallace broke the mold, but their erratic, singular approaches rarely built machines or legacies beyond their own usually brief time in the spotlight.

Americans became less likely to hurt each other over electoral politics. The nineteenth-century tradition of post-election day newspaper reports detailing all the shootings, stabbings, and "knock-downs" that took place at a city's polls evaporated. Even the White supremacist riots that tore apart Black communities in Tulsa, Springfield, and Chicago in the early twentieth century were less overtly tied to party politics than the equivalent nineteenth-century conflicts in Memphis, New Orleans, or Colfax.[53] Across the early decades of the twentieth century, while the national murder rate climbed, partisan political violence fell. It's not that twentieth-century America was a peaceful place, but that disturbances of the peace were less tied to campaigns or elections.

There were still assassinations. The spectacular Alderman's Wars of 1920s Chicago, for instance, saw Florie's old nemesis Johnny Powers barely survive the bombing of his home. But in the twentieth century, violence within the political system became rarer. Six U.S. congressmen were murdered in office in the forty-six years between 1859 and 1905, often by political rivals. The three congressmen killed over the next three quarters of a century—Huey Long, Robert F. Kennedy, and Leo Ryan—were each shot by a stranger. A system in which Will Kelley could have been slashed by a congressman in downtown Washington, and fired on by a mob in Mobile, and yet most of his eulogists deemed neither incident worthy of mention, is hard to imagine in another era.[54]

This restrained model helps explain, in part, how America managed to avoid the brutal mass politics that ravaged much of the rest of the world in the twentieth century. While Europe and Asia found themselves enthralled by the spectacles of fascism and communism, America's political system had just spent decades setting limits against a similar style of public participation. Putting on a uniform, lighting a torch, and parading in formation appealed to crowds in Germany, Russia, or China in ways that Americans had worked hard to contain. The United States was in the rare position of experiencing the twentieth century as generally calmer than the nineteenth. The downside of this skepticism toward public politics was the hostility directed at those who marched for civil rights or against the Vietnam War as new forms of political speech emerged later in the century.

Those forms kept changing. The relative restraint of the twentieth century heated into the politics of the twenty-first, rhetorically dominated by "telling it like it is," performative dissent, and manipulated fear. All of these features loudly reject the restrained style of the twentieth-century politics—a politics that was itself a rejection of the convulsions of the nineteenth century. The most striking aspect of this three-century arc is not where we are now or where we may go, but how winding the road has been. Our political system looks stiff and unyielding, governed by rigid checks and balances, but the history of American democracy proves how much capacity for change lies dormant in it. Taking the long view, "This Is Not Normal" might as well be our national motto.

It's tempting to tell this story solely as an evolution of law, of amendments ratified granting wider and wider access. But the driving force behind our changing system has been America's popular political culture, the way we *use* politics. Frederick Douglass knew this, warning Will Kelley in his 1871 letter: "The country is ruled by sentiment as well as law, while the spirit is much more important than the letter." "The best laws on the statute book," Douglass predicted, "are of the merest mockery in the hands of men who hate them." Douglass had good reason, as Reconstruction crested, to fear the whims of popular political culture. (And he was right: the Fifteenth Amendment remained in the Constitution even as it became nearly impossible for most African Americans to actually vote.) But the dramatic cleaning and calming of American democracy around 1900 also grew from the same power of "sentiment" above "statute book." A few narrow legal and bureaucratic changes coincided with a colossal rethinking of how citizens interacted with their democracy. As Theodore Roosevelt wrote in 1888, "no law can give us good government; at the utmost, they can only give us the opportunity to get good government." Getting good government has been the longest-running cultural project in American history, one with no end in sight.[55]

The deep history of American electoral politics can seem static and flat—a succession of dull, inconsequential presidents with gray beards and silly names—punctuated by the single crisis of the Civil War. This makes it feel as if any conflict means impending collapse, that the only two options for our democracy are doldrums or disunion. But our political system is not nearly so brittle. There is incredible variability in how we have used our democracy, with plenty of room for ugliness without apocalypse, and for reform without utopia. The lesson of the Age of Acrimony in American politics is that the range of normal feelings is far broader than the detached calm insisted on for much of the twentieth century. The capacity for positive or negative change lies with the American people ourselves.

In 1943, in the midst of a war for democracy, the Writers' War Board asked the *New Yorker* to compose a statement on "the meaning of democracy." The magazine put its best writer to the task. E. B. White responded with a beautiful, humanistic definition, including these lines:

> Democracy is the recurrent suspicion that more than half of the people are right more than half of the time. It is the feeling of privacy in the voting booths, the feeling of communion in the libraries, the feeling of vitality everywhere. Democracy is a letter to the editor . . . Democracy is a request from a War Board, in the middle of a morning in the middle of a war, wanting to know what democracy is.[56]

White was born in 1899, the year after the Gillespie voting machine's fluttering green curtain introduced "privacy in the voting booths." How much of his soaring definition is inherent to democracy? How much of it would have been familiar in the nineteenth century, to a man like Will Kelley? And how much was the result of an earlier war, fought not for democracy but within it?

CHAPTER EIGHTEEN

"It Runs in Our Blood to Be Leaders"

K o's Ma sent a letter. Pages of black ink, a bubbling tide of persistent questions and irreverent jokes. Just how his Ma talked. There had been a lot of letters since Ko started at Harvard, but this one was different. In it, Florie mused about "the very best day of my life, that day twenty one years ago tomorrow, which brought you to us."[1]

Looking back from 1906 at 1885, peering from the new dawn of the twentieth century into the depths of the Gilded Age, Florie reminisced about how much the world had changed. So much had transpired since those dark days when she had been pregnant in Zurich, feuding with her family and scorning American democracy. "As for the good, it is more than can be said," Florie wrote, pointing to the growing international movement for women's suffrage, the liberal reforms in Russia, the economic emergence of Asia, incredible scientific breakthroughs, and, of course, "the rising of the tide of Socialism thro out the civilized world."[2]

Florie sounded little like the prickly woman she had been in 1885. She was among the most enthusiastic heralds of the progressive dawn that was altering American democracy and her own personal life. "History is making very fast in these days!" she cheered, returning to her girlhood love of exclamation points. While her father had warned, in 1865, "these are terrible times for timid people," by 1906 Florie was cheering to Ko, "It certainly is the most interesting period in the history of the world!"[3]

Even as she worked to reform the era, Florie was reforming her relationship with her family. As she traveled the world, she poured out a torrent of affectionate letters to her three children, Ko especially. She sent the same kind of ranty, loving, opinionated missives that her father had once mailed to her. Like Will, Florie refused to shield her children from her work, writing to Ko about speeches given, fights picked, legislation passed. She sounds like her father in the 1870s, informing his own curious daughter about his anger at the Grant administration, or the foods served at a Chinese banquet in San Francisco. Florie teased and cajoled for replies from her busy college-student son, joking about "my greed for letters." Ko wrote back affectionately, gamely reading the Marxist tracts she recommended and sighing: "There is nobody at all like you in the world. I am so proud of being your son." Margaret and John were more distant; like Will Kelley, Florie had chosen one child to share her intellectual and political life with, for good and bad.[4]

In those same years, Florie worked to remake her relationship with her past. Having repaired her bond with her mother, Florie spent extended stretches with Carrie, working to atone for the "selfish sins" of her youth. In her 1906 birthday letter to Ko, Florie addressed her son, herself, and also her mother and father when she wished: "If sons and daughters could only know their power of giving pleasure—and pain—how differently most of them would act!"[5]

Also like her father, Florie became a political nomad, forever setting out for her next speaking engagement, factory inspection, or consumer campaign. She kept a spare room in the Henry Street Settlement House on New York's hectic Lower East Side, but was never there for long. She would bounce around the nation, then reconnect with her chicks for summers at Henry Demarest Lloyd's Rhode Island beach house, spending hours on the rooftop widow's walk, breathing in bracing Atlantic air and plotting her next campaign.

Those calm moments fit into a busy, happy life of public activism. In middle age Florie seemed mobilized; not since her studies with her father, and then at Cornell, in the 1870s, had she sounded so energized. "I am so well that it seems as though I might live to be a hundred!" she exulted to Ko at forty-seven. Ideas for books were "seething in my mind," and invitations flooded in. She wrote Ko about a visit to the progressive activist Frederic Howe's home in Cleveland: "Behold your parent staying with Senator Howe of Ohio, in a most agreeable house." Her hosts chauffeured her to events "automobilewise," and invited her to elaborate soirees. Florie remained bemused about it all, rolling her eyes about attending a formal luncheon of blue-blooded suffragists, struggling to imagine any chore "less to my liking" than nibbling tea sandwiches in polite company. Her children laughed back, amused by the idea of their mother lecturing to the "multitude of the fashionable" in her worn black dresses. She even returned to Washington, helping to draft child labor legislation and enjoying the courtesy of congressmen who had heard legends about her father. It was a triumphant return for Florie, harking back to the early 1880s, when she boarded with Will at the Riggs House and intimidated Washington's debutantes and congressmen alike.[6]

Florie built friendships with the new icons of the progressive age, from Louis Brandeis to W. E. B. Du Bois. She won over, and then grew to disdain, Teddy Roosevelt; what she once admired as "fearlessness" came to seem like "reckless egotism." But she was a woman more defined by her rivalries. Her friend and ally Frances Perkins, the future secretary of labor and creator of Social Security, fondly recalled working with the "explosive, hot-tempered, determined" Florence Kelley, chuckling, "she was no gentle saint." Another friend wrote about the fun of watching Florie set upon some opponent of child labor protections. She had a tell—her wide mouth would begin to quiver in meetings, as if she were fighting a losing battle to spare some poor, misinformed speaker. When on the offensive, "she was unrivaled," her friend wrote. "No other man or woman I have ever heard so blended knowledge of facts, wit, satire, burning indignation, prophetic denunciation—all poured out at white heat in a voice varying from flute-like tones to deep organ tones." In photographs, she looks like a wise old alligator, grinning, but ready to strike.[7]

Du Bois was most impressed. When Florie joined the board of the fledgling NAACP, the civil rights leader assumed that she would be another absentee do-gooder, lending her name to a board she rarely attended. But she made public war on racism, attacking New York realtors who refused to sell to African Americans or Jews, and willingly losing the support of southern members of the National Consumer League who complained about "the mongrelization of this splendid country of ours." Du Bois recalled her presence at NAACP meetings with wonder—"I remember time and time again in our board, when meetings were drawing on drowsily to conventional conclusions, Florence Kelley would burst in with a question." After a torrent of Florie's persistent asking, "I have seen a dead board galvanized." For her boldness, her antiracism, her socialism, and her unrestrained desire for answers, Florence Kelley "paid in bitter dislike, in determined misunderstanding, and in the loss of nearly every reward that smug respectability and calculated conformity bring," Du Bois wrote with admiration.[8]

Many politicians, jurists, and businessmen certainly found her challenging. Florie was a far more combative politician than her father, who preferred to dance around opponents. Unhappy with one verdict, she attacked the "senile" conservatives on the Supreme Court, "whose average age is 74 years!" Annoyed at the House of Representatives' refusal to appropriate funds for infant and maternity aid, she publicly demanded: "Why does Congress wish babies to die?" In her papers, one-half of a delicious back and forth with the U.S. War Department exists. In response to her call to banish some incompetent employee, a decorous bureaucrat carefully replied: "I am afraid I shall have to argue with you. I do not know where Timbuctoo is, but the colleague to whom you refer has some admitted blind-spots, but some very robust virtues."[9]

And a friend once overheard two businessmen whispering at a meeting about one of Florie's labor bills. One man asked the other why he kept silent despite disliking the legislation, to which the other shot back: "What, and let that fire-eater in the black dress make a monkey of me!"[10]

Florie's efforts paid off in legislative victories that would have made her father proud. She found increasing political influence, building over the 1900s and 'tos. With her support, Congress created the U.S. Children's Bureau, limited the sale of goods produced by child labor, and provided for maternal and infant care—the first federal step toward later Social Security legislation. Building on her generation's willingness to tinker with the Constitution, Florie campaigned ceaselessly for amendments protecting children and female workers and guaranteeing women's suffrage. By the

1910s and '20s she was operating on an impressive national scale, much as her father had when he used tariff schedules to shape the entire American economy. She boldly pressed the NCL: "In 1925, forty-two legislatures will be in session. If we do not make a nation-wide drive for the 8 hours day in 1925, who will?"[11]

Florie influenced American public life in ways that simply did not exist in her father's day. Perhaps no figure made better use of the new model of politics. She continued to be frustrated by electoral democracy, asking Ko, "How do you account for the fact that the city proletariat in this country, instead of being Socialist is corruptly democratic? That is a problem which I find wholly baffling." Yet she rejoiced that the rise of independent voting had "destroyed the political careers" of many of her conservative opponents. The beauty of the new era, to Florie, was that the whims of voters mattered less. Lloyd's prediction of "government without politics" seemed to be coming true. Legislators were more likely to bypass the voters and go straight to experts. To her, politicians were often just "a funnel" for interest groups "to pour their ideas through." When queried about her views on a presidential race, Florie replied that Americans cared too much about elections. They should focus more on "wise and faithful administrative work." Lobbying, Florie's friend Julia Lathrop wrote to her, "is an alluring indoor sport if properly played."[12]

What Florie never seemed to mention, and certainly did not mourn, was the crash in voter turnout and participation that brought about this new political model. Very few progressives did; the problem of the stay-at-homes rarely came up. With so much activity, it was easy to ignore the quieting of the old model's hubbub. This explains how the memory of the previous era evaporated so thoroughly. A large mass of working people found themselves less able or inclined to participate in government in the twentieth century, a loss Florie thoroughly ignored.

Like his mother before him, Ko Kelley took great interest in his parent's work. At Harvard, he helped form a political club, and the letters of mother and son hark back to Will Kelley's enthusiasm for Florie's social science club at Cornell thirty years before. "By all means, push the Political Club!" she prodded, recommending that they study the work of her friends Howe, Addams, and Du Bois. Excited by her son's reformist leanings, she begged that Ko consider the issues of race and gender, asking how he tolerated a system that continued "dis-franchising Dr. Du-Bois and myself," practically hollering into her letter to him. "It is <u>white</u>, <u>male</u> democracy!" (Tellingly, she complained in that same letter about the ease with which Italian and Jewish immigrants could vote.) Ko was a receptive son and even took up his mother's advice to read Marx's massive *Capital*, beaming, "When you next see me, I shall be a full fledged Marxian socialist!"[13]

Taking a more serious tone with her daughter Margaret, Florie sent her a pep talk on her entrance into Smith College in 1905, reminding the sometimes snarky girl: "It runs in our blood to be leaders. You will yourself be one without setting out to be one. And your jests will count, a keen wit is a terrible weapon." Hoping to fire her daughter with some of the passions she shared with Ko, Florie pushed: "The future of this Republic depends largely on the college students of to-day; and my children owe it to their grandfather, and to me, and to themselves, to line up on the right side now."[14]

Florie would ride the tide of decades. Across the 1900s, 'tos, and '20s she remained a prominent, divisive presence and an affectionate, pushy mother. When Ko named his daughter Florence, in 1920, the new grand-mother was thrilled: "I keep wondering what Florence will be going to see presidential candidates about when she is my age." Ko built a little empire of his own, as a lawyer, civil servant, and civic leader. Only in the Kelley family could his career as assistant treasury secretary, vice president of the Chrysler Corporation, and board member of dozens of labor and reform organizations seem like a small contribution, compared to what his mother and grandfather had achieved.[15]

Florie would fight on into the 1930s, barreling through the conservative backlash of the '20s, when she was denounced as a revolutionary communist trained by Engels himself (to which she replied that she was not: she was a revolutionary *socialist* trained by Engels himself). In between public campaigns she would enjoy the seclusion of the only possession that interested her, a seaside cottage on the Maine coast. There she watched the morning light from a glassed-in sunroom while writing to Ko, or Eleanor Roosevelt, or a factory laborer with concerns about her working conditions. Eventually colon cancer began its slow assault. She would go on writing and joking until the end. In 1932 she would die in Philadelphia, not far from the Elms. It is a shame that she would pass away on the threshold of the New Deal, a revolution in social democracy enacted by many of her friends and adherents. The Supreme Court justice Felix Frankfurter would memorialize Florie as "the woman who has probably the largest single share in shaping the social history of the United States during the first thirty years of this century."[16]

Some eulogists mentioned her famous father, yet few saw the full depth of their relationship and its contribution to American democracy over a full century. From the day in 1835 when a lanky Will Kelley pushed his way onto a Boston stage to speak out for workingmen's democracy, until Florie's death in 1932, at least one Kelley was hammering away for the rights of laboring people.

Florence Kelley spent half her life in the nineteenth century and half in the twentieth. The difference is striking. In that 1906 birthday letter to Ko, Florie spelled out her sense that a new age was dawning. "Life itself,—the human organism—registers some of the greatest gains," Florie wrote, recalling how "my childhood and youth were darkened by the horror of diphtheria. That is gone, forever, from human experience." Florie was so bold that she hoped, tragically, "if you reach the years of your grandfather, old age will have lost its terrors and cancer, one of its blackest shadows, will be under control."[17]

That change would not come, but in 1906 Florie could confidently look back on 1885 and sense the re-forming of American life. Something had been left behind in the nineteenth century. It was most notable in what Florie did not mention in her letter to her soon-to-be twenty-one-year-old. She ignored the topic that most parents of sons like Ko had focused on in similar letters over the previous decades. She made no mention of his first vote.

Yet try as she might to leave the old politics behind, Florie dragged a crucial element with her into the new era. She was still the girl raised by her father to feel an intimate bond between her personal identity and her nation's politics. This intimacy was the fuel that drove nineteenth-century democracy. It was the power that bosses held over voters, living among them and "knowing them intimately," as Addams put it, while reformers kept at a distance. It was the force that pushed young men to wrap their bodies in party uniforms, a fixation that physically pained Americans during anxious moments like the fluttering 1876 election. The politics of a nineteenth-century citizen, wrote an annoyed British wife about her partisan American husband, "are as inseparable from him as his clothes."[18]

For the Kelley family, this intimacy was a congenital and chronic condition. It had scarred Will's body with his enemy's knives; it had shaken Florie to her core as she sat in her first socialist meeting, clutching the sides of her chair and trembling. From father to daughter and from mother to son, the Kelleys interwove their love for each other with their passion for the nation. In bubbling letters and dinner table debates, in sunny afternoons reading in the Elms's library, and in the U.S. Congress where Will spoke on the floor while Florie mouthed the words from the galleries, they connected through that bond. A century of political acrimony could not spoil it. And now Florie passed it down to Ko. She linked his birth and growth—from the little boy in the wicker pram into a Harvard man and a full-fledged socialist—to the developments of "the most interesting period in the history of the world!" Family and democracy; the private and the public; the Kelleys were never very good at keeping them separate. It ran in their blood.

Florie concluded her birthday note to the son:

> Nothing can rob me of my pride and joy in the chapter of your life which closes to-day, or my proud and confident hope for the new chapter which opens tomorrow.
> Your loving old mother
> Florence Kelley[19]

ACKNOWLEDGMENTS

This was a five A.M. book, written in gulps before my infant son woke up each morning. Maybe it was the sleep deprivation, or the over-caffeination, but those hours feel dreamlike and joyful to me now. I started collaborating with Bloomsbury just as my son was born, and ever since then my publishers, my colleagues, my friends, my family, and most especially my incredible wife have all worked to help me write this book about a parent-child relationship while I've been building one of my own.

The Smithsonian's National Museum of American History aided and abetted this book in surprising ways. Spending years among the objects this book describes has been a rare privilege for a historian, allowing me to experience these materials as living actors with their own stories. Attending protests, rallies, conventions, caucuses, and primaries for the museum sharpened my engagement with the past. Watching Donald Trump accept the Republican nomination at the 2016 Republican National Convention, while reading Murat Halstead's accounts of the 1860 convention in the nosebleed seats, was an experience I never expected. By asking me to collect from the ugly politics of the twenty-first and nineteenth centuries simultaneously, the museum pushed me to try to articulate the relationship between past and present.

A museum is made up of people, not just objects, and wonderful coworkers helped me write this book. I'm lucky to have benefitted from the expertise of my colleagues who study electoral politics, including Lisa Kathleen Graddy, Claire Jerry, Harry Rubenstein, Larry Bird, Bethanee Bemis, Sara Murphy, Barbara Clark Smith, and Debbie Hashim. Other curators and historians talked shop, talked history, and occasionally talked trash, especially Eric Hintz, Ken Cohen, Peter Manseau, Lexi Lord, Theresa McCulla, Tim Winkle, and Peter Liebhold. Most of all, Ellen Feingold helped this book along, offering her curiosity, her counsel, and her humor. My supervisors gave me the priceless gifts of trust and time.

Other Smithsonian employees, including Valeska Hilbig, Roberta Walsdorf, Bennie Burton, and Alex Gutierrez, helped navigate the bureaucracy and get this book out into the world. Many more colleagues provided friendship and wisdom, whether we discussed this project or their own exciting work.

Archivists, librarians, and digitizers at a host of libraries and historical societies helped me access the sources that built this book. I owe a depth of gratitude to the caretakers of the Kelley family papers at the Historical Society of Pennsylvania, the New York Public Library, and the Columbia University Libraries, as well as the archives of the Connecticut Historical Society, Harvard's Houghton Library, the Huntington, the Minnesota Historical Society, the Nebraska State Historical Society, the University of North Carolina Libraries, University of Virginia Special Collections Library, the Wisconsin Historical Society, and Yale University's Special Collections. David Holcomb's unparalleled collection of photographs provided an angle on the past that I had not seen before. And Charlie Annand, the intrepid curator of the Milford New Hampshire History Society who identified George Holt's Wide Awake materials, joined me in collaboration, detective work, and a rewarding friendship.

And many thanks, of course, to Mike Caires, for his constant encouragement and gentle corrections on the finer points of Gilded Age monetary policy. His gift of a bound volume of Memorial Addresses on the Life and Character of William D. Kelley helped launch this project.

The work of a modern historian involves uncovering new voices, but also stewarding existing knowledge, and this book is built on decades of scholarship. In particular, Kathryn Kish Sklar's inquisitive, humane study of Florence Kelley's life provided the narrative soul of this work, while Michael McGerr's *The Decline of Popular Politics* and Mark Wahlgren Summers's many works guided me towards a thesis. I hope I did them justice.

Bloomsbury Publishing turned this project from a hunch and a rant into a beautiful finished product. Ben Hyman has been a wise and creative editor, enthusiastic and imaginative, but also firm and clear-eyed. It's been a joy to create this book together with him. The rest of the staff at Bloomsbury deserve many thanks as well. Katherine Flynn, my agent at

Kneerim & Williams, had the good judgement to connect me with Ben and Bloomsbury, and I owe her thanks yet again. Her taste, creativity, and willingness to tackle daunting challenges (including tangling with the federal bureaucracy!) has shaped my career over the years.

My parents and siblings kept me sharp and relevant. They are often the first audience I imagine when I write: if a story couldn't entertain a tableful of shouting Grinspans, it's probably not worth printing. Keiana Mayfield has joined that noisy table, and my life, keeping me honest and alert, remaining a loving, challenging, rewarding presence. Through parenting and pandemics, we produced this book together. On that note, I have to thank my son's daycare teachers, who made so much of it possible. Oh, and I'd like to thank my mother-in-law, Janene, who specifically asked to be thanked.

Finally, I have to thank Solomon, this book is for him. I can't quite articulate how he helped this project, but he did. It seems counterintuitive, running against the cliché that children slow down writing projects, but somehow raising Solomon while writing this book has made me a better historian. I'm so happy that he's joined us at that noisy table.

IMAGE PLATE CREDITS

Page 1: "Exciting Scene In the House of Representatives," February 18, 1865, Collections of the Division of Political History, National Museum of American History, Smithsonian Institution, Washington, D.C.

Page 2: Library of Congress, Manuscript Division, Brady-Handy Collection.

Page 3: Manuscripts and Archives Division, The New York Public Library.

Page 4, top left and right: Collections of the Division of Political and Military History, National Museum of American History, Smithsonian Institution, Washington, D.C.

Page 4, bottom: Collections of the Division of Political and Military History, National Museum of American History, Smithsonian Institution, Washington, D.C.

Page 5, top and bottom: Courtesy of The David Holcomb Political Americana Collection.

Page 6, top: Thomas Nast, "Uncle Sam's Thanksgiving Dinner," *Harper's Weekly*, November 22 1869, Collections of the Division of Political and Military History, National Museum of American History, Smithsonian Institution, Washington, D.C.

Page 6, bottom: Miriam and Ira D. Wallach Division of Art, Prints and Photographs: Picture Collection, New York Public Library.

Page 7: Library of Congress, Prints and Photographs Division.

Page 8, top: Miriam and Ira D. Wallach Division of Art, Prints and Photographs: Picture Collection, New York Public Library.

Page 8, bottom: Thomas Nast, "'Keep Cool!' Ten Days After the Election," *Harper's Weekly*, December 2, 1876, Collections of the Division of Political and Military History, National Museum of American History, Smithsonian Institution, Washington, D.C.

Page 9: Thomas Nast, "Iron and Blood," *Harper's Weekly*, July 31, 1875. Personal collection of Jon Grinspan.

Page 10, top: Library of Congress, Geography and Map Division.

Page 10, bottom: "1789 to 1889—The Progress of Time," *Judge*, Collections of the Division of Political and Military History, National Museum of American History, Smithsonian Institution, Washington, D.C..

Page 11, top: "A Harmless Explosion," *Puck*, May 25, 1881, U.S. Senate Collection.

Page 11, bottom: "An American Invention for Blowing Up Bosses," *Puck*, November 11, 1881," Collections of the Division of Political and Military History, National Museum of American History, Smithsonian Institution, Washington, D.C.

Page 12, top: Florence Kelley Wischnewetzky (pregnant) and Lazare Wischnewetzky in Europe, ca. 1885, Kelley Family Papers, Rare Book & Manuscript Library, Columbia University in the City of New York.

Page 12, bottom: Manuscripts and Archives Division, The New York Public Library.

Page 13, top: Miriam and Ira D. Wallach Division of Art, Prints and Photographs: Picture Collection, New York Public Library.

Page 13, bottom: Collections of the Division of Political and Military History, National Museum of American History, Smithsonian Institution, Washington, D.C.

Page 14, top: William Allen Rogers, "1881–1897," *Harper's Weekly*, October 24, 1896.

Page 14, bottom: Library of Congress, National Child Labor Committee (Lewis Hine photographs).

Page 15, top: Milford Historical Society, Milford, New Hampshire.

Page 15, bottom: Miriam and Ira D. Wallach Division of Art, Prints and Photographs: Picture Collection, New York Public Library.

Page 16, top: Gillespie Voting Machine, 1898, Collections of the Division of Political and Military History, National Museum of American History, Smithsonian Institution, Washington, D.C.

Page 16, bottom left: "The Man Who Will Elect the Next President," *Leslie's: The People's Weekly*, June 27, 1912, Collections of the Division of Political and Military History, National Museum of American History, Smithsonian Institution, Washington, D.C.

Page 16, bottom right: "How to Use the Voting Machine," *Popular Science Monthly*, November 1920, Collections of the Division of Political and Military History, National Museum of American History, Smithsonian Institution, Washington, D.C.

BIBLIOGRAPHY

PRIMARY SOURCE MATERIALS

Archival Papers and Collections

Columbia University Libraries, Archival Collections, New York, NY
  • Kelley Family Papers

Connecticut Historical Society, Hartford, CT
  • Chaney, Jane
  • Gilman Family Papers
  • Peck, Tracey
  • Wilcox, Jeremiah A.

Historical Society of Pennsylvania, Philadelphia, PA
  • Bigler, William
  • Kelley, William Darrah
  • Keyser, Edmund
  • Marshall, Samuel R.
  • Moore, Joseph Hampton
  • Randall, Samuel J.
  • Sinclair, Robert Lincoln

Houghton Library, Harvard Special Collections, Cambridge, MA
  • Howells, William Dean

Milford Historical Society, Milford, NH
  • Holt, George P. Papers

Minnesota Historical Society, St. Paul, MN
  • Donnelly, Ignatius

Nebraska State Historical Society, Lincoln, NE
  • Uriah W. Oblinger Family Collection

New York Public Library, New York, NY
  • Kelley, Florence Papers
  • Kelley, Nicholas Papers

Southern Historical Collection, University of North Carolina, Chapel Hill, NC
  • Schenck, David

University of Virginia Special Collections, Charlottesville, VA
  • Ashworth, Susan M. Eaton
  • Baker, Richard Henry
  • Graham, Bettie Ann
  • Gray, Susan B.
  • Gregory, Mary Susan
  • Hunton, John
  • Johnston, Mary
  • Minor, Louisa A.
  • Parrish, Stephen
  • Peyton, John W.
  • Springer, Thomas W.

Wisconsin Historical Society, Madison, WI
  • Lloyd, Henry Demarest Papers

Yale Special Collections, Sterling Library, New Haven, CT
  • Campbell, Michael F.

Published Diaries

"A Funnie Place, No Fences," Teenagers' Views of Kansas 1867–1900. Edited by C. Robert Haywood and Sandra Jarvis. Lawrence: University of Kansas, 1992.

Andrews, Sidney. The South Since the War, as Shown by Fourteen Weeks of Travel and Observation in Georgia and the Carolinas. Boston: Ticknor & Co., 1866.

Beadle, Erastus Flavel. Ham, Eggs, and Corn Cake: A Nebraska Territory Diary. Edited by Ronald Naugle. Lincoln: University of Nebraska Press, 2001.

Beardsley, David. "Birthday Commentaries on His Life." Visions of the Western Reserve. Edited by Robert A. Wheeler. Columbus: Ohio State University Press, 2000.

Blackwell, Alice Stone. Growing Up in Boston's Gilded Age. New Haven: Yale University Press, 1990.

Bradford Eppes, Susan. *Through Some Eventful Years*. Macon, GA: J. W. Burke Co., 1926.

Bridgman Conant Bierce, Chloe. *Journal and Biological Notice of Chloe B. Conant Bierce*. Cincinnati: Elm Street Printing, 1869.

Brokmeyer, Henry Conrad. *A Mechanic's Diary*. Washington, D.C.: privately published, 1910.

Channing, Elizabeth Parsons. *Autobiography and Diary of Elizabeth Parsons Channing: Gleanings of a Thoughtful Life*. Boston: American Unitarian Association, 1907.

Claytor, William Quesenbury. *Diary of William Claytor, 1849–1896*. Alexandria, VA: Alexander Street Press, 2002.

Cohen, Rose. *Out of the Shadow*. New York: George H. Doran, 1918.

Donnelly, Ignatius. *The Diary of Ignatius Donnelly*. Edited by Theodore Ludwig Nydahl. Minneapolis: University of Minnesota, 1941.

Doten, Alfred. *The Journals of Alfred Doten, 1849–1903*. Reno: University of Nevada Press, 1973.

Eastman, Elaine Goodale. *Journal of a Farmer's Daughter*. New York: G. P. Putnam's Sons, 1881.

Farnsworth, Martha. *Plains Woman: The Diary of Martha Farnsworth, 1882–1922*. Edited by Marlene Springer and Haskell Springer. Bloomington: Indiana University Press, 1986.

Gillespie, Emily Hawley. *A Secret to Be Buried: The Diary and Life of Emily Hawley Gillespie*. Iowa City: University of Iowa Press, 1989.

Grimké, Charlotte L. Forten. *The Journals of Charlotte Forten Grimké*. Edited by Brenda Stevenson. Oxford: Oxford University Press, 1988.

Havens, Catherine Elizabeth. *The Diary of a Little Girl in Old New York*. New York: Henry Collins Brown, 1919.

Hayes, Rutherford B. *Diary and Letters of Rutherford Birchard Hayes*. Columbus: Ohio State Archaeological and Historical Society, 1922.

Jackson, Oscar Lawrence. *The Colonel's Diary; Journals kept Before and During the Civil War*. Edited by David P. Jackson. Sharon, PA: privately published, 1922.

Johnson, Rolf. *Happy as a Big Sunflower: Adventures in the West, 1876–1880.* Edited by Richard E. Jensen. Lincoln: University of Nebraska Press, 2000.

Mayne, Isabella Maud Rittenhouse. *Maud.* Edited by Richard Lee Strout. New York: Macmillan & Co., 1939.

McDowell Burns, Amanda. *Fiddle in the Cumberland.* Edited by Amanda McDowell and Lela McDowell Blankenship. New York: Richard R. Smith, 1943.

Mersman, Joseph J. *The Whiskey Merchant's Diary.* Edited by Linda A. Fisher. Athens: Ohio University Press, 2007.

Private Pages: Diaries of American Women, 1830s–1970s. Edited by Penelope Franklin. New York: Ballantine Books, 1986.

Ridgely, Anna. "A Girl in The Sixties." *Journal of the Illinois State Historical Society* 2 (October 1929).

Seward, Francis. "Diary of Fanny Seward." Edited by Patricia C. Johnson. *University of Rochester Library Bulletin* 16 (Autumn 1960).

Spottswood, Wilson Lee. *Brief Annals.* Harrisonburg, VA: Publishing Department M.E. Book Room, 1888.

Stanton, Elizabeth Cady. *Elizabeth Cady Stanton, As Revealed in Her Letters, Diary and Reminiscences, vol. 2.* Edited by Harriot Stanton Blatch and Theodore Stanton. New York: Harper & Brothers, 1922.

Strong, George Templeton. *Diary.* Edited by Allan Nevins and Milton Halsey Thomas. New York: Macmillan Press, 1952.

Thomas, Ella Gertrude Clanton. *Secret Eye: The Journal of Elle Gerturde Clanton Thomas, 1848–1889.* Edited by Virginia Ingraham Burr. Chapel Hill: University of North Carolina Press, 1990.

Ward, Lester. *Young Ward's Diary.* Edited by Bernhard J. Stern. New York: G. P. Putnam's Sons, 1935.

Wells, Ida Barnett. *The Memphis Diary of Ida B. Wells: An Intimate Portrait of the Activist as a Young Woman.* Edited by Miriam Decosta-Willis. Boston: Beacon Press, 1995.

Youmans Van Ness, Anne L. *Diary of Annie L. Youmans Van Ness, 1864–1881.* Alexandria, VA: Alexander Street Press, 2004.

Published Memoirs, Reminiscences, and Autobiographies

Abbott, Lyman. *Reminiscences.* Boston: Houghton Mifflin Company, 1914.

Adams, Charles Francis Junior. *Charles Francis Adams, 1835–1915; An Autobiography.* Boston: Houghton Mifflin Company, 1916.

Albee, John. *Confessions of Boyhood.* Boston: Gorham Press, 1910.

America's Immigrants: Adventures in Eyewitness History. Compiled by Rhonda Hoff. New York: H. Z. Walck, 1967.

Anderson, Rasmus Bjorn. *Life Story of Rasmus Bjorn Anderson.* Madison, WI: privately published, 1915.

Barbour, Sylvester. *Reminiscences.* Hartford, CT: Lockwood & Brainard Company, 1908.

Bisno, Abraham. *An Autobiographical Account of Bisno's Early Life and the Beginnings of Unionism in the Women's Garment Industry.* Berkeley: University of California Press, 1967.

Bok, Edward W. *The Americanization of Edward Bok.* New York: Scribner & Sons, 1920.

Bourne, Randolph S. "The Two Generations," *Atlantic Monthly,* May 1911.

Bruce, Henry Clay. *The New Man: Twenty-Nine Years A Slave, Twenty-Nine Years a Free Man, Recollections of Henry Clay Bruce.* York, PA: P. Anstadt & Sons, 1895.

Canby, Henry Seidel. *The Age of Confidence: Life in the Nineties.* New York: Farrar & Rinehart, 1934.

Cobb, Ned. *All God's Dangers: The Life of Nate Shaw.* Compiled by Theodore Rosengarten. Chicago: University of Chicago Press, 1974.

Cole, Cornelius. *Memoirs of Cornelius Cole.* New York: McLoughlin Brothers, 1908.

Culp, Frederick M. *Gibson County, Past and Present.* Paducah, KY: Turner Publishing Company, 1961.

Curley, James Michael. *I'd Do it Again.* New York: Arno Press, 1976.

DePew, Chauncey Mitchell. *My Memories of Eighty Years*. New York: C. Scribner's Sons, 1922.

Ellis, W. T. *Memories: My Seventy-Two Years in the Romantic County of Yuba, California*. Eugene: University of Oregon Press, 1939.

Graham, Jared Benedict. *Handset Reminiscences: Recollections of an Old-Time Printer and Journalist*. Salt Lake City: Century Printing Company, 1915.

Graves, Jackson A. *My Seventy Years in California*. Los Angeles: Times Mirror Press, 1927.

Haugen, Nils. *Pioneer and Political Reminiscences*. Evansville, WI: Antes Press, 1930.

Haven, Alice Bradley. *Cousin Alice: A Memoir of Alice B. Haven*. Edited by Cornelia Richards. New York: D. Appleton & Co., 1868.

Howard, Robert M. *Reminiscences*. Columbus, GA: Gilbert Printing Company, 1912.

Howe, Frederic. *The Confessions of a Reformer*. New York: C. Scribner's Sons, 1925.

Howells, William Dean. *Imaginary Interviews*. New York: Harper & Brothers Publishers, 1910.

Howells, William Dean. *Years of My Youth*. New York: Harper & Brothers, 1916.

Johnston, William G. *Life and Reminiscences from Birth to Manhood*. New York: Knickerbocker Press, 1901.

Kernan, J. Frank. *Reminiscences of Old Fire Laddies and Volunteer Fire Departments of New York and Brooklyn*. New York: M. Crane, 1885.

Kelley, Florence. *The Autobiography of Florence Kelley: Notes of Sixty Years*. Edited by Kathryn Kish Sklar. Chicago: Illinois Labor History Society, Charles H. Kerr Publishing Company, 1986.

Kellie, Luna. *The Praire Populist: The Memoirs of Luna Kellie*. Edited by Jane Taylor Nelsen. Iowa City: University of Iowa Press, 1992.

Kildare, Owen. *My Mamie Rose: The Story of My Regeneration*. New York: Baker and Taylor Company, 1903.

King, William Fletcher. *Reminiscences*. New York: Abingdon Press, 1915.

Leach, Frank. *Recollections of a Newspaperman; A Record of Life and Events in California*. San Francisco: S. Levinson Co., 1917.

Logan, Mary A. *Reminiscences of a Soldier's Wife*. New York: Charles Scribner's Sons, 1916.

Lynch, John Roy. *The Reminiscences of an Active Life: The Autobiography of John Roy Lynch*. Edited by John Hope Franklin. Chicago: University of Chicago Press, 1970.

Marx, Harpo. *Harpo Speaks. . . . about New York*. Edited by Rowland Barber. New York: Limelight Editions, 1985.

The Mexican Immigrant, His Life-Story. Edited by Manuel Gamio. Chicago: University of Chicago Press, 1931.

Murdock, Charles A. *A Backward Glance at Eighty*. San Francisco: P. Elder and Company, 1921.

Parsons, Albert R. *Life of Albert Parsons: With a Brief History of the Labor Movement in America*. Edited by Lucy Parsons. Chicago: privately published, 1903.

Pomeroy, Marcus. *Reminiscences and Recollections of "Brick" Pomeroy*. New York: Advance Though Company, 1890.

Poore, Ben Perley. *Reminiscences of Sixty Years at the National Metropolis, Vol II*. Philadelphia: Hubbard Brothers Publisher, 1886.

Riis, Jacob. *Making of an American*. New York: Macmillan Company, 1901.

Roosevelt, Theodore, Jr. *Theodore Roosevelt—An Autobiography*. New York: Charles Scribner, 1913.

Schurz, Carl. *The Reminiscences of Carl Schurz*. New York: McClure Co., 1907.

Selby, Julian A. *Memorabilia and Anecdotal Reminiscences of Columbia South Carolina*. Columbia: R. L. Bryan Company, 1905.

Shields, Art. *My Shaping-Up Years: The Early Years of Labor's Great Reporter*. New York: International Publishers, 1983.

Sobieski, John. *The Life Story and Personal Reminiscences of Col. John Sobieski*. Shelbyville, IL: J. L. Douthit & Son, 1900.

Steffens, Lincoln. *The Autobiography of Lincoln Steffens.* New York: Harcourt and Brace, 1937.

Stephenson, Isaac. *Recollections of a Long Life, 1829–1915.* Chicago: privately published, 1915.

Thompson, B. F. "The Wide Awakes of 1860." *The Magazine of History with Notes and Queries,* November 1909. 293–96.

Ueland, Andreas. *Recollections of an Immigrant.* New York: Minton, Balch & Co., 1929.

Wallace, Lew. *An Autobiography.* New York: Harper & Brothers, 1906.

White, Andrew Dickson. *Autobiography of Andrew Dickinson White.* New York: Century Co., 1904.

White, William Allen. *The Autobiography of William Allen White.* New York: Macmillan, 1947.

Willard, Frances E. *Glimpses of Fifty Years: The Autobiography of an American Woman.* Chicago: Women's Temperance Publication Association, H. J. Smith & Co., 1889.

Witham, James. *Fifty years on the Firing line: My part in the farmers' movement.* Chicago: privately published, 1924.

Published Letters

Adams, Henry. *The Letters of Henry Adams, Volume II 1868–1885.* Edited by Jacob Claver Levenson. Cambridge: Harvard University Press, 1982.

Anthony, Susan B. *The Life and Work of Susan B. Anthony: Including Public Addresses, Her Own Letters and Many from Her Contemporaries During Fifty Years.* Edited by Ida Husted Harper. Indianapolis: Hollenbeck Publishing, 1899.

Botta, Anne Charlotte Lynch. *Memoirs of Anne C. L. Botta Written by her friends.* Edited by Vincenzo Botta. New York: J. Selwin Tait & Sons, 1893.

Child, Lydia Maria. *Letters of Lydia Maria Child.* Edited by Wendell Phillips. Cambridge: Riverside Press, 1882.

Chronicles from the Nineteenth Century: Family Letters of Blanche Butler and Adelbert Ames, Volume One. Compiled by Blanche Butler Ames. Clinton, MA: privately published, 1957.

Dickinson, Emily Elizabeth. *The Letters of Emily Dickinson, Vol 1.* Edited by Mabel Todd Loomis. Boston: Roberts Bros., 1894.

FitzGerald, Emily McCorkle. *An Army Doctor's Wife on the Frontier: Letters from Alaska and the Far West, 1874–1878.* Pittsburgh: University of Pittsburgh Press, 1962.

Fleet, Maria Louisa Wacker. *Green Mount after the War: The Correspondence of Maria Louisa Wacker Fleet and her family, 1865–1900.* Edited by Betsy Fleet. Charlottesville: University Press of Virginia, 1978.

Grierson, Alice Kirk. *The Colonel's Lady on the Western Frontier: The Correspondence of Alice Kirk Grierson.* Edited by Shirley A. Leckie. Lincoln: University of Nebraska Press, 1989.

Howard Conant, Charlotte. *A Girl of the Eighties at College and at Home.* Edited by Martha Pike Conant. Boston: Houghton, Mifflin & Co., 1931.

Howells, William Dean. *Selected Letters of William Dean Howells, Vol 1.* Edited by George Arms. Boston: Twayne Publishing, 1979.

Judson, Emily Chubbuck. *The Life and Letters of Mrs. Emily C. Judson.* New York: Sheldon & Co., 1860.

Letters from the Promised Land: Swedes in America 1840–1915. Edited by H. Arnold Barton. Minneapolis: University of Minnesota, 1975.

Lincoln, Abraham. *Abraham Lincoln, The Collected Works, 9 Vol.* Edited by Roy P. Basler. New Brunswick, NJ: Rutgers University Press, 1953.

McMullen, William. In *Letters from an Irish Ward Leader: William McMullen to Samuel J. Randall, 1864–1890.* Edited by Harry C. Silcox. Philadelphia: Historical Society of Pennsylvania, 1985.

Roosevelt, Theodore, Jr. *The Selected Letters of Theodore Roosevelt.* Edited by H. W. Brands. New York: Rowman & Littlefield Publisher, 2013.

Tilden, Samuel J. *Letters and Literary Memorials of Samuel J. Tilden.* Edited by John Bigelow. New York: Harper and Brothers Pub., 1908.

Sumner, Charles. *The Works of Charles Sumner*. Boston: Lee and Shephard, 1875–83.

Their Own Saga: Letters From the Norwegian Global Migration. Edited by Frederick Hale. Minneapolis: University of Minnesota Press, 1986.

Tilden, Samuel J. *The Writings and Speeches of Samuel J. Tilden*. Edited by John Bigelow. New York: Harper & Brothers, 1885.

Tucker Emerson, Ellen. *The Letters of Ellen Tucker Emerson*. Edited by Edith W. Gregg. Kent, OH: Kent State University Press, 1982.

The Welsh in America, Letters from the Immigrants. Edited by Alan Conway. Minneapolis: University of Minnesota Press, 1961.

Primary Books

Abbott, Lyman. *The Spirit of Democracy*. New York: Houghton Mifflin Co., 1910.

Abbott, Lyman. *Silhouettes of My Contemporaries*. New York: Doubleday, 1921.

Addams, Jane. *Democracy and Social Ethics*. New York: Macmillan and Co., 1902.

Addams, Jane. *The Spirit of Youth and the City Streets*. New York: Macmillan Company, 1909.

Before he is Twenty: Five Perplexing Phases of Boyhood Considered. Edited by Edward Bok. New York: F. H. Revell, 1894.

Beveridge, Albert J. *The Young Man and the World*. New York: D. Appleton and Company, 1905.

Bigelow, John. *The Life of Samuel J. Tilden*. New York: Harper & Brothers, 1895.

Blaine, Harriet Bailey. *Letters of Mrs. James G. Blaine*. Edited by Harriet S. Blaine Beale. New York: Duffield & Co., 1908.

Blaine, James G. *Life and Public Services of Hon. James G. Blaine*. Edited by James P. Boyd. Philadelphia: Publishers Union, 1893.

Bodine, Lester. *Off the Face of the Earth*. Omaha: Festner Printing Co., 1894.

Brigham, Johnson. *Blaine, Conkling and Garfield: A Reminiscence and a Character Study*. New York: G. E. Stechert & Co., 1919.

Browne, Junis Henri. *The Great Metropolis: A Mirror of New York*. Hartford, CT: American Publishing Company, 1869.

Bryce, James. *Bryce on America Democracy: Selections from "The American Commonwealth" and "The Hindrances to Good Citizenship."* New York: Macmillan Publishing Co., 1919.

Carpenter, Frank. *Carp's Washington*. New York: McGraw-Hill Book Company, 1960.

Chapin, Elizabeth Moore. *American Court Gossip, or, Life at the National Capitol*. Marshalltown, IA: Chapin & Hartwell Bros., 1887.

Chapman, John Jay. *Practical Agitation*. New York: Charles Scribner's Sons, 1900.

Conkling, Roscoe. *Life and Letters of Roscoe Conkling: Orator, Stateman, Advocate*. Edited by Alfred R. Conkling. New York: Charles L. Webster & Co, 1889.

Dickens, Charles. *American Notes for General Circulation*. London: J. M. Dent & Co., 1907.

Dineen, Joseph F. *Ward Eight*. New York: Harper & Brothers, 1936.

Du Bois, W. E. B. *The Philadelphia Negro: A Social Study*. Philadelphia: University of Pennsylvania, 1899.

Foster, Lilian. *Andrew Johnson: President of the United States*. London: Richardson Press, 1866.

George, Henry. *Progress and Poverty: An Inquiry into the Cause of Industrial Depressions and of Increase of Want with Increase of Wealth*. New York: Sterling Publishing Company, 1879.

Godkin, Edwin Lawrence. *The Problems of Modern Democracy*. New York: Charles Scribner's Sons, 1896.

Harper, Frances Ellen Watkins. *The Underground Rail Road: A Record of Facts, Authentic Narratives, Letters, &c*. Philadelphia: Porter & Coates, 1872.

Hay, John. *The Life and Letters of John Hay, Volume 1*. Edited by William Roscoe Thayer. Boston: Houghton Mifflin Company, 1908.

Ivin, William Mills. *Machine Politics and Money in Elections in New York City*. New York: Harper & Brothers, 1887.

Kelley, Florence. *Some Ethical Gains Through Legislation*. New York: Macmillan Co., 1905.

Kelley, Florence. *Twenty Questions about the Federal Amendment Proposed by the National Woman's Party*. New York: National Consumers' League, 1922.

Kelley, William D. in *The Equality of All Men before the Law, Claimed and Defended in Speeches by Hon. William D. Kelley, Wendell Phillips, and Frederick Douglass*. Boston: Press of Geo. C. Rand & Avery, 1865.

Kelley, William D. *National Centennial Celebration and Exposition*. Washington: F. & J. Rives & G. A. Bailey, 1871.

Kelley, William D. *The Old South and the New: A Series of Letters*. New York: G. P. Putnam's Sons, 1888.

Kelley, William D. *Speeches, Addresses, and Letters on Industrial and Financial Questions*. New York: H. C. Baird, 1872.

Kipling, Rudyard. *American Notes*. New York: Frank F. Lovell Company, 1889.

Leland, Charles G. *Pipps Among the Wide Awakes*. New York: Wevill & Chapin, 1860.

Liddell, Henry. *The Evolution of a Democrat: A Darwinian Tale*. New York: Paquet & Co., 1888.

Linn, James Weber. *Jane Addams: A Biography*. New York: D. Appleton & Co., 1935.

Lippmann, Walter. *Drift and Mastery: An Attempt to Diagnose the Current Unrest*. New York: Mitchell Kennerley, 1914.

Lloyd, Henry Demarest. *Man, The Social Creator*. New York: Doubleday, Page, 1906.

Lloyd, Henry Demarest. *Wealth Against Commonwealth*. New York: Harper Brothers Publishing, 1894.

Locke, David Ross. *Nasby: Divers Views, Opinions and Prophecies of Petroleum v. Nasby*. Cincinnati: R. W. Carroll & Co., 1867.

Lowell, James Russell. *Lowell's Works, Literary and Political Addresses*. Boston: Houghton, Mifflin, and Co., 1886.

Memorial Addresses on the Life and Character of William D. Kelley, Delivered in the House of Representatives and the Senate, Fifty-First Congress, First Session. Washington, DC: Government Printing Office, 1890.

Nordhoff, Charles. *Politics for Young Americans*. New York: Harper & Brothers, 1875.

Post, Louis F. *The Ethics of Democracy: A Series of Optimistic Essays on the Natural Laws of Human Society*. Indianapolis: Bobbs-Merrill Company, 1916.

Raymond, Walter Marion. *Rebels of the New South*. Chicago: Charles H. Kerr & Co., 1905.

Reid, Whitelaw. *Horace Greeley*. New York: Charles Scribner's Sons, 1879.

Riordan, William L. *Plunkitt of Tammany Hall: A Series of Very Plain Talks on Very Practical Politics*. New York: E. P. Dutton & Co., 1963.

Roosevelt, Theodore. *Essays on Practical Politics*. New York: G. P. Putnam's Sons, 1888.

Scudder, Horace Elisha. *James Russell Lowell: A Biography*. Boston: Houghton & Mifflin Company, 1901.

Shapley, Rufus Edmonds. *Solid for Mulhooly*. New York: G. W. Carleton & Co., 1881.

Sherman, William Tecumseh and Sherman, John. *The Sherman Letters: Correspondence Between General and Senator Sherman from 1837 to 1891*. Edited by Rachel Sherman Thorndike. New York: Charles Scribner's Sons, 1894.

Steffens, Lincoln. *Upbuilders*. New York: Doubleday, Page, 1909.

Strong, Josiah. *Our Country: Its Possible Future and its Present Crisis*. New York: Baker & Taylor Co., 1885.

Tourgée, Albion Winegar. *Letters to a King*. Cincinnati: Cranston and Stowe, 1888.

Twain, Mark and Charles Dudley Warner. *The Gilded Age: A Tale of Today*. New York: American Publishing Company, 1873.

Vance, James Isaac. *The Young Man Foursquare*. New York: F. H. Revell Co., 1894.

Weyl, Walter. *The New Democracy*. New York: Macmillan and Co., 1914.

White, William Allen. *The Old Order Changeth: A View of American Democracy*. Milwaukee: Young Churchman Co., 1917.

Newspapers and Magazines

Albany Evening Register
American Federationist
American Heritage
American Monthly Review
American Nonconformist
American Reformer
American Review: Arizona Journal-Miner
Atchinson Daily Globe
Atlanta Daily Constitution
Atlantic Monthly
Augusta Daily Chronicle & Sentinel
Baltimore Afro-American
Baltimore Patriot
Baltimore Sun
Bangor Daily Whig & Courier
Bismarck Tribune
Boston Daily Advertiser
Boston Daily Atlas
Boston Investigator
Boston Transcript
Brooklyn Daily Eagle
Burlington Hawkeye
Cincinnati Gazette
Cincinnati Commercial Tribune

Chicago Inter Ocean
Chicago Tribune
Chronicle, Student Magazine of University of Michigan
Cleveland Gazette
Cleveland Herald
Colored American
Congressional Globe
Congregationalist
Continent; an Illustrated Weekly Magazine
Daily Arkansas Gazette
Daily Boomerang
Daily Evening Bulletin
Daily National Intelligencer
Central City, Colorado, Daily Register-Call
Denver Rocky Mountain News
Des Moines Daily State Register
Duluth News-Tribune
Emancipator and Weekly Chronicle
Emporia Daily Gazette
Frank Leslie's Illustrated Newspaper
Galveston Daily News
Georgia Journal & Messenger

Georgia Press
Georgia Weekly Telegraph
Grand Forks Herald
Harper's Weekly
Harper's Young People
Hartford Daily Courant
Hinds County Gazette
Houston Union
Huntsville Gazette
Idaho Avalanche
Independent
Indiana School Journal
Indianapolis Freeman
Indianapolis Sentinel
Irish World and American Industrial
    Liberator
Kansas City Evening Star
Keith County News
Knoxville Journal
La Follette's Weekly Magazine
Le Petit Temps
Liberator
Little Rock Morning Republican
London Daily News
Los Angeles Daily Times
Lowell Citizen and News
Macon Telegraph and Messenger
Memphis Enquirer
Milwaukee Daily Journal
Milwaukee Sentinel
Mississippian and State Gazette
Montana Morning Republican
Morning Oregonian
Nation
National Police Gazette
New Haven Journal and Courier
New Haven Register

New Mississippian
New Orleans Times Picayune
New Yorker
New York Evening Post
New York Freeman
New York Herald
New York Sun
New York Times
New York Tribune
New York World
New-York Spectator
Newark Evening News
News and Courier
North American
North American Review
North Star
Ogallala Reflector
Ohio State Journal
Ohio Statesman
Omaha World Herald
Outlook
Overland Monthly and Out
    West Magazine
Owatonna Journal
Pennsylvania Inquirer and Daily Courier
Philadelphia Inquirer
Philadelphia Ledger
Pittsfield Sun
Pomeroy's Democrat
Provincial Freeman
Puck
Raleigh Register, and North-Carolina
    Gazette
Republican Magazine
Review of Reviews
Richmond News and Observer
Richmond Plane

Salt Lake Tribune
San Francisco Argonaut
San Jose Evening News
School Board Journal
St. Louis Dispatch
St. Louis Globe-Democrat
St. Paul Daily News
Tariff Review
Trenton State Gazette

United States Magazine and Democratic
   Review
Vermont Patriot
Vermont Watchman
Washington Bee
Washington Post
Weekly Patriot and Union
Wheeling Register
Wisconsin State Register
Youth's Companion

American Life Histories Interviews, Federal Writers' Project

Acosta, St. Elmo W. Interviewed by Rose Shepherd. July 17, 1938.

Boyter, W. A. Interviewed by Ethel Deal. September 4, 1939.

Dowling, James. Interviewed by Edward Welch. December 22, 1938.

Hines, DeWitt. Interviewed by Adyleen G. Merrick. February 2, 1939.

Huyck, Mrs. Charley. Interviewed by Harold J. Moss. January 24, 1939.

Kaiser, Emil R. Interviewed by Francis Donovan Thomaston. December 15, 1938.

Lovell, Cora. Interviewed by Rosalie Smith. January 4, 1939.

Mathews, B. G. Interviewed by Bessie Jollensten. November 5, 1938.

McCarthy, John J. "A speech made by J. J. McCarthy at Kearney, Nebraska." Collected by Bessie Jollensten. October 19, 1938.

McCarthy, John J. "When I first voted the Democratic Ticket." Collected by Bessie Jollensten. October 19, 1938.

McCarthy, Mary. Interviewed by Bessie Jollensten. October 19, 1938.

Perciful, Frank. Interviewed by Annie McAulay. September 1, 1938.

Powers, Don and Susie. Interviewed by John William Prosser. February 6, 1939.

Pringle, Sarah Ann Ross. Interviewed by Effie Cowan.

Slave Narratives

Bryant, Robert. *Born in Slavery: Slave Narratives from the Federal Writers' Project, 1936–1938. Missouri Narratives*, Volume X, 61.

Cancer, Polly Turner. Transcribed by Ann Allen Geoghegan. *Mississippi Narratives Prepared by the Federal Writers' Project of the Works Progress Administration For the State of Mississippi*. Last accessed October 28, 2020. http://msgw.org/slaves /cancer-pollyt-xslave.htm.

Davis, Louis. Transcribed by Ann Allen Geoghegan. *Mississippi Narratives Prepared by the Federal Writers' Project of the Works Progress Administration For the State of Mississippi*. Last accessed October 28, 2020. http://msgw.org/slaves /davis-xslave.htm.

Gray, Callie. Transcribed by Ann Allen Geoghegan. *Mississippi Narratives Prepared by The Federal Writer's Project of The Works Progress Administration For the State of Mississippi*. Last accessed October 28, 2020. http://msgw.org/slaves /gray-xslave.htm.

Hill, Louis. Farmington, Missouri. *Born in Slavery: Slave Narratives from the Federal Writers' Project, 1936–1938. Missouri Narratives*, Volume X, 186.

Holsell, Rhody. *Born in Slavery: Slave Narratives from the Federal Writers' Project, 1936–1938: Missouri Narratives, Volume X*, 191.

Jones, Aaron. Transcribed by Ann Allen Geoghegan. *Mississippi Narratives Prepared by the Federal Writers' Project of the Works Progress Administration For the State of Mississippi*. Last accessed October 28, 2020. http://msgw.org/slaves /jones-aaron-xslave.htm.

Nealy, Wylie. Interview by Irene Robertson, Biscoe, Arkansas. *Born in Slavery: Slave Narratives from the Federal Writers' Project, 1936–1938. Arkansas Narratives*, Volume II, 188.

Pope, John. Interview by Irene Robertson, Biscoe, Arkansas. Arkansas. *Born in Slavery: Slave Narratives from the Federal Writers' Project, 1936–1938. Arkansas Narratives*, Volume II, Part 5, 359.

Ramsay, George Washington. Transcribed by Ann Allen Geoghegan. *Mississippi Narratives Prepared by the Federal Writers' Project of the Works Progress*

Administration For the State of Mississippi. Last accessed October 28, 2020. http://msgw.org/slaves/ramsey-xslave.htm.

Wamble, Reverend. Interviewed by Archie Koritz, Valparaiso, Indiana. *Born in Slavery: Slave Narratives from the Federal Writers' Project, 1936–1938. Indiana Narratives*, Volume V, 198.

Young, John I. Interviewed by Henry Muir, Montgomery County, Ohio. Works Progress Administration, Ex-Slave Narratives. Ohio Historical Society, "The African-American Experience in Ohio, 1850–1920."

SECONDARY SOURCE MATERIALS
Books and Dissertations

Altschuler, Glenn C. and Stuart M. Blumin. *Rude Republic: Americans and their Politics in the Nineteenth Century*. Princeton, NJ: Princeton University Press, 2000.

Bensel, Richard Franklin. *The American Ballot Box in the Mid-Nineteenth Century*. Cambridge: Cambridge University Press, 2004.

Bensel, Richard Franklin. *The Political Economy of American Industrialization, 1877–1900*. Cambridge: Cambridge University Press, 2000.

Bernstein, Iver. *The New York City Draft Riots: Their Significance in American Society and Politics in the Age of the Civil War*. New York: Oxford University Press, 1990.

Biddle, Daniel R. and Murray Dubin. *Tasting Freedom: Octavius Catto and the Battle for Equality in Civil War America*. Philadelphia: Temple University Press, 2010.

Blight, David. *Frederick Douglass: Prophet of Freedom*. New York: Simon and Schuster, 2018.

Burlingame, Sara Lee. "The Making of A Spoilsman: The Life and Career of Roscoe Conkling from 1829–1873." PhD dissertation, Johns Hopkins University, 1974.

Burnham, Walter Dean. *Presidential Ballots: 1836–1892*. Baltimore: Johns Hopkins Press, 1955.

Chambers, John Whiteclay. *Tyranny of Change: America in the Progressive Era, 1890–1920.* New Brunswick, NJ: Rutgers University Press, 2000.

Chidsey, Donald Barr. *The Gentleman from New York: A Life of Roscoe Conkling.* New Haven: Yale University Press, 1935.

Chudacoff, Howard. *The Age of the Bachelor.* Princeton, NJ: Princeton University Press, 1999.

Corder, J. Kevin and Christina Wolbrecht. *Counting Women's Ballots: Female Voters from Suffrage through the New Deal.* Cambridge: Cambridge University Press, 2016.

Curti, Merle. *The Making of an American Community: A Case Study in Democracy in a Frontier County.* Stanford: Stanford University Press, 1959.

Destler, Chester M. *Henry Demarest Lloyd and the Empire of Reform.* Philadelphia: University of Pennsylvania Press, 1963.

Eastman, Carolyn. *A Nation of Speechifiers.* Chicago: University of Chicago Press, 2009.

Edwards, Rebecca. *Angels in the Machinery: Gender in American Party Politics from the Civil War to the Progressive Era.* New York: Oxford University Press, 1997.

Edwards, Rebecca. *New Spirits: Americans in the Gilded Age.* New York: Oxford University Press, 2006.

Egerton, Douglas. *Wars of Reconstruction: The Brief, Violent History of America's Most Progressive Era.* New York: Bloomsbury Publishing, 2015.

Field, Corinne T. *The Struggle for Equal Adulthood: Gender, Race, Age, and the Fight for Citizenship in Antebellum America.* Chapel Hill: University of North Carolina Press, 2015.

Filler, Louis. *The Muckrackers.* San Francisco: Stanford University Press, 1993.

Foner, Eric. *Free Labor, Free Soil, Free Men.* Oxford: Oxford University Press, 1970.

Foner, Eric. *Freedom's Lawmakers: A Directory of Black Officeholders during Reconstruction.* Rev. ed. Baton Rouge: Louisiana State University Press, 1996.

Foner, Eric. *The Second Founding: How the Civil War and Reconstruction Remade the Constitution.* New York: W. W. Norton, 2019.

Franklin, John Hope. *Reconstruction After the Civil War.* Chicago: University of Chicago Press, 1962.

Fraser, Steve, *The Age of Acquiescence: The Life and Death of American Resistance to Organized Wealth and Power.* New York: Little, Brown, and Co., 2015.

Freeman, Joanne. *The Field of Blood: Violence in Congress and the Road to Civil War.* New York: Farrar, Strauss, & Giroux, 2018.

Gallagher, Gary. *The Union War.* Cambridge: Harvard University Press, 2012.

Gallman, J. Matt. *America's Joan of Arc, The Life of Anna Elizabeth Dickinson.* New York: Oxford University Press, 2006.

Gambill, Edward Lee. *Conservative Ordeal: Northern Democrats and Reconstruction, 1865–1868.* Ames: Iowa State University Press, 1981.

Greco, Michael Robert. "William Darrah Kelley: The Ante-bellum Years," PhD dissertation, University of Michigan, 1975, 197.

Green, James. *Death in the Haymarket: A Story of Chicago, the First Labor Movement and the Bombing that Divided Gilded Age America.* New York: Anchor Books, 2006.

Greenberg, Amy. *Cause for Alarm: The Volunteer Fire Department in the Nineteenth-Century City.* Princeton, NJ: Princeton University Press, 1998.

Grinspan, Jon. *The Virgin Vote: How Young Americans Made Democracy Social, Politics Personal, and Voting Popular in the Nineteenth Century.* Chapel Hill: University of North Carolina Press, 2016.

Goldmark, Josephine. *Impatient Crusader: Florence Kelley's Life Story.* Champaign: University of Illinois Press, 1953.

Goodwin, Doris Kearns. *The Bully Pulpit: Theodore Roosevelt, William Howard Taft, and the Golden Age of Journalism.* New York: Simon & Schuster, 2013.

Hofstadter, Richard. *The Age of Reform.* New York: Vintage Books, 1955.

Holt, Michael Fitzgibbon. *By One Vote: The Disputed Election of 1876.* Lawrence: University of Kansas Press, 2009.

Holt, Michael Fitzgibbon. *Forging a Majority: the Formation of the Republican Party in Pittsburgh, 1848–1860.* New Haven: Yale University Press, 1969.

Hoogenboom, Ari. *Outlawing the Spoils: A History of Civil Service Reform Movement.* New York: Praeger, 1982.

Jacobs, Kathryn Allamong. *King of the Lobby: The Life and Times of Sam Ward, Man about Town in Gilded-Age Washington,* Baltimore: John Hopkins University Press, 2010.

Jordan, David M. *Roscoe Conkling of New York: Voice in the Senate.* Ithaca: Cornell University Press, 1971.

Josephson, Matthew. *The Politicos: 1865–1896.* New York: Harcourt, Brace and Company, 1938.

Keller, Morton. *Affairs of State.* Cambridge: Belknap Press of Harvard University Press, 1977.

Keller, Morton. *America's Three Regimes.* New York: Oxford University Press, 2007.

Keyssar, Alexander. *The Right to Vote: The Contested History of Democracy in the United States.* New York: Basic Books, 2009.

Kleppner, Paul. *Who Voted? The Dynamics of Electoral Turnout, 1870–1980.* New York: Praeger, 1982.

Kleppner, Paul. *The Third Electoral System, 1853–1892: Parties, Voters, and Political Cultures.* Chapel Hill: University of North Carolina Press, 2010.

Klinghard, Daniel. *Nationalization of American Politics 1880–1896.* Cambridge: Cambridge University Press, 2010.

Kornbluh, Mark Lawrence. *Why America Stopped Voting: The Decline of Participatory Democracy and the Emergence of Modern American Politics.* New York: New York University Press, 2000.

Lane, Roger. *The Roots of Violence in Black Philadelphia.* Cambridge: Harvard University Press, 1989.

Lloyd, Caro. *Henry Demarest Lloyd, a Biography.* New York: Knickerbocker Press, 1912.

McCarty, Nolan; Poole, Keith T. and Rosenthal, Howard. *Polarized America: The Dance of Ideology and Unequal Riches.* Cambridge: Massachusetts Institute of Technology Press, 2006.

McGerr, Michael E. *The Decline of Popular Politics, The American North 1865–1928*. Oxford: Oxford University Press, 1986.

McGerr, Michael. *A Fierce Discontent: The Rise and Fall of the Progressive Movement in America, 1870–1920*. New York: Free Press, 2003.

McKivigan, John. *Forgotten Firebrand: James Redpath and the Making of Nineteenth-Century America*. Ithaca: Cornell University Press, 2008.

Mead, Rebecca, *How the Vote Was Won: Women Suffrage in the Western United States*. New York: New York University Press, 2006.

Merriman, John. *Massacre: The Life and Death of the Paris Commune*. New York: Basic Books, 2014.

Millard, Candice. *The Destiny of the Republic: A Tale of Madness, Medicine, and the Murder of a President*. New York: Doubleday, 2011.

Montgomery, David. *Citizen Worker: The Experience of Workers in the United States with Democracy and the Free Market During the Nineteenth Century*. Cambridge: Cambridge University Press, 1993.

Morris, Edwin. *The Rise of Theodore Roosevelt*. New York: Modern Library, 1979.

Morris, Roy, Jr. *The Fraud of the Century: Rutherford B. Hayes, Samuel J. Tilden, and the Stolen Election of 1876*. New York: Simon & Schuster, 2003.

Murphy, Kevin. *Political Manhood: Red Bloods, Mollycoddles, and the Politics of Progressive Era Reform*. New York: Columbia University Press, 2010.

Neely, Mark E., Jr. *The Boundaries of American Political Culture in the Civil War Era*. Chapel Hill: University of North Carolina Press, 2005.

Oller, John. *American Queen: The Rise and Fall of Kate Chase Sprague—Civil War "Belle of the North" and Gilded Age Woman of Scandal*. New York: Da Capo Press, 2014.

Perman, Michael. *Struggle for Mastery: Disfranchisement in the South, 1888–1908*. Chapel Hill: University of North Carolina Press, 2001.

Phelan, Craig. *Grand Master Workman: Terence Powderly and the Knights of Labor*. New York: Praeger Co., 2000.

Postel, Charles. *Equality: An American Dilemma, 1866–1896.* New York: Farrar, Straus, and Giroux, 2019.

Postel, Charles. *The Populist Vision.* Oxford: Oxford University Press, 2007.

Powers, Madelon. *Faces Along the Bar: Lore and Order in the Workingman's Saloon, 1870–1920.* Chicago: University of Chicago Press, 1999.

Pressly, Thomas. *Americans Interpret their Civil War.* New York: Free Press, 1965.

Putnam, Robert. *Bowling Alone: The Collapse and Revival of American Community.* New York: Simon & Schuster, 2001.

Quigley, David. *Second Founding: New York City, Reconstruction, and the Making of American Democracy.* New York: Hill & Wang, 2004.

Ridge, Martin. *Ignatius Donnelly: Portrait of a Politician.* St. Paul: Minnesota Historical Society Press, 1991.

Rorabaugh, W. J. *The Alcoholic Republic: An American Tradition.* New York: Oxford University Press, 1979.

Rose, Kenneth D. *Unspeakable Awfulness: America Through the Eyes of European Travelers, 1865–1900.* New York: Routledge, 2013.

Rosen, Jeffrey. *Louis D. Brandeis: American Prophet.* New Haven: Yale University Press, 2016.

Rosenblum, Nancy L. *On the Side of the Angels: An Appreciation of Parties and Partisanship.* Princeton, NJ: Princeton University Press, 2010.

Ruling America: History of Wealth and Power in a Democracy. Edited by Steve Fraser and Gary Gerstle. Cambridge: Harvard University Press, 2005.

Rugoff, Milton, *America's Gilded Age: Intimate Portraits from an Era of Extravagance and Change, 1850–1890.* New York: Henry Holt, 1989.

Ryan, Mary. *Civic Wars.* Berkeley: University of California Press, 1998.

Ryan, Mary. *Cradle of the Middle Class.* Cambridge: Cambridge University Press, 1981.

Ryan, Mary. *Women in Public: Between Banners and Ballots, 1825–1880.* Baltimore: Johns Hopkins University Press, 1992.

Sanders, M. Elizabeth. *The Roots of Reform: Farmers, Workers, and the American State, 1877–1917*. Chicago: University of Chicago Press, 1999.

Schwantes, Carlos. *Coxey's Army: An American Odyssey*. New York: Caxton Press, 1985.

Sellers, Charles. *The Market Revolution*. Oxford: Oxford University Press, 1991.

Shelden, Rachel. *Washington Brotherhood: Politics, Social Life, and the Coming of the Civil War*. Chapel Hill: University of North Carolina Press, 2013.

Silbey, Joel. *The American Political Nation, 1838-1893*. Stanford: Stanford University Press, 1994.

Silcox, Harry C. *Philadelphia Politics from the Bottom Up: The Life of Irishman William McMullen, 1824–1901*. Philadelphia: Balch Institute Press, 1989.

Sklar, Kathryn Kish. *Florence Kelley & the Nation's Work: The Rise of Women's Political Culture*. New Haven: Yale University Press, 1995.

Smith, Adam I. P. *No Party Now: Politics in the Civil War North*. New York: Oxford University Press, 2006.

Southern Black Leaders of the Reconstruction Era. Edited by Howard N. Rabinowitz. Champaign: University of Illinois Press, 1982.

Sproat, John. *The Best Men: The Liberal Reformers of the Gilded Age*. New York: Oxford University Press, 1968.

Stiles, T. J. *Jesse James: Last Rebel of the Civil War*. New York: Vintage Books, 2003.

Summers, Mark Wahlgren. *A Dangerous Stir: Fear, Paranoia, and the Making of Reconstruction*. New York: Oxford University Press, 2009.

Summers, Mark Wahlgren. *The Ordeal of Reunion: A New History of Reconstruction*. Chapel Hill: University of North Carolina Press, 2014.

Summers, Mark Wahlgren. *Party Games: Getting, Keeping, and Using Power in Gilded Age Politics*. Chapel Hill: University of North Carolina Press, 2004.

Summers, Mark Wahlgren. *The Press Gang: Newspapers and Politics, 1865–1878*. Chapel Hill: University of North Carolina Press, 1994.

Tebeau, Mark. *Eating Smoke: Fire in Urban America, 1800–1950*. Baltimore: Johns Hopkins University Press, 2003.

Thomas, John L. *Alternative America: Henry George, Edward Bellamy, Henry Demarest Lloyd and the Adversary Tradition*. Cambridge: Harvard University Press, 1983.

Tucker, David M. *Mugwumps: The Public Moralists of the Gilded Age*. Columbia: University of Missouri Press, 1998.

Valelly, Richard M. *The Two Reconstructions: The Struggle for Black Enfranchisement*. Chicago: University of Chicago, 2004.

Vorenberg, Michael. *Final Freedom: The Civil War, the Abolition of Slavery, and the Thirteenth Amendment*. Cambridge: Cambridge University Press, 2001.

Wendt, Lloyd and Herman Kogan. *Lords of the Levee: The Story of Bathhouse John and Hinky Dink*. Chicago: Northwestern University Press, 2005.

White, Jonathan W. *Emancipation, the Union Army, and the Reelection of Abraham Lincoln*. Baton Rouge: Louisiana State University, 2014

White, Richard. *The Republic for Which It Stands: The United States During Reconstruction and the Gilded Age, 1865–1896*. New York: Oxford University Press, 2017.

Wiebe, Robert H. *The Search for Order, 1877–1920*. New York: Hill and Wang, 1967.

Wiebe, Robert H. *Self-Rule: A Cultural History of American Democracy*. Chicago: University of Chicago Press, 1995.

Wilentz, Sean. *Chants Democratic: New York City and the Rise of the American Working Class*. New York: Oxford University Press, 1984.

Winch, Julie. *A Gentleman of Color: The Life of James Forten*. New York: Oxford University Press, 2002.

Young, Jeremy C. *The Age of Charisma: Leaders, Followers, and Emotions in American Society, 1870–1940*. Cambridge: Cambridge University Press, 2016.

Ziparo, Jessica. *This Grand Experiment: When Women Entered the Federal Workforce in Civil War–Era Washington, D.C.* Chapel Hill: University of North Carolina, 2017.

Articles and Essays

Alexander, Thomas B. "The Dimensions of Voter Partisan Consistency in Presidential Elections from 1840 to 1860." *Essays on American Antebellum Politics, 1840–1860*. Edited by Stephen E. Maizlish. College Station: Texas A&M University Press, 1982.

Amer, Mildred. "Members of the U.S. Congress Who Have Died of Other Than Natural Causes While in Office." *Congressional Research Service, Report for Congress*, Library of Congress, March 13, 2002.

Argersinger, Peter. "A Place on the Ballot: Fusion Politics and Antifusion Laws." *American Historical Review* (January 1980), 287–306.

Barreyre, Nicolas. "The Politics of Economic Crises: The Panic of 1873, the End of Reconstruction, and the Realignment of American Politics." *Journal of the Gilded Age and the Progressive Era* 10, no. 4 (October 2011): 403–423.

Benedict, Michael Les. "Reform Republicans and the Retreat from Reconstruction." *Preserving the Constitution: Essays on Politics and the Constitution in the Reconstruction Era*. New York: Fordham University Press, 2006, 168–185.

Brown, Ira V. "William D. Kelley and Radical Reconstruction." *Pennsylvania Magazine of History and Biography* 85, no. 3 (July 1961): 316–329.

Carr, Nicholas. "'I Have Not Abandoned Any Plan': The Rage in Francis Parkman." *Massachusetts Historical Review* 17 (2015): 1–34.

Clark, Krissy and McGhee, Geoff. "Did the West Make Newspapers, or Did Newspapers Make the West?" Stanford University, Rural West Initiative. Last modified February 22, 2013. http://www.stanford.edu/group/ruralwest /cgi-bin/drupal/content/rural-newspapers-history.

Crain, Patricia. "Potent Papers: Secret Lives of the Nineteenth-Century Ballot." *CommonPlace* 9 (October 2008). Last accessed October 24, 2020. http:// commonplace.online/article/potent-papers/.

Croly, Herbert. "Memoirs of Herbert Croly." *New York History* 58, no. 3 (July 1977): 313–329.

Davis, Susan G. "'Making the Night Hideous': Christmas Revelry and Public Disorder in Nineteenth-Century Philadelphia." *American Quarterly* 34, no. 2 (June 1982): 185–199.

Diemer, Andrew. "Reconstructing Philadelphia: African Americans and Politics in the Post-Civil War North." *Pennsylvania Magazine of History and Biography* 11, no. 1 (January 2009): 29–58.

Donald, David Herbert. "An Excess of Democracy." *Lincoln Reconsidered: Essays on the Civil War Era.* 3rd ed. New York: Vintage Books, 2001.

Drago, Edmund. "Georgia's 1st Black Voter Registrars During Reconstruction." *Georgia Historical Quarterly* 78, no. 4 (Winter 1994): 760–793.

Dupre, Daniel. "Barbeques and Pledges." *The Journal of Southern History* 60 (August 1994): 470–512.

Durrill, Wayne K. "Political Legitimacy and Local Courts: 'Politicks at Such a Rage' in a Southern Community during Reconstruction." *Journal of Southern History* 70, no. 3 (2004): 577–617.

Edwards, Rebecca. "Politics, Social Movements, and the Periodization of U.S. History." *Journal of the Gilded Age and Progressive Era* 8, no. 4 (October 2009): 463–473.

Engstromm, Erik. "The Rise and Decline of Turnout in Congressional Elections." *American Journal of Political Science* 56, no. 2 (April 2012): 373–386.

Field, Corinne T. "Are Women . . . All Minors? Women's Rights and the Politics of Aging in the Antebellum United States." *Journal of Women's History* 12 (Winter 2001): 113–137.

Gienapp, William E. "Politics Seem to Enter into Everything: Political Culture in the North, 1840–1860." *Essays on American Antebellum Politics, 1840–1860.* Edited by Stephen E. Maizlish. College Station: Texas A&M University Press, 1982.

Grinspan, Jon. "'Young Men for War': The Wide Awakes and Lincoln's 1860 Presidential Campaign." *Journal of American History* 96 (September 2009): 357–378.

Hoogenboom, Ari. "The Pendleton Act and the Civil Service." *American Historical Review* Vol. 64, no. 2 (January 1959): 301–318.

Huckabee, David C. "Reelection Rates of House Incumbents: 1790–1994." *Congressional Research Service, Report for Congress,* Library of Congress, March 8, 1995.

Kernell, Samuel. "Toward Understanding 19th Century Congressional Careers: Ambition, Competition, and Rotation." *American Journal of Political Science* 21, no. 4 (November 1977): 669–693.

Kingsdale, Jon. "The 'Poor Mans Club': Social Functions of the Urban Working-Class Saloon." *American Quarterly* 25, no. 4 (October 1973): 472–489.

Lowe, Richard. "The Freedmen's Bureau and Local Black Leadership." *Journal of American History* 80, no. 3 (December 1993): 989–998.

McCormick, Richard. "The Discovery that Business Corrupts Politics: A Reappraisal of the Origins of Progressivism." *American Historical Review* 86, no. 2 (April 1981): 247–274.

Perkins, Frances. "My Recollections of Florence Kelley." *Social Service Review* 28, no. 1 (March 1954): 12–19.

Peterson, R. Eric and Jennifer E. Manning. "Violence Against Members of Congress and Their Staff: Selected Examples and Congressional Responses." *Congressional Research Service, Report for Congress*, Library of Congress, August 17, 2017.

Rathbun, Julius G. "'The Wide Awakes': The Great Political Organization of 1860." *Connecticut Quarterly* 1 (October 1895).

Robinson, Nick. "The Decline of the Lawyer." *Buffalo Law Review* 65 (August 2017): 657–737.

Russ, William A., Jr. "Registration and Disfranchisement Under Radical Reconstruction." *Mississippi Valley Historical Review* 21, no. 2 (September 1934): 163–180.

Silcox, Harry. "The Black 'Better Class' Political Dilemma: Philadelphia Prototype Isaiah C. Wears." *Pennsylvania Magazine of History and Biography* 113, no. 1 (January 1989): 45–66.

Ware, Alan. "Anti-Partyism and Party Control of Political Reform in the United States: The Case of the Australia Ballot." *British Journal of Political Science* 30, no. 1 (January 2000): 1–29.

Wiggins, Sarah Woolfolk. "The 'Pig Iron' Kelley Riot in Mobile, May 14, 1867." *Alabama Review* 22, no. 1 (January 1970): 45–56.

Winther, Oscar O. "The Soldier Vote in the Election of 1864." *New York History* 25 (October 1944).

Wood, Nic. "A Sacrifice on the Altar of Slavery: Doughface Politics and Black Disenfranchisement in Pennsylvania, 1837–1838." *Journal of the Early Republic* 31, no. 1 (Spring 2011): 75–106.

NOTES

PREFACE

1. Significantly, those turnouts grew higher after the Civil War. Eligible voter turnout for the eight elections leading up to the Civil War (1832 through 1860) was an already high 71.6 percent, but for the eight elections after the war (1868–96) it shot up 6 percent to an unprecedented 77.6 percent. And while across American history the average winner of a popular presidential election (1824–2016) won by a margin of 8.5 percent of the popular vote, from 1876 through 1888, each election was won by the loser of the popular vote or less than 1 percent of the popular vote. No victorious president, from 1876 through 1892, won a majority of the popular vote. Meanwhile, control of Congress shifted between the Republicans and Democrats six times in twenty-four years. See John P. McIver, *Historical Statistics of the United States, Millennial Edition*, ed. Susan B. Carter and Scott Sigmund Gartner (Cambridge: Cambridge University Press, 2006), Series Eb62–113; Gerhard Peters and John Woolley, "Presidential Elections Data," American Presidency Project, University of California, Santa Barbara, accessed September 1, 2020, http://www.presidency.ucsb.edu/elections.php.

Political violence is harder to track, but we know that thousands died during the wars of Reconstruction, hundreds more in interparty political conflicts nationwide (especially in cities in the lower North and in the West), and the National Guard was called out 328 times between 1886 and 1895 to suppress labor activism, often violently. Of the congressmen murdered in office across American history, a plurality died between 1859 and 1905. During this era Americans often expressed a blasé attitude toward election day shootings, stabbings, and beatings, shrugging "in some places there will be rioting." See "How It Looks to a Foreigner from the London Daily News," reprinted in *Boston Daily Advertiser* (Boston, Massachusetts), June 8, 1872; Douglas Egerton, *Wars of Reconstruction: The Brief, Violent History of America's Most Progressive Era* (New York: Bloomsbury, 2015); Mildred Amer, "Members of the U.S. Congress Who Have Died of Other Than Natural Causes While in Office," Congressional Research Service, Report for Congress, Library of Congress, March 13, 2002; R. Eric Peterson and Jennifer E. Manning, "Violence Against Members of Congress and Their Staff: Selected Examples and Congressional

Responses," Congressional Research Service, Report for Congress, Library of Congress, August 17, 2017.

None of this is to claim that the political tensions of the decades after the Civil War were somehow *worse* than those of the antebellum era or the war years. There is no parallel to the dangers of the 1850s or the devastation wrought between 1861 and 1865. But the political process during Reconstruction and the Gilded Age could be louder, closer, more tumultuous, and more violent without slanting toward the disaster of disunion and war. The challenge was, in many ways, the opposite: American democracy was a sustainable train wreck, a source of constant convulsion with no clear resolution in sight. As the dour editor E. L. Godkin put it in 1897, "No government has ever come upon the world from which there seemed so little prospect of escape." Edwin Lawrence Godkin, *Problems of Modern Democracy: Political and Economic Essays* (New York: Charles Scribner's Sons, 1897), 202.

2. John Jay Chapman, "The Capture of Government by Commercialism," *Atlantic Monthly*, February 1898, 154; William Dean Howells, "Politics," *Atlantic Monthly*, January 1872, 124; Jacob Riis, "Reform by Humane Touch," *Atlantic Monthly*, December 1899, 752.

3. McIver, *Historical Statistics*.

4. Paul Kleppner, *Who Voted? The Dynamics of Electoral Turnout, 1870–1980* (New York: Praeger, 1982), 34; Jon Grinspan, *The Virgin Vote: How Young America Made Democracy Social, Politics Personal, and Voting Popular in the Nineteenth Century* (Chapel Hill: University of North Carolina Press, 2016).

5. Henry Childs Merwin, "Tammany Points the Way," *Atlantic Monthly*, November 1894, 685.

6. Many great works in the past have tackled this question, including Michael E. McGerr, *The Decline of Popular Politics: The American North, 1865–1928* (Oxford: Oxford University Press, 1986); Mark Lawrence Kornbluh, *Why America Stopped Voting: The Decline of Participatory Democracy and the Emergence of Modern American Politics* (New York: New York University Press, 2000); Morton Keller, *America's Three Regimes* (New York: Oxford University Press, 2007); Robert H. Wiebe, *Self-Rule: A Cultural History of American Democracy* (Chicago: University of Chicago Press, 1995); Robert H. Wiebe, *The Search for Order, 1877–1920* (New York: Hill and Wang, 1967).

7. Kleppner, *Who Voted?*, 68–69; Kornbluh, *Why America Stopped Voting*, 108–10.

8. For the purposes of this book, *politics* is defined as most nineteenth-century Americans used it, in terms of topics related to elections, campaigns, and the

chief political parties. The story of this book is largely a history of the widening of the term *politics* to encompass social issues outside those chosen by parties and politicians.

9. This point was originally made in Rebecca Edwards's extremely wise *New Spirits: Americans in the Gilded Age* (New York: Oxford University Press, 2006), 5. Edwards further rethought the legacy of the Gilded Age in creative ways in "Politics, Social Movements, and the Periodization of U.S. History," *Journal of the Gilded Age and Progressive Era* 8, no. 4 (2009): 463–473.

10. Josephine Goldmark, *Impatient Crusader: Florence Kelley's Life Story* (Champaign: University of Illinois Press, 1953), 73.

11. E. P. H., "Doings of Women Folk," *Galveston Daily News*, June 11, 1889; Frances Perkins, "My Recollections of Florence Kelley," *Social Service Review* 28, no. 1 (1954): 19.

CHAPTER ONE: "THE ONE QUESTION OF THE AGE IS *SETTLED*"

1. William Kelley to Caroline Kelley, January 22, 1865, William Darrah Kelley Papers, Historical Society of Pennsylvania, Philadelphia (hereafter cited as WDK Papers); William Kelley to Caroline Kelley, January 26, 1865, WDK Papers; William Kelley to Caroline Kelley, February 4, 1865, WDK Papers; Caroline Kelley to Florence Kelley, February 23, 1864, Florence Kelley Papers, New York Public Library (hereafter cited as FK Papers).

2. *The Autobiography of Florence Kelley: Notes of Sixty Years*, ed. Kathryn Kish Sklar (Chicago: Illinois Labor History Society, Charles H. Kerr, 1986), 20–26; "Personal and General Notes," *New York Tribune*, July 19, 1875; "Judge Kelley," *Daily Picayune*, March 17, 1890.

3. Caroline Kelley to Florence Kelley, February 23, 1864, FK Papers.

4. Florence Kelley to William Kelley, n.d., FK Papers; Florence Kelley to unknown, November 28, 1881, FK Papers.

5. William Kelley to Caroline Kelley, January 31, 1865, FK Papers; William Kelley to Caroline Kelley, January 22, 1865, WDK Papers.

6. Frank Carpenter, "A Tariff-Day in the House," *Milwaukee Sentinel*, May 18, 1884; "A Pig Iron Orator," *Georgia Weekly Telegraph and Georgia Journal & Messenger*, March 10, 1874; Michael Robert Greco, "William Darrah Kelley: The Ante-bellum Years" (PhD diss., University of Michigan, 1975), 197.

7. William Kelley to Caroline Kelley, January 31, 1865, FK Papers.

8. William Kelley to Caroline Kelley, January 31, 1865, FK Papers; Michael Vorenberg, *Final Freedom: The Civil War, the Abolition of Slavery, and the Thirteenth Amendment* (Cambridge: Cambridge University Press, 2001), 205–7.

9. William Kelley to Caroline Kelley, January 31, 1865, FK Papers.

10. J. Matt Gallman, *America's Joan of Arc: The Life of Anna Elizabeth Dickinson* (New York: Oxford University Press, 2006), 30–41; William Kelley, "Speech of Hon. William D. Kelley of Pennsylvania in Support of His Proposed Amendment to the Bill 'To Guarantee to Certain States, Whose Governements Have been Usurped or Overthrown, A Republican Form of Government,'" Delivered in the House of Representatives, January 16, 1865, in *The Equality of All Men before the Law, Claimed and Defended in Speeches by Hon. William D. Kelley, Wendell Phillips, and Frederick Douglass* (Boston: Press of Geo. C. Rand & Avery, 1865), 6.

11. Ira V. Brown, "William D. Kelley and Radical Reconstruction," *Pennsylvania Magazine of History and Biography* 85, no. 3 (1961): 319; Greco, "William Darrah Kelley."

12. "Obituary Day in Congress," *Milwaukee Daily Journal*, January 26, 1885; Charles O'Neill, *Memorial Addresses on the Life and Character of William D. Kelley, Delivered in the House of Representatives and the Senate, Fifty-First Congress, First Session* (Washington, D.C.: Government Printing Office, 1890), 17.

13. "Philadelphia, Prominent Keystone State Politicians," *Chicago Tribune*, October 21, 1868.

14. Will's plan did not call for immediate suffrage for all African Americans. Instead he proposed "an entering wedge," which would enable Black men who had fought in the Union Army or who could read the Constitution. From there, he hoped it would soon expand to "the whole mass" of the population. Though certainly far short of full representation, in 1865 it was likely the most radical step toward Black suffrage put forward in Congress. Kelley, "Speech of Hon. William D. Kelley," 5–28.

15. Greco, "William Darrah Kelley," 84–85; Kelley, "Speech of Hon. William D. Kelley," 6, 24; Brown, "William D. Kelley and Radical Reconstruction," 319, 321.

16. Brown, "William D. Kelley and Radical Reconstruction," 321; James W. Ashton to William Kelley, January 23, 1865, FK Papers.

17. Field's attack on Will came in the context of his own fight to get into Congress. Field had been elected to Congress in the reconstructed state of Louisiana;

however, the state was brought back into the Union under the lax standards of President Lincoln's 10 percent plan. Congress, controlled by Radical Republicans, blocked Louisiana's readmission, including Alexander Pope Field's admission to Congress. Will—as he pointed out midconfrontation—was not on the committee responsible for keeping Field out. But Will was a prominent, noticeable, very audible radical who had just staked his name on Black suffrage, making himself a prominent face of all Radical Republicans, which is probably why Field chose to attack him. During the fight, Will refused to strike Field, considering his sixty-five-year-old assailant "too old a man for me to strike." William Kelley to Caroline Kelley, January 22, 1865, FK Papers; "Assault of Hon. W. D. Kelley," February 21, 1865, *Congressional Globe containing Debates and Proceedings of the Second Session of the Thirty Eighth Congress, Special Session of Senates* (Washington, D.C.: F & J Rives, Congressional Globe Printing Office, 1865), 971–74; "Attack on Judge Kelley," *North American*, January 23, 1865; *Evening Star*, January 21, 1865; J. R. McCurdy to William Kelley, January 25, 1865, WDK Papers; Frank E. Stevens, "Alexander Pope Field," *Journal of the Illinois State Historical Society* 4 (April 1911): 7–38.

18. William Kelley to Caroline Kelley, January 22, 1865, FK Papers; William Kelley to Caroline Kelley, January 26, 1865, FK Papers.

19. O'Neill, *Memorial Addresses on the Life and Character of William D. Kelley*, 3; Eric Foner, *The Second Founding: How the Civil War and Reconstruction Remade the Constitution* (New York: W. W. Norton, 2019), 99.

20. William Kelley to Caroline Kelley, January 31, 1865, FK Papers.

21. Michael Vorenberg, *Final Freedom: The Civil War, the Abolition of Slavery, and the Thirteenth Amendment* (Cambridge: Cambridge University Press, 2001), 207.

22. William Kelley to Caroline Kelley, January 31, 1865, FK Papers.

23. Vorenberg, *Final Freedom*, 210; *Memoirs of Cornelius Cole* (New York: McLoughlin Brothers, 1908), 220.

24. "An Address by Hon Wm D Kelley—an Interesting Occasion," *North American*, March 23, 1865.

25. *Life and Letters of Roscoe Conkling: Orator, Stateman, Advocate*, ed. Alfred R. Conkling (New York: Charles L. Webster, 1889), 254, 270.

26. David Quigley, *Second Founding: New York City, Reconstruction, and the Making of American Democracy* (New York: Hill & Wang, 2004), 44.

27. Michael F. Holt, *The Political Crisis of the 1850s* (New York: W. W. Norton, 1978); Nic Wood, "A Sacrifice on the Altar of Slavery: Doughface Politics and

Black Disenfranchisement in Pennsylvania, 1837–1838," *Journal of the Early Republic* 31, no. 1 (2011): 75–106; William Freehling, *The Road to Disunion: Secessionists at Bay, 1776–1854* (New York: Oxford University Press, 1990), 287–337; Rachel Shelden, *Washington Brotherhood: Politics, Social Life, and the Coming of the Civil War* (Chapel Hill: University of North Carolina Press, 2013); Martin Van Buren to Thomas Ritchie, January 13, 1827, The Papers of Martin Van Buren, Series 5, Library of Congress.

28. McIver, *Historical Statistics*.

29. Gary Gallagher, *The Union War* (Cambridge, MA: Harvard University Press, 2012); Joanna Freeman, *The Field of Blood: Violence in Congress and the Road to Civil War* (New York: Farrar, Straus & Giroux, 2018); James McPherson, *What They Fought For, 1861–1865* (New York: Holt McDougal, 1995).

30. "Is Democracy a Failure?," *New York Times*, March 14, 1861.

31. Henry Wilson, "New Departure and the Republican Party," *Atlantic Monthly*, January 1871, 104; Jonathan Baxter Harrison, "Certain Dangerous Tendencies in American Life," *Atlantic Monthly*, October 1878, 389–403; "An Address by Hon Wm D Kelley"; Carl Schurz, "The True Problem," *Atlantic Monthly*, March 1867, 371–72.

32. To understand Johnson's political philosophy, and White supremacy writ large, it's important to remind oneself that "the people" meant "the White people." See Lilian Foster, *Andrew Johnson: President of the United States* (London: Richardson, 1866), 104.

33. Henry Demarest Lloyd, *Wealth Against Commonwealth* (New York: Harper Brothers, 1894), 508.

34. Richard Selcer, *Civil War America, 1850 to 1875 (Almanacs of American Life)* (New York: Facts on File, 2006), 114, 106, 217.

35. Henry Adams, *The Education of Henry Adams* (Boston: Houghton Mifflin Co., 1918), 239.

36. "The Next President," *Atlantic Monthly*, May 1868, 639; Martin Ridge, *Ignatius Donnelly: Portrait of a Politician* (St. Paul: Minnesota Historical Society Press, 1991), 129; Joseph Hubert Debar, *The West Virginia Hand-Book and Immigrant's Guide: A Sketch of the State of West Virginia* (Parkersburg, WV: Gibbens Brothers, 1870).

37. Adam I. P. Smith, *No Party Now: Politics in the Civil War North* (New York: Oxford University Press, 2006); Jonathan W. White, *Emancipation, the Union Army, and the Reelection of Abraham Lincoln* (Baton Rouge: Louisiana State University Press, 2014); Ignatius Donnelly, January 1, 1865, in *The Diary of*

Ignatius Donnelly, ed. Theodore Ludwig Nydahl (Minneapolis: University of Minnesota Press, 1941).

38. Kelley, "Speech of Hon. William D. Kelley," 3; William Kelley, "Speech of Hon Wm D Kelley of PA on Freedmens Affairs: Delivered in the House of Representatives," February 23, 1864, 2; Kelley, "Speech of Hon. William D. Kelley," 25.

39. Kelley, "Speech of Hon. William D. Kelley," 25.

40. *Education of Henry Adams*, 249.

41. Kelley, "Speech of Hon. William D. Kelley," 3.

CHAPTER TWO: "THE GREAT AMERICAN GAME"

1. Ignatius Donnelly, October 20, 1865; Donnelly, November 1866; Donnelly, October 15, 1872, in *Diary of Ignatius Donnelly*.

2. Ignatius Donnelly, October 28, 1865, in *Diary of Ignatius Donnelly*, 296, 295, 235, 503.

3. Donnelly, October 28, 1865, 330.

4. Donnelly, October 28, 1865, 307.

5. Excerpt from *Owatonna Journal*, in *Diary of Ignatius Donnelly*, 99; *Autobiography of William Allen White* (New York: Macmillan, 1946), 104; Andreas Ueland, *Recollections of an Immigrant* (New York: Minton, Balch, 1929), 262.

6. Ignatius Donnelly, September 16, 1866, in *Diary of Ignatius Donnelly*, 258, 330.

7. Ignatius Donnelly, *Diary of Ignatius Donnelly*, 330; Donnelly, *Diary of Ignatius Donnelly*, 242.

8. Ignatius Donnelly, *Diary of Ignatius Donnelly*, 204.

9. "Mr. Lowell's Politics," *Atlantic Monthly*, August 1888, 274.

10. William H. McElroy, "An Old War Horse to a Young Politician," *Atlantic Monthly*, June 1880, 762.

11. McElroy, "Old War Horse to a Young Politician," 762.

12. "How It Looks to a Foreigner," *London Daily News*, reprinted in *Boston Daily Advertiser*, June 8, 1872; Kenneth D. Rose, *Unspeakable Awfulness: America through the Eyes of European Travelers, 1865–1900* (New York: Routledge, 2013), 210–14.

13. "How It Looks to a Foreigner"; August Segerberg, September 28, 1884, in *Letters from the Promised Land: Swedes in America, 1840–1915*, ed. H. Arnold Barton (Minneapolis: University of Minnesota Press, 1975), 194; "Tableau of

'the Thirteen Original States,'" *Frank Leslie's Illustrated Newspaper*, November 18, 1876.

14. "How It Looks to a Foreigner."

15. Joel Silbey, *The American Political Nation, 1838–1893* (Stanford, CA: Stanford University Press, 1994), 126; Jacob Frey, *Reminiscences of Baltimore* (Baltimore: Maryland Book Concern, 1893), 53; Robert Gray Gunderson, *The Log Cabin Campaign* (Lexington: University Press of Kentucky, 1957); Jon Grinspan, "'Young Men for War': The Wide Awakes and Lincoln's 1860 Presidential Campaign," *Journal of American History* 96 (September 2009): 357–78; Ignatius Donnelly, September 16, 1866, in *Diary of Ignatius Donnelly*, 258.

16. *Life and Letters of Roscoe Conkling*, 682; "The Ohio Canvas," *Georgia Weekly Telegraph and Georgia Journal & Messenger*, August 2, 1875.

17. Ignatius Donnelly, in *Diary of Ignatius Donnelly*, 571.

18. "Letter from Pleasant Riderhood," *Daily Picayune*, August 25, 1878.

19. Segerberg, September 28, 1884, 194; Anonymous Norwegian Immigrant, "Letter from Anonymous Norwegian Immigrant in Chicago, 1883," in *Their Own Saga: Letters from the Norwegian Global Migration*, ed. Frederick Hale (Minneapolis: University of Minnesota Press, 1986), 183.

20. Frances Ellen Watkins Harper, May 13, 1867, in *The Underground Rail Road: A Record of Facts, Authentic Narratives, Letters, &c: Narrating the Hardships, Hair-breadth Escapes, and Death Struggles of the Slaves in Their Efforts for Freedom* (Philadelphia: Porter & Coates, 1872), 767–68.

21. John McKivigan, *Forgotten Firebrand: James Redpath and the Making of Nineteenth-Century America* (Ithaca, NY: Cornell University Press, 2008), 123, 122; Jeremy C. Young, *The Age of Charisma: Leaders, Followers, and Emotions in American Society, 1870–1940* (Cambridge: Cambridge University Press, 2016).

22. Merwin, "Tammany Points the Way," 685.

23. Will Kelley normally spoke with proper grammar, in elaborate, clause-heavy sentences. The idea that he attributed his career to "me magnificent voice," probably comes from the bigoted and mistaken depiction of Kelley as an uneducated Irish Catholic who spoke in the stereotypical dialect often attributed to that population. Kelley was in fact descended from Scottish and English Presbyterians and Quakers, and the use of this accent to diminish his intellect says more about the anti-Irish biases of the newspaper than it does about Kelley, or Irish Americans. See "Clippings," *Macon Telegraph and Messager*, May 19, 1882.

24. J. Donald Cameron, *Memorial Addresses on the Life and Character of William D. Kelley*, 71; Greco, "William Darrah Kelley," 56.

25. William Kelley, "Remarks of Hon. William D. Kelley of Pennsylvania in Support of the Bill Equalizing Pay, Rations, Clothing, and Arming of Our Soldiers," delivered in the House of Representatives, April 30, 1864, in *Speeches Concerning Politics and Government During the Civil War Period*, 3:6; Julie Winch, *A Gentleman of Color: The Life of James Forten* (New York: Oxford University Press, 2002), 115.

26. Greco, "William Darrah Kelley," 35–36; Kathryn Kish Sklar, *Florence Kelley and the Nation's Work: The Rise of Women's Political Culture* (New Haven, CT: Yale University Press, 1995), 6.

27. Greco, "William Darrah Kelley," 35–36; "The Tariff," *St. Louis Globe-Democrat*, October 26, 1880.

28. Sean Wilentz, *Chants Democratic: New York City and the Rise of the American Working Class* (New York: Oxford University Press, 1984); Jonathan H. Earle, *Jacksonian Antislavery and the Politics of Free-Soil, 1824–1854* (Chapel Hill: University of North Carolina Press, 2004); Edward Widmer, *Young Americans: The Flowering of Democracy in New York City* (New York: Oxford University Press, 1998).

29. Cameron, *Memorial Addresses on the Life and Character of William D. Kelley*, 71; Greco, "William Darrah Kelley," 56.

30. Cameron, *Memorial Addresses on the Life and Character of William D. Kelley*, 72; "Political Portraits with Pen and Pencil," *United States Magazine and Democratic Review* 26 (June 1851): 553; Greco, "William Darrah Kelley," 61.

31. "S. W.," *New York Tribune*, July 8, 1864; Sklar, *Florence Kelley and the Nation's Work*, 35.

32. "Judge Kelley," *St. Paul Daily News*, January 7, 1890.

33. Sklar, *Florence Kelley and the Nation's Work*, 13.

34. "What Mr. Kelley Wants to See in Ohio," *New York Tribune*, July 19, 1875; "Personal and General Notes," *Daily Picayune*, March 17, 1890; William Kelley to Albert Kelley, December 13, 1881, WDK Papers.

35. "The Curse of the Bonsall Family of Pennsylvania?," *Hidden Histories* (blog), Historical Society of Pennsylvania, March 2, 2010; Sklar, *Florence Kelley and the Nation's Work*, 27.

36. William Kelley to Caroline Kelley, February 4, 1865, WDK Papers; Florence Kelley to William Kelley, December 2, 1865, FK Papers.

37. Greco, "William Darrah Kelley," 223.

38. Daniel R. Biddle and Murray Dubin, *Tasting Freedom: Octavius Catto and the Battle for Equality in Civil War America* (Philadelphia: Temple University Press, 2010), 236; Greco, "William Darrah Kelley," 227, 219.

39. Brown, "William D. Kelley and Radical Reconstruction," 318.

40. Brown, "William D. Kelley and Radical Reconstruction," 318; William Kelley to Abraham Lincoln, Philadelphia, November 29, 1860, Abraham Lincoln Papers, Library of Congress.

41. *Autobiography of Florence Kelley*, 23–24.

42. *Autobiography of Florence Kelley*, 23–24.

43. "Pig Iron Orator"; George William Curtis to William Darrah Kelley, September 10, 1869, WDK Papers.

44. Richard M. Valelly, *The Two Reconstructions: The Struggle for Black Enfranchisement* (Chicago: University of Chicago Press, 2004), 24, 40; Edmund Drago, "Georgia's First Black Voter Registrars during Reconstruction," *Georgia Historical Quarterly* 78, no. 4 (1994): 760–93.

45. William Darrah Kelley, "The Kelley Riot," *Chicago Inter-Ocean*, May 14, 1888; "Washington," *Milwaukee Sentinel*, March 18, 1888; Brown, "William D. Kelley and Radical Reconstruction," 325; Sarah Woolfolk Wiggins, "The 'Pig Iron' Kelley Riot in Mobile, May 14, 1867," *Alabama Review* 22, no. 1 (1970): 45–56.

46. Kelley, "Kelley Riot"; Wiggins, "'Pig Iron' Kelley Riot."

47. Kelley, "Kelley Riot"; Brown, "William D. Kelley and Radical Reconstruction," 325; Wiggins, "'Pig Iron' Kelley Riot."

48. Kelley, "Kelley Riot"; Brown, "William D. Kelley and Radical Reconstruction," 319, 325; Wiggins, "'Pig Iron' Kelley Riot."

49. Kelley, "Kelley Riot"; Brown, "William D. Kelley and Radical Reconstruction," 325; Wiggins, "'Pig Iron' Kelley Riot."

50. Kelley, "Kelley Riot."

51. Kelley, "Kelley Riot."

52. "The Mobile Riot," *New York Times*, May 16, 1867.

CHAPTER THREE: "THE GAME GOING ON
AT WASHINGTON"

1. *The Life and Letters of John Hay*, ed. William Roscoe Thayer (Boston: Houghton Mifflin, 1908), 1:147; Kathryn Allamong Jacobs, *King of the Lobby: The Life and Times of Sam Ward, Man about Town in Gilded-Age Washington* (Baltimore:

Johns Hopkins University Press, 2010), 67–68; Rachel Shelden, *Washington Brotherhood* (Chapel Hill: University of North Carolina Press, 2013).

2. Joanna Freeman, *The Field of Blood: Violence in Congress and the Road to Civil War* (New York: Farrar, Straus & Giroux, 2018), 181.

3. Jacobs, *King of the Lobby*, 70.

4. Frank Carpenter, *Carp's Washington* (New York: McGraw-Hill, 1960), 5, 6.

5. *Education of Henry Adams*, 243.

6. *Education of Henry Adams*, 256; Carpenter, *Carp's Washington*, 3.

7. Ridge, *Ignatius Donnelly*, 129–31.

8. Ridge, *Ignatius Donnelly*, 111, 133.

9. Mark W. Summers, *A Dangerous Stir* (Chapel Hill: University of North Carolina Press, 2012), 91; William Tecumseh Sherman to John Sherman, February 25, 1868, in *The Sherman Letters: Correspondence Between General and Senator Sherman from 1837 to 1891*, ed. Rachel Sherman Thorndike (New York: Charles Scribner's Sons, 1894), 398.

10. Carpenter, *Carp's Washington*, 87, 6, 114; Jacobs, *King of the Lobby*.

11. Elizabeth Moore Chapin, *American Court Gossip, or, Life at the National Capital* (Washington, D.C.: Chapin & Hartwell Bros., 1887), 32.

12. Harriet Bailey Blaine to Walker Blaine, March 18, 1872, in *Letters of Mrs. James G. Blaine*, ed. Harriet S. Blaine Beale (New York: Duffield, 1908), 1:105.

13. Harriet Bailey Blaine to Alice B. Coppinger, January 8, 1872, in *Letters of Mrs. James G. Blaine*, 1:78.

14. Harriet Bailey Blaine to Alice B. Coppinger, January 8, 1872, in *Letters of Mrs. James G. Blaine*, 1:78.

15. Carpenter, *Carp's Washington*, 25; Don Piatt, *Georgia Weekly Telegraph and Georgia Journal & Messenger*, May 24, 1870; "Philadelphia, Prominent Keystone State Politicians," *Chicago Tribune*, October 21, 1868.

16. William D. Kelley to Florence Kelley, June 15, 1878, FK Papers.

17. Carpenter, *Carp's Washington*, 111.

18. Henry Adams, *The Education of Henry Adams*, ed. Henry Cabot Lodge (Boston: Massachusetts History Society, 1918), 239.

19. Freeman, *Field of Blood*; Carpenter, *Carp's Washington*, 14; Mapheus Smith and Marian L. Brockway, "Some Political Characteristics of American Congressmen, 1800–1919," *Southwestern Social Science Quarterly* 22, no. 3 (1941): 209–22; Nick Robinson, "The Decline of the Lawyer," *Buffalo Law Review* 65 (August 2017): 4.

20. David C. Huckabee, "Reelection Rates of House Incumbents: 1790–1994," Congressional Research Service, March 8, 1995; Samuel Kernell, "Toward Understanding Nineteenth Century Congressional Careers: Ambition, Competition, and Rotation," *American Journal of Political Science* 21, no. 4 (1977): 660–93.

21. Henry Wilson, "New Departure and the Republican Party," *Atlantic Monthly*, January 1871, 107; Morton Keller, *America's Three Regimes* (New York: Oxford University Press, 2007), 148.

22. Ridge, *Ignatius Donnelly*, 130.

23. Brown, "William D. Kelley and Radical Reconstruction," 319; David M. Jordan, *Roscoe Conkling of New York: Voice in the Senate* (Ithaca, NY: Cornell University Press, 1971), 1.

24. Donald Barr Chidsey, *The Gentleman from New York: A Life of Roscoe Conkling* (New Haven, CT: Yale University Press, 1935), 309.

25. Chidsey, *Gentleman from New York*, 1; Ben Perley Poore, *Reminiscences of Sixty Years at the National Metropolis* (Philadelphia: Hubbard Brothers, 1886), 2:206; Sara Lee Burlingame, "The Making of a Spoilsman: The Life and Career of Roscoe Conkling from 1829–1873" (PhD diss., Johns Hopkins University, 1974), 121; *Life and Letters of Roscoe Conkling*, 32.

26. Chidsey, *Gentleman from New York*, 5; Horace Greeley, *New York Tribune*, May 19, 1871; Chidsey, *Gentleman from New York*, 272, 119.

27. Chidsey, *Gentleman from New York*, 259, 20.

28. *Life and Letters of Roscoe Conkling*, 30, 254; Frederick Douglass, "Address by Hon. Frederick Douglass," delivered in the Congregational Church, Washington, D.C., April 16, 1883, Library of Congress.

29. Chidsey, *Gentleman from New York*, 11; *Life and Letters of Roscoe Conkling*, 16; Chidsey, *Gentleman from New York*, 18; *Life and Letters of Roscoe Conkling*, 95.

30. Chidsey, *Gentleman from New York*, 81.

31. Chidsey, *Gentleman from New York*, 80–91.

32. Chidsey, *Gentleman from New York*, 259; "Presidential Electioneering in the Senate," *Atlantic Monthly*, March 1879, 373.

33. Chauncey Mitchell DePew, *My Memories of Eighty Years* (New York: C. Scribner's Sons, 1922), 75–77.

34. Edmund Keyser, Diary, October 13, 1868, Historical Society of Pennsylvania, Philadelphia; Richard White, *The Republic for Which It Stands: The United States During Reconstruction and the Gilded Age, 1865–1896* (New York: Oxford University Press, 2017), 98; Uriah Oblinger to Mattie Thomas, October 25,

1866, Uriah W. Oblinger Family Collection, Nebraska State Historical Society, Lincoln.

35. DePew, *My Memories of Eighty Years*, 79.

CHAPTER FOUR: "I BOAST OF PHILADELPHIA AT ALL TIMES"

1. Carrie Kelley to William Kelley, February 20, 1867, WDK Papers.

2. Florence Kelley to William Kelley, October 10, 1869, WDK Papers; *Autobiography of Florence Kelley*, 30.

3. Carrie Kelley to Will Kelley, July 1, 1868, WDK Papers.

4. Elizabeth Pugh to William Kelley, on back of Florence Kelley to William Kelley, January 12, 1869, WDK Papers.

5. *Autobiography of Florence Kelley*, 24, 26, 27.

6. Josephine Goldmark, *Impatient Crusader: Florence Kelley's Life Story* (Champaign: University of Illinois Press, 1953), 6; William Kelley to Florence Kelley, July 2, 1869, WDK Papers.

7. William Kelley to Florence Kelley, July 2, 1869, FK Papers.

8. *Autobiography of Florence Kelley*, 25, 34.

9. *Autobiography of Florence Kelley*, 25–26.

10. *Autobiography of Florence Kelley*, 35.

11. *Autobiography of Florence Kelley*, 34; Greco, "William Darrah Kelley," 61.

12. George A. Smith to William Kelley, April 6, 1866, WDK Papers.

13. William Kelley to Florence Kelley, June 22, 1871; February 5, 1875; June 1, 1875; June 22, 1876, WDK Papers; William Kelley to Florence Kelley, June 20, 1876, FK Papers.

14. Florence Kelley to Josephine Goldmark, in Goldmark, *Impatient Crusaders*, 56.

15. Gallman, *America's Joan of Arc*, 30–39; Sklar, *Florence Kelley and the Nation's Work*, 46.

16. Sklar, *Florence Kelley and the Nation's Work*, 29.

17. *Autobiography of Florence Kelley*, 42.

18. Florence Kelley to Josephine Goldmark, in Goldmark, *Impatient Crusaders*, 56.

19. J. W. Forney to William Kelley, April 27, 1867, WDK Papers; Kelley, "Remarks of Hon. William D. Kelley of Pennsylvania in Support of the Bill Equalizing Pay, Rations, Clothing, and Arming of Our Soldiers," 3:6; Winch, *Gentleman of Color*, 115; Biddle and Murray, *Tasting Freedom*, 149, 236, 307.

20. Roger Lane, *The Roots of Violence in Black Philadelphia* (Cambridge, MA: Harvard University Press, 1989), 59; "Philadelphia," *Chicago Tribune*, October 21, 1868; Ignatius Donnelly, December 2, 1879, *Diary of Ignatius Donnelly*, 774.

21. Donnelly, in *Diary of Ignatius Donnelly*, 886.

22. W. E. B. Du Bois, *The Philadelphia Negro: A Social Study* (Philadelphia: University of Pennsylvania Press, 1899); Biddle and Murray, *Tasting Freedom*; Harry Silcox, "The Black 'Better Class' Political Dilemma: Philadelphia Prototype Isaiah C. Wears,"*Pennsylvania Magazine of History and Biography* 113, no. 1 (1989): 45–66; Andrew Diemer, "Reconstructing Philadelphia: African Americans and Politics in the Post Civil War North," *Pennsylvania Magazine of History and Biography* 133, no. 1 (2009): 29–58.

23. Biddle and Murray, *Tasting Freedom*; Silcox, "Black 'Better Class' Political Dilemma," 45–66; Diemer, "Reconstructing Philadelphia"; Nicholas Wood, "'A Sacrifice on the Altar of Slavery': Doughface Politics and Black Disenfranchisement in Pennsylvania, 1837–1838," *Journal of the Early Republic* 31, no. 1 (2011): 75–106.

24. William Kelley, "The Safeguards of Personal Liberty: An Address by Hon. Wm. D. Kelley" (Philadelphia, 1865), 2–3. This pamphlet was published by the Social, Civil and Statistical Association of Colored People of Pennsylvania.

25. Silcox, "Black 'Better Class' Political Dilemma," 45–66; Biddle and Murray, *Tasting Freedom*; Diemer, "Reconstructing Philadelphia."

26. Diemer, "Reconstructing Philadelphia," 38, 50; Kelley, "Safeguards of Personal Liberty," 2–3.

27. Diemer, "Reconstructing Philadelphia," 38; Silcox, "Black 'Better Class' Political Dilemma," 49.

28. Quigley, *Second Founding*, 72–84; Silcox, "Black 'Better Class' Political Dilemma," 49; William D. Kelley, Cong. Globe, 40th Cong., 2d Sess. (Feb. 11, 1868), 1347.

29. Diemer, "Reconstructing Philadelphia," 50; Foner, *Second Founding*, 99; Biddle and Murray, *Tasting Freedom*, 398; *Life and Letters of Roscoe Conkling*, 386.

30. "The Demonstration of Colored Citizens," *Frank Leslie's Illustrated Newspaper*, April 30, 1870; "Celebration at Helena," *Morning Republican*, May 3, 1870.

31. Isaiah C. Wears, quoted in *The Press*, October 9, 1870; Silcox, "Black 'Better Class' Political Dilemma," 49; Biddle and Murray, *Tasting Freedom*, 410; "The Constitution Amendment!," 1866 political cartoon, Library of Congress, Photographs and Prints.

32. Biddle and Murray, *Tasting Freedom*, 410.
33. Silcox, "Black 'Better Class' Political Dilemma," 46, 74; Grinspan, *Virgin Vote*, 66.
34. Frederick Douglass to William Kelley, May 2, 1871, WDK Papers.
35. Silcox, "Black 'Better Class' Political Dilemma," 49–50.
36. Harry C. Silcox, *Philadelphia Politics from the Bottom Up: The Life of Irishman William McMullen, 1824–1901* (Philadelphia: Balch Institute Press, 1989), 25–30, 43.
37. Silcox, *Philadelphia Politics from the Bottom Up*, 70.
38. Silcox, *Philadelphia Politics from the Bottom Up*, 82, 42, 30–50.
39. Silcox, *Philadelphia Politics from the Bottom Up*, 70.
40. Rudyard Kipling, *American Notes* (New York: Frank F. Lovell, 1889), 48; Thomas Mador Gilmore, "The Saloon as a Club," *North American Review* 157, no. 443 (1893): 511–12; Jon Kingsdale, "The 'Poor Mans Club': Social Functions of the Urban Working-Class Saloon," *American Quarterly* 25, no. 4 (1973): 472–89.
41. Silcox, *Philadelphia Politics from the Bottom Up*, 60.
42. Silcox, *Philadelphia Politics from the Bottom Up*, 68.
43. William McMullen, *Letters from an Irish Ward Leader: William McMullen to Samuel J. Randall, 1864–1890*, ed. Harry C. Silcox, Historical Society of Pennsylvania; Silcox, *Philadelphia Politics from the Bottom Up*, 75.
44. Silcox, *Philadelphia Politics from the Bottom Up*, 77–96; Biddle and Murray, *Tasting Freedom*, 421–40.
45. Biddle and Murray, *Tasting Freedom*, 429.
46. Silcox, "Black 'Better Class' Political Dilemma," 53; Lane, *Roots of Violence in Black Philadelphia*, 57–60; Silcox, *Philadelphia Politics from the Bottom Up*, III, 145.
47. Amy Greenberg, *Cause for Alarm: The Volunteer Fire Department in the Nineteenth-Century City* (Princeton, NJ: Princeton University Press, 1998), 110–14.
48. "William D. Kelley, writing to the Philadelphia Press of the mineral wealth of the Rocky Mountain region," *Little Rock Morning Republican*, October 25, 1871.
49. Fanny M. Jackson Coppin to William Kelley, February 13, 1872, FK Papers.
50. Frederick Douglass to William Kelley, May 2, 1871, WDK Papers.

CHAPTER FIVE: "SWALLOW IT DOWN"

1. Edwards, *New Spirits*, 1–2.

2. Thomas Nast, "The Brains," *Harper's Weekly*, October 21, 1871.

3. Merle Curti, *The Making of an American Community: A Case Study in Democracy in a Frontier County* (Stanford, CA: Stanford University Press, 1959), 68; White, *Republic for Which It Stands*, 525, 474–76.

4. Mark Twain and Charles Dudley Warner, *The Gilded Age: A Tale of Today* (New York: American Publishing, 1873).

5. Nicolas Barreyre, "The Politics of Economic Crises: The Panic of 1873, the End of Reconstruction, and the Realignment of American Politics," *Journal of the Gilded Age and the Progressive Era* 10, no. 4 (2011): 403–23; White, *Republic for Which It Stands*, 269.

6. Roger Finke and Rodney Stark, "Turning Pews into People: Estimating Nineteenth Century Church Membership," *Journal for the Scientific Study of Religion* 25, no. 2 (1986): 180–92.

7. W. T. Stead, "Mr. Richard Croker and Greater New York," *Review of Reviews*, October 1897, 345.

8. Walter Weyl, *The New Democracy* (New York: Macmillan, 1914), 60.

9. Lydia Maria Francis Child to Sarah Blake Sturgis Shaw, 1869, in *Letters of Lydia Maria Child with a Biographical Introduction by John G. Whittier and Appendix by Wendell Phillips* (Boston: Houghton, Mifflin, 1883), 199–200; Jane Addams, *Democracy and Social Ethics* (New York: Macmillan, 1902), 267.

10. Matthew Josephson, *The Politicos* (New York: Harcourt, Brace, 1938), 341; *Life and Letters of Roscoe Conkling*, 394; Mark Wahlgren Summers, *The Ordeal of Reunion: A New History of Reconstruction* (Chapel Hill: University of North Carolina Press, 2014), 245–55.

11. *The Life Story and Personal Reminiscences of Col. John Sobieski* (Shelbyville, IL: J. L. Douthit & Son, 1900), 384.

12. Frances Elizabeth Willard, October 29, 1866, in *Glimpses of Fifty Years: The Autobiography of an American Woman* (Chicago: Woman's Temperance Publication Association, 1889), 192–93; Jacob Riis, *Making of an American* (New York: Macmillan, 1901), 108.

13. Warrington Dawson, "General Butler's Campaign in Massachusetts," *Atlantic Monthly*, December 1871, 745; Jonathan Baxter Harrison, "Limited Sovereignty in the United States," *Atlantic Monthly*, February 1879, 184.

14. John Jay Chapman, *Practical Agitation* (New York: Charles Scribner's Sons, 1900), 2; Mark Wahlgren Summers, *The Press Gang: Newspapers and Politics, 1865–1878* (Chapel Hill: University of North Carolina Press, 1994), 68.

15. "Young Men in Council," *Boston Daily Advertiser*, August 27, 1878.

16. Michael G. Mulhall, ed., *The Dictionary of Statistics*, 4th ed. (Farmington Hills, MI: Gale Research, 1969), 50; James Witham, *Fifty Years on the Firing Line: My Part in the Farmers' Movement* (Chicago: self-published, 1924), 61.

17. Letter to editor, *New York Tribune*, December 1, 1876; James S. Clarkson, "The Politician and the Pharisee," *North American Review* 152, no. 41 (1891): 616; "Independent: His Purpose in Politics," *Boston Daily Globe*, April 14, 1888.

18. Thomas Nast, "The Third-Term Panic," *Harper's Weekly*, November 7, 1874.

19. "Young Men in Politics," *Daily Rocky Mountain News*, May 8, 1874; "A Time for Independence," *New York Tribune*, November 12, 1875.

20. *Life and Letters of Roscoe Conkling*, 388.

21. Paul Kleppner, *The Third Electoral System, 1853–1892: Parties, Voters, and Political Cultures* (Chapel Hill: University of North Carolina Press, 2010), 33, 41.

22. *Reminiscences of an Active Life: Autobiography of John Roy Lynch*, ed. John Hope Franklin (Jackson: University Press of Mississippi, 2010).

23. Quigley, *Second Founding*, 94–100.

24. John I. Young, interview by Henry Muir, Montgomery County, Ohio, Works Progress Administration, Ex-Slave Narratives, "The African-American Experience in Ohio, 1850–1920," Ohio Historical Society, Columbus.

25. Chidsey, *Gentleman from New York*, 1.

26. Blanche Bruce to Roscoe Conkling, April 1879, in *Life and Letters of Roscoe Conkling*, 583; John Oller, *American Queen: The Rise and Fall of Kate Chase Sprague—Civil War "Belle of the North" and Gilded Age Woman of Scandal* (New York: Da Capo, 2014), 178–79.

27. Witham, *Fifty Years on the Firing Line*, 10.

28. Kelley, "Speech of Hon Wm D Kelley of PA on Freedmens Affairs," 2.

29. Florence Kelley to Isaac and Elizabeth Pugh, Los Angeles, August 7, 1872, FK Papers; Sklar, *Florence Kelley and the Nation's Work*, 43.

30. Florence Kelley to Isaac and Elizabeth Pugh, Colorado Springs, July 21, 1872; Florence Kelley to Isaac and Elizabeth Pugh, Los Angeles, August 7, 1872, FK Papers; Sklar, *Florence Kelley and the Nation's Work*, 43.

31. J. C. Rowland to William Kelley, January 28, 1873, WDK Papers; George P. McLean to William Kelley, March 1, 1873, WDK Papers; A. R. Nettleton to William Kelley, October 3, 1872, FK Papers; Joseph Keppler, "Credit

Mobilier," *Frank Leslie's Illustrated Newspaper*, March 3, 1873; William Kelley to Caroline Kelley, January 9, 1873, WDK Papers.

32. William Kelley to William Cullen Bryant, February 11, 1873, WDK Papers; William Kelley to Elizabeth Cady Stanton, December 13, 1872, WDK Papers; Kelley, "Speech of Hon. William D. Kelley," 3.

33. Richard Bensel, *The Political Economy of American Industrialization, 1877–1900* (Cambridge: Cambridge University Press, 2000), 5–6, 134.

34. "The Inflationists," *New York Times*, August 28, 1875; William Kelley to Florence Kelley, January 15, 1875, WDK Papers.

35. "The Men Who Voted for the Force Bill," *Daily Evening Bulletin*, March 4, 1875; William Kelley to Florence Kelley, February 5, 1875, WDK Papers.

36. "Hasty Action Regretted," *Boston Daily Advertiser*, April 30, 1875; "Judge Kelley and the South," *Galveston Daily News*, May 1, 1875; "Pig-Iron Kelley," *Georgia Weekly Telegraph and Georgia Journal & Messenger*, May 4, 1875.

37. "Judge Kelley's Views," *Galveston Daily News*, May 15, 1875; Brown, "William D. Kelley and Radical Reconstruction," 325; Wiggins, "'Pig Iron' Kelley Riot."

38. "Judge Kelley's Views," *Philadelphia Enquirer*, cited in "Washington," *Galveston Daily News*, May 2, 1875.

39. James C. Baylis to William Kelley, May 4, 1875, WDK Papers; William Kelley, "The Silver Question: Speech of Hon. William D. Kelley of Pennsylvania in the House of Representatives, May 10, 1879," pamphlet in State Library of Pennsylvania; "Pig Iron Kelley on Finance," *Daily Evening Bulletin*, December 12, 1874.

40. H. H. Colquitt to William Kelley, July 22, 1875, WDK Papers; "Not 'Pig-Iron,'" *Georgia Press*, November 16, 1875; William Kelley, *The Old South and the New: A Series of Letters* (New York: G. P. Putnam and Sons, 1888).

41. G. Haines Haddow to William Kelley, January 25, 1867, WDK Papers; Henry Hill and George B. Halsted to William Kelley, July 18, 1875, FK Papers.

42. "The Evil of Gold Dollar Worship," *New York Times*, July 12, 1875; "The Only Issue in Ohio," *New York Tribune*, July 21, 1875.

43. Greco, "William Darrah Kelley," 84–85; "The Evil of Gold Dollar Worship," *New York Times*, July 12, 1875.

44. "Sign of the Times," *Daily Evening Bulletin*, May 8, 1875; "Going Abroad for Economy's Sake," *Galveston Daily News*, April 7, 1875; "The Only Issue in Ohio," *New York Tribune*, July 21, 1875; Thomas Nast, "Iron and Blood," *Harper's Weekly*, July 1875.

45. "Kelley," *St. Louis Globe-Democrat*, June 23, 1875.

46. "The Inflationists," *New York Times*, August 28, 1875; "Judge Kelley," *Chicago Inter-Ocean*, August 14, 1875.

47. "Judge Kelley at Home," *New York Tribune*, July 19, 1875; "What Mr. Kelley Wants to See in Ohio," interview in *Cincinnati Gazette*, reprinted in *New York Tribune*, August 16, 1875.

48. "The Greenback Convention," *Atlanta Daily Constitution*, August 28, 1875; "Judge Kelley at Home," *New York Tribune*, July 19, 1875.

49. *Autobiography of William Allen White*, 83.

50. Summers, *Press Gang*, 65–66; "Between the Devil and the Deep Blue Sea," *New York Tribune*, March 20, 1875.

51. "Between the Devil and the Deep Blue Sea."

52. Witham, *Fifty Years on the Firing Line*, 21–22.

53. Ignatius Donnelly, March 13, 1870, in *Diary of Ignatius Donnelly*, 370.

54. Ignatius Donnelly, January 15, 1870, in *Diary of Ignatius Donnelly*, 362, 509, 362.

55. Ignatius Donnelly, March 13, 1870, in *Diary of Ignatius Donnelly*, 370.

56. Ignatius Donnelly, *Diary of Ignatius Donnelly*, 376.

57. Ignatius Donnelly, *Diary of Ignatius Donnelly*, 376.

CHAPTER SIX: "IF ANYBODY SAYS ELECTION TO ME, I WANT TO FIGHT"

1. Florence Kelley to William Kelley, July 29, 1876, FK Papers.

2. White, *Republic for Which It Stands*, 288.

3. William Kelley, *National Centennial Celebration and Exposition* (Washington, DC: F. & J. Rives & G. A. Bailey, 1871); William Kelley to Florence Kelley, June 1, 1875, WDK Papers; Florence Kelley to William Kelley, July 29, 1876, FK Papers.

4. Florence Kelley to William Kelley, July 29, 1876, FK Papers; Frances Perkins, "My Recollections of Florence Kelley," *Social Service Review* 28, no. 1 (1954): 15.

5. *Autobiography of Florence Kelley*, 48.

6. Turnout statistics drawn from McIver, *Historical Statistics*.

7. McIver, *Historical Statistics*; Michael F. Campbell, October 9, 1876, Sterling Library, Yale Special Collections, New Haven, CT; Rolf Johnson, November 6, 1876, in *Happy as a Big Sunflower: Adventures in the West, 1876–1880*, ed. Richard E. Jensen (Lincoln: University of Nebraska Press, 2000), 33; "What Is Democracy? To the Young Voters of the United States," *Pomeroy's Democrat*,

June 3, 1876; Samuel Tilden, "To perfect the organization of the Democracy of this state," circular to New York State Democrats, March 31, 1868, Printed Ephemera Collection, Library of Congress.

8. "Our Young Voters," *Trenton State Gazette*, October 30, 1884; Democratic Party Platforms, "1876 Democratic Party Platform Online," The American Presidency Project, https://www.presidency.ucsb.edu/node/273179.

9. Tilden, "To perfect the organization of the democracy of this state," 43, 61; White, *Republic for Which It Stands*, 331; Robert Kelley, "The Thought and Character of Samuel J. Tilden: The Democrat as Inheritor," *Historian* 26 (Spring 1964): 189; John Bigelow, *The Life of Samuel J. Tilden* (New York: Harper & Brothers, 1895), 47.

10. Henry Adams to Charles Milnes Gaskell, June 14, 1876, in *The Letters of Henry Adams, Volume II, 1868–1885*, ed. Jacob Claver Levenson (Cambridge, MA: Harvard University Press, 1982), 276; Michael Fitzgibbon Holt, *By One Vote: The Disputed Election of 1876* (Lawrence: University Press of Kansas, 2009), 70; Rutherford Birchard Hayes, April 22, 1877, *Diary and Letters of Rutherford Birchard Hayes, Nineteenth President of the United States, 1865–1883*, ed. Charles Richard William (Columbus: Ohio State Archaeological and Historical Society, 1924), 3:433; John Sproat, *The Best Men: Liberal Reformers in the Gilded Age* (New York: Oxford University Press, 1968), 94.

11. The Political Campaign Collections in the Smithsonian Institution's National Museum of American History contain an incredible variety of 1876 campaign merchandise, including the Hayes and Wheeler mug mentioned, a wide variety of torches from 1876, and the fireworks catalogs. For the "Tilden and Hendricks scarf," see *Autobiography of William Allen White*, 9.

12. Grinspan, "'Young Men for War,'" 360; Julius G. Rathbun, "'The Wide Awakes': The Great Political Organization of 1860," *Connecticut Quarterly* 1 (October 1895): 335; "The young man who deposited his maiden vote on Nov. 7 was easily recognized," *Milwaukee Daily Sentinel*, December 11, 1876; Michael F. Campbell, August 27, 1880, and September 4, 1880, Sterling Library, Yale Special Collections, New Haven, CT.

13. Henry Conrad Brokmeyer, September 1856, in *A Mechanic's Diary* (Washington, D.C.: privately published, 1910), 239; Daniel Klinghard, *Nationalization of American Politics, 1880–1896* (Cambridge: Cambridge University Press, 2010), 117; "Elections and Suffrage: The Congressional Investigation," *New York Times*, August 9, 1879.

14. "Election in Chicago," *Lillehammers Tilskuer*, December 27, 1883; Richard Franklin Bensel, *The American Ballot Box in the Mid-Nineteenth Century* (Cambridge: Cambridge University Press, 2004).

15. "Election in Chicago," *Lillehammers Tilskuer*, December 27, 1883; Frank Leach, *Recollections of a Newspaperman; A Record of Life and Events in California* (San Francisco: S. Levinson, 1917), 17–21; Abbott, *Reminiscences*, 110. The best information on ballot tricks can be found in Mark Wahlgren Summers, *Party Games: Getting, Keeping, and Using Power in Gilded Age Politics* (Chapel Hill: University of North Carolina Press, 2004), 94–130; Patricia Crain, "Potent Papers: Secret Lives of the Nineteenth-Century Ballot," *Common-Place* 9 (October 2008), http://commonplace.online/article/potent-papers, Last accessed October 24, 2020.

16. Andreas Ueland, *Recollections of an Immigrant* (New York: Minton, Balch, 1929), 51; Charles A. Murdock, *A Backward Glance at Eighty* (San Francisco: Paul Elder, 1921), 122–23; William L. Riordan, *Plunkitt of Tammany Hall: A Series of Very Plain Talks on Very Practical Politics* (New York: McClure, Phillips, 1905), 19.

17. "Religion in Politics," *Weekly Register-Call* (Central City, CO), September 5, 1890; Bensel, *American Ballot Box*; Daniel J. Ryan, "Clubs in Politics," *North American Review* 146, no. 375 (1888): 176; "The Bull-Dozed State: Louisiana as Seen by Judge Kelley," *St. Louis Post-Dispatch*, December 8, 1876.

18. James Michael Curley, *I'd Do It Again* (New York: Arno, 1976), 18; Andreas Ueland, *Recollections of an Immigrant*, 51; Leach, *Recollections of a Newspaperman*, 14.

19. Paul Kleppner, *Who Voted? Dynamics of Electoral Turnout, 1870–1980* (Greenwood, NY: Praeger, 1982), 24.

20. Roy Morris Jr., *Fraud of the Century: Rutherford B. Hayes, Samuel Tilden, and the Stolen Election of 1876* (New York: Simon & Schuster, 2007), 11–12; Ulysses S. Grant to John A. Logan, November 10, 1876, telegraph in Collections of Political History, National Museum of American History, Smithsonian Institution, Washington, D.C.

21. Morton Keller, *Affairs of State* (Cambridge, MA: Belknap Press of Harvard University Press, 1977), 241; C. A. Stephens, "The Rival Bonfires," *The Youth's Companion*, October 16, 1884, 57.

22. Alice Kirk Grierson to Benjamin Henry Grierson, November 3, 1876, in *The Colonel's Lady on the Western Frontier: The Correspondence of Alice Kirk Grierson*, ed. Shirley A. Leckie (Lincoln: University of Nebraska Press, 1989), 91–93.

23. Elizabeth Cady Stanton to Harriot Eaton Stanton Blatch, November 8, 1876, in *Elizabeth Cady Stanton, As Revealed in Her Letters, Diaries and Reminiscences*, ed. Harriot Stanton Blatch and Theodore Stanton (New York: Harper & Brothers, 1922), 2:149; William Dean Howells to William Cooper Howells, November 12, 1876, in *Selected Letters of William Dean Howells*, ed. George Arms (Boston: Twayne, 1979), 2:141.

24. Maria Louisa Wacker Fleet to James William Fleet, March 11, 1877, in *Green Mount after the War: The Correspondence of Maria Louisa Wacker Fleet and Her Family, 1865–1900*, ed. Betsy Fleet (Charlottesville: University Press of Virginia, 1978), 160.

25. White, *Republic for Which It Stands*, 330–31; Sklar, *Florence Kelley and the Nation's Work*, 54; "Bull-Dozed State"; Morris, *Fraud of the Century*, 209.

26. "The Strong Government Idea," *Atlantic Monthly*, February 1880, 276.

27. *Life and Letters of Roscoe Conkling*, 529–30.

28. Holt, *By One Vote*, 240–50; Morris, *Fraud of the Century*, 234.

29. The election of 1876 certainly wasn't a fair vote—no election saw as much violent suppression of Black voters in the South. But Democrats also won the popular vote more peacefully in key northern states like New York, Indiana, and New Jersey. Even in states like Pennsylvania, which they failed to win, Democrats did 11 percent better in 1876 than in 1872. Nationwide, Democrats won 50 percent more popular votes than in 1872. It seems fair to conclude that, bearing in mind both the suppression of Black Republicans in the South but also the large growth of White Democrats in both North and South, the Democrats were the larger, more popular party overall in 1876.

30. Holt, *By One Vote*, 240–50; Morris, *Fraud of the Century*, 234; Michael Les Benedict, "Reform Republicans and the Retreat from Reconstruction," in *Preserving the Constitution: Essays on Politics and the Constitution in the Reconstruction Era* (New York: Fordham University Press, 2006), 168–85.

31. Summers, *Ordeal of Reunion*, 385–88; White, *Republic for Which It Stands*, 334–35.

32. "Nothing but News," *Milwaukee Daily Sentinel*, March 7, 1877; *Life and Letters of Roscoe Conkling*, 529–30.

33. Josiah Strong, *Our Country: Its Possible Future and Its Present Crisis* (New York: Baker & Taylor, 1885), 124; James Green, *Death in the Haymarket: A Story of Chicago, the First Labor Movement, and the Bombing That Divided Gilded Age America* (New York: Anchor Books, 2006), 69; Eric Wakin, "From Flintlock to 'Tramps' Terror: Guns and Gun Control in the Nineteenth-Century New York City" (PhD diss., Columbia University, 2010).

34. Joel Tyler Headley, *The Great Riots of New York* (New York: Basic Books, 2004), 110; Herman Melville, "The House-top, A Night Piece (July 1863)," in *Battle Pieces and Aspects of the War* (New York: Harper & Brothers, 1866), 86.

35. John Merriman, *Massacre: The Life and Death of the Paris Commune* (New York: Basic Books, 2014); F. J. W., "The Third Party," *Washington Post*, May 10, 1880.

36. *Life and Letters of Roscoe Conkling*, 254, 270.

37. Francis Parkman, "The Failure of Universal Suffrage," *North American Review* 263 (July–August 1878): 18.

38. Harrison, "Limited Sovereignty in the United States," 186–87.

39. James Garfield, "A Century of Progress," *Atlantic Monthly*, July 1877, 63; William Dean Howells, "Politics," *Atlantic Monthly*, January 1872, 124.

40. James Russell Lowell to Joel Benton, January 19, 1876, in Horace Elisha Scudder, *James Russell Lowell: A Biography* (Boston: Houghton & Mifflin, 1901), 194.

41. James Russell Lowell, "The World's Fair, 1876," in Scudder, *James Russell Lowell*, 192; Lowell, "Tempora Mutantor," in *The Writings of James Russell Lowell: Poems* (Boston: Houghton, Mifflin, 1890), 4:394.

42. Albion Winegar Tourgée, *Letters to a King* (Cincinnati: Cranston & Stowe, 1888), 83; James Russell Lowell to Joel Benton, January 19, 1876, in Scudder, *James Russell Lowell*, 195; Russell Kirk, *The Conservative Mind* (New York: Gateway Editions, 2001), 348.

43. Nicholas Carr, "'I Have Not Abandoned Any Plan': The Rage in Francis Parkman," *Massachusetts Historical Review* 17 (2015): 1–34; Eileen K. Cheng, *The Plain and Noble Garb of Truth: Nationalism and Impartiality in American Historical Writing, 1784–1860* (Athens: University of Georgia Press, 2008).

44. Parkman, "Failure of Universal Suffrage," 2.

45. Parkman, "Failure of Universal Suffrage," 2, 4.

46. Parkman, "Failure of Universal Suffrage," 5, 4.

47. Francis Parkman to Thomas Wentworth Higginson, June 5, 1876, in Charles Haight Farnham, *A Life of Francis Parkman* (Boston: Little, Brown, 1907), 272; Parkman, "Failure of Universal Suffrage," 10.

48. Parkman, "Failure of Universal Suffrage."

49. "The Failure of Universal Suffrage," *Chicago Daily Tribune*, July 8, 1878; "Is Universal Suffrage a Failure?," *Galveston Daily News*, July 20, 1878; "The Failure of Universal Suffrage," *Rocky Mountain News*, July 10, 1878.

50. Harrison, "Limited Sovereignty in the United States," 187, 190; William Dean Howells, "Politics," *Atlantic Monthly*, January 1872, 126; Keyssar, *Right to Vote*, 117–62.

51. "Presidential Electioneering in the Senate," *Atlantic Monthly*, March 1879, 369; "A Fresh Suggestion," *Chicago Inter Ocean*, March 30, 1876.

52. Michael McGerr, *The Decline of Popular Politics: The American North, 1866–1928* (New York: Oxford University Press, 1984), 49–51; Keyssar, *Right to Vote*, 132.

53. "A True Republic," *Atlantic Monthly*, 716.

54. "Presidential Electioneering in the Senate," *Atlantic Monthly*, March 1879, 369.

55. Goldwin Smith, "Is Universal Suffrage a Failure," *Atlantic Monthly*, January 1879, 82.

CHAPTER SEVEN: "BOTHER POLITICS!"

1. "William D. Kelley, Jr.," *Philadelphia Ledger*, November 30, 1877; "The Shooting of Judge Kelley's Son," *New York Times*, December 2, 1877.

2. "William D. Kelley, Jr."; "Shot by a colored man," *North American*, November 30, 1877.

3. Sklar, *Florence Kelley and the Nation's Work*, 80; William Kelley to Florence Kelley, April 15, 1871, WDK Papers.

4. "William D. Kelley, Jr."; "Shooting of Judge Kelley's Son."

5. "Shot by a colored man"; *Idaho Avalanche*, December 1, 1877; "Notes about Town," *North American*, December 15, 1877.

6. Sklar, *Florence Kelley and the Nation's Work*, 80.

7. In the latter half of the Gilded Age, from the Haymarket affair in 1886 to the election of 1896, many of these conflicts would be addressed more directly.

8. Charles Nordhoff, *Politics for Young Americans* (New York: Harper & Brothers, 1875), 48.

9. *Autobiography of Florence Kelley*, 45; Florence Kelley to William Kelley, July 29, 1876, FK Papers.

10. Sklar, *Florence Kelley and the Nation's Work*, 80; Goldmark, *Impatient Crusader*, 72.

11. Sklar, *Florence Kelley and the Nation's Work*, 50–51.

12. Florence Kelley to Caroline Kelley, October 29, 1876, FK Papers; *Autobiography of Florence Kelley*, 49, 53.

13. Sklar, *Florence Kelley and the Nation's Work*, 56; William Kelley to Caroline Kelley, February 23, 1879, WDK Papers.

14. Goldmark, *Impatient Crusader*, 72

15. Florence Kelley to Caroline Kelley, October 29, 1876, FK Papers.

16. *Autobiography of Florence Kelley*, 49; Florence Kelley to William Kelley, November 3, 1877, FK Papers; *Autobiography of Florence Kelley*, 49.

17. Florence Kelley to William Kelley, December 2, 1878, FK Papers; Sklar, *Florence Kelley and the Nation's Work*, 342n24; "Denis Kearney," *New York Tribune*, September 7, 1878.

18. Sklar, *Florence Kelley and the Nation's Work*, 64.

19. "Judge Kelley's Views," *Chicago Inter Ocean*, March 1, 1884; George Rogers Starkey, *The Compound Oxygen Treatment* (Philadelphia: Starkey & Palen, 1881); Florence Kelley to Caroline Kelley, September 29, 1876, in *The Selected Letters of Florence Kelley*, ed. Kathryn Kish Sklar and Beverly Wilson Palmer (Champaign: University of Illinois Press, 2009), 11.

20. "A Political Day," *North American*, September 12, 1878.

21. "A Close Rub for Pig-Iron Kelley," *Chicago Daily Tribune*, September 12, 1878; "Political Day."

22. Robert Ellis Thompson, "William Darragh Kelley," *Irish World and American Industrial Liberator*, January 25, 1890; "Political Duty"; "Close Rub for Pig-Iron Kelley."

23. "Political Day"; "Close Rub for Pig-Iron Kelley."

24. "Political Day."

25. D. H. Mason to Henry Carey, July 3, 1878, WDK Papers; "Political Day."

26. "Judge Kelley Accepts," *North American*, September 19, 1878.

27. Florence Kelley to William Kelley, November 3, 1877, FK Papers.

CHAPTER EIGHT: "WHEN A MAN WORKS IN POLITICS, HE SHOULD GET SOMETHING OUT OF IT"

1. Ben Perley Poore, *Reminiscences of Sixty Years at the National Metropolis*, vol. 2 (Philadelphia: Hubbard Brothers, 1886), 206; *Life and Letters of Roscoe Conkling*, 286.

2. DePew, *My Memories of Eighty Years*, 80–81; *Life and Letters of Roscoe Conkling*, 306.

3. Greco, "William Darrah Kelley," 227, 219.

4. There was, to be fair, a great deal of mythmaking in the distinctions Conkling was drawing. Curtis was a committed Republican, not turning his back on party politics but trying to reform from within. Conkling, at the same time, came

from a wealthy old family and held his position as senator because the legislature of his state selected him, not because he won it in a general election.

5. "Practical Politics," *Frank Leslie's Illustrated Newspaper*, January 16, 1875, 306; Ari Hoogenboom, *Outlawing the Spoils: A History of Civil Service Reform Movement* (New York: Praeger, 1982), 77–78; Johnson Brigham, *Blaine, Conkling, and Garfield: A Reminiscence and a Character Study* (New York: G. E. Stechert, 1919), 14–15.

6. Chidsey, *Gentleman from New York*, 39; "Speech," *New York Times*, September 27, 1877, September 28, 1877.

7. *Life and Letters of Roscoe Conkling*, 538.

8. *Life and Letters of Roscoe Conkling*, 541, 540.

9. *Life and Letters of Roscoe Conkling*, 540.

10. *Life and Letters of Roscoe Conkling*, 541.

11. *Life and Letters of Roscoe Conkling*, 549; "Speech."

12. DePew, *My Memories of Eighty Years*, 80–81; Hoogenboom, *Outlawing the Spoils*, 248.

13. Amos Cummings, "Curtis Speech," *New York Sun*, September 27, 1877; "Speech."

14. *Life and Letters of Roscoe Conkling*, 540.

15. "The Independent Voter," *New York Tribune*, April 9, 1875.

16. *Life and Letters of Roscoe Conkling*, 540.

17. Ari Hoogenboom, "The Pendleton Act and the Civil Service," *American Historical Review* 64, no. 2 (1959): 303; William L. Riordon, *Plunkitt of Tammany Hall: A Series of Very Plain Talks on Very Practical Politics* (New York: E. P. Dutton, 1963), 38.

18. White, *Republic for Which It Stands*, 356; Crandall Shifflett, *Victorian America, 1876 to 1913, Almanacs of American Life* (New York: Facts on File, 1996), 61

19. "The American Anomaly," *Washington Post*, December 20, 1885.

20. Carpenter, *Carp's Washington*, 120–21.

21. Jessica Ziparo, *This Grand Experiment: When Women Entered the Federal Workforce in Civil War–Era Washington, D.C.* (Chapel Hill: University of North Carolina Press, 2017), 45, 51.

22. Rolf Johnson, October 16, 1876; November 6, 1876; November 26, 1877; in Jensen, *Happy as a Big Sunflower*, 31, 33, 76.

23. William McMullen, January 21, 1886, in Silcox, *Letters from an Irish Ward Leader: William McMullen to Samuel J. Randall*.

24. John Roy Lynch, *Reminiscences of an Active Life: Autobiography of John Roy Lynch*, ed. John Hope Franklin (Jackson: University Press of Mississippi, 2010), 172.

25. "Black Officeholders in the South," Facing History and Ourselves, last accessed October 24, 2020, https://www.facinghistory.org/reconstruction -era/black-officeholders-south; Eric Foner, *Freedom's Lawmakers: A Directory of Black Officeholders during Reconstruction*, rev. ed. (Baton Rouge: Louisiana State University Press, 1996), xi–xxxii; Philip F. Rubio, *There's Always Work at the Post Office: African American Postal Workers and the Fight for Jobs, Justice, and Equality* (Chapel Hill: University of North Carolina Press, 2010).

26. Lane, *Roots of Violence in Black Philadelphia*, 61–62; Silcox, "Black 'Better Class' Political Dilemma," 60.

27. David M. Tucker, *Mugwumps: The Public Moralists of the Gilded Age* (Columbia: University of Missouri Press, 1998); White, *Republic for Which It Stands*, 172–213.

28. *Life and Letters of Roscoe Conkling*, 513; Rutherford Birchard Hayes, April 22, 1877, in *Diary and Letters of Rutherford Birchard Hayes*, 3:433.

29. Theodore Roosevelt Jr., *Theodore Roosevelt—An Autobiography* (New York: Charles Scribner, 1913), 7.

30. Chidsey, *Gentleman from New York*, 110.

31. Doris Kearns Goodwin, *The Bully Pulpit: Theodore Roosevelt, William Howard Taft, and the Golden Age of Journalism* (New York: Simon & Schuster, 2013), 45; *Theodore Roosevelt—an Autobiography*, 133.

32. *Theodore Roosevelt—an Autobiography*, 23–24.

33. Kearns Goodwin, *Bully Pulpit*, 45–46.

34. Robert H. Wiebe, *Self-Rule: A Cultural History of American Democracy* (Chicago: University of Chicago Press, 1995), 17–113.

35. Wiebe, *Search for Order*, 21; Henry George, *Progress and Poverty: An Inquiry into the Cause of Industrial Depressions and of Increase of Want with Increase of Wealth* (New York: Sterling, 1879), 7–8; Edwards made strong use of this same concept of "the wedge" in *New Spirits*, 9–10.

36. John Whiteclay Chambers, *Tyranny of Change: America in the Progressive Era, 1890–1920* (New Brunswick, NJ: Rutgers University Press, 2000), 5; Edwards, *New Spirits*, 60–79; David Montgomery, *Fall of the House of Labor* (Cambridge: Cambridge University Press, 1987).

37. Parkman, "Failure of Universal Suffrage," 4; Strong, *Our Country*, 124.

38. "A Tragedy in Two Acts," *New York Tribune*, June 12, 1888; "A Great State," *New York Herald*, November 9, 1877.

39. McElroy, "An Old War Horse to a Young Politician"; Kevin Murphy, *Political Manhood: Red Bloods, Mollycoddles, and the Politics of Progressive Era Reform* (New York: Columbia University Press, 2010), 11–12; "Johnny Powers," *Milwaukee Sentinel*, January 28, 1898.

40. Chidsey, *Gentleman from New York*, 236, 239, 161; Chapin, *American Court Gossip*, 22.

41. Jordan, *Roscoe Conkling of New York*, 203; Oller, *American Queen*.

42. *Life and Letters of Roscoe Conkling*, 513; Oller, *American Queen*, 176.

43. Oller, *American Queen*, 183–87.

44. Oller, *American Queen*, 206.

45. "A Great State," *New York Herald*, November 9, 1877.

46. James Garfield, "A Century of Congress," *Atlantic Monthly*, July 1877, 63.

47. *Theodore Roosevelt—an Autobiography*, 86.

CHAPTER NINE: "WHERE DO ALL THESE CRANKS COME FROM?"

1. Carpenter, *Carp's Washington*, 163.

2. Candice Millard, *The Destiny of the Republic: A Tale of Madness, Medicine, and the Murder of a President* (New York: Doubleday, 2011), 50, 63.

3. Mary Densel, "The Grand Procession," *Harper's Young People*, November 9, 1880; *Puck*, September 22, 1880, 34.

4. Millard, *Destiny of the Republic*, 95, 57.

5. James Blaine, *Eulogy of James Garfield* (New York: J. S. Ogilvie, 1882), 42.

6. Millard, *Destiny of the Republic*, 96, 118, 127.

7. Chidsey, *Gentleman from New York*, 346–50; Chapin, *American Court Gossip*, 48.

8. Millard, *Destiny of the Republic*, 113.

9. Letter from Harriet Bailey Blaine, July 3, 1881, in *Letters of Mrs. James G. Blaine*, 1:211.

10. Harriet Bailey Blaine to Walker Blaine, 1881, in *Letters of Mrs. James G. Blaine*, 1:229.

11. Millard, *Destiny of the Republic*, 128.

12. "Letter-Writing Cranks: Queer Folk Who Ask Questions and Make Suggestions," *St. Louis Globe-Democrat*, March 18, 1886; "The Crank," *Los*

Angeles Times, December 22, 1881; "Guiteau's Ambassador," *Chicago Daily Tribune*, March 17, 1882; "'Cranks' Some of Those Who Infest Washington," *Cleveland Herald*, July 13, 1881.

13. "Colorado Cranks," *Los Angeles Times*, February 28, 1894; "A Reservation for Cranks," *Galveston Daily News*, September 15, 1883; Robert Jones Burdette, "Deal Gently with the Cranks," *Daily Evening Bulletin*, July 25, 1884; "Deal Gently with the Cranks," *Idaho Avalanche*, August 16, 1884; "Deal Gently with the Cranks," *Vermont Watchman*, October 1, 1884; John Fiske, "Some Cranks and Crotchets," *Atlantic Monthly*, March 1899, 299; "Crank Is Not Slang," *Chicago Daily Tribune*, May 18, 1887.

14. "Origin of 'Cranks,'" *Morning Oregonian*, May 22, 1899; "Cranks Shooting Cranks," *Milwaukee Sentinel*, February 4, 1885; "The Crank and His Inspiration," *Washington Post*, January 4, 1894; "A Pen Portrait," *Augusta Chronicle*, January 25, 1904.

15. "Race Cranks," *New York Freeman*, January 16, 1886; "A Negro Cranks Letter to the Gov," *Galveston Daily News*, July 17, 1885; H. S. Fulkerson, *The Negro: As He Was; as He Is; as He Will Be* (Vicksburg, MS: Commercial Herald printers, 1887), 81; Atticus Greene Haygood, "The Negro a Citizen," in *Sermons and Speeches* (Nashville, TN: Southern Methodist Publication House, 1883); John Ambrose Price, *The Negro: Past Present and Future* (New York: Neale, 1907), 206–7; "Greenbackers as 'Cranks,'" *Indianapolis Sentinel*, May 30, 1884; "Reservation for Cranks."

16. Nydahl, *Diary of Ignatius Donnelly*, 820–21, 56.

17. Ridge, *Ignatius Donnelly*, 197–264.

18. Nydahl, *Diary of Ignatius Donnelly*, 75.

19. National Council of Women of the United States, "Transactions of the National Council of Women of the United States," assembled in Washington, D.C., February 22–25, 1891, ed. Rachel Foster Avery (Philadelphia: J. B. Lippincott, 1891), 344.

20. Carrie Chapman Catt to Susan B. Anthony, September 1890, in *The Life and Work of Susan B. Anthony: Including Public Addresses, Her Own Letters and Many from Her Contemporaries During Fifty Years*, ed. Ida Husted Harper (Indianapolis: Hollenbeck, 1899), 2:693.

21. "State at Large," *Rocky Mountain News*, December 26, 1883.

22. Kipling, *American Notes*, 32.

23. Bensel, *Political Economy of American Industrialization*, xx–xxi, 457–519; Rebecca Edwards, *Angels in the Machinery: Gender in American Party Politics*

from the Civil War to the Progressive Era (New York: Oxford University Press, 1997).

24. O'Neill, *Memorial Addresses on the Life and Character of William D. Kelley*, 16; Carpenter, *Carp's Washington*, 25; "The Tariff Is the Cause of Bribery in Elections," *Milwaukee Sentinel*, April 17, 1889.

25. Letters of William Kelley, February 16, 1882, WDK Papers; Summers, *Rum, Romanism, and Rebellion: The Making of the 1884 Election* (Chapel Hill: University of North Carolina Press, 2003), 94.

26. Crandall Shifflett, ed., *Victorian America, 1876 to 1913 (Almanacs of American Life)* (New York: Facts on File, 1996), 58.

27. The Mongrel tariff placed a fee on the import of vegetables but not fruit. The ensuing legal case—*Nix v. Hedden*—led the U.S. Supreme Court to officially designate the tomato as a vegetable. "The Pennsylvania Puzzle," *Milwaukee Daily Journal*, April 14, 1887; "Democratic Principles and the Speakership," *Galveston Daily News*, November 11, 1883; Mr. Breckenridge, *Memorial Addresses on the Life and Character of William D. Kelley*, 60; Summers, *Rum, Romanism, and Rebellion*, 104-6.

28. Henry Loomis Nelson, "The Political Horizon," *Atlantic Monthly*, March 1900, 309.

CHAPTER TEN: "NOW WE SHALL HAVE THE WORST AGAIN"

1. *Autobiography of Florence Kelley*, 61-62.

2. *Autobiography of Florence Kelley*, 62.

3. *Autobiography of Florence Kelley*, 62.

4. "'Cranks' Some of Those Who Infest Washington," *Cleveland Herald*, July 13, 1881; Sklar, *Florence Kelley and the Nation's Work*, 62; "Judge Kelley's Daughter," *Boston Daily Globe*, August 31, 1886.

5. "Judge Kelley's Daughter."

6. "Judge Kelley's Daughter."

7. Sklar, *Florence Kelley and the Nation's Work*, 63-64.

8. "General," *Daily Inter Ocean*, January 31, 1880; William Kelley to Caroline Kelley, December 2, 1882, FK Papers.

9. Sklar, *Florence Kelley and the Nation's Work*, 66-67.

10. *Autobiography of Florence Kelley*, 65; Sklar, *Florence Kelley and the Nation's Work*, 80-81.

11. Caroline Kelley to William Kelley, May 4, 1883, Kelley Family Letters, Columbia University.

12. *Autobiography of Florence Kelley*, 65–67.

13. Florence Kelley to Susan B. Anthony, January 21, 1884, Kelley Family Letters, Columbia University.

14. Caroline Kelley to Florence Kelley, October 19, 1883, FK Papers; *Autobiography of Florence Kelley*, 69.

15. Sklar, *Florence Kelley and the Nation's Work*, 84.

16. *Autobiography of Florence Kelley*, 72, 71.

17. *Autobiography of Florence Kelley*, 73.

18. *Autobiography of Florence Kelley*, 73–74.

19. *Autobiography of Florence Kelley*, 71.

20. William D. Kelley, Cong. Rec., 48th Cong., 1st Sess. (June 3, 1884), 4774; and William D. Kelley, Cong. Rec., 48th Cong., 1st Sess. (June 19, 1884), 5354–55.

21. Anthony had a bad habit of using Will's love and regard for Florie to manipulate him, later accusing Will that "it is cruel for you to leave your daughter, so full of hope and resolve, to suffer the humiliations of disfranchisement she already feels so keenly, and which she will find more and more galling as she grows into the stronger and grander woman she is sure to be." Susan B. Anthony to William Darrah Kelley, January 6, 1886, in *The Life and Words of Susan B. Anthony: Including Public Addresses, Her Own Letters and Many from her Contemporaries During Fifty Years*, Vol. 2, ed. Ida Husted Harper (Indianapolis: Bowen-Merrill Company, 1898), 584

22. Florence Kelley to Susan B. Anthony, January 21, 1884, FK Papers.

23. "Miss Florence Kelley's Complaint," *Washington Post*, April 27, 1884.

24. "Miss Florence Kelley's Complaint."

25. Charlotte Howard Conant to Chester C. Conant, June 1, 1884, and October 30, 1884, in *A Girl of the Eighties at College and at Home from the Family Letters of Charlotte Howard Conant and from Other Records*, ed. Martha Pike Conant (Boston: Houghton, Mifflin, 1931), 163–64, 178–79.

26. Charlotte Howard Conant to Chester C. Conant, October 30, 1884, in *Girl of the Eighties at College and at Home*, 178–79.

27. *Life Story and Personal Reminiscences of Col. John Sobieski*, 229.

28. William Dean Howells to William Cooper Howells, June 8, 1884, in *Selected Letters of William Dean Howells*, 3:101; "Letter to the Editor from 'Old '56,'" *New York Times*, June 8, 1884.

29. Joseph Keppler, "The Tattooed Man," *Puck*, June 4, 1884.

30. Charlotte Howard Conant to Chester C. Conant, October 30, 1884, in *Girl of the Eighties at College and at Home*, 178–79.

31. Brooklyn Young Republican Club, *Young Republican Campaign Song Book*, comp. Henry Camp (Brooklyn: Harrison & Morton, 1888), 34.

32. Summers, *Rum, Romanism, and Rebellion*, 182–83.

33. "The Morals of the Campaign," *Congregationalist*, August 28, 1884, 4.

34. William Dean Howells to Thomas Perry, August 15, 1884, in *Selected Letters of William Dean Howells*, 3:108; William Dean Howells to Mark Twain, August 10, 1884, in *Selected Letters of William Dean Howells*, 3:107.

35. For campaign uniforms in 1884, see the Unexcelled Campaign Fireworks Company's *Illustrated Campaign Handbook Manual of Arms and Tactics* (New York, 1884), in the Political Campaign Collections, Smithsonian Institution, National Museum of American History, Washington, D.C.; Greg Hand, "Cincinnati's 1884 Election Was a Real Riot," *Cincinnati Magazine*, October 27, 2020.

36. Segerberg, September 28, 1884; Edward W. Bok, *The Americanization of Edward Bok* (New York: Scribner & Sons, 1920), 441–46.

37. Harriet Bailey Blaine, December 24, 1881, in Harriet Bailey Blaine to Walker Blaine, March 18, 1872, in *Letters of Mrs. James G. Blaine*, 1:275–77.

38. Harriet Bailey Blaine to Alice B. Coppinger, November 30, 1884, in *Letters of Mrs. James G. Blaine*, 119–21.

39. Harriet Bailey Blaine to Walker Blaine, August 18, 1879, in *Letters of Mrs. James G. Blaine*, 161–62.

40. Jordan, *Roscoe Conkling of New York*, 420.

41. Martha Farnsworth, November 8, 1884, in *Plains Woman: The Diary of Martha Farnsworth, 1882–1922*, ed. Marlene Springer and Haskell Springer (Bloomington: Indiana University Press, 1986), 19; William Dean Howells to William Cooper Howells, November 9, 1884, in *Selected Letters of William Dean Howells*, 3:113.

42. E. V. Smalley, "The Political Field," *Atlantic Monthly*, January 1884, 124.

43. Josephson, *Politicos*, 364–65.

CHAPTER ELEVEN: "A YOUNG LADY, NOW IN EUROPE, WHO BEARS MY NAME"

1. Kipling, *American Notes*, 13.

2. Kipling, *American Notes*, ix.

3. Kipling, *American Notes*, 10.

4. Kipling, *American Notes*, 10.

5. Kipling, *American Notes*, 11.

6. Kipling, *American Notes*, 13.

7. Kipling, *American Notes*, 10.

8. Kipling, *American Notes*, 13.

9. Democracy was, to be sure, in greater danger during the Civil War itself. But many pursued the war, especially on the Union side, driven by their zealous faith in preserving America's political system. In the 1880s, democracy faced less an overall threat of collapse than the kind of rot and drift that could undermine popular confidence. For a brilliant summation of these concerns, see Tourgée, *Letters to a King*.

10. *Memoirs of Cornelius Cole*, 220; "Do Our Votes Count?," *Los Angeles Times*, May 2, 1894.

11. "A Talk with Ingalls," *St. Louis Post-Dispatch*, April 13, 1890.

12. Kelley, "Speech of Hon. William D. Kelley," 3; Frederic Howe, *The Confessions of a Reformer* (New York: C. Scribner's Sons, 1925), 173.

13. Howe, *Confessions of a Reformer*, 2, 148.

14. Kipling, *American Notes*, 37, 36.

15. Godkin, *Problems of Modern Democracy*, 202; Hoogenboom, *Outlawing the Spoils*, 266.

16. Caroline Kelley to William Kelley, June 1884, Kelley Family Papers, Columbia University.

17. William Kelley to Florence Kelley, June 18, 1884, WDK Papers.

18. Greco, "William Darrah Kelley," 223.

19. "Judge Kelley's Daughter"; Sklar, *Florence Kelley and the Nation's Work*, 93–94.

20. Sklar, *Florence Kelley and the Nation's Work*, 94; Caroline Kelley to Will Kelley, February 24, 1888, WDK Papers.

21. Sklar, *Florence Kelley and the Nation's Work*, 93.

22. Sklar, *Florence Kelley and the Nation's Work*, 94.

23. William Kelley to Florence Kelley, June 18, 1884, WDK Papers; "Judge Kelley's Daughter"; "Gotham Gossip," *Daily Picayune*, November 26, 1887.

24. Florence Kelley to Mary Thorne Lewis, February 12, 1885, FK Papers.

25. Florence Kelley to Mary Thorne Lewis, June 10, 1885, FK Papers; "Judge Kelley's Daughter."

26. Florence Kelley to Mary Thorne Lewis, March 19, 1885, FK Papers.

27. Florence Kelley to Mary Thorne Lewis, March 19, 1885, FK Papers; Florence Kelley to William Kelley, February 1885, Kelley Family Letters, Columbia University.

28. Florence Kelley to Mary Thorne Lewis, March 19, 1885, FK Papers.

29. Florence Kelley to Mary Thorne Lewis, March 19, 1885, FK Papers; Frank Carpenter, "Public Men as Authors: Carp in Cleveland Leader," *Daily Evening Bulletin*, May 14, 1885; "Judge Kelley's Illness," *North American*, November 24, 1884.

30. Florence Kelley to Mary Thorne Lewis, February 12, 1885, FK Papers; Florence Kelley to Mary Thorne Lewis, June 4, 1885, FK Papers.

31. Florence Kelley to Mary Thorne Lewis, March 19, 1885, FK Papers.

32. Florence Kelley to Mary Thorne Lewis, March 19, 1885, FK Papers.

33. Florence Kelley to Mary Thorne Lewis, March 19, 1885, FK Papers.

34. Florence Kelley to Mary Thorne Lewis, June 4, 1885, FK Papers.

35. Florence Kelley to Mary Thorne Lewis, June 4, 1885, FK Papers.

36. Sklar, *Florence Kelley and the Nation's Work*, 96; Florence Kelley to Caroline Kelley, December 16, 1885, FK Papers.

37. Florence Kelley to Mary Thorne Lewis, March 19, 1885, FK Papers.

38. Florence Kelley to Friedrich Engels, June 9, 1886, in *Selected Letters of Florence Kelley*, 31, 32.

39. Florence Kelley to Friedrich Engels, June 9, 1886, in *Selected Letters of Florence Kelley*, 31.

40. Florence Kelley to Friedrich Engels, January 10, 1886, in *Selected Letters of Florence Kelley*, 30; Florence Kelley to Friedrich Engels, June 9, 1886, in *Selected Letters of Florence Kelley*, 31.

41. William Kelley to Elizabeth Pugh, December 20, 1887, WDK Papers.

42. William Kelley Jr. to Caroline Kelley, February 27, 1885, FK Papers.

43. Florence Kelley to Friedrich Engels, June 9, 1886, in *Selected Letters of Florence Kelley*, 31; Florence Kelley to Mary Thorne Lewis, March 19, 1885, FK Papers; Francis Parkman, "Failure of Universal Suffrage," 2.

44. "Women of the World," *St. Louis Post-Dispatch*, April 29, 1885.

45. John Jay Chapman, *Practical Agitation* (New York: C. Scribner's Sons, 1900), 10.

CHAPTER TWELVE: "REFORMERS WHO EAT ROAST BEEF"

1. Burlingame, "Making of a Spoilsman," 15; *Life and Letters of Roscoe Conkling*, 672.

2. White, *Republic for Which It Stands*, 368–70.

3. "New York Helpless in a Tornado of Wind and Snow," *New York Times*, March 13, 1888.

4. Chidsey, *Gentleman from New York*, 384.

5. *Life and Letters of Roscoe Conkling*, 701.

6. *Life and Letters of Roscoe Conkling*, 703.

7. "Conkling," *New York Herald*, April 19, 1888; Chidsey, *Gentleman from New York*, 346–48.

8. Charles Henry Lea, "The Lesson of the Pennsylvania Election," *Atlantic Monthly*, January 1891, 98; James Michael Curley, *I'd Do It Again* (New York: Arno, 1976), 22.

9. "Independent: His Purpose in Politics," *Boston Daily Globe*, April 14, 1888, 1.

10. "Independent: His Purpose in Politics."

11. "Mr. Lowell's Politics," 275; "How to Rule Cities: Sunset Club," *Chicago Daily Tribune*, November 23, 1894.

12. Sproat, *Best Men*, 272; George Frederic Parsons, "The Saloon in Politics," *Atlantic Monthly*, September 1886, 406.

13. Gary Gerstle, *Liberty and Coercion: The Paradox of American Government from the Founding to the Present* (Princeton, NJ: Princeton University Press, 2015), 165; Hoogenboom, "Pendleton Act and the Civil Service," 315; Josephson, *Politicos*, 345.

14. "How to Rule Cities: Sunset Club."

15. Kearns Goodwin, *Bully Pulpit*, 66–67.

16. Edwin Morris, *The Rise of Theodore Roosevelt* (New York: Modern Library, 1979), xxi; *Theodore Roosevelt—an Autobiography*, 56.

17. *Theodore Roosevelt—an Autobiography*, 55, 56.

18. Young, *Age of Charisma*, 61.

19. Kearns Goodwin, *Bully Pulpit*, 126–27.

20. Theodore Roosevelt to Jonas Van Duzer, November 20, 1883, in *The Selected Letters of Theodore Roosevelt*, ed. H. W. Brands (New York: Rowman & Littlefield, 2013), 29; Theodore Roosevelt to Anna Roosevelt, June 8, 1884, in *Selected Letters of Theodore Roosevelt*, 33; "Filling Roosevelt's Ranks," *New York Times*, October 21, 1886.

21. *Theodore Roosevelt—an Autobiography*, 86, 147, 88.

22. Theodore Roosevelt to Walter Camp, March 11, 1895, in *Selected Letters of Theodore Roosevelt*, 100.

23. *Theodore Roosevelt—an Autobiography*, 151.

24. Theodore Roosevelt to Anna Roosevelt, June 8, 1884, in *Selected Letters of Theodore Roosevelt*, 34; Theodore Roosevelt, *Essays on Practical Politics* (New York: G. P. Putnam's Sons, 1888), 20.

25. R. D. Støve, June 9, 1888, in Hale, *Their Own Saga*, 183.

26. "The Rape of the Party," *Milwaukee Daily Journal*, September 26, 1888.

27. Kornbluh, *Why America Stopped Voting*, 39; Ignatius Donnelly, November 3, 1886, in *Diary of Ignatius Donnelly*.

28. Goldwin Smith, "Is Universal Suffrage a Failure," *Atlantic Monthly*, January 1879, 82.

29. M. Elizabeth Sanders, *The Roots of Reform: Farmers, Workers, and the American State, 1877–1917* (Chicago: University of Chicago Press, 1999); Craig Phelan, *Grand Master Workman: Terence Powderly and the Knights of Labor* (New York: Praeger, 2000). See the Knights of Labor beer steins in the Political Campaign Collections, Smithsonian Institution, National Museum of American History, Washington, D.C.

30. Howe, *Confessions of a Reformer*, 173.

31. Luna Kellie, *The Prairie Populist: The Memoirs of Luna Kellie*, ed. Jane Taylor Nelsen (Iowa City: University of Iowa Press, 1992), 110.

32. Kellie, *Prairie Populist*, 111.

33. Kellie, *Prairie Populist*, 111.

CHAPTER THIRTEEN: "A MAN WHO HAS BEEN THROUGH AS MUCH AS I HAVE"

1. William Kelley to Elizabeth Pugh, December 20, 1887, WDK Papers; "Congressman Kelley Returns," October 28, 1883, *New York Times*.

2. Sklar, *Florence Kelley and the Nation's Work*, 136; Florence Kelley to Caroline Kelley, December 20, 1887, in *Selected Letters of Florence Kelley*, 35; Florence Kelley to William Kelley, March 20, 1888, FK Papers.

3. William Kelley to Elizabeth Pugh, December 20, 1887, WDK Papers.

4. Sklar, *Florence Kelley and the Nation's Work*, 138.

5. E. P. H., "Doings of Women Folk."

6. Florence Kelley to William Kelley, March 20, 1888, FK Papers.

7. "The Last Session of the Fiftieth Congress: How the Lobbyists Arrange Things," *Milwaukee Daily Journal*, December 5, 1888.

8. "Last Session of the Fiftieth Congress."

9. Will seems to have been misquoted here. There seems to be no evidence that he was ever shot. It is more likely that he discussed once being slashed (by Alexander Pope Fields in 1865). See J. Donald Cameron, *Memorial Addresses on the Life and Character of William D. Kelley*, 75; "Last Session of the Fiftieth Congress"; "Washington," *Milwaukee Sentinel*, March 18, 1888.

NOTES TO PAGES 189–99 345

10. *Autobiography of Florence Kelley*, 29; "Judge Kelley," *St. Paul Daily News*, January 7, 1890.

11. "Telegraphic Notes," *Daily Evening Bulletin*, June 7, 1887.

12. "Washington"; Wiggins, "'Pig Iron' Kelley Riot."

13. "Giving Up Places," *Milwaukee Sentinel*, December 4, 1889; "The Hon. W. D. Kelley," *Daily Inter Ocean*, January 11, 1890.

14. O'Neill, *Memorial Addresses on the Life and Character of William D. Kelley*, 20.

15. "William D. Kelley Dead," *North American*, January 10, 1890; "Judge Kelley Sinking," *Atchinson Daily Globe*, January 7, 1890.

16. Florence Kelley to William Kelley, December 11, 1889, in *Selected Letters of Florence Kelley*, 43.

17. "Judge William D. Kelley," *Huntsville Gazette*, January 11, 1890; "Washington Affairs," *Indianapolis Freeman*, January 18, 1890.

18. "William D. Kelley Dead"; William McKinley, *Memorial Addresses on the Life and Character of William D. Kelley*, 36; Carpenter, *Carp's Washington*.

19. "The Death of Judge Kelley," *Morning Oregonian*, January 10, 1890; Joseph McKenna, *Memorial Addresses on the Life and Character of William D. Kelley*, 50; William L. Wilson, *Memorial Addresses on the Life and Character of William D. Kelley*, 43.

20. McKinley, *Memorial Addresses on the Life and Character of William D. Kelley*, 36.

21. Kelley, "Speech of Hon. William D. Kelley," 3.

22. Joseph Cannon, *Memorial Addresses on the Life and Character of William D. Kelley*, 46.

23. "Hon. W. D. Kelley"; "Judge William D Kelleys Estate," *New York Times*, February 1, 1891.

24. Thomas E. Heenan, U.S. Consul to Odessa, to William Kelley, April 4, 1889, WDK Papers.

CHAPTER FOURTEEN: "SOME CHANGE MUST OCCUR VERY SOON NOW"

1. Florence endured years of mounting emotional and physical abuse from Lazare before these incidents in 1891. These appear to be the first and second large incidents in which he struck her, but they build on a pattern of abuse that lasted from the late 1880s into 1891. See "The Daughter of Pig-Iron Kelley Forced to Run from Home," *Chicago Tribune*, March 25, 1892; Sklar, *Florence Kelley and the Nation's Work*, 167–68.

2. Florence Kelley to Caroline Kelley, February 24, 1892, FK Papers.

3. *Autobiography of William Allen White*, 215.

4. Kipling, *American Notes*, 139; Green, *Death in the Haymarket*, 3.

5. William Dean Howells, *New York Tribune*, November 12, 1887; Green, *Death in the Haymarket*, 118; "The Craze for Cranks," *Chicago Daily Tribune*, October 19, 1900; Green, *Death in the Haymarket*, 4.

6. Florence Kelley to Friedrich Engels, May 27, 1892, in *Selected Letters of Florence Kelley*, 26; *Autobiography of Florence Kelley*, 77–78.

7. Jane Addams, *The Spirit of Youth and the City Streets* (New York: Macmillan, 1909), 9.

8. Sklar, *Florence Kelley and the Nation's Work*, 230.

9. Abraham Bisno, *An Autobiographical Account of Bisno's Early Life and the Beginnings of Unionism in the Women's Garment Industry* (Berkeley: University of California Press, 1967), 115; Goldmark, *Impatient Crusader*, 47–48.

10. Alice Hamilton to Agnes Hamilton, March 30, 1898, in Sicherman, *Alice Hamilton: A Life in Letters* (Cambridge: Harvard University Press, 1984), 113; Sklar, *Florence Kelley and the Nation's Work*, 185–86.

11. John L. Thomas, *Alternative America* (Cambridge, MA: Harvard University Press, 1983), 19.

12. Michael E. McGerr, *The Decline of Popular Politics: The American North, 1865–1928* (New York: Oxford University Press, 1986), 120; "The Independent Newspaper," *Washington Post*, November 28, 1895.

13. Henry Demarest Lloyd, *Wealth Against Commonwealth* (New York: Harper & Brothers, 1894), 4, 2, 495; Chester M. Destler, *Henry Demarest Lloyd and the Empire of Reform* (Philadelphia: University of Pennsylvania Press, 1963), 125.

14. Caro Lloyd, *Henry Demarest Lloyd, a Biography* (New York: Knickerbocker Press, 1912), 320.

15. White, *Republic for Which It Stands*, 748.

16. Charles Postel, *The Populist Vision* (Oxford: Oxford University Press, 2007), 140, 156.

17. William Dean Howells to William Cooper Howells, November 6, 1892, in *Selected Letters of William Dean Howells*, 4:29.

18. *Education of Henry Adams*, 179; Peter Argersinger, "A Place on the Ballot: Fusion Politics and Antifusion Laws," *American Historical Review*, January 1980, 289; 1892 Presidential General Election Data, National, Dave Leip's Atlas of U.S. Presidency Elections, last accessed October 24, 2020, https://uselectionatlas.org

/RESULTS/data.php?year=1892&datatype=national&def=1&f=0&off=0&e lect=0.

19. 1892 Presidential General Election Data; Anonymous Norwegian Immigrant in Brooklyn, October 1, 1892, in Hale, *Their Own Saga*, 183.

20. Josephson, *Politicos*, 503, 480.

21. *Autobiography of William Allen White*, 132, 83.

22. *Autobiography of William Allen White*, 86, 116.

23. Sklar, *Florence Kelley and the Nation's Work*, 224.

24. Lloyd, *Wealth Against Commonwealth*, 495.

CHAPTER FIFTEEN: "THE SECRET CAUSE"

1. "First Regiment Armory," *Chicago Tribune*, May 12, 1889.

2. White, *Republic for Which It Stands*, 165; Frances Hodgson Burnett, "When He Decides," in *Before He Is Twenty: Five Perplexing Phases of Boyhood Considered* (New York: F. H. Revell, 1894), 31.

3. David Montgomery, *Citizen Worker: The Experience of Workers in the United States with Democracy and the Free Market During the Nineteenth Century* (Cambridge: Cambridge University Press, 1993), 95–96.

4. James Bryce, *Bryce on America Democracy: Selections from "The American Commonwealth" and "The Hindrances to Good Citizenship"* (New York: Macmillan, 1919), 34; McGerr, *Decline of Popular Politics*, 80.

5. McGerr, *Decline of Popular Politics*, 78.

6. "Mr. Lowell's Politics," 275.

7. "Johnny Powers," *Milwaukee Sentinel*, January 28, 1898; Murphy, *Political Manhood*, 60.

8. McGerr, *Decline of Popular Politics*, 83; Klinghard, *Nationalization of American Politics*, 128.

9. "The Hamilton Club," in *The History of the National Republican League of the United States*, ed. John F. Hogan (Detroit: National Republican League Press, 1898), 375.

10. Silcox, "Black 'Better Class' Political Dilemma," 53; Lane, *Roots of Violence in Black Philadelphia*, 57–59.

11. *Life Story and Personal Reminiscences of Col. John Sobieski*, 268; "Why the Campaign Is Quiet," *Washington Post*, October 13, 1892; McGerr, *Decline of Popular Politics*, 69–106.

12. McGerr, *Decline of Popular Politics*, 104.

13. "Ballot Reform Applied to the Election," *New York Times*, November 4, 1889; Keyssar, *Right to Vote*, 142–43; Alan Ware, "Anti-Partyism and Party Control of Political Reform in the United States: The Case of the Australia Ballot," *British Journal of Political Science* 30, no. 1 (2000): 1–29.

14. Septima Maria Levy Collis, *A Woman's Trips to Alaska: Being an Account of a Voyage through the Inland Seas of the Sitkan Archipelago, in 1890* (New York: Cassell, 1890), 186–94; "The Australian Ballot and the Independent Voter," *Los Angeles Times*, November 15, 1898.

15. Edward J. Blum, *Reforging the White Republic: Race, Religion, and American Reconstruction* (Baton Rouge: Louisiana State University, 2005), 201; Merwin, "Tammany Points the Way," 681; Lyman Abbott, *The Spirit of Democracy* (New York: Houghton Mifflin, 1910), 19.

16. Keyssar, *Right to Vote*, 89.

17. Michael Perman, *Struggle for Mastery: Disfranchisement in the South, 1888–1908* (Chapel Hill: University of North Carolina Press, 2001), 25; Young White Men's League of Jackson, "A Blast from the Youth: The Young Men of Jackson Utter Their Ultimatum" (Jackson, MS, 1890).

18. Keyssar, *Right to Vote*, 91.

19. *All God's Dangers: The Life of Nate Shaw*, ed. Theodore Rosengarten (New York: Alfred A. Knopf, 1974), 42–44.

20. "The Exact Truth," *New York Times*, December 7, 1896.

21. Young, *Age of Charisma*, 62.

22. William Allen White, "What's the Matter with Kansas?," *Emporia Gazette*, August 15, 1896.

23. Richard Hofstadter, *The Age of Reform* (New York: Vintage Books, 1955), 107; Theodore Roosevelt to Cecil Spring Rice, October 8, 1896, in *Selected Letters of Theodore Roosevelt*, 124.

24. Young, *Age of Charisma*, 97.

25. *Autobiography of William Allen White*, 142.

26. *Autobiography of William Allen White*, 142.

27. Young, *Age of Charisma*, 32.

28. Merwin, "Tammany Points the Way," 685.

29. *Autobiography of William Allen White*, 172; White, *Republic for Which It Stands*, 836.

30. Josephson, *Politicos*, 699; McGerr, *Decline of Popular Politics*, 142.

31. The Political Campaign Collections of the Smithsonian's National Museum of American History house a particularly useful collection of buttons from the

1896 election, as well as a large amount of Bryan and McKinley silver-versus-gold paraphernalia, jewelry, and paperweights.

32. "On the Eve of Battle," *Los Angeles Times*, October 31, 1896.

33. Ignatius Donnelly, November 6, 1896, in *Diary of Ignatius Donnelly*; Lloyd, *Henry Demarest Lloyd, a Biography*, 295.

CHAPTER SIXTEEN: "INVESTIGATE, AGITATE, LEGISLATE"

1. Florence Kelley to Henry Demarest Lloyd, July 13, 1893, Henry Demarest Lloyd Papers, University of Wisconsin; Sklar, *Florence Kelley and the Nation's Work*, 237.

2. Sklar, *Florence Kelley and the Nation's Work*, 237–38.

3. Sklar, *Florence Kelley and the Nation's Work*, 237–38.

4. James T. Young, "The Basis of Present Reform Movements," *Annals of the American Academy of Political and Social Science* 21 (March 1903): 91.

5. James Weber Linn, *Jane Addams: A Biography* (New York: D. Appleton, 1935).

6. Goldmark, *Impatient Crusader*, 37; Sklar, *Florence Kelley and the Nation's Work*, 37;

7. Sklar, *Florence Kelley and the Nation's Work*, 242; Frances Perkins, "My Recollections of Florence Kelley," *Social Service Review* 28, no. 1 (1954): 18.

8. "Report card of John Kelley," November 29, 1899, FK Papers.

9. Florence Kelley to Caroline Kelley, February 24, 1893, FK Papers; Florence Kelley to Carolina Kelley, December 31, 1893, in *Selected Letters of Florence Kelley*, 70.

10. William Allen Rogers, "Guiteau Was a Power in Washington for One Day: Shall Altgeld be a Power There for Four Years?," *Harper's Weekly*, October 24, 1896; Florence Kelley to Henry Demarest Lloyd, October 1, 1896, in *Selected Letters of Florence Kelley*, 84.

11. Florence Kelley to Henry Demarest Lloyd, October 1, 1896, in *Selected Letters of Florence Kelley*, 84.

12. "Johnny Powers," *Milwaukee Sentinel*, January 28, 1898; Lloyd Wendt and Herman Kogan, *Lords of the Levee: The Story of Bathhouse John and Hinky Dink* (Chicago: Northwestern University Press, 2005), 38–39.

13. H. W. Brands, *The Reckless Decade: America in the 1890s* (Chicago: University of Chicago Press, 2002), 120; Sklar, *Florence Kelley and the Nation's Work*, 218.

14. "Raked in His Ward: Independent Club of the Nineteenth Scores Powers," *Chicago Tribune*, January 15, 1898; Sklar, *Florence Kelley and the Nation's Work*, 302.

15. Donnelly, November 6, 1896, in *Diary of Ignatius Donnelly*; Sklar, *Florence Kelley and the Nation's Work*, 218; Florence Kelley, *Some Ethical Gains Through Legislation* (New York: Macmillan, 1905), 182, 195.

16. Sklar, *Florence Kelley and the Nation's Work*, 291; McKinley, *Memorial Addresses on the Life and Character of William D. Kelley*, 36; Florence Kelley to Caroline Kelley, August 27, 1898, FK Papers.

17. Sklar, *Florence Kelley and the Nation's Work*, 293.

18. Florence Kelley to Henry Demarest Lloyd, January 31, 1899, in Henry Demarest Lloyd Papers, University of Wisconsin, Madison.

19. Eric Foner, *The Story of American Freedom* (New York: W. W. Norton, 1998), 124.

20. *The Autobiography of Lincoln Steffens* (New York: Harcourt and Brace, 1937), 41.

21. *Autobiography of Lincoln Steffens*, 509, 179.

22. Louis Filler, *The Muckrakers* (San Francisco: Stanford University Press, 1993), 24.

23. *Autobiography of William Allen White*, 186.

24. Lincoln Steffens, *The Shame of the Cities* (New York: McClure, Phillips, 1904); Howe, *Confessions of a Reformer*, 182.

25. *Autobiography of Lincoln Steffens*, 414.

26. *Autobiography of Lincoln Steffens*, 400.

27. *Autobiography of Lincoln Steffens*, 407, 220.

28. "Memoirs of Herbert Croly," *New York History* 58, no. 3 (1877): 326.

29. *Autobiography of Lincoln Steffens*, 518; *Teddy Roosevelt—an Autobiography*, 153.

30. Howe, *Confessions of a Reformer*, 57, 111, 93.

31. Steffens, *Shame of the Cities*, 205; Howe, *Confessions of a Reformer*, 58.

32. William Allen White, *The Old Order Changeth: A View of American Democracy* (Milwaukee: Young Churchman, 1917), 28.

33. Steffens, *Shame of the Cities*, 3, 4.

34. Steffens, *Shame of the Cities*, 4, 14.

35. Steffens, *Shame of the Cities*, 280.

36. Merwin, "Tammany Points the Way," 681; Young, "Basis of Present Reform Movements," 94; White, *Old Order Changeth*, 68; Addams, *Democracy and Social Ethics*; Walter Lippmann, *Drift and Mastery: An Attempt to Diagnose the Current Unrest* (New York: Mitchell Kennerley, 1914).

37. Parkman, "Failure of Universal Suffrage," 4; Addams, *Democracy and Social Ethics*, 256; Howe, *Confessions of a Reformer*, 3.

38. Kelley, "Speech of Hon. William D. Kelley," 24.

39. Addams, *Democracy and Social Ethics*, 224.

40. Florence Kelley to Eustace Percy, February 2, 1913, FK Papers; Florence Kelley, "The Right of Women to the Ballot," in *Some Ethical Gains Through Legislation*, 183; Weyl, *New Democracy*, 4; Mapheus Smith and Marian L. Brockway, "Some Political Characteristics of American Congressmen, 1800–1919," *Southwestern Social Science Quarterly* 22, no. 3 (1941): 209–22.

41. Henry Demarest Lloyd, *Man, The Social Creator* (New York: Doubleday, Page, 1906), 163.

42. Lloyd, *Man*, 75.

43. "Voting by Machinery," *Harper's Weekly*, December 29, 1894, 1245.

44. Owen Edwards, "When Pulling a Lever Tallied the Vote," *Smithsonian Magazine*, November 2004. The Myers and Gillespie machines, as well as a large variety of descriptive and promotional material, are preserved in the Political Campaign Collections of the Smithsonian's National Museum of American History.

CHAPTER SEVENTEEN: "THE RIGHT NOT TO VOTE"

1. George Holt's torch, along with his Wide Awakes cape and an impressive selection of his letters and photographs, were discovered in an attic by the Milford Historical Society in 2016. They were carefully preserved by the intrepid curator Charlie Annand, and the cape and torch were donated to the Smithsonian's National Museum of American History, where they are currently preserved in the Political Campaign Collections.

2. A. M. Duneklee, "Memorial to George P. Holt," Milford Historical Society, November 1918, Collections of Milford Historical Society, Milford, New Hampshire.

3. See photograph in Collections of Milford Historical Society.

4. "This Quiet Campaign," *Washington Post*, September 25, 1900; "A Quiet Campaign," *Cincinnati Commercial Tribune*, October 15, 1904; "A Quiet Campaign," *New York Times*, October 18, 1908.

5. "The Quiet Campaign," *Hartford Courant*, October 27, 1906; "A Quiet Campaign," *New York Times*, October 18, 1908.

6. "The Quiet Campaign Methods," *Los Angeles Times*, October 19, 1904; "Politicians Cut Red Fire," *Los Angeles Times*, October 26, 1910.

7. Frank M. Loomis, "The Right Not to Vote," *New York Times*, November 3, 1900; "The Stay-at-Home Voter," *Atlanta Constitution*, October 21, 1912;

"Stay-at-Home Duty Shirkers," *Los Angeles Times*, April 7, 1913; "Election Crowd Small," *New York Tribune*, November 6, 1907.

8. "The American Citizen," *Chicago Daily Tribune*, November 4, 1908; "Election Quietest in History," *St. Louis Post-Dispatch*, August 3, 1910; Wiebe, *Self-Rule*, 134.

9. Turnout statistics drawn from McIver, *Historical Statistics*.

10. Erik Engstromm, "The Rise and Decline of Turnout in Congressional Elections," *American Journal of Political Science* 56, no. 2 (2012): 381; Emil R. Kaiser, interviewed by Francis Donovan Thomaston, December 15, 1938, American Life Histories: Manuscripts from the Federal Writers' Project, last accessed October 24, 2020, https://www.loc.gov/resource/wpalho.08070404/?st=gallery; Alan Ware, "Anti-Partyism and Party Control of Political Reform in the United States: The Case of the Australia Ballot," *British Journal of Political Science* 30, no. 1 (2000): 1–29.

11. Kornbluh, *Why America Stopped Voting*, 98, 95.

12. Paul Kleppner, *Who Voted? Dynamics of Electoral Turnout, 1870–1980* (New York: Praeger, 1982), 33–34; Kornbluh, *Why America Stopped Voting*, 108–11; Grinspan, *Virgin Vote*, 129–52.

13. Abbott, *Reminiscences*, 99–112.

14. Abbott, *Reminiscences*, 112.

15. Abbott, *Spirit of Democracy*, 1.

16. Chapman, *Practical Agitation*, 8; White, *Old Order Changeth*, 146.

17. John Jay Chapman, "The Capture of Government by Commercialism," *Atlantic Monthly*, February 1898, 156; White, *Old Order Changeth*, 184.

18. White, *Old Order Changeth*, 17; *Autobiography of William Allen White*, 215; White, *Old Order Changeth*, 49–50.

19. Woodrow Wilson, "Democracy and Efficiency," *Atlantic Monthly*, March 1901, 289; Abbott, *Spirit of Democracy*, 21–22.

20. Young, *Age of Charisma*, 200.

21. William Dean Howells, *A Boy's Town: Described for Harper's Young People* (New York: Harper & Brothers, 1890), 228; Louis F. Post, *The Ethics of Democracy: A Series of Optimistic Essays on the Natural Laws of Human Society* (Indianapolis: Bobbs-Merrill, 1916), 345; Chapman, *Practical Agitation*, 32–33.

22. Chapman, *Practical Agitation*, 32–33; *Autobiography of William Allen White*, 225.

23. Abbott, *Spirit of Democracy*, 1.

24. McGerr, *Decline of Popular Politics*, 107–38.

25. Shifflett, *Victorian America*, 74, 87; Robert Putnam, *Bowling Alone: The Collapse and Revival of American Community* (New York: Simon & Schuster, 2001), 387.

26. Shifflett, *Victorian America*, 331.

27. Young, "Basis of Present Reform Movements," 86–89.

28. John Jay Chapman, "Between Elections," *Atlantic Monthly*, January 1900, 30.

29. Wiebe, *Self-Rule*, 136.

30. Kornbluh, *Why America Stopped Voting*, 109.

31. Rose Cohen, *Out of the Shadow* (New York: George H. Doran, 1918), 100–101; Manuel Gamio, ed., *The Mexican Immigrant, His Life-Story* (Chicago: University of Chicago Press, 1931).

32. Robert Staughton Lynd and Helen Merrell Lynd, *Middletown: A Study in Contemporary American Culture* (New York: Harcourt, Brace, 1929), 414; Don Powers and Susie Powers, interview by John William Prosser, Columbia, SC, February 6, 1939, American Life Histories: Manuscripts from the Federal Writers' Project.

33. Lane, *Roots of Violence in Black Philadelphia*, 76–77.

34. Nearly half of New York's aldermen ran saloons, and in the 1884 election, two-thirds of New York's political conventions and primaries were held in or next to a saloon. See Jon Kingsdale, "The 'Poor Mans Club': Social Functions of the Urban Working-Class Saloon," *American Quarterly* 25, no. 4 (1973): 472–73; Madelon Powers, *Faces Along the Bar: Lore and Order in the Workingman's Saloon, 1870–1920* (Chicago: University of Chicago Press, 1999), 30–31, 54.

35. George Frederic Parsons, "The Saloon in Politics," *Atlantic Monthly*, September 1886, 406; Walter Hawley, "The Making of Politicians," *Independent*, October 24, 1895, 4.

36. Michael Lewis, "Access to Saloons, Wet Voter Turnout, and Statewide Prohibition Referenda, 1907–1919," *Social Science History* 32, no. 3 (2008): 373–404.

37. "After the Ball That Didn't Happen," *Illinois Issue*, December 17, 1909, 3; Arthur J. Bilek, *The First Vice Lord Big Jim Colosimo* (Nashville, TN: Cumberland House, 2008); "After the Ball That Didn't Happen," 3.

38. Bilek, *First Vice Lord Big Jim Colosimo*, 69.

39. "After the Ball That Didn't Happen," 3; "Hinky Dink Kenna and Bath House Coughlin," *Household Guest* 28 (1910): 24.

40. "After the Ball That Didn't Happen," 3.

41. "After the Ball That Didn't Happen," 3.

42. Israel "Izzy" Klein, "To Make the House of Representatives Work Again, Make It Bigger," *Hill*, August 17, 2018, last accessed October 24, 2020, https://thehill.com/opinion/campaign/402234-to-make-the-house-of-representatives-work-again-make-it-bigger.

43. Erik Engstromm, "The Rise and Decline of Turnout in Congressional Elections," *American Journal of Political Science* 56, no. 2 (2012): 376–77.

44. The authors of this eye-opening study were able to chart income inequality, and the percentage of the U.S. population that was born overseas, to this same U-curve, implying a correlation between these factors and polarization in Congress. However, a polarized Congress is not the same as political division in the country at large. It is a useful tool to try to quantify something deeply qualitative and should not be interpreted as a chart of political ill will writ large. See Nolan McCarty, Keith T. Poole, and Howard Rosenthal, *Polarized America: The Dance of Ideology and Unequal Riches* (Cambridge, MA: MIT Press, 2006).

45. Young, "Basis of Present Reform Movements," 97; Young, *Age of Charisma*, 191–92.

46. Weyl, *New Democracy*, 108.

47. Lincoln Steffens, *Upbuilders* (New York: Doubleday, Page, 1909), 287–88.

48. John Chamberlain, *Farewell to Reform: Being a History of the Rise, Life, and Decay of the Progressive Mind in America* (New York: Liveright, 1932), 201; William Howard Taft, *Liberty Under Law: An Interpretation of the Principles of Our Constitutional Government* (New Haven, CT: Yale University Press, 1922), 27–28.

49. Carrie Chapman Catt to Susan B. Anthony, September 1890, in *Life and Work of Susan B. Anthony*, 2:693.

50. Auguste Marie Michel, *A Mutilated Life Story: Strange Fragments of an Autobiography* (Chicago: privately published, 1911), 171.

51. Jeffrey Rosen, *Louis D. Brandeis: American Prophet* (New Haven, CT: Yale University Press, 2016), 25; Peter Stearn, *American Cool: Constructing a Twentieth-Century Emotional Style* (New York: New York University Press, 1994).

52. "Klan Fought in Florida," *New York Times*, January 29, 1949.

53. The brutal massacre of dozens of Black Floridians in Ocoee on election day, 1920, stands as an atrocious exception.

54. Mildred Amer, "Members of the U.S. Congress Who Have Died of Other Than Natural Causes While in Office," Congressional Research Service, Report for Congress, Library of Congress, March 13, 2002; R. Eric Peterson

and Jennifer E. Manning, "Violence Against Members of Congress and Their Staff: Selected Examples and Congressional Responses," Congressional Research Service, Report for Congress, Library of Congress, August 17, 2017.

55. Frederick Douglass to William Kelley, May 2, 1871, WDK Papers; Roosevelt, *Essays on Practical Politics*, 3.

56. E. B. White, "The Meaning of Democracy," *New Yorker*, July 3, 1943.

CHAPTER EIGHTEEN: "IT RUNS IN OUR BLOOD TO BE LEADERS"

1. Florence Kelley to Nicholas Kelley, July 11, 1906, FK Papers.
2. Florence Kelley to Nicholas Kelley, July 11, 1906, FK Papers.
3. Florence Kelley to Nicholas Kelley, July 14, 1906, FK Papers.
4. Florence Kelley to Nicholas Kelley, July 15, 1905, in *Selected Letters of Florence Kelley*, 129, 195.
5. Florence Kelley to Nicholas Kelley, July 11, 1904, in *Selected Letters of Florence Kelley*, 123; Florence Kelley to Nicholas Kelley, July 11, 1906, in *Selected Letters of Florence Kelley*, 140.
6. Florence Kelley to Nicholas Kelley, July 1, 1907, in *Selected Letters of Florence Kelley*, 152; Florence Kelley to Nicholas Kelley, February 18, 1906, in *Selected Letters of Florence Kelley*, 137; Florence Kelley to Nicholas Kelley, January 1906, FK Papers; Florence Kelley to Nicholas Kelley, January 1906, in FK Papers; Florence Kelley to Caroline Kelley, January 19, 1901, in *Selected Letters of Florence Kelley*, 107.
7. Florence Kelley to Lillian Wald, January 24, 1899, in *Selected Letters of Florence Kelley*, 95; Florence Kelley to Newton D. Baker, in *Selected Letters of Florence Kelley*, 237; Frances Perkins, "My Recollections of Florence Kelley," *Social Service Review* 28, no. 1 (1954): 19; Goldmark, *Impatient Crusader*, 72.
8. Jean M. Gordon to Florence Kelley, January 11, 1921, FK Papers; Herbert Aptheker, "Du Bois on Florence Kelley," *Social Work* 11, no. 4 (1966): 99.
9. Florence Kelley to Nicholas Kelley, July 1, 1907, in *Selected Letters of Florence Kelley*, 151–52; Goldmark, *Impatient Crusader*, 8–9; U.S. War Department to Florence Kelley, June 21, 1919, FK Papers.
10. Goldmark, *Impatient Crusader*, 73.
11. Florence Kelley to Molly Dewson, February 17, 1924, in *Selected Letters of Florence Kelley*, 331.

12. Florence Kelley to Nicholas Kelley, August 18, 1904, FK Papers; Florence Kelley to Nicholas Kelley, November 12, 1906, FK Papers; Florence Kelley to Nicholas Kelley, October 1, 1920, in *Selected Letters of Florence Kelley*, 256; Florence Kelley to Henry Beckett, March 21, 1920, FK Papers; Julia Lathrop to Florence Kelley, April 28, 1923, FK Papers.

13. Florence Kelley to Nicholas Kelley, January 1906, FK Papers; Florence Kelley to Nicholas Kelley, February 1906, FK Papers; Sklar, *Selected Letters of Florence Kelley*, foonote 2,126.

14. Florence Kelley to Margaret Kelley, September 20, 1905, in *Selected Letters of Florence Kelley*, 133.

15. Florence Kelley to Nicholas Kelley, October 1, 1920, in *Selected Letters of Florence Kelley*, 256.

16. Sandra D. Harmon, "Florence Kelley in Illinois," *Journal of the Illinois State Historical Society* 74, no. 3 (1981): 163.

17. Florence Kelley to Nicholas Kelley, July 11, 1906, FK Papers.

18. Addams, *Democracy and Social Ethics*, 224; Frances Anne Kemble, *Journal of Frances Anne Butler* (Philadelphia: Carey, Lea & Blanchard, 1835), 1:112.

19. Florence Kelley to Nicholas Kelley, July 11, 1906, FK Papers.

INDEX

Note: throughout the index, "Will" and "Florie" refer to William D. and Florence Kelley, respectively.

A NOTE ON THE AUTHOR

JON GRINSPAN is curator of political history at the Smithsonian's National Museum of American History. He is the author of the award-winning *The Virgin Vote: How Young Americans Made Democracy Social, Politics Personal, and Voting Popular in the Nineteenth Century*. He frequently contributes to the *New York Times* and has been featured in the *New Yorker*, the *Washington Post*, and elsewhere. He lives in Washington, D.C., but travels the country collecting historic objects—from nineteenth- and twenty-first-century campaigns, conventions, and protests—for the Smithsonian.